H

D0439677

NASHVILLE & MEMPHIS

SUSANNA HENIGHAN POTTER

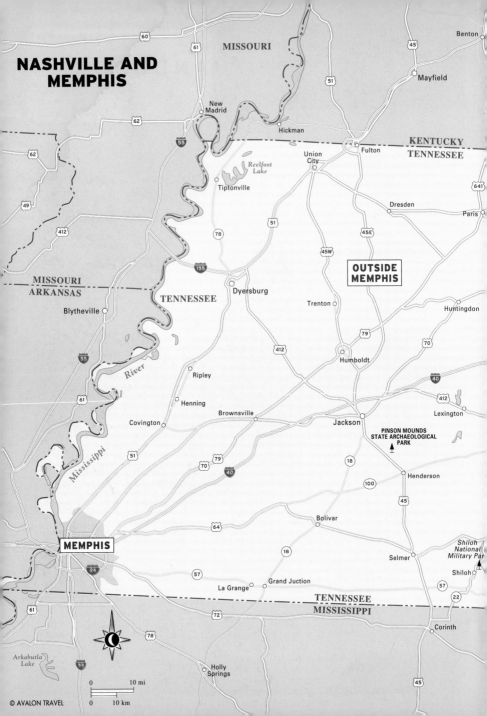

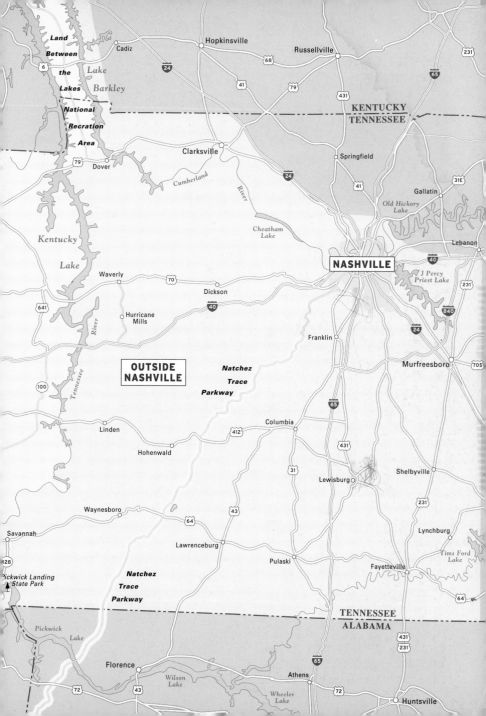

Contents

Discover Nashville & Memphis

Nashville and Memphis are capital cities on America's musical map. One the pinnacle of country music, the other the birthplace of the blues (and adopted hometown of Elvis Presley), these Tennessee towns deliver their weight in gold records.

But it is somewhere in the territory between blues and country that you will find the magical appeal of these cities. When two musical forms that, on the face of things, could not be more different emerge within the same state and a short two-hour drive from one another – there's something more to the story.

That story is the hard life of the South, experienced differently but no less acutely during the last century by poor blacks and whites of Tennessee, Mississippi, and the Appalachian Mountains. Blues men and women came to Memphis to sing songs of hard life and bad love on a street named Beale. Working-class Nashvillians turned out on Saturday nights to let loose at the Grand Ole Opry. And a boy from Tupelo combined country, blues, and gospel to give birth to a whole new musical art form.

You cannot enjoy Nashville or Memphis on mute. Music is what keeps these cities alive. Nashville is the place where you can pay homage to the kings and queens of country, where going out in cowboy boots is not a passing style – it's a tradition. Memphis music is rough and ready, Beale

Street vibrating with the sounds of the blues. At Graceland, you relive the miracle and tragedy of Elvis Presley.

While music is the pulse of any trip to Nashville and Memphis, there is more to the melody than that. The cities are monuments to the past – both troubled and triumphant. Elegant old homes evoke the glory days of the Old South, Civil War monuments remember spilled blood, and the landmarks of the Civil Rights Movement bear witness to the triumph of right over wrong.

Memphis and Nashville defy stereotype: Nashville is not a hillbilly haven – it is a cosmopolitan town where business is big. And Memphis is far more than Beale Street or Graceland – peel away the layers to find a city with surprising sophistication and an unstoppable spirit of survival. With a little planning and a sense of adventure, you can explore a Memphis and Nashville that visitors don't always see. You can dine in fine restaurants, or at classic meat-and-three diners. You can listen to undiscovered talent in a Nashville listening room or Memphis juke joint. And you can delve into the social history that gave rise to the music that has drawn you to these cities in the first place.

The ideal Nashville and Memphis vacation is the one that you make, and one you'll want in your playlist for years to come.

Planning Your Trip

▶ WHERE TO GO

Nashville

Music City USA is the epicenter of the country music industry and home base for its fans. The Country Music Hall of Fame, honky-tonks of Lower Broadway, and the Ryman Auditorium are landmarks of country music history. Listen to great live music at the Grand Ole Opry, the Bluebird Cafe, or other clubs about town. But Nashville is more than music. The Athens of the South has museums, historic homes, and a full-size replica of the Parthenon. The Hermitage on the city's outskirts was the home of U.S. President Andrew Jackson and is one of the best historic sites in the state.

The Grand Ole Opry, in Nashville

Outside Nashville

Hit the road to find beautiful natural areas, cozy towns, and the rolling hills of Walking Horse Country. Just down the interstate is Franklin, a destination for shopping, arts, and Civil War history lovers. Drive down the Natchez Trace Parkway to find inviting towns like Leiper's Fork and the Tennessee Museum of Early Farm Life in Spring Hill. The most famous small town in Tennessee is Lynchburg, home of the Jack Daniel's Distillery. A few miles down the road is the lesser-known and better-for-it George Dickel Distillery. Northeast of Nashville is Land Between the Lakes, a natural area with camping, hiking, fishing, hunting, and The Homeplace, a functioning frontier homestead.

Carnton Plantation, in Franklin

Memphis

The metropolis of the mid-South, this Mississippi River city is rough around the edges but has a heart of gold. With Southern plate lunch diners, barbecue joints, and some of the best fried chicken in all of Dixie, Memphis is a feast for the stomach—and the ears. Beale Street is where the blues were born, and the music still sounds from clubs along Beale and juke joints around the city. Memphis was Elvis Presley's home, and his Graceland mansion

Elvis Presley's Graceland mansion, in Memphis

is a monument to this music hero. The site of Martin Luther King's 1968 assassination, Memphis has turned that dark history into the National Civil Rights Museum, a tribute to Dr. King and the Civil Rights Movement he led.

Outside Memphis

The Tennessee Delta is at once spare and richly populated. The hard life of Delta farmers gave birth to blues musicians, whose story is told at the West Tennessee Delta Heritage Center in Brownsville. Visit the Alex Haley House Museum in Henning, where the author of *Roots* first heard tales of his African ancestors. Drive south of Jackson to discover Pinson Mounds, built by ancient Indians. In the state's northwest corner is Reelfoot Lake, an eerie landscape of knob-kneed cypress trees. Across the Delta is the Tennessee River and the charming town of Savannah. Farther south, near the Mississippi border, is Shiloh, the village that erupted in battle in 1864, one of the most iconic of the Civil War.

▶ WHEN TO GO

Summer is the peak travel season to Nashville and Memphis. The CMA Music Festival in June is the single biggest event of the year in Nashville, and Elvis Week in August in Memphis is that city's biggest single draw. Be prepared for some sweltering heat—the thermometer may read 90 degrees, but it will feel like more than 100 in these two humid-as-heck cities.

The best time to visit both cities is spring or fall, when the temperatures are more comfortable and crowds a bit less intense.

Memphis in May is a series of super festivals and events worth planning for.

During winter, most attractions cut back their hours and some outdoor attractions close all together. Despite this, the winter months can be a great time to visit, especially if you are looking for good deals and the fewest crowds. Special Christmas events in Nashville put a one-of-a-kind spin on country music, and Elvis's Birthday Week in January is a cooler and less frenzied celebration of the King.

► BEFORE YOU GO

Nashville or Memphis?

Nashville and Memphis are distinct destinations, separated by more than 200 miles of interstate. If you plan to visit both in a single trip, you will need at least two weeks, a car, and a lot of energy.

If you have limited time, then choose one city to focus on. For many people, it is an easy decision that comes down to the type of music you prefer. Blues lovers pick Memphis and country fans choose Nashville. Elvis fans don't even have to ask. If you love all music, consider these facts: Nashville has better antebellum homes and a more polished image. Memphis has better barbecue, the Mississippi River, and the National Civil Rights Museum. Both cities have great restaurants, quirky attractions, and friendly people.

If you have time, budget in a few days to explore the countryside between the two cities, where you will find historical, cultural, and musical attractions, plus a culture that is totally different from the urban atmosphere of Nashville and Memphis.

Getting Around

A car is an asset in both cities. In Memphis you can get around downtown on the public trolleys, and there's a free shuttle to Graceland. But to get to midtown restaurants, parks, and museums, you'll need a car. In Nashville, you can explore downtown on foot, but you'll need wheels to get to Music Valley, the Grand Ole Opry, and historic homes like Belle Meade and Travellers Rest.

And a car is essential if you plan any excursions into the countryside.

What to Bring

If you want to go hear live music, pack some going-out clothes. In Nashville, this means cowboy boots and western wear, or the closest thing you have to it. In Memphis, it could mean anything from blue jeans to a sexy dress.

In the summer it is hot and humid, so dress accordingly. Lightweight cotton and hats are the way to go. During spring and fall, versatility is the key. The weather is changeable in these seasons, so pack clothes that can easily layer. Include a light jacket for cool evenings. In winter, you'll need a coat plus long pants and warm shirts or sweaters. Even though this is the south, it does get cold.

If you're going to be driving around the cities, get a good road map before you leave home; the hand-out road maps provided by most car rental agencies leave a lot to be desired.

You can get around downtown Memphis on public trolleys.

Explore Nashville & Memphis

▶ THE BEST OF NASHVILLE AND MEMPHIS

Spanning two weeks and hundreds of miles, this itinerary includes the highlights of Nashville, Memphis, and the countryside in between. A car is a must, and a comfortable one at that since you'll be doing a lot of driving. This trip provides a pleasant mix of history, music, culture, and nature.

Day 1

Arrive in Nashville. Check into a downtown hotel, such as the Hermitage or Union Station. Eat dinner in Germantown at the award-winning Mad Platter and stroll lower Broadway and the District on your first night in town.

Day 2

Visit the Country Music Hall of Fame to see country music history up close, and tour the original home of the Grand Ole Opry, the Ryman Auditorium. Have lunch at Jack's Bar-B-Que on Broadway. See the Grand Ole Opry in the evening.

Day 3

Head towards West Nashville. Drive through Music Row on your way to Centennial Park and The Parthenon. Eat lunch at Martha's at the Plantation at Belle Meade, and then spend the afternoon at Cheekwood Museum and Gardens, where you see special exhibits plus a collection of Nashville art, including work by folk sculptor William Edmondson. Star gaze at the Sunset Grill in Hillsboro Village, or opt for steak over at Jimmy Kelly's in midtown. Catch the show at the Bluebird Cafe, which books up-and-coming singer-songwriters.

The Bluebird Cafe, in Nashville

plate lunch at Swett's, in Nashville

road visit the Ancestral Home of James Knox Polk in Columbia, where you'll also overnight.

Day 8

Drive to Savannah and visit the Tennessee River Museum. Learn about the freshwater pearl industry and the early river steamboats. Overnight in Savannah and dine at the Worleybird Cafe.

Day 9

Spend the morning at Shiloh National Military Park, the site of the deadliest Civil War battle in Tennessee. Hike to the Shiloh Indian Mounds or take the audio tour of the battlefield. Lunch along the river at World Famous Hagy's Catfish Restaurant, and then drive to Pinson Mounds State Archaeological Park to learn about prehistoric Tennesseans. Drive on to Memphis, and check into a downtown hotel, such as the Talbot Heirs Guest House or the Peabody Memphis.

Day 4

Go uptown to the Tennessee State Capitol and the Civil Rights Room at the Nashville Public Library, where you will learn about Nashville's important role in the U.S. Civil Rights Movement. Then head west along Jefferson to eat soul food at Swett's. In the afternoon, visit Fisk University to see the excellent O'Keeffe-Stieglitz art collection, plus the university's collection of African art.

Day 5

Depart Nashville. Drive south to Franklin and visit the Carnton Plantation, epicenter of the Battle of Franklin, one of the most devastating defeats for the Southern army during the Civil War. Eat lunch at Monell's, and then spend the afternoon shopping downtown and at the Factory. Eat dinner at Saffire and overnight in Franklin.

Day 6

Drive to Normandy and visit the George Dickel Distillery. Eat dinner at the Bell Buckle Cafe and overnight at the Walking Horse Hotel in Wartrace.

Day 7

Drive to Spring Hill and visit the Tennessee Museum of Early Farm Life and the Rippavilla Plantation. A few miles down the

Pinson Mounds State Archaeological Park

GOING WHOLE HOG: THE BEST EATS

BARBECUE

Real barbecue joints are places that smoke their meat – almost always a whole hog – slowly over real wood. Traditional Tennessee Q generally falls closer to the vinegary Eastern North Carolina type than the sticky-sweet Kansas City style. But you'll find plenty of both.

Truly good barbecue will usually come "dry" with sauce available on the side. Meat that has been smoked for hours over wood coals will be smoky, tender, and moist. Some Memphis eateries serve barbecue spaghetti – a plate of soft spaghetti noodles dressed with sweet barbecue sauce. Wow!

For the best barbecue, try:

· **Cozy Corner** (Memphis): People come in droves for barbecued Cornish hens and ribs. You'll know they are open by the sight of smoke and the smell of barbecuing meat.

· **Interstate Bar-B-Que** (Memphis): The best of sweet-style barbecue. The pulled pork is tender and spicy. They also serve barbecue spaghetti.

HOT CHICKEN

This west Tennessee specialty is irresistible: spicy, seasoned chicken pan-fried in batches in a cast-iron skillet until it is the color of mahogany. The meat is juicy and the flavor out-of-this-world spicy. Each hot chicken establishment carefully guards its recipe, and each delivers a slightly different combination of flavors.

Hot chicken is served piping hot on a bed of white bread. Coleslaw and potato salad are optional, but an ice-cold drink is not.

For the best hot chicken, try:

· **Gus's World Famous Fried Chicken** (Mason): The original location of a growing Memphis chain of fried chicken joints (in Memphis, they don't really call it hot chicken), this is a roadside restaurant with a juke joint feel.

· **Prince's Hot Chicken Shack** (Nashville): The mother-ship of hot chicken. Period. This north Nashville institution does not advertise, but it's always full of people waiting patiently for made-to-order spicy fried chicken.

Memphis's favorite food: barbecue

MEAT-AND-THREE

Meat-and-three, also called plate lunch, is a style of restaurant that implies a style of food. Traditionally, patrons choose one "meat," or main dish, from a selection of daily specials, plus three (or two, or four) "vegetables," or side dishes, plus a serving of fresh rolls, biscuits, or cornbread (or all three!).

The food is invariably home-style Southern cooking: meatloaf, fried chicken, chipped beef, chicken and dumplings for the meats; turnip greens, mashed potatoes, fried okra, green beans, fried apples for the vegetables. Dessert, which is usually included, may be a fruit cobbler or cream pie. Meat-and-threes are lunchtime eateries.

For the best meat-and-threes, try:

· **The Little Tea Shop** (Memphis): Welcoming, cozy, and casual. The corn sticks are to die for.

· **Cupboard Restaurant** (Memphis): Homemade food with lots of fresh vegetables.

· **Arnold's Country Kitchen** (Nashville): Served cafeteria style, so you can see all the lovely choices before your very eyes. Try the flat pancake-style cornbread.

Day 10

Take the Beale Street Walking Tour in the morning, stopping at the W. C. Handy Museum. Take your picture with the Elvis statue, and go treasure-hunting at A. Schwab. Eat lunch at the Little Tea Shop downtown, and then head over to Mud Island for the afternoon. Explore the Mississippi River Museum and the River Walk. Eat dinner in Harbor Town on Mud Island.

Day 11

Go to the National Civil Rights Museum in the morning, eat lunch along South Main, and then go to the Stax Museum of American Soul Music in the afternoon. Drive south to find Interstate Bar-B-Que for dinner.

Stax Museum of American Soul Music, in Memphis

Day 12

Make it Elvis Day. Start early at Graceland to avoid the crowds and then visit Sun Studio, where Elvis recorded his first hit. Eat a burger at Dyer's on Beale Street in memory of the King.

and eat dinner in Cooper-Young at the Young Avenue Deli (casual) or the Beauty Shop (contemporary).

Day 13

Start out at Elmwood Cemetery with the audio tour, and then drive east. Visit the Memphis Brooks Museum of Art and lounge in Overton Park. Visit the Dixon

Day 14

Drive back to Nashville along I-40, making a pit stop in Brownsville, to visit the West Tennessee Delta Heritage Center, to gain an understanding of the music and history of the delta region.

► FROM BLUEGRASS TO THE BLUES: A MUSICAL JOURNEY

Music is what keeps Nashville and Memphis alive. And it's what many visitors want to experience more than anything else.

Because of the broad spectrum of musical genres present in the two cities—bluegrass to the blues—music fans should not just stick to what they know and love. Take a gander on something different and you might just discover a new favorite. At the very least, you will come to see that connection

that exists between even the most varied musical forms.

Memphis
DOWNTOWN

Beale Street is still the place to start if you want to find the birthplace of the blues. Visit the W. C. Handy Museum to see where the father of the blues lived while he was in Memphis. The Memphis Rock 'n' Soul

Memphis's Beale Street, home of the blues

No place in Memphis is more important to American musical history than Graceland, home of Elvis Presley. Here the King lived with his parents, wife, extended family, and his buddies, the Memphis Mafia. See his remarkable taste in decor and pay your respects over his grave in the meditation garden.

MIDTOWN

Sun Studio is where early blues records were made, where Elvis recorded his first hit, and where the likes of Jerry Lee Lewis and Johnny Cash laid records. It's hallowed ground in musical history.

Not far from Sun Studio is Lauderdale Courts, the public housing project where Elvis lived with his parents when they moved to Memphis. The Overton Park Shell was one of the first places Elvis Presley performed after he was discovered. It's getting a major overhaul.

One of Memphis best-loved juke joints Wild Bill's is found in midtown. It gets kicking late on Friday and Saturday nights.

Several good rock 'n' roll clubs keep you honest. The Young Avenue Deli and the Hi-Tone are stalwarts. Stroll in for a cold beer and a refreshing dose of rock.

Museum just off Beale Street is a good introduction to the story of the blues (and other types of music). Watch guitars being made at the Gibson Guitar Factory, and see a performance at the historic Orpheum Theatre at the head of Beale Street.

Visit the Center for Southern Folklore for one of its regular concerts or events; enjoy some genuine blues and support the preservation of the arts.

After dark, stroll Beale Street to find live blues and jazz at clubs like the King's Palace and B. B. King's.

SOUTH MEMPHIS

The single best musical museum in Memphis is the Stax Museum of American Soul Music. Here you will learn not only about the remarkable story of Stax, but also soul's musical roots in gospel and country music.

Visit the Church of the Full Gospel Tabernacle, founded by Rev. Al Green in 1979. The Sunday morning service begins at 11 A.M.

This photograph of Jerry Lee Lewis, Carl Perkins, Johnny Cash, and Elvis Presley was taken at Sun Studio in Memphis.

The Delta
BROWNSVILLE

It was the landscape and hardship of country living that really gave birth to the blues. Drive the rural routes in Haywood County to breathe in the Delta air. Stop in Nutbush, the childhood home of Tina Turner. Then stop in Brownsville at the West Tennessee Delta Heritage Museum for exhibits about the music and culture of this region. Overnight in Brownsville or drive on to Jackson.

JACKSON

The International Rock-a-Billy Hall of Fame has exhibits and tours, but the best deal is to come on Monday or Saturday nights for the live music and dancing lessons. Rock-a-billy never sounded so good!

Nashville
DOWNTOWN

No part of Nashville says country music quite like Lower Broadway. Colorful honky-tonks like Tootsie's Orchid Lounge offer live music beginning at 10 A.M. every day, and the Wildhorse Saloon is where pretty cowgirls and handsome cowboys go to have fun. Get off the beaten track at the Douglas Corner Cafe, a listening room, or 3rd and Lindsley, a club that books up-and-coming Americana, soul, and R&B acts. For the more serious of mind, start at the Country Music Hall of Fame for an introduction to all things country. Visit the Mother Church of Country Music, the Ryman Auditorium, buy your new boots at one of the half-dozen clothiers on Lower Broadway, and stock up on CDs at Ernest Tubb's. Admire the hardware at Gruhn Guitars, and buy a retro-print poster at Hatch Show Print.

Now for something completely different, don your best duds and enjoy a night at the Nashville Symphony. The delightful sounds

Country Music Hall of Fame, in Nashville

of one of the south's best symphonies will ease the mind and clean the musical palate.

MUSIC VALLEY

Explore wax museums, souvenir shops, and the Opryland Hotel by day. Or take a cruise along the Cumberland on the General Jackson Showboat, a superior dining and entertainment experience. Spend your evening at the Grand Ole Opry, and your late-night at Ernest Tubb's Midnite Jamboree, still going strong.

MIDTOWN

Sandwiched between downtown and Hillsboro Village is Music Row, the business center of Nashville. While you're unlikely to see a star, it's still worth the gamble. Take a stroll and then grab a table at the Sunset Grill for more star-watching. At night check out the Bluebird Cafe for the next big thing.

SOUTH NASHVILLE

Go shopping for just the right outfit at Katy K's Ranch Dressing. Bar hop in trendy South Nashville neighborhoods: check out the Station Inn (bluegrass and roots music), the Mercy Lounge (rock, country, soul, and more) and the Basement (indy rock) just for starters.

► AFRICAN-AMERICAN HERITAGE

Nashville and Memphis experienced the Civil Rights Movement of the 1960s first-hand. They also have rich African-American histories. This itinerary brings you closer to this history.

Downtown Nashville

Nashville's greatest Civil Rights story is the downtown sit-ins and economic boycott that successfully desegregated city services in 1960. Learn about the events of that year and what followed at the Civil Rights Room at the Nashville Library.

Visit the Tennessee State Museum to learn about Tennessee history, including slavery, emancipation, and freedom. Learn about African-American contributions to country music at the Country Music Hall of Fame.

North Nashville

Fisk University is the oldest university in Nashville and one of the oldest institutions of learning for African Americans. Visit Jubilee Hall, built from the proceeds of the Fisk Jubilee Singers' first tour, and the Aaron Douglas Gallery, named for the esteemed muralist and educator.

Across the road from Fisk is Meharry Medical College, which at one time graduated half the African-American doctors in America. A bit farther down the road is Tennessee State University, a historically black state-funded university.

South Nashville

Fort Negley, a Union fortification built to protect Nashville during the Civil War, was constructed by free blacks and slaves who were pressed into service. Hundreds died during its construction.

West Nashville

Tour guides at Belle Meade Plantation highlight the importance of slaves and African-American staff at the grand estate. A slave cabin has been re-created on the grounds.

Cheekwood is home to a permanent collection of African-American folk artist William Edmondson, whose stone sculptures are fascinating and imaginative.

Hermitage

The Hermitage east of Nashville has

Cheekwood, in West Nashville

NATURE ESCAPE

For cities, Memphis and Nashville have a lot of nature. Nashville may be the greenest city in the nation, with its myriad parks and leafy neighborhoods. Memphis has the Mississippi River, a natural landmark of mammoth proportions.

Natural getaways can be close or far; head to the city park or take a weekend getaway to the woods.

DOWNTOWN NASHVILLE

For a quick retreat in the middle of town **Centennial Park** is your best choice. This well-loved and well-used park is home to the Parthenon, but also has a lovely pond and lots of walking trails. Bring a picnic and enjoy.

WEST NASHVILLE

Cheekwood Museum and Gardens may be the most beautiful setting for a picnic in all of Nashville. The estate built by the Maxwell House fortune is lovely, but it is the grounds that really take the cake. Hike the sculpture trail or visit the Japanese garden. Bring a picnic and make a day of it.

Nashville is well endowed with parks. The **Edwin and Percy Warner Parks** are twin city parks next to each other. You can hike, jog, ride horseback, and visit the nature center. Just a bit farther down the road is the **Radnor Lake State Natural Area.** Preserved thanks to local ornithologists and other environmentalists, this is a perfect place for a family hike or solo expedition.

EAST NASHVILLE

J. Percy Priest Lake on the east side of Nashville provides lots of opportunities for outdoor adventure. Hike the shoreline, go for a swim, or get out on a boat. The lake is a magnet for Nashville residents in the summertime. Hike or camp at **Long Hunter State Park.**

NATCHEZ TRACE

The two-lane scenic parkway that begins a few miles west of Nashville is perfect for a bike ride. If you're driving, enjoy passing through quiet and unspoiled countryside. Take a detour at **Leiper's Fork** and hike part of the old Natchez Trace.

LAND BETWEEN THE LAKES

This glory-land of outdoor recreation is located on the slim finger of land between the Cumberland and Tennessee Rivers. Camping, hiking, fishing, hunting, and horseback riding are the most popular pursuits. You can see wild elk and bison and experience an 1850s-era frontier farm.

Plan to spend at least two nights **camping.** Go for a hike on one day and then rent a boat to explore the lake shore.

REELFOOT LAKE

Truly a natural paradise. Escape from the daily grind at the Airpark Inn on the lake front. Gaze at the lake-scape of cypress trees, birds, and the beautiful west Tennessee sky. Go for a float on the lake, or a hike along the shore. Fuel up on catfish and hushpuppies.

Reelfoot Lake

MEMPHIS

Visit Mud Island and the **Mississippi River Walk** to see a scale model of the Mississippi, from Minnesota to New Orleans. Take a **river cruise** to get up close to the Big Muddy.

Head east to the **Dixon** and the **Memphis Botanic Garden** to see classic southern gardens, with colorful flowers and lots of greenery. For a more rustic experience, go to **Shelby Farms** to hike, mountain bike, or play with the dog.

The Hermitage, the home of Andrew Jackson, east of Nashville

comprehensive exhibits about slave life on the presidential estate. Archaeological studies have been done to learn more about the lives of the hundreds of slaves who made Andrew Jackson's retreat profitable.

Franklin

The McLemore House was built by Harvey McLemore, a former slave and farmer, in 1880 and has housed five generations of the McLemore family. It is now a museum about African Americans in Williamson County.

Brownsville

Learn about the way of life of the Tennessee Delta at the West Tennessee Delta Heritage Center. See the way that cotton was grown and harvested, and learn about the culture of the region.

Henning

See the Alex Haley House Museum in a quiet sawmill town in the Tennessee Delta. It was around the kitchen table that Haley first heard stories of his African ancestors. He went on to write the Pulitzer Prize–winning novel *Roots*.

Along the Mississippi River, Fort Pillow State Park preserves the Civil War battlefield where hundreds of black Union soldiers were killed, even after their commander had surrendered. The event, dubbed a massacre by Union supporters, remains controversial.

Memphis

The National Civil Rights Museum at the Lorraine Motel is comprehensive and moving. It uses audio, video, and the words of participants to tell the story of the Civil Rights Movement. A true must-see.

The home where the Slavehaven Underground Railroad Museum is housed is said to have been a stop on the Underground Railroad. Today it is a museum that celebrates the ways in which slaves resisted and escaped slavery.

While music is the centerpiece, civil rights and the racial dynamics of the day are not far from the fore at the Stax Museum of American Soul Music in South Memphis. Learn how music erased racial conceptions, until the assassination of Martin Luther King, Jr. changed everything.

Visit the W. C. Handy Home and Museum and explore Beale Street to discover the African-American heritage of the blues.

▶ WEEKEND GETAWAYS

Nashville

If all you have is a long weekend, don't de-spair. This get-away itinerary is the perfect blend of excitement and restoration.

DAY 1

Arrive in Nashville. If you've flown in, rent a car. Check into a downtown hotel, such as the Hermitage, the Hilton, or the Union Station. Eat dinner downtown at the elegant Capitol Grill and then make your first night one you'll remember: head to Music Valley and catch the Grand Ole Opry.

DAY 2

Sleep in after your night out, and then fuel up with breakfast at the legendary Pancake Pantry in Hillsboro Village. Take a tour of the Mother Church of Country Music, Ryman Auditorium, where the Grand Ole Opry was born. See the evening show at the Bluebird Cafe, where you just might catch the next big star on their way up.

DAY 3

Soak up some of Nashville's history by spending the day at The Hermitage. Explore the home and the grounds of this estate belonging to Andrew Jackson, and learn about how a 19th-century plantation worked. On your last night in town, treat yourself to dinner at F. Scott's, a jazz club and superb restaurant.

Memphis

So the boss won't give you a whole week off. Don't be blue. Memphis has the cure for what ails you.

DAY 1

Arrive in Memphis. Grab a taxi to your down-town hotel, such as the Peabody Memphis or the Talbot Heirs Guest House. If you're in time, watch the duck march at 5 P.M. at the Peabody, and then walk to Beale Street for dinner at E. P. Delta Kitchen and a night of music at B. B. King's.

DAY 2

Get an early start at Graceland and beat the crowds. Ponder the meaning of Elvis over barbecue from the Interstate Bar-B-Que at lunch. Make a detour to Sun Studio, where Elvis cut his first records, and then take an afternoon stroll along the Mighty Mississippi at Tom Lee Park. Enjoy a fine dinner at the Inn at Hunt Phelan.

DAY 3

Ride the trolley to the National Civil Rights Museum. Spend the afternoon at the Stax Museum of American Soul Music. Go back to Beale Street for a late afternoon stroll. Grab a cold one and listen to the blues. Make it an early or a late night: your choice.

Sun Studio, in Memphis

NASHVILLE

Nashville is the home of country music. This city of 600,000 on the banks of the Cumberland River is where tomorrow's hits are made and where you can hear them performed on the stage of the longest-running live radio variety show, the Grand Ole Opry.

There is a twang in the air all around the city—in the honky-tonks along lower Broadway, on the streets of downtown Nashville, and in Music Valley, modern home of the Opry. During the annual Country Music Association Festival in June, the whole city is alive with the foot-tapping rhythm of country music.

Nashville is also the city where performers and songwriters come to make it in the music business. Listening rooms and nightclubs all over the city are the beneficiaries of this abundance of hopeful talent. There is no excuse to stay home after night falls.

It is wrong to think that country music is all there is to Nashville. After the Civil War and Reconstruction, Nashville became known as the Athens of the South because it was a center for education and the arts. Still today, Nashville offers visitors much more than a night at the Opry. Excellent art museums include the Frist Center for Visual Arts and the Cheekwood. The Nashville Symphony Orchestra plays in the elegant and acclaimed Schermerhorn Center downtown.

Come to watch the Tennessee Titans play football, or to play golf at one of the award-winning courses nearby. Admire the Parthenon in Centennial Park, or drive to the southern

HIGHLIGHTS

◖ **Country Music Hall of Fame:** Pay homage to the kings and queens of country music while you trace its evolution from old-time Appalachian mountain music to today's mega-hits (page 27).

◖ **Civil Rights Room at the Nashville Public Library:** The public library houses the best exhibit about the historic Nashville sit-ins of 1960 (page 33).

◖ **The Parthenon:** First built in 1897 to mark the 100th anniversary of the state of Tennessee, this life-sized replica of the Greek Parthenon is as beautiful as it is unusual (page 35).

◖ **Cheekwood:** Art and nature are perfectly balanced in this exceptional museum and botanic garden built on an estate financed by Maxwell House coffee (page 41).

◖ **The Hermitage:** The home of U.S. president Andrew Jackson is much more than a beautiful home; it is a museum of the 19th-century way of life (page 51).

◖ **The Grand Ole Opry:** The live radio variety show that's been on the air for more than 80 years is still the best place to be entertained in Music City (page 55).

◖ **The Bluebird Cafe:** The quintessential Nashville listening room, the Bluebird hosts intimate music sessions every night of the week (page 57).

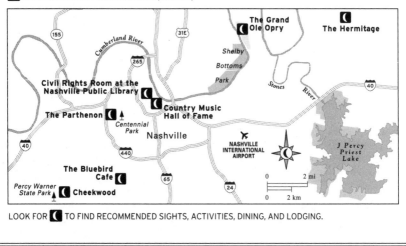

LOOK FOR ◖ TO FIND RECOMMENDED SIGHTS, ACTIVITIES, DINING, AND LODGING.

outskirts of the city for a hike at Radnor Lake State Natural Area.

Downtown is dominated by tall office towers and imposing government buildings, including the state Capitol. Meat-and-three restaurants serve irresistible Southern-style meals, while eateries along Nolensville Pike reflect the ethnic diversity of the city.

Nashville is a city that strikes many notes, but sings in perfect harmony.

PLANNING YOUR TIME

Nashville is a popular destination for weekend getaways. Over two days you can see a few of the city's attractions and catch a show at the Grand Ole Opry. Musical pilgrims and history enthusiasts should plan to spend more time in Music City. Even the most disciplined explorers will find themselves happily occupied if they choose to stay a full week.

Downtown is a good home base for many

visitors. Hotels here are within walking distance of many attractions, restaurants, and nightclubs. They are also the most expensive accommodations in the city. Visitors who are primarily interested in seeing a show at the Grand Ole Opry or shopping at Opry Mills should shack up in Music Valley, where you will find a smorgasbord of affordable hotel rooms.

Visitors with a car can also look for accommodation outside of the city center. There are affordable hotels in midtown, and charming bed-and-breakfasts in Hillsboro and East Nashville. All these neighborhoods are nicely off the tourist track. The city's lone hostel is in midtown and is a good choice for budget travelers.

When to Go

Summer is the most popular time to visit Nashville. The CMA Music Festival in June draws thousands to the city. Temperatures in August top out around 90 degrees, although it can feel much hotter.

Spring and fall enjoy mild temperatures, and are the best time to visit Nashville. You will avoid the largest crowds but still sample all that the city has to offer. In spring you will enjoy sights of tulips, dogwoods, and magnolias in bloom. Beginning in mid-October, foliage around the city starts to turn blazing red, brown, and yellow.

In winter, temperatures range from 30 to 50 degrees. During November and December, holiday concerts and decorations liven up the city. Many attractions cut back hours during winter, and some outdoor attractions are closed altogether.

ORIENTATION

For a city of its size, Nashville takes up a lot of space. In fact, Nashville has the second-largest footprint of any major American city. But don't picture a scene of concrete: Nashville is a leafy, suburban city. Outside downtown is a patchwork of traffic lights, strip malls, and tree-lined residential neighborhoods, several of which are incorporated towns with their own elected officials, city halls, and police.

Nashville's attractions are spread out among the city's various neighborhoods. Learn the locations and identities of a few parts of town, and you are well on your way to understanding Music City.

City Center

Nashville straddles the Cumberland River, a waterway that meanders a particularly uneven course in this part of Tennessee. Downtown Nashville sits on the west bank of the river, climbing a gradual incline from Broadway to the Tennessee State Capitol. It is defined by landmarks including the BellSouth tower, the tallest building in Tennessee, better known by many as the Batman building for the two tall antennae that spring from the top.

Downtown is divided into two general areas: **Broadway and the District** is the entertainment area, and where you will find major attractions like the Country Music Hall of Fame, the Ryman Auditorium, and Printer's Alley, a hotbed of clubs and bars. **Downtown** refers to the more traditional city zone, where you'll find office buildings, the Tennessee State Museum, and city parks.

It is a good plan to walk around central Nashville since traffic and parking are about as difficult here as in any city of this size. But do remember that Nashville is built on a hill. Walking between Broadway and the state Capitol is perfectly doable, but on a hot summer day, or with small children in tow, you may think otherwise.

East Nashville

Shelby Street Pedestrian Bridge spans the Cumberland at McGavock Street and takes you straight to the heart of East Nashville. Now dominated by humongous LP Field, home of the Tennessee Titans, the eastern reaches of Nashville are also home to some of the most charming residential neighborhoods. **Edgefield,** Nashville's oldest suburb, was a separate city when it first sprang up in the 19th century. Many of its most elegant homes were destroyed in the great East Nashville fire of 1916, but it still boasts a lovely mix of

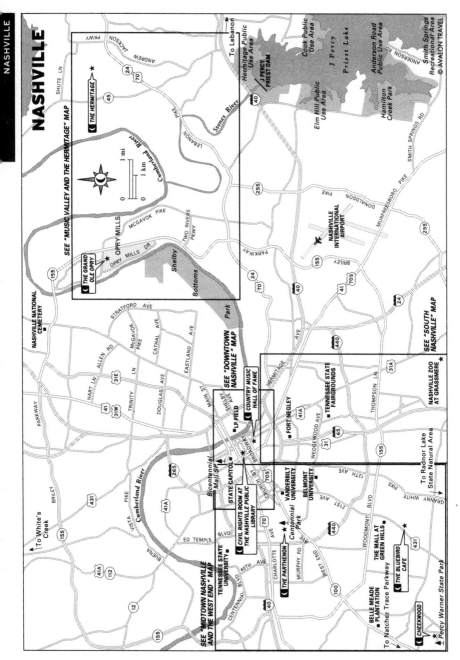

NASHVILLE

SEE "MUSIC VALLEY AND THE HERMITAGE" MAP

★ THE HERMITAGE

To Lebanon

Cumberland River

SEE "DOWNTOWN NASHVILLE" MAP

SEE "SOUTH NASHVILLE" MAP

SEE "MIDTOWN NASHVILLE AND THE WEST END" MAP

© AVALON TRAVEL

© SUSANNA HENIGHAN POTTER

Downtown Nashville sits on the west bank of the Cumberland River.

Victorian, Princess Anne, and Colonial Revival homes. Farther east is **Lockeland Springs.**

While there are no blockbuster attractions in East Nashville, visitors should consider the growing number of bed-and-breakfast accommodations here. The neighborhoods are close to downtown, but also boast their own unique nightlife, restaurants, and character.

North Nashville

North of the state Capitol and Bicentennial Mall is **Germantown,** a quaint, compact neighborhood now awash with galleries, restaurants, and studios, once the home of European immigrants. Heading west from Germantown, **Jefferson Street** takes you past several of Nashville's African-American landmarks, including Fisk University and Meharry Medical College.

A neighborhood created entirely for the tourist trade, **Music Valley** is the zone of hotels, restaurants, and retail that has popped up around the Opryland Hotel and the Grand Ole Opry House. Located inside a narrow loop of the Cumberland River, Music Valley lies northeast of downtown Nashville. It is convenient to the airport along the Briley Parkway.

If Music Valley is actually a valley, you wouldn't know it. The strip of hotels, restaurants, souvenir shops, and malls is just about as far removed from the natural environment as you can get. The Grand Ole Opry is the best thing that Music Valley has going for it. Opryland Hotel is an attraction in its own right, however, and Opry Mills is a discount shopper's paradise. Music Valley is also home to a wide variety of hotel accommodations, including some budget-friendly choices.

West Nashville

Perhaps the most famous neighborhood in all of Nashville, **Music Row** is where country music deals are done. The tree-lined streets of 16th and 17th Avenues, a few blocks southwest of downtown, shade dozens of different recording studios, record labels, and producers.

Lying just west of downtown, **Elliston Place** is a block of nightclubs, restaurants, and two famous Nashville eateries: Elliston Place Soda Shop and Rotier's.

The neighborhood is surrounded by medical complexes, and is a few blocks from the city's only downtown hostel. Centennial Park, Nashville's best urban park, is a few blocks farther west.

The youthful energy of nearby Vanderbilt University and Belmont College keep **Hillsboro Village** one of the most consistently hip neighborhoods in Nashville. Located on both sides of 21st Avenue, Hillsboro and the related neighborhood of Belmont are about as far away from the Grand Ole Opry as you can get in Nashville.

Hillsboro is home to one of Nashville's finest used book stores, stylish and pricey boutiques, and notable restaurants, including the upscale Sunset Grill, the down-home Pancake Pantry, and Fido, a coffeehouse for all seasons. Hillsboro is also where you will find the alternative movie house the Belcourt, which screens independent and arts movies every day of the week.

South of Hillsboro is **Green Hills,** whose primary attraction is a shopping mall. Together, Hillsboro, Elliston Place, and Green Hills are Nashville's **Midtown.**

Sylvan Park is an old suburb of the city, located between Charlotte Avenue and Murphy Road, just west of the city center. Noted for neat homes and state-named roads, the neighborhood is quiet and residential.

Along Charlotte Avenue, facing Sylvan Park, you will find antiques and thrift stores, the Darkhorse Theater, and Rhino Books,

specializing in used and rare books. Farther out along Charlotte is the Goodwill Superstore, a dream come true for thrift store aficionados, and a burgeoning number of ethnic eateries.

West End refers to the neighborhoods along West End Avenue. It includes Belle Meade, an incorporated city and one of the wealthiest in the whole state. Head in this direction to find good restaurants, the Belle Meade Plantation, and Cheekwood.

South Nashville

South of the city center are several distinct neighborhoods. **8th Avenue South,** close to downtown, is the antiques district. Restaurants like Arnold's Country Kitchen and clubs including the Douglas Corner Cafe draw people to this neighborhood.

Follow 12th Avenue as it heads south from downtown to find **the Gulch.** Rising from what was once a railroad wasteland, the Gulch is now the city's hot spot for high-rise housing and urban condos.

A few miles farther south along 12th Avenue is **12 South,** another of Nashville's most newly gentrified neighborhoods. An influx of young professional property owners has given rise to new restaurants, boutiques, and coffee shops.

There is not much greenery left in **Green Hills,** a retail hot spot south of Hillsboro Village. If you can stand the traffic jam, follow 21st Avenue south to find upscale Green Hills Mall and the venerable Bluebird Cafe, tucked away in a strip mall a few blocks farther south.

Sights

BROADWAY AND THE DISTRICT

This is the entertainment and retail hub of Nashville. Walk along lower Broadway, as the blocks from 5th Avenue to the river are called, and you will pass a dozen different bars, restaurants, and shops catering to visitors. The District, located along 2nd Avenue near where it crosses Broadway, is a neighborhood where old warehouses have been converted to nightclubs, shops, office space, and loft condominiums.

◖ Country Music Hall of Fame

The distinctive design of the Country Music Hall of Fame and Museum (222 5th Ave. S., 615/416-2001, www.countrymusichalloffame.com, daily 9 A.M.–5 P.M., $15.95–19.95) is the first thing you will notice about this monument to country music. Vertical windows at the front and back of the building resemble

piano keys; the sweeping arch on the right side of the building portrays a 1950s Cadillac fin; and from above, the building resembles a bass clef. The Hall of Fame was first established in 1967, and its first inductees were Jimmie Rodgers, Hank Williams, and Fred Rose. The original Hall was located on Music Row, but in 2002 it moved to this brand-new signature building two blocks off Broadway in downtown Nashville.

Country music fans are drawn by the carload to the Hall of Fame, where they can pay homage to country's greatest stars, as well as the lesser-known men and women who influenced the music. The hall's slogan is "Honor Thy Music."

The museum is arranged chronologically, beginning with country's roots in the Scotch-Irish ballads sung by the southern mountains' first settlers, and ending with displays on some of the genre's hottest stars of today. In between,

PHOTO COURTESY THE TENNESSEE DEPARTMENT OF TOURIST DEVELOPMENT

Guitars and fringed jackets are some of the things on display at the Country Music Hall of Fame.

exhibits detail themes including the rise of bluegrass, honky tonk, and the world-famous Nashville Sound, which introduced country music to the world.

There are a half-dozen private listening booths where you can hear studio-quality recordings of seminal performances, as well as a special display of a few of the genre's most famous instruments. Here you can see Bill Monroe's mandolin, Maybelle Carter's Gibson, and Johnny Cash's Martin D-355.

If you are truly interested in learning something about country music while you're here, splurge on the $5 audio guide, which adds depth to the exhibits and helps to drown out distractions caused by your fellow museumgoers.

The Hall of Fame itself is set in a rotunda. Brass plaques honor the 100 inductees, and around the room are the words "Will the Circle Be Unbroken," from the hymn made famous by the Carter Family.

The Ryman Auditorium

Thanks to an $8.5 million renovation in the 1990s, the historic Ryman Auditorium (116 5th Ave. N., 615/889-3060, www.ryman.com, daily 9 A.M.–4 P.M., $12.50–16.25) remains one of the best places in the United States—let alone Nashville—to hear live music. Built in 1892 by Captain Thomas Ryman, the Union Gospel Tabernacle, as the Ryman was then called, was designed as a venue for the charismatic preaching of Rev. Samuel P. Jones, to whom Ryman owed his own conversion to Christianity.

Managed by keen businesswoman Lula C. Naff during the first half of the 20th century, the Ryman began to showcase music and performances. In 1943, Naff agreed for the Ryman to host a popular barn dance called the Grand Ole Opry. The legacy of this partnership gave the Ryman its place in history as the so-called Mother Church of Country Music.

The Opry remained at the Ryman for the next 31 years. After the Opry left in 1974, the Ryman fell into disrepair and was virtually condemned when Gaylord Entertainment, the same company that owns the Opry, decided to invest in the grand old tabernacle. Today, it is a

popular concert venue, booking rock, country, and classical acts, and performers still marvel at the fabulous acoustics of the hall.

Seeing a show at the Ryman is by far the best way to experience this historic venue, but if you can't do that, pay the $12.50 admission to see a short video and explore the auditorium on your own. You can sit a few minutes on the old wooden pews and even climb on stage to be photographed in front of the classic Opry backdrop. A guided tour that takes you backstage costs $16.25.

Shelby Street Pedestrian Bridge

Built in 1909, the Sparkman Street Bridge was slated for demolition in the 1998 after inspectors called its condition "poor." But citing the success of the Walnut Street Bridge in revitalizing downtown Chattanooga, Tennessee, advocates succeeded in saving the bridge. The Shelby Street Bridge reotpened in 2003 as a pedestrian and bike bridge.

The Shelby Street Bridge connects East

The Ryman Auditorium is also called the Mother Church of Country Music.

Nashville neighborhoods with downtown. It is also convenient on Titan game days since the eastern terminus is a few hundred yards from LP Field. Perhaps most significant for visitors, however, is the fact that the views of the downtown cityscape are excellent from here.

Fort Nashborough

Fort Nashborough (170 1st Ave., 615/862-8400, Mon.–Sat. 10 A.M.–5:30 P.M., Sun. 1–5 P.M., free) is a one-quarter-sized replica of the fort erected by James Robertson and John Donelson when they first settled what was then called French Lick on Christmas Day 1779. Visitors here will get the feeling that this site has seen better days. While the replica fort is open, it is mostly left unattended and there is little to see or learn here. The interiors of the five cabins have been gated with iron bars, seemingly to prevent neighborhood vagrants from settling in. The site is mostly fascinating simply because it looks so out of place among Nashville's skyscrapers and the Tennessee Titans' stadium nearby. It has a nice view of the river too.

Tennessee Sports Hall of Fame

Sports fans will enjoy the Tennessee Sports Hall of Fame (Nashville Arena, 615/242-4750, www.tshf.net, Mon.–Sat. 10 A.M.–5 P.M., $3). Located in a state-of-the-art 7,500-square-foot exhibit space, the hall chronicles the history of sports in Tennessee from the 1800s to today's heroes.

Customs House

Located at 701 Broadway, the old Nashville Customs House is a historic landmark and architectural beauty. Construction on the Customs House began in 1875 and President Rutherford B. Hayes visited Nashville to lay the cornerstone in 1877. The building is an impressive example of the Victorian Gothic style. It was designed by Treasury architect William Appleton Potter and was completed in 1916. Although it is called a customs house, the building served as the center of federal government operations in the city:

Federal government offices, courts, and treasury offices were housed in the building. For many years it held the city's U.S. Post Office.

Ownership transferred from the federal to the city government in 1979 and the building was later leased for redevelopment. It currently houses federal bankruptcy court and other offices.

Hume Fogg

Located across Broadway from the Customs House is Hume Fogg Magnet School. It sits on land formerly occupied by Hume School, Nashville's first public school. The four-story stone-clad 1912 building was designed by William Ittner of St. Louis in the Norman Gothic style with Tudor Gothic details. Today, it is a public magnet school with a reputation for high academic standards.

The Frist Center for the Visual Arts

Nashville's foremost visual art space is the Frist Center for the Visual Arts (919 Broadway, 615/744-3247, www.fristcenter.org, Mon.–Sat. 10 A.M.–5:30 P.M., Thurs. and Fri. until 9 P.M., Sun. 1–5 P.M., adults $8.50, seniors and military $7.50, students $6.50). The Frist is located in a stately building that once housed the 1930s downtown post office. High ceilings, art deco finishes, and unique hardwood tiles distinguish the museum.

With no permanent collection of its own, the Frist puts on about 12 different major visiting exhibitions annually. At any given time, you will see between three and four different exhibits. ArtQuest, a permanent part of the Frist, is an excellent hands-on arts activity room for children and their parents.

DOWNTOWN

The greater part of downtown is dominated by large office buildings and federal, state, and city government structures. From Commerce Street northward to the state Capitol, you will find historic churches, museums, and hordes of office workers.

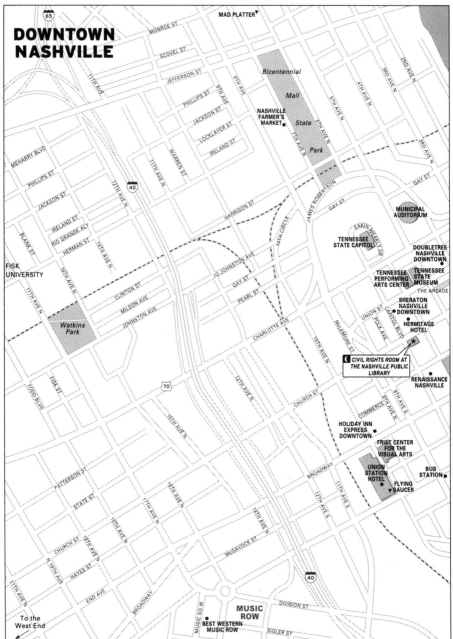

DOWNTOWN NASHVILLE

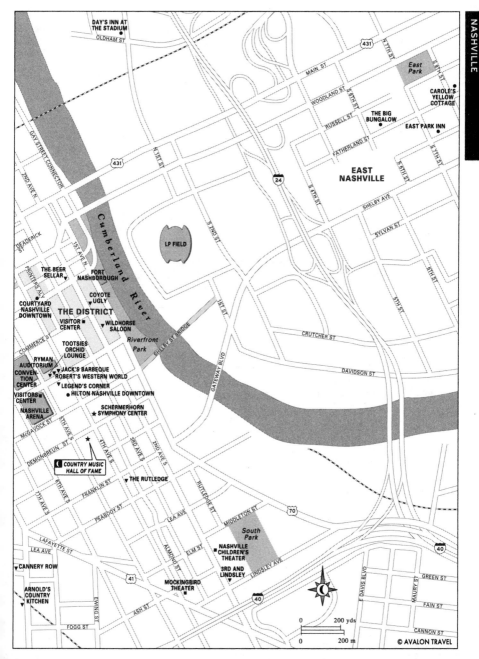

© SUSANNA HENIGHAN POTTER

The Tennessee Senate chambers are inside the State Capitol.

Tennessee State Capitol

Set on the top of a hill and built with the formality and grace of classic Greek architecture, the capitol building of Tennessee strikes a commanding pose overlooking downtown Nashville. Construction of the Capitol began in 1845, two years after the state legislature finally agreed that Nashville would be the permanent capital city. Even with the unpaid labor of convicts and slaves, it took 14 years to finish the building.

The Capitol is built of limestone, much of it from a quarry located near present-day Charlotte and 13th Avenues. In the 1950s, extensive renovations were carried out and some of the original limestone was replaced. The interior marble came from Rogersville and Knoxville, and the gasoliers were ordered from Philadelphia. The Capitol was designed by architect William Strickland, who considered it his crowning achievement and is buried in a courtyard on the north end of the Capitol.

Visitors are welcome at the Capitol. Ask at the information desk for a printed guide that identifies each of the rooms and many of the portraits and sculptures both inside and outside of the building. If the legislature is not in session, you can go inside both the House and Senate chambers, which look much as they did back in the 19th century. In the 2nd-floor lobby, you can see two bronze reliefs depicting the 19th and 14th amendments to the United States Constitution, both of which were ratified by the State of Tennessee in votes held at the Capitol.

Guided tours of the Capitol depart hourly Monday–Friday 9 A.M.–3 P.M. Ask at the information desk inside for more information.

Other important State buildings surround the Capitol. The **Library and Archives** sits directly west of the Capitol, and next to the **Tennessee Supreme Court.** The **Tennessee War Memorial** is a stone plaza on the south side of the Capitol, and a nice place to people-watch. A number of State office buildings are nearby, and State employees can be seen walking to and fro, especially at lunchtime.

Tennessee State Museum

If you are used to the flashy multimedia exhibits found in many of today's top museums, the Tennessee State Museum (5th Ave., 615/741-2692, www.tnmuseum.org, Tues.–Sat. 10 A.M.–5 P.M., Sun. 1–5 P.M., free) will seem like a musty throwback to the past. The displays are largely straightforward combinations of text and images, and they require visitors to read and examine on their own. There are but a few video presentations. But for patrons with enough patience to give the displays their due, the museum offers an excellent overview of Tennessee history from the Native Americans to the New South era of the 1880s.

Exhibits detail the state's political development, the Revolutionary and Civil Wars, and profile famous Tennesseans including Andrew Jackson and Davy Crocket. They also cast a spotlight on the lifestyles and diversions of Tennesseans of various eras, from the early frontiersmen and -women to a free African-American family before emancipation. Special artifacts include the top hat worn by Andrew Jackson at his presidential inauguration, a musket that belonged to Daniel Boone, and the jaw bone of a mastodon.

The **Tennessee Military Museum** (Legislative Plaza, 615/741-2692, Tues.–Sat. 10 A.M.–5 P.M., free) is associated with the Tennessee State Museum and highlights America's overseas conflicts, beginning with the Spanish-American War in 1989 and ending with World War II. The exhibits examine the beginnings of the wars, major battles, and the outcomes. There is a special exhibit about Alvin C. York, the Tennessee native and World War I hero. The military museum is located in the War Memorial Building on the south side of the Capitol.

◖ Civil Rights Room at the Nashville Public Library

The Nashville Public Library (615 Church St., 615/862-5800, Mon.–Thurs. 9 A.M.–8 P.M., Fri. 9 A.M.–6 P.M., Sat. 9 A.M.–5 P.M., Sun. 2–5 P.M., free) houses the city's best exhibit on the movement for civil rights that took place in Nashville in the 1950s and '60s. Nashville was the first Southern city to desegregate public services, and it did so relatively peacefully, setting an example for activists throughout the south.

The story of the courageous men and women who made this change happen is told through photographs, videos, and displays in the Civil Rights Room at the public library. The library is a fitting location for the exhibit, since the block below on Church Street was the epicenter of the Nashville sit-ins during 1960.

Inside the room, large-format photographs show school desegregation, sit-ins, and a silent march to the courthouse. A circular table at the center of the room is symbolic of the lunch counters where young students from Fisk, Meharry, American Baptist, and Tennessee A&I sat silently and peacefully at sit-ins. The table is engraved with the ten rules of conduct set out for sit-in participants, including rules to be polite and courteous at all times, regardless of how you are treated. A timeline of the national and Nashville civil rights movements is presented above the table.

Inside a glass-enclosed viewing room you can choose from six different documentary videos, including an hour-long 1960 NBC news documentary about the Nashville sit-ins. Many of the videos are 30 minutes or longer, so plan on spending several hours here if you are keenly interested in the topics.

The centerpiece of the Civil Rights Room is a glass inscription by Martin Luther King, who visited the city in 1960 and said, during a speech at Fisk University: "I came to Nashville not to bring inspiration, but to gain inspiration from the great movement that has taken place in this community."

Nashville is planning a new and much-needed museum dedicated to its African-American history and culture, which will be located at the corner of Jefferson and 8th Avenues, near the farmer's market. Until this museum is built, the Nashville Public Library is the best place to learn about the city's racially segregated past and the movement that changed that.

NASHVILLE SIT-INS

Greensboro, North Carolina, is often named as the site of the first sit-ins of the American civil rights movement. In truth, activists in Nashville carried out the first "test" sit-ins in late 1959. In these test cases, protesters left the facilities after being refused service and talking to management about the injustice of segregation. In between these test sit-ins and the moment when Nashville activists would launch a full-scale sit-in campaign, students in Greensboro took that famous first step.

The Nashville sit-ins began on February 13, 1960, when a group of African-American students from local colleges and universities sat at a downtown lunch counter and refused to move until they were served. The protesting students endured verbal and physical abuse, and were arrested.

Community members raised money for the students' bail, and black residents of the city began an economic boycott of downtown stores that practiced segregation. On April 19, the home of Z. Alexander Looby, a black lawyer who was representing the students, was bombed. Later the same day, students led a spontaneous, peaceful, and silent march through the streets of downtown Nashville to the courthouse. Diane Nash, a student leader, asked Nashville mayor Ben West if he thought it was morally right for a restaurant to refuse to serve someone based on the color of his or her skin. Mayor West said no.

The march was an important turning point for the city. The combined effect of the sit-ins, the boycott, and the march caused, in 1960, Nashville to be the first major Southern city to experience widespread desegregation of its public facilities. The events also demonstrated to activists in other parts of the South that non-violence was an effective tool of protest.

The story of the young people who led the Nashville sit-ins is told in the book *The Children* by David Halberstam. In 2001, Nashville resident Bill King was so moved by the story of the protests that he established an endowment to fundraise for a permanent civil rights collection at the Nashville Public Library. In 2003, the Civil Rights Room at the Nashville Public Library was opened. It houses books, oral histories, audio-visual records, microfilm, dissertations, and stunning photographs of the events of 1960. The words of one student organizer, John Lewis, who went on to become a congressman from Georgia, are displayed over the entryway: "If not us, then who; if not now, then when?"

The Civil Rights Room is located on the 2nd floor of the library, adjacent to the room that houses its Nashville collection.

The Arcade

One of Nashville's most unique urban features is the covered arcade that runs between 4th and 5th Avenues and parallel to Union Street. The two-story arcade with a gabled glass roof was built in 1903 by developer Daniel Buntin, who was inspired by similar arcades he saw in Italy.

From the moment it opened, the Arcade was a bustling center for commerce. Famous for its peanut shop, the Arcade has also been the location of photo studios, jewelers, and a post office for many years. Today, restaurants crowd the lower level, while professional offices line the 2nd floor.

Downtown Presbyterian Church

William Strickland, the architect who designed the Tennessee State Capitol, also designed the Downtown Presbyterian Church (154 5th Ave. N., 615/254-7584, www.dpchurch.com), a place of worship now on the National Register of Historic Places. Built in 1848 to replace an earlier church destroyed by fire, the church is in the Egyptian revival style that was popular at the time. It is, however, one of only three surviving churches in the country to be built in this style.

Downtown Presbyterian, which added the word "Downtown" to its name in 1955, was used as a Union hospital during the Civil War, and it is where James K. Polk was inaugurated as Tennessee governor in 1839. Visitors are welcome to come for a self-guided tour during regular business hours. Groups of five or more can call in advance for a guided tour of the building.

MUSIC ROW

Home to the business end of the country music industry, Music Row can be found along 16th and 17th Avenues south of where they cross Broadway. While there are few bona fide attractions here, it is worth a jaunt to see the headquarters of both major and independent music labels all in one place.

Music Row's most famous, or infamous, landmark is *Musica,* the sculpture at the Music Row traffic circle. The Alan LeQuire sculpture caused a stir when it was unveiled in 2003 for the larger-than-life anatomically correct men and women it depicts. Regardless of your views on art and obscenity, it is fair to say that *Musica* speaks more to Nashville's identity as the Athens of the South than as Music City USA.

RCA Studio B

As a rule, the music labels in Music Row are open for business, not tours. The lone exception is Historic RCA Studio B (Music Square W., 615/416-2001, www.countrymusichalloffame. com, $12.95). The RCA studio was the second recording studio in Nashville and the place where artists including the Everly Brothers, Roy Orbison, Dolly Parton, Elvis Presley, and Hank Snow recorded hits. Also called the RCA Victor Studio, this nondescript studio operated from 1957 to 1977. Visitors on the one-hour tour, which departs from the Country Music Hall of Fame downtown, hear anecdotes about recording sessions at the studio and see rare footage of a 1960s Dottie West recording session. The studio no longer operates, but it is used in courses at nearby Belmont College.

Tours can only be purchased in conjunction with admission to the Country Music Hall of Fame. Tours depart hourly Sunday–Thursday 10:30 A.M.–2:30 P.M. On Friday and Saturday, tours leave every half-hour 10:30 A.M.–2:30 P.M.

The Upper Room

Three million Christians around the world know the *Upper Room Daily Devotional Guide,* a page-a-day pocket devotional available in 106 countries and 40 languages. Headquartered in Nashville, the Upper Room Ministry has established a bookstore, museum, and chapel to welcome visitors. **The Upper Room Chapel and Museum** (1908 Grand Ave., 615/340-7207, www.upperroom.org/chapel, Mon.–Fri. 8 A.M.–4:30 P.M., free) features a small museum of Christian-inspired art, including a wonderful collection of nativity scenes from around the world made from materials ranging from needlepoint to camel bone. Visitors may also tour the chapel, with its 8-foot-by-20-foot stained-glass window and 8-foot-by-17-foot wood carving of Leonardo da Vinci's *The Last Supper.* A 15-minute audio presentation discusses features of the carving and tells the history and mission of the Upper Room.

Admission to the Upper Room is free; donations are accepted.

MIDTOWN

Encompassing the neighborhoods of Elliston Place, Hillsboro Village, and Green Hills, midtown refers to the parts of Nashville between downtown and the West End.

◖ The Parthenon

In 1893, efforts began to raise funds for a mighty exposition that would celebrate the 1896 centennial of the state of Tennessee. Though the exposition would start a year late—in 1897—it would exceed all expectations. The old West Side Race Track was converted to a little city, with exhibit halls dedicated to transportation, agriculture, machinery, minerals, forestry, and African Americans, among other themes. There were Chinese, Cuban, and Egyptian villages, a midway, and an auditorium. The exposition attracted 1.7 million people between May 1 and October 31.

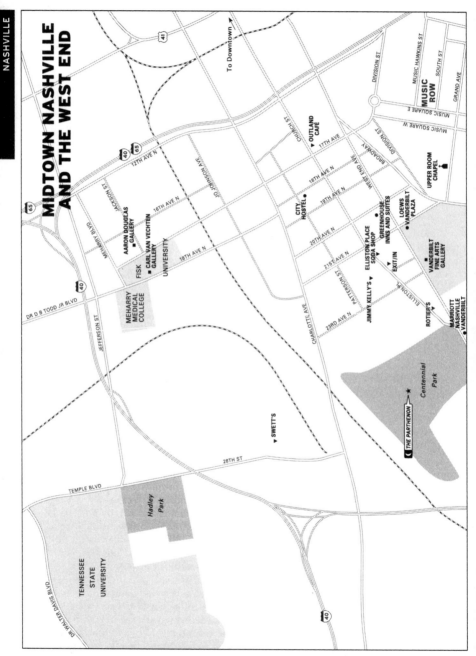

MIDTOWN NASHVILLE AND THE WEST END

NASHVILLE

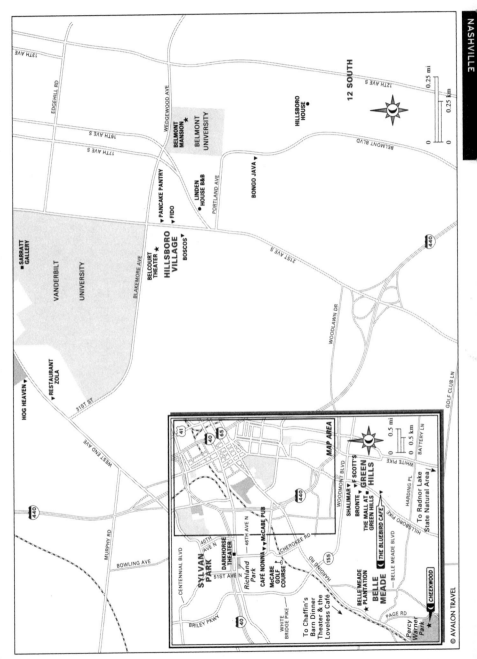

© AVALON TRAVEL

© SUSANNA HENIGHAN POTTER

The Parthenon in Centennial Park is one of Nashville's most extraordinary structures.

While the event turned only a modest profit for its organizers, it no doubt contributed in other ways to the local economy and to the stature of the state.

When the exposition closed in the fall of 1897, all the exhibit halls were torn down, except for a life-sized replica of the Greek Parthenon, which had housed an art exhibit during the centennial. The exposition grounds were made into a public park, aptly named Centennial Park, and Nashvillians continued to admire their Parthenon.

The Parthenon replica had been built out of wood and plaster, and it was designed only to last through the centennial. Remarkably, it survived well beyond that. But by the 1920s, the Parthenon was crumbling. City officials, responding to public outcry to save the Parthenon, agreed to restore it, and they hired a contractor to rebuild the replica. The contractor did so using tinted concrete.

Today, the Parthenon remains one of Nashville's most iconic landmarks. It is a monument to the creativity and energy of the New

South, and also to Nashville's distinction as the Athens of the South.

You can see and walk around the Parthenon simply by visiting Centennial Park. It is, in many respects, most beautiful from the outside. You can also pay to go inside.

The Parthenon (Centennial Park, 2600 West End Ave., 615/862-8431, Tues.–Sat. 9 A.M.–4:30 P.M., Sun. June–Aug. only 12:30–4:30 P.M., adults $5, seniors and children $2.50) has three gallery spaces; the largest is used to display works from its permanent collection of 63 pieces of American art. The other two galleries host changing exhibits. Visitors to the museum are also able to go inside the Parthenon to view the 42-foot statue of Athena Parthenos.

Belmont Mansion

The elaborate "summer home" of Adelicia Acklen was constructed in 1853 and was named Belle Monte. Belmont Mansion (1900 Belmont Blvd., 615/460-5459, www.belmont-mansion.com, Mon.–Sat. 10 A.M.–4 P.M., Sun.

1–4 P.M., adults $10, seniors $9, children 6–12 $3), as it is known today, is a monument to the excesses of the Victorian age.

Adelicia was born to a wealthy Nashville family in 1817. When she was 22, Adelicia married Isaac Franklin, a wealthy bachelor 28 years her senior. When Franklin died seven years later, Adelicia inherited his substantial wealth. Adelicia remarried to Joseph Acklen, a young lawyer, and together they planned and built Belmont Mansion. The home was built in the Italian style, with touches of Egyptian revival style.

The home boasted 36 rooms and 16,000 square feet of space including a grand gallery where the Acklens hosted elaborate balls and dinner parties. The property included a private art gallery, aviary, zoo, and conservatory, as well as a lake and acres of manicured gardens. After the Civil War, Adelicia traveled to Europe, where she purchased a number of paintings and sculptures that are now on display in her restored mansion.

Shortly before her death, Adelicia sold Belmont to two female educators who ran a girls school from the property for 61 years. Later, it was purchased by the founders of Belmont College, a private college known for its music and music business programs.

Visitors to the mansion are given a 45-minute guided tour of the property, which includes the downstairs sitting and entertaining rooms and three of the upstairs bedrooms.

Vanderbilt University

Named for philanthropist Commodore Cornelius Vanderbilt, who donated $1 million in 1873 to found a university that would "contribute to strengthening the ties which should exist between all sections of our common country," Vanderbilt University (www.vanderbilt.edu) is now one of the region's most respected institutions of higher education.

A private research university, Vanderbilt has an enrollment of 6,300 undergraduates and 5,200 graduates. The university comprises 10 schools, a medical center, public policy center, and The Freedom Forum First Amendment Center. Originally just 75 acres, the university had grown to 250 acres by 1960. When the

McKISSACK AND McKISSACK ARCHITECTS

The oldest African-American architectural firm in Tennessee can trace its roots to Moses McKissack (1790-1865), a member of the West African Ashanti tribe, who was sold into slavery to William McKissack of North Carolina. Later, McKissack moved to Middle Tennessee. Moses became a master builder, and he passed his knowledge on to his son, Gabriel Moses McKissack, born in 1840. Gabriel Moses passed his knowledge of the building trade to his own son, Moses McKissack III, born in 1879.

Moses McKissack III was born in Pulaski, where he received a basic education in the town's segregated schools. In 1890 he was hired by a local white architect. From then until 1905, McKissack designed and built homes throughout the area, including many in Mount Pleasant in Maury County. He devel-oped a reputation as an excellent architect and tradesman.

In 1905 McKissack moved to Nashville, where he started his own construction company. Within a few years, he was working on major projects. He built a home for the dean of architecture and engineering at Vanderbilt University and the Carnegie Library at Fisk University. In 1922, Moses's brother, Calvin, joined him and they opened McKissack and McKissack, Tennessee's first black architectural firm.

The McKissacks have continued to distinguish themselves in the building industry, and they have also kept the business in the family. Since 1991 the company has been led by Cheryl McKissack, a fifth-generation McKissack. The firm employs more than 100 people and has corporate offices in Philadelphia and New York City.

George Peabody School for Teachers merged with Vanderbilt in 1979, another 53 acres were added.

Vanderbilt's campus life is vibrant, and there is a daily roll call of lectures, recitals, exhibits, and other special events. Check http://calendar.vanderbilt.edu for an up-to-date listing of all campus events.

Prospective students and their parents can sign up for a campus tour. Vanderbilt also offers a self-guided tour of the campus's trees, which form the Vanderbilt Arboretum. Most trees on the tour are native trees common to Nashville and middle Tennessee. This is a nice activity for people who want to hone tree identification skills. Download a podcast or print a paper copy of the tour from the website or contact the university for more information.

Vanderbilt University also has two excellent art galleries: The **Sarratt Gallery** (Sarratt Student Center, Vanderbilt Place near 24th Ave., 615/322-2471, Mon.–Fri. 9 A.M.–9 P.M., Sat.–Sun. 11 A.M.–10 P.M.) has a more contemporary bent than the **Vanderbilt Fine Arts Gallery** (Fine Arts Bldg., Mon.–Fri. noon–4 P.M., Sat.–Sun. 1–5 P.M., free), which includes works that demonstrate the development of both Eastern and Western art, plus six different traveling exhibits annually. The Fine Arts Gallery is located near the intersection of West End and 23rd Avenues. Both galleries are closed or limit their hours during university holidays and semester breaks, so it's a good idea to call ahead.

There is designated visitor parking in several lots on the Vanderbilt campus. Look on the eastern edge of the sports facilities parking lot off Natchez Trace, in the Wesley Place parking lot off Scarritt Place, or in the Terrace Place parking lot between 20th and 21st Avenues north of Broadway.

Belmont University

The school for girls founded in the Belmont Mansion in 1890 evolved in 1913 to the Ward-Belmont School for Women and in 1951 to coed Belmont College. Since 1991, it has been Belmont University, a higher-education institution with links to the Tennessee Baptist Convention. Belmont is a fast-growing university with highly respected music and music business programs. It has a student enrollment of 4,800.

WEST END

Nashville's most posh neighborhood, Belle Meade, is actually a city with its own government. Named after an antebellum plantation, Belle Meade the city is home to Nashville's elite, and famously possesses one of the most wealthy zip codes in America. Drive through to spy on mansions that look more like museums and lawns that look like botanical gardens.

Around Belle Meade are other nice neighborhoods where Nashville's professionals and upper class live. West End Avenue, the area's thoroughfare, is home to lots of nice restaurants. As you head westward, you pass Cheekwood, the Warner Parks, and eventually run into the Natchez Trace Parkway.

Belle Meade Plantation

The mansion at the former Belle Meade Plantation is the centerpiece of present-day Belle Meade Plantation and one of the finest old homes in the city. Its name means "beautiful pasture," and indeed it was Belle Meade's pastures that gave rise to the plantation's fame as the home of a superb stock of horses. Purchased as 250 acres in 1807 by Virginia farmer John Harding and his wife, Susannah, the estate grew to 5,400 acres at its peak in the 1880s and 1890s.

Belle Meade was never a cotton plantation, although small amounts of the cash crop were grown here, along with fruits, vegetables, and tobacco. Instead it was the horses, including the racehorse Iroquois, that made Belle Meade famous. The mansion was built in 1820 and expanded in 1853. Its grand rooms are furnished with period antiques, more than 60 percent of which are original to the house. The estate also includes outbuildings, including a smokehouse, dairy, and the original log cabin that Harding built for his family when they moved to Belle Meade in 1807.

The plantation also includes a slave cabin, which houses an exhibit on Belle Meade's enslaved population, which numbered more than 160 at its peak. Two of these slaves are described in detail. Susanna Carter was the mansion's housekeeper for more than 30 years, and remained with the family even after the end of slavery. On her deathbed, Selena Jackson, the mistress of Belle Meade for many years, called Susanna "one of the most faithful and trusted of my friends." The other African American who features prominently at the museum is Bob Green, whose skill and experience as a hostler earned him one of the highest salaries ever paid to a horse hand of the day.

Visitors to Belle Meade are given a one-hour guided tour of the mansion and then visit the outbuildings and grounds on their own.

(Cheekwood

Plan to spend a full morning or afternoon at Cheekwood (1200 Forrest Park Dr., 615/356-8000, www.cheekwood.org, Tues.–Sat. 9:30 A.M.–4:30 P.M., Sun. 11 A.M.–4:30 P.M.,

adults $10, seniors $8, students and children $5) so you can experience the full scope of this magnificent art museum and botanical garden. Galleries in the Cheekwood mansion house the museum's American and European collections, including an excellent contemporary art collection. Cheekwood has the largest public collection of works by Nashville artist William Edmondson, the sculptor and stoneworker. Cheekwood usually displays items from its permanent collection as well as traveling exhibitions from other museums. Many exhibits have special ties with Nashville.

But the Cheekwood is far more than just an art museum. The mansion overlooks hundreds of acres of gardens and woods, and it is easy to forget that you are near a major American city when you're at the Cheekwood. Walk the mile-long Carell Woodland Sculpture Trail past works by 15 internationally acclaimed artists, or stroll past the water garden to the Japanese garden. There are dogwood gardens, an herb garden, a delightful boxwood garden, and much more. Wear comfortable shoes and

© SUSANNA HENIGHAN POTTER

The gardens at Cheekwood are a joy to explore.

WILLIAM EDMONDSON

The first African-American artist to have a one-man show at the Museum of Modern Art in New York was Nashville-born sculptor William Edmondson.

Edmondson was born around 1870 in the Hillsboro area of Nashville. He worked for decades as a laborer on the railroads, a janitor at Women's Hospital, and in other similar jobs before discovering his talent for sculpture in 1929. Edmondson told the Nashville *Tennessean* that his talent and passion were God-given: "God appeared at the head of my bed and talked to me, like a natural man, concerning the talent of cutting stone He was about to bestow. He talked so loud He woke me up. He told me He had something for me."

Edmondson was a prolific sculptor. He worked exclusively with limestone, and he created angels, women, doves, turtles, rabbits, and other "varmints." He also made tombstones. Edmondson never learned to read or write, and he called many of his works "mirkels" because they were inspired by God.

In the 1930s, Louise Dahl-Wolfe, a photographer for *Harper's Bazaar* magazine, brought Edmondson and his work to the attention of Alfred Barr, the director of the Museum of Modern Art. Barr and other trustees of the museum admired what they termed as Edmondson's "modern primitive" work, and they invited him to display a one-man show at the museum in 1938. In 1941, the Nashville Art Museum put on an exhibit of Edmondson's work.

Edmondson continued to work until the late 1940s, when he became ill with cancer. He died in 1951 and is buried in an unmarked grave at Mt. Ararat Cemetery in Nashville. The city park at 17th Avenue North and Charlotte Avenue is named in honor of William Edmondson.

You can see an exhibit of Edmondson's work at the Cheekwood Museum.

pack a bottle of water so you can enjoy the grounds in comfort.

The Cheekwood owes its existence to the success of the coffee brand Maxwell House. During the 1920s, Leslie Cheek and his wife, Mabel Wood, invested in the new coffee brand being developed by their cousin, Joel Cheek. Maxwell House proved to be a success and earned the Cheeks a fortune, which they used to buy 100 acres of land in West Nashville. The family hired New York residential and landscape architect Bryant Fleming to create a 30,000-square-foot mansion and neighboring gardens. Cheekwood was completed in 1933.

Leslie Cheek lived in the mansion just two years before he died, and Mabel lived there for another decade before deeding it to her daughter and son-in-law, who later offered it as a site for a museum and garden. Cheekwood opened to the public in 1960.

Visitors pay admission at a guard gate at the entrance; there is a total family cap of $30 per car. Once inside, drive to parking lot B so you can explore the art museum and grounds. Parking lot A is for the museum shop and restaurant.

SOUTH NASHVILLE

Head south on 4th Avenue, which becomes Nolensville Pike, towards a diverse array of attractions.

Fort Negley

Early in the Civil War, the Union army determined that taking and holding Nashville was a critical strategic link in their victory. So after Nashville fell in 1862, the Federals wasted no time fortifying the city against attacks. One of the city's forts was Fort Negley, built between August and December 1862 on St. Cloud Hill south of the city center.

Fort Negley owes its existence to the 2,768 men who were enrolled to build it. Most were blacks, some free and some slave, who were pressed into service by the Union army. These men felled trees, hauled earth, and cut and laid limestone for the fort. They slept in the open and enjoyed few, if any, comforts while they labored. Between 600 and 800 men died while building the fort, and only 310 received payment.

When it was completed, Fort Negley was the largest inland masonry fortification in North America. It was never challenged. Fort Negley was abandoned by the military after the war, but it remained the cornerstone of one of Nashville's oldest African-American communities, now known as Cameron-Trimble. During the New Deal, the Works Progress Administration rebuilt large sections of the crumbling fort, and it became a public park.

In 2007, the city opened a visitors center to tell the story of the fort. **Fort Negley Park** (Fort Negley Dr., 615/862-8470, Tues.–Sat. 9 A.M.–4:30 P.M., free) includes a museum about the fort and Nashville's role in the Civil War. There is a short paved loop trail around the base of the fort, plus raised boardwalks through the fortifications themselves. Historic markers tell the story of the fort's construction and detail its military features.

City Cemetery

Right next to Fort Negley Park, off Chestnut Street, is the old City Cemetery. Opened in 1822, City Cemetery (1001 4th Ave. S., www.thenashvillecitycemetery.org) was the final resting place of many of Nashville's most prominent early citizens, including founder James Robertson; William Driver, the U.S. Navy captain who named the flag "Old Glory"; Mabel Lewis Imes and Ella Sheppard, members of the original Fisk Jubilee Singers; and 14 Nashville mayors.

During the Civil War, the cemetery was contracted to bury more than 15,000 Union and Confederate dead, although they were later reinterred in different cemeteries.

Visitors are welcome 8 A.M.–5 P.M. daily. Consult the information board in the Keeble Building for help with your self-guided tour. Guided tours and special events, such as living history tours, garden tours, and historical lectures, take place on the second Saturday of

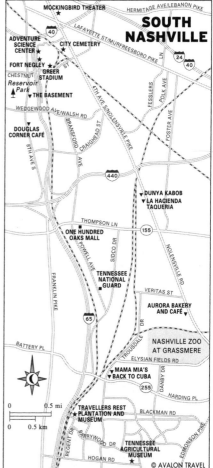

each month. The events are aimed at telling the history of Nashvillians who are buried at this historical cemetery.

Adventure Science Center

Children will enjoy learning about science at the Adventure Science Center (800 Fort Negley Blvd., 615/862-5160, Mon.–Sat. 10 A.M.–5 P.M., Sun. 12:30–5:30 P.M., adults $9, children $7). Interactive exhibits explore how the body works, the solar system, and other scientific

THE BATTLE OF NASHVILLE

During most of the Civil War, Nashville was occupied by Federal forces. After Fort Donelson, 90 miles northeast of Nashville, fell in mid-February 1862, Nashville was in Union hands. The Federals turned Nashville into an important goods depot for the Northern cause, and set strict rules for city residents during occupation.

As the war drew to a close in late 1864, Nashville was the site of what war historians now say was the last major battle of the Western Theater.

The Battle of Nashville came after a string of defeats for the Confederate army of Tennessee, commanded by John Bell Hood. After his bloody and humiliating losses at Spring Hill and Franklin a few miles south, Hood moved north and set up headquarters at Travellers Rest, the home of John Overton. His plan was to set up his troops in an arc around the southern side of the city. Union Maj. Gen. George H. Thomas did not plan to wait for Hood's attack, however. He devised to attack first and drive the Confederates away from Nashville.

A winter storm and frigid temperatures delayed the battle. For two weeks, from December 2 to 14, 1864, the two armies peered at one another across the no-man's-land between the two lines. Then, at dawn on December 15, 1864, the Union attack began. Union troops on foot and horse, including at least four U.S. Colored Infantry brigades, attacked various Confederate posts around the city. By the close of the first day of fighting, Hood withdrew his troops two miles farther south from the city.

The dawn of the second day of battle augured more losses for the Confederates. Unable to hold their line against the Union assault, they fell back again. As darkness fell, Union Maj. Gen. Thomas wired Washington to announce his victory. Pursued by a Union cavalry commanded by Maj. Gen. James Wilson, what remained of the Confederate army of Tennessee marched south and on the day after Christmas crossed the Tennessee River into Alabama. Four months later, the war was over.

COURTESY OF LIBRARY OF CONGRESS

An artist depicts the 1864 Battle of Nashville.

areas. The center's new Sudekum Planetarium opened in June 2008. With 164 seats, it is the largest planetarium in Tennessee.

Tennessee Central Railway Museum

Railroad enthusiasts should make a detour to the Tennessee Central Railway Museum (220 Willow St., 615/244-9001, www.tcry.org, Tues., Thurs., and Sat. 9 A.M.–3 P.M., free). This institution is best known for its special railroad excursions (see *Tours* later in this chapter), but they also collect railroad equipment and paraphernalia, which are on display at the museum. The museum is located in an otherwise industrial area between the interstate and the railroad tracks, one block north of Hermitage Avenue and east of Fairfield Avenue.

Nashville Zoo at Grassmere

See familiar and exotic animals at the Nashville Zoo at Grassmere (3777 Nolensville Pike, 615/833-1534, www.nashvillezoo.org, adults $13, seniors $11, children 3–12 $8, children under 3 free). From April 1 to October 15, the zoo is open daily 9 A.M.–6 P.M. The rest of the year, opening hours are daily 9 A.M.–4 P.M. The zoo is closed Thanksgiving, Christmas, and New Year's Days. Parking is free.

Many of the zoo's animals live in beautiful habitats like Lorikeet Landing, Gibbon Islands, and Bamboo Trail. The zoo's meerkat exhibit, featuring the famously quizzical and erect animals, is one of its most popular. The Wild Animal Carousel is an old-time carousel with 39 different brightly painted wooden animals. Two of the newest exhibits feature African wild dogs and Eurasian Lynx.

The zoo is located at Grassmere, the one-time home and farm of the Croft family. The historic Croft farmhouse has been preserved and is open for guided tours in October and December every year.

Travellers Rest Plantation and Museum

Travellers Rest (636 Farrell Pkwy., 615/832-8197, www.travellersrestplantation.org, Tues.–Sat. 10 A.M.–4 P.M., Sun. 1–4 P.M., $2–10) was the home of John Overton, a Nashville lawyer who helped found Memphis, served on the first Tennessee Supreme Court, and was a trusted advisor to Andrew Jackson, the seventh U.S. president and the first from Tennessee.

Overton was born in Virginia and studied law in Kentucky before he decided to move to Middle Tennessee, what was then the western frontier of the United States. When workmen were digging the cellar for the original home in 1799, they uncovered Native American skeletons and artifacts—Overton had chosen a Mississipian-era Indian mound for the site of his home. But the archaeological finds did not stop Overton, who initially named his home Golgotha, or hill of skulls. The name did not stick, however; tradition has it that Overton later named the home Travellers Rest because it was his place of rest between long trips as a circuit judge in Middle and East Tennessee.

Travellers Rest underwent two major expansions in its lifetime: one in 1808 and another 20 years later. The additions allowed Overton first to accommodate a growing number of young law students who wished to study law with him, later his wife, Mary, and their children, and, finally, the elaborate parties that Overton hosted to further the political career of Andrew Jackson.

John Overton was many different things in his lifetime. Among them was slave owner. Records show that between 30 and 80 slaves lived at Travellers Rest before emancipation. While Overton's plantation was not the primary source of his wealth, it no doubt contributed to his status and prominence. Sadly, when the L&N Railroad purchased the Overton property in the 1940s, the company destroyed not only the Overton family burial ground and peach orchard, but also the slave cabins that remained at the rear of the house.

Visitors to Travellers Rest may choose to skip the mansion tour; admission to the grounds alone is just $3. But to get the full story and flavor of the property, choose the 45-minute guided tour.

Tennessee Agricultural Museum

The Tennessee Agricultural Museum (Ellington Agricultural Center, 615/837-5197, www.tnagmuseum.com, Mon.–Fri. 9 A.M.–4 P.M., free) celebrates the ingenuity and dedicated labors of farm life from the 17th to the 20th century. Operated by the Tennessee Department of Agriculture and set on the department's pleasant south Nashville campus, the museum depicts various facets of Tennessee farm life. There are exhibits about clothes-washing, blacksmithing, coopers, plows, and weaving, just to name a few. Outside, there is a small kitchen garden with heirloom vegetables, and replicas of a log cabin, one-room schoolhouse, and outdoor kitchen. There is also a short self-guided nature trail illustrating the ways that settlers used various types of native Tennessee trees.

Admission to the museum is free, but you can pre-arrange demonstrations for a fee. Staff are also available to answer any questions. This is a good choice for families.

JEFFERSON STREET

Jefferson Street runs from downtown through northwestern Nashville, past several of the city's African-American landmarks.

Bicentennial Mall

Just as Tennessee celebrated its 100th anniversary in 1896 with the construction of Centennial Park, Tennessee celebrated its 200th anniversary in much the same way. The **Bicentennial Capitol Mall State Park** occupies 19 acres on the north side of the capitol building. It offers excellent views of the Capitol, which towers over the mall. The mall and the Capitol are separated by a steep hill and more than 200 steps, which prove daunting to all but the fittest among us.

The mall has dozens of features that celebrate Tennessee and Tennesseans, including a 200-foot granite map of Tennessee embedded in concrete; a River Wall with 31 fountains, each representing one of Tennessee's rivers; and a timeline with Tennessee events, inscriptions,

The Tennessee State Capitol overlooks the Bicentennial Mall, built in 1996 to commemorate Tennessee's 200th anniversary.

THE JUBILEE SINGERS

In 1871, Fisk University needed money. Buildings at the school established in old Union army barracks in 1866 were decaying while more and more African Americans came to seek education.

So, the school choir withdrew all the money from the University's treasury and left on a world tour. The nine singers were Isaac Dickerson, Maggie Porter, Minnie Tate, Jennie Jackson, Benjamin Holmes, Thomas Rutling, Eliza Walker, Green Evans, and Ella Sheppard. Remembering a biblical reference to the Hebrew "year of the jubilee," Fisk treasurer and choir manager George White gave them their name, the Fisk Jubilee Singers.

The singers struggled at first, but before long audiences were praising them. They toured first the American South, then the North, and in 1873 sailed to England for a successful British tour. Their audiences included William Lloyd Garrison, Wendell Phillips, Ulysses S. Grant, William Gladstone, Mark Twain, Johann Strauss, and Queen Victoria. Songs like "Swing Low, Sweet Chariot" and "Nobody Knows the Trouble I've Seen" moved audiences to tears. The singers introduced the spiritual to mainstream white audiences and erased negative misconcep-

Jubilee Hall on the Fisk University campus was paid for by the proceeds of the Fisk Jubilee Singers.

tions about African Americans and African-American education.

In 1874 the singers returned to Nashville. They had raised enough money to pay off Fisk's debts and build the University's first permanent structure, an imposing Victorian Gothic six-story building now called Jubilee Hall. It was the first permanent structure built solely for the education of African Americans in the United States.

Every October 6, the day in 1871 that the singers departed Fisk, the University recalls their struggle and their triumph with a convocation featuring the modern-day Jubilee Singers.

and notable quotes from 1796 to 1996. There is also a monument to Tennessee's WWII veterans and casualties, and a walk of counties that depicts each of the state's 95 counties. A one-mile path that circles the mall's perimeter is popular with walkers and joggers, and a 2,000-seat amphitheater is used for special events. The park may be a civics lesson incarnate, but it is also a pleasant place to pass the time.

To the west of the mall is the **Nashville Farmer's Market,** where you can buy fresh produce, hot food, and arts and crafts.

Fisk University

Founded in 1866 to educate newly freed slaves, Fisk University (www.fisk.edu) has a long and proud history as one of the United States' foremost black colleges. W. E. B. Du Bois attended Fisk, graduating in 1888, and Booker T. Washington married a Fisk alumna and sent his own children to Fisk. In more modern times, Knoxville native and poet Nikki Giovanni attended Fisk.

Fisk sits at the corner of Jefferson Street and Dr. D. B. Todd Jr. Boulevard, about 10 blocks west of downtown Nashville. The campus is a smattering of elegant redbrick buildings set on open green lawns, although a few more modern buildings, including the library, detract from the classical feel. One of the oldest Fisk buildings is **Jubilee Hall,** on the north

a Fisk University class in 1899

end of the campus, which is said to be the first permanent building constructed for the education of African Americans in the country. It was built with money raised by the Fisk Jubilee Singers, who popularized black spirituals during a world tour from 1871 to 1874. Another notable building is the **Fisk Little Theatre,** a white clapboard building that once served as Union hospital during the Civil War.

At the corner of Jackson Street and Todd Boulevard is the **Carl Van Vechten Gallery,** named for the art collector who convinced artist Georgia O'Keeffe to donate to Fisk a large portion of the work and personal collection of her late husband, Alfred Stieglitz. The college still retains much of this collection, although they have sought to sell parts of it to raise funds for the cash-strapped private school. The legal and financial uncertainty over this art collection has forced the college to put it in storage for the time being. The collection, previously housed at the Van Vechten Gallery, includes works by Stieglitz and O'Keeffe, as well as

acclaimed European and American artists including Pablo Picasso, Paul Cezanne, Pierre-Auguste Renoir, Diego Rivera, Arthur Dove, Gino Severini, and Charles Demuth. It is truly a remarkable collection.

The **Aaron Douglas Gallery** (Jackson St. and 17th Ave. N., Tues.–Fri. 11 A.M.–4 P.M., Sat. 1–4 P.M., Sun. 2–4 P.M., free) houses Fisk's collection of African, African-American, and folk art works. It also hosts visiting exhibits, and others by Fisk students and faculty. It is named after painter and illustrator Aaron Douglas, who also established Fisk's first formal art department. The gallery is located on the top floor of the Fisk library.

Fisk welcomes visitors, but there is no central information desk or printed guide. A map is posted just inside the library, and this is the best place to go to start your visit. Historical markers provide details of each of the main campus buildings. To see the famous painting of the Jubilee Singers, enter Jubilee Hall and bear right to the Appleton Room, where it hangs at the rear.

FISK'S STIEGLITZ COLLECTION

When photographer Alfred Stieglitz died in 1946, his wife, Georgia O'Keeffe, herself one of the most important artists of her generation, was left with the responsibility of giving away his massive art collection. Stieglitz had collected more than 1,000 works by artists including Arthur Dove, Marsden Hartley, O'Keeffe, Charles Demuth, and John Marin. He also owned several African sculptures.

Stieglitz's instructions regarding this art collection were vague. In his will he asked O'Keeffe to select the recipients "under such arrangements as will assure to the public, under reasonable regulations, access thereto to promote the study of art."

O'Keeffe selected several obvious recipients for parts of the collection: the Library of Congress, the National Gallery of Art in Washington, the Metropolitan Museum of Art, the Art Institute of Chicago, and the Philadelphia Museum of Art. Fisk University in Nashville was a surprise, and Carl Van Vechten, a writer, photographer, and friend of Stieglitz and O'Keeffe, is credited with making the suggestion. Van Vechten was keenly interested in African-American art and was close friends with Fisk president Charles Johnson.

O'Keeffe and Fisk were not an easy partnership. According to an account by C. Michael Norton, when she first visited the university a few days before the Carl Van Vechten Gallery would open on campus, O'Keeffe ordered major changes to the gallery space, eventually flying in a lighting designer from New York on the day before the opening. At the opening ceremony on November 4, 1949, held at the Memorial Chapel at Fisk, O'Keeffe declined President Johnson's invitation to the lectern and spoke from her chair, saying curtly: "Dr. Johnson wrote and asked me to speak and I did not answer. I had and have no intention of speaking. These paintings and sculptures are a gift from Stieglitz. They are for the students. I hope you go back and look at them more than once."

The Stieglitz Collection at Fisk consists of 101 works of art, including two by O'Keeffe, 19 Stieglitz photographs, prints by Cezanne and Renoir, and five pieces of African tribal art.

Cash-strapped Fisk has sought to sell parts of the collection to raise funds. A proposal to sell a 50 percent share in the collection for $30 million to Wal-Mart heiress Alice Walton's Crystal Bridges Museum in Bentonville, Arkansas, has been rejected by a court, but Fisk continues to press its case. In 2008, an alternative proposal was made to house the collection in the planned museum of African-American culture, art, and history, to be located near the Bicentennial Mall. But that idea offered no immediate financial relief for Fisk and raised many unanswered questions. Meanwhile, Fisk was ordered to repair the Van Vechten Gallery and again open the collection to the public, or risk losing Stieglitz's bequest altogether.

Meharry Medical College

Just across Dr. D. B. Todd Jr. Boulevard from Fisk is Meharry Medical College, the largest private, comprehensive, historically black institution educating medical professionals. It was founded in 1876 as the Medical Department of the Central Tennessee College of Nashville, under the auspices of the Freeman's Aid Society of the Methodist Episcopal Church.

Meharry was at one time responsible for graduating more than half of all African-American doctors and nurses in the United States. Today it has an enrollment of more than 700 students.

Hadley Park

Founded in 1912, Hadley Park is believed to be the oldest public park developed for African Americans in the South and, most likely, the United States. The park got its start when Fisk University president George Gates requested that the city buy land and create a park for its black citizens. This was in the era of segregation, so other city parks were not open to blacks. The request was granted, and the park opened in July 1912. An old farmhouse was converted into a community center, and benches and a playground were installed. It is now home to a state-of-the-art gym and fitness center, computer labs, meeting rooms, and tennis courts.

Tennessee State University

Founded in 1912 as a normal school for blacks, Tennessee State University (www.tnstate.edu) is now a comprehensive university with more than 9,000 students. In 1979, as a result of a court order to desegregate the state's universities, TSU merged with the Nashville campus of the University of Tennessee. Today, TSU's student body is 75 percent African American.

MUSIC VALLEY

A knot of tourist attractions separated from the rest of Nashville by the Cumberland River, Music Valley has little to recommend it other than the Grand Ole Opry. A strip of motels, restaurants, and dubious country music "museums," this is one tourist zone that you will be just as happy to skip. Unless, of course, you just want to soak up the trashy side of Music City tourism.

If you're game, however, head straight for **Cooter's** (2613 McGavock Pk., 615/872-8358, Mon.–Thurs. 9 A.M.–7 P.M., Fri.–Sat. 9 A.M.–8 P.M., Sun. 9 A.M.–6 P.M., free), a gift shop and museum dedicated to the *Dukes of Hazzard* television show. The museum features a mind-boggling array of toys, ornaments, and model cars manufactured in the 1970s and '80s to profit off the Dukes' wild popularity. You can also see one of the bright-orange Dodge Chargers that became the Dukes' icon. In the gift shop, buy a pair of "official" Daisy Dukes, or any number of General Lee souvenirs. Cooters is operated by Ben Jones who played Cooter, the affable sidekick mechanic, in the original television series. In recent years, Jones has been one of the forces behind DukeFest, a wildly popular annual celebration of fast cars and the General Lee held at the Nashville Motor Speedway.

A few doors down from Cooters, you will find **Willie Nelson and Friends Museum** (2613 McGavock Pike, 615/885-1515, summer daily 9 A.M.–8 P.M., winter daily 9 A.M.–7 P.M.,

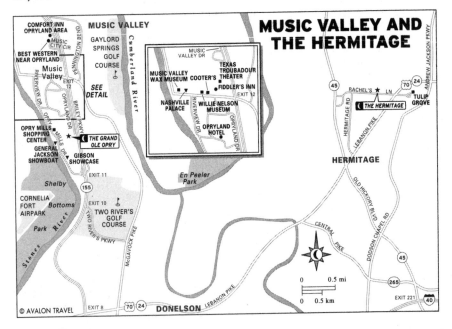

$10), which showcases a number of things that once belonged to Willie Nelson, including his golf bag, a replica of his tour bus, and the guitar he played during his first performance on the Grand Ole Opry. Many of the Willie Nelson items were purchased by museum operators Jeannie and Frank Oakley at an IRS auction.

Another choice is the **Music Valley Wax Museum of the Stars** (2515 McGavock Pike, 615/884-7876, daily 9 A.M.–5 P.M., $12), which advertises itself thus: "As close as you can get to Nashville's biggest stars without being slapped with a restraining order." Enough said.

The Grand Ole Opry

Since 1974, the Grand Ole Opry (2802 Opryland Dr., 615/871-6779, www.opry.com) has been performed at the specially built Grand Ole Opry House in Music Valley.

The Opry performs at least two times a week, Friday and Saturday, with additional shows on Tuesday night most weeks. If you don't come to see a show, you can stop at the **Grand Ole Opry Museum** (2802 Opryland Dr., 615/889-6611, Mon., Wed., and Thurs. 10 A.M.–6 P.M., Tues. 10 A.M.–7:30 P.M., Fri. 10 A.M.–8:30 P.M., Sat. 10 A.M.–10 P.M., Sun. noon–5 P.M., free). The museum has exhibits about many early Opry members and performers, including Minnie Pearl and Roy Acuff. It also emphasizes the important link between the Opry and WSM radio, which still broadcasts the Opry live in Nashville and on the Internet. The museum is closed in January and February.

If the Opry isn't occupied with a performance or special event, you can take a backstage tour for $11.

EAST OF NASHVILLE
◖ The Hermitage

Andrew Jackson's plantation and home 16 miles east of Nashville is the area's best historical tourist attraction. The Hermitage (4580 Rachel's Ln., 615/889-2941, www.thehermitage.com, daily 9 A.M.–5 P.M., $7–15, family pass $40) is

The Hermitage was the home of Andrew Jackson, the seventh president of the United States.

OLD HICKORY

Andrew Jackson, the seventh president of the United States, was one of the most important American political figures of the first half of the 19th century. His impact was so great that we now refer to his era as the Age of Jackson and his ideology as Jacksonian Democracy.

Jackson was born in 1767 on the American frontier in South Carolina. His father, an immigrant from Northern Ireland, died before Jackson was born. At age 12, Jackson volunteered for the American army in the Revolutionary War. Jackson's two brothers, Hugh and Robert, died during the war. His mother, Elizabeth, died of smallpox in 1781. Jackson was 14 years old, and alone in the world.

Remarkably, Jackson not only survived; he flourished. In 1784 he moved to Salisbury, North Carolina, where he studied law. In 1787 he became a licensed lawyer and moved west, to Washington County, now part of Tennessee. In 1788 he was appointed the district attorney for the Mero District, now Middle Tennessee.

In Nashville, a city that was founded less than 10 years earlier, Jackson met Rachel Donelson, the daughter of John Donelson. Jackson fell in love with Rachel and in 1781 they were married. Later, when they learned that Rachel's earlier, unhappy marriage to Lewis Robards of Kentucky was not legally dissolved, they remarried in 1794 before a Davidson County justice of the peace.

The Jacksons set about to establish a home and livelihood. Jackson practiced law, speculated in land, and dabbled in politics. They bought farmland in Davidson County where they built the Hermitage, which would be the

Andrew Jackson

COURTESY OF LIBRARY OF CONGRESS/ALEXANDER HAY RITCHIE

Jacksons' home for the rest of their lives. The couple never had children of their own, but they adopted a nephew, who was known as Andrew Jackson Jr., and reared several indian orphans.

By 1798 Jackson was a circuit-riding judge on the Tennessee Superior Court, but he also developed a reputation for resolving his own conflicts through violence. He brawled with a set of brothers, killed a man in a duel, caned another, and ran a sword through a third. In 1803 he quarreled publicly with governor John Sevier and nearly dueled him as well.

where Jackson retired following his two terms as president of the United States, and it is where he and his beloved wife, Rachel, are buried.

Jackson bought the property in 1809; he and Rachel initially lived in a rustic log cabin, which has since been restored. Jackson first named the home and property Rural Retreat, and later he chose the more poetic name, the Hermitage. Jackson ran a successful cotton plantation on the property, owning as many

as 150 slaves. In 1819 he and Rachel started construction of what is now the mansion. They moved in 1821.

In 1831, two years after he became the nation's seventh president, Jackson expanded the mansion so it was more suitable for presidential entertaining. While Jackson was in Washington, his adopted son, Andrew Jackson Jr., managed the property, and when a chimney fire damaged the house in 1834, Jackson

Jackson's violent temper was better suited for the battlefield. In 1802 he was elected Major General of the Tennessee militia and with the outbreak of war in 1812, his leadership was required. Jackson earned the nickname "Old Hickory" in 1812 when he disobeyed orders and refused to dismiss his Tennessee soldiers in Natchez, Mississippi, marching them back to Tennessee under great hardship instead. He earned national fame three years later when he marched his men from Florida to New Orleans, where he resoundingly defeated the British. The American public was so pleased with their new war hero that they did not mind when they learned the British had actually surrendered two weeks earlier. Neither did they mind some of his tactics: military executions, imposition of martial law, suspension of habeas corpus, and defiance of a federal court order.

In the succeeding years, Jackson fought battles with Native American tribes, and negotiated land treaties with them. By 1821, he quit his post as Major General and came home to the Hermitage for a short retirement.

In 1822 the Tennessee state legislature nominated Jackson for U.S. president and his nomination was seconded by other states. In the 1824 contest, Jackson received more votes than any other contender in the crowded field. But when the U.S. House of Representatives gave the presidency to John Quincy Adams, Jackson called the decision a "corrupt bargain" that violated the will of the voters. His 1828 presidential campaign had begun.

The 1828 campaign was spirited and dirty.

Opponents found seemingly countless stories of Jackson's indiscretions, and they accused him and Rachel of committing adultery by marrying before Rachel's divorce was final. When Rachel Jackson died on December 22, 1828, Jackson accused his opponents of hastening her death by slander.

Jackson was raised as a Presbyterian and held strong religious beliefs throughout his life. He resisted Rachel Jackson's encouragements to formally join a church, however, saying that he feared the charge of hypocrisy that could be leveled against him as a public churchgoer. Jackson promised Rachel that when he left public life he would join the church, and he was true to his word. In July 1838, Jackson, then in his 70s, joined the church.

During his two terms as president, Jackson enraged his opponents and delighted supporters. He took unprecedented actions in the name of reform, including several controversial banking decisions. He believed in a strong federal government and stood in the way of state nullification of federal laws. By the end of his eight years in the White House, Jackson was known by his opponents as "King Andrew," while his supporters still saw him as a spokesman of the common man.

Jackson, who never remarried, spent the remaining eight years of his life at the Hermitage, where he entertained guests, helped to manage the farm, and dispensed advice to politicians. His health declined, though, and in 1845, at age 78, he died and was buried in the Hermitage garden, next to his beloved Rachel.

Jr. and his wife, Sarah, saw to its restoration. At the end of Jackson's second term in office in 1837, he retired to the Hermitage and lived here happily until his death in 1845.

Following President Jackson's death, the Hermitage remained in family hands until 1853, when it was sold to the State of Tennessee to pay off the family's debts. It opened as a museum in 1889 and was restored largely due to the persistence of the Ladies Hermitage Association. Because the property never left family hands before it was sold to the State, many of the furnishings are original and even the wallpaper in several rooms dates back to the years when Andrew Jackson called it home.

One major strength of the present-day Hermitage tour and museum is that it focuses not only on Jackson and the construction and decoration of the mansion, but also the African-American slaves who worked at the

Hermitage plantation. Curators and archaeologists have studied the Hermitage to learn about the hundreds of men and women who made the Hermitage profitable and successful for so many years. The tour of the grounds takes visitors to Alfred's Cabin, a slave cabin occupied until 1901 by former Hermitage slave Alfred Jackson. You also learn about the agriculture that took place on the Hermitage, and can see cotton being cultivated during the summer months. To learn even more about the Hermitage's slaves, take an add-on wagon tour, offered from April to October.

Visitors to the Hermitage begin with a video about Andrew Jackson and the Hermitage, and can continue on to a museum. You take an audio tour of the grounds, and guided tours are offered of the mansion. You wind up in the gift shop and café. Plan on spending at least three hours here to make the most of your visit. Try to come when the weather is good.

TOURS
Nash Trash Tours
Nashville's most notorious tour guides are Sheri Lynn and Brenda Kay Jugg, sisters who ferry thrill-seekers around Nashville in a big pink school bus. The Nash Trash Tour (615/226-7300 or 800/342-2123, www.nashtrash.com, $30) is a raunchy, rollicking, rib-tickling tour of city attractions, some of which you won't even find in this guidebook. Be prepared to be the butt of some of the jokes yourself; their "I Got Trashed" T-shirts have a double meaning. You'll snack on canned cheese and there's a pit stop to buy beer. Not appropriate for children or adults who aren't comfortable laughing at themselves and others. As Sheri Lynn says: "If we haven't offended you, just give us some time."

Gray Line Tours
Nashville's largest tour company, Gray Line (2416 Music Valley Dr., 615/883-5555 or

800/251-1864), offers no fewer than 12 different sightseeing tours of the city. The three-hour Discover Nashville tour costs $40 per adult and includes entrance to the Ryman Auditorium, the Country Music Hall of Fame, and stops at other city landmarks.

The three-hour Homes of the Stars tour takes you past the homes of stars including Alan Jackson, Vince Gill, Dolly Parton, and the late Tammy Wynette for $35. There is also a one-hour downtown trolley tour for $12 and a 90-minute downtown walking tour for $20.

General Jackson Showboat
Enjoy lunch or dinner, live entertainment, and a cruise along the Cumberland on the General Jackson Showboat (2812 Opryland Dr., 615/458-3900, www.generaljackson.com). Midday tickets range $30–50 and include lunch. Evening tickets are $35–90 and include a three-course dinner. You can cruise and skip the meal at midday or in the evening for $17.

Tennessee Central Railway
The Tennessee Central Railway Museum (220 Willow St., 615/244-9001, www.tcry.org) offers an annual calendar of sightseeing and themed railway rides in central Tennessee. Excursions include fall foliage tours, Christmas shopping expeditions, and trips to scenic small towns. All trips run on the Nashville and Eastern Railroad, which runs east, stopping in Lebanon, Watertown, and Cookville, and terminates in Monterrey.

Trips sell out early, so book your tickets well in advance.

Nashville Black Heritage Tours
Call ahead to book a tour for your family or group with Bill Daniel of Nashville Black Heritage Tours (5188 Almaville Rd., Smyrna, 615/890-8153), who will craft a tour of the city's most important African-American heritage sites.

Entertainment

From shopping to live music, Nashville offers visitors plenty of diversions. Even if you are not a fan of country music, you will find plenty to do in Music City.

LIVE MUSIC AND CLUBS

No trip to Nashville is complete without listening to some live music. Music City overflows with musicians and opportunities to hear them. So whether you catch a show at the Opry, stake out a seat at the Bluebird Cafe, or enjoy a night at the symphony, be sure to make time for music during your visit.

Even before you arrive in the city, you can plan out your nights thanks to the Nashville Convention and Visitors Bureau (www.nashvillecvb.com). Through a handy feature on the bureau's website you can check out upcoming concerts a month or more in advance. Many venues will let you buy tickets in advance over the phone or online.

Published on Wednesday, the *Nashville Scene* always includes detailed entertainment listings and recommendations. The *Tennessean,* the city's daily paper, publishes its entertainment insert on Friday.

◖ The Grand Ole Opry

If there's anything you really must do while in Nashville, it's go to see the Grand Ole Opry (2802 Opryland Dr., 615/871-6779 or 800/733-6779, www.opry.com, $35–50). For more than 80 years this weekly radio showcase of country music has drawn crowds to Nashville. Every show at the Opry is still broadcast live on WSM, a Nashville AM radio station. Shows are also streamed online and some are televised on cable. But nothing quite beats being there.

The Opry runs on Friday and Saturday night, with two two-and-a-half-hour shows each night. The early show starts at 6:30 P.M. and the late show starts at 9:30 P.M. Sometimes there is a bonus show on Tuesday evening.

Since this is a radio broadcast, shows start and end right on time.

Every Opry show is divided into 30-minute segments, each of which is hosted by a different member of the Opry. This elite country music fraternity includes dozens of stars that you've heard of and others you haven't. The host performs two songs; one at the beginning of their half-hour segment and one at the end. In between they will introduce two or three other performers, each of whom will sing about two songs. In between segments, the announcers read radio commercials and stagehands change around the stage set.

All in all, it is a fast-paced show that keeps your toes tapping. Even if there's an act that you don't like, they won't be on the stage for too long. Of course, the flip side is that if it's an act you love, well, they're only on the stage for two songs too. Even when the biggest stars appear on the Opry stage, they rarely sing more than a few numbers.

The Opry usually releases the full line-up for each show about a week in advance. Some fans wait until then to buy their tickets so they're sure to catch a big-name artist. My advice is to forget about bragging to your friends back home about who you saw at the Opry and buy tickets to any show at all. Each show is carefully balanced to include bluegrass, classic country, popular country, and, sometimes, gospel. It is a true showcase that every fan of country music will enjoy.

Most Opry shows take place in the Grand Ole Opry House, a 4,400-seat auditorium in Music Valley. The interior of the hall was designed to look like the Ryman Auditorium, although the seats are much more comfortable. A circle of the original stage from the Ryman was cut out and placed in the center of the Opry House stage, and it is here that artists stand when they perform. Several months out of the year the Opry returns to the Ryman for its Opry at the Ryman season.

THE GRAND OLE OPRY

Nashville's most famous broadcast can trace its roots to October 1925, when Nashville-based National Life and Accident Insurance Company opened a radio station in town. Its call letters, WSM, stood for "We Shield Millions," the company's motto.

WSM hired George D. Hay, a radio announcer who had worked in Memphis and Chicago, to manage the station. Hay – who, while in Chicago, had announced one of the nation's first live country radio shows – planned to create a similar such program in Nashville.

On November 25, 1925, Hay invited a 78-year-old fiddler, Uncle Jimmy Thompson, to perform live on Saturday night over the radio waves. The response was electric, and WSM continued to broadcast live old-time music every Saturday night. In May 1927, the program developed the name the Grand Ole Opry, practically by chance. An announcer named Judge Hay was segueing from the previous program of classical opera to the barn dance. "For the past hour, we have been listening to music taken largely from Grand Opera. From now on, we will present the Grand Ole Opry," he said. The name stuck.

During the first few years, most Opry performers were unknowns who worked day jobs in and around Nashville. But as the show gained popularity, some acts were able to make it professionally, including Uncle Dave Macon, the Vagabonds, and the Delmore Brothers. By 1939, the Opry gained a slot on the nationwide NBC radio network, allowing it to reach a national audience every week.

Always a live audience show, the Opry was performed in several different venues over the years. It started in the WSM studio, then moved to the Hillsboro Theater (now the Belcourt), the Dixie Tabernacle on Fatherland Street, and the War Memorial Auditorium downtown. In 1943 it moved to the Ryman Auditorium, where it remained until 1974, when National Life built a new 5,000-seat auditorium in a rural area north of Nashville. The first show from the new Opry House in Music Valley was broadcast on March 16, 1974. President Richard Nixon attended. In 1983, the Opry was acquired by Oklahoma-based Gaylord Broadcasting Company. The Opry is still owned by Gaylord Entertainment.

The music that flows from the Opry's stage on a Saturday night (and now, Tuesday and Friday too) has changed since the first fiddler took the airwaves. Just as country music broadened its appeal by softening its hard edges, the Opry has evolved with its audience. Today it is a showcase for all types of country and country-inspired music, including bluegrass, gospel, honky-tonk, and zydeco. It remains, however, one of the most esteemed and celebrated institutions in country music.

The Opry is the most famous stage in country music.

Ernest Tubb Midnite Jamboree

Texas Troubadour Ernest Tubb started a tradition when he set up a live radio show at the back of his Broadway record shop. The show was broadcast after the Opry shut down across the street, and it lived up to its name, the Midnite Jamboree. The Jamboree continues, now broadcast from the **Texas Troubadour Theatre** (Music Valley Village, 2416 Music Valley Dr., 615/889-2472, www.ernesttubb. com, no cover). Located across the street from the Opryland Hotel, the Jamboree gets started early in the evening, while the Opry is still on, but things really get swinging after midnight.

The Texas Troubadour Theatre is also home to the **Cowboy Church** (2416 Music Valley Dr., 615/859-1001, www.nashvillecowboychurch. org). Every Sunday morning at 10 A.M., locals and tourists dressed in anything from shorts to Stetsons gather here for a lively praise-and-worship country gospel church service led by Dr. Harry Yates and Dr. Joanne Cash Yates. The church was founded in 1990 with just six souls; today it attracts hundreds to its weekly services. Country and gospel music legends make cameo performances now and again, but the real star is Jesus.

The Gibson Showcase

Guitar manufacturer Gibson has a concert venue next to its Nashville retail store. The Gibson Showcase (161 Opry Mills Dr., 615/514-2200, ext. 231, cover varies) puts on weekday bluegrass concerts, evening dinner events, and special shows. Bluegrass jams start at 8 P.M. on Monday nights; there's no cover charge and reservations are not accepted. Just Country and More is a showcase of country music classics, pop tunes, and family entertainment performed while guests chow on a Southern dinner menu. Special events include performances by jazz, blues, bluegrass, and country greats.

The Ryman Auditorium

The most famous music venue in Nashville, the Ryman Auditorium (116 5th Ave. N., www. ryman.com, cover varies) continues to book

some of the best acts in town, of just about every genre you can imagine. On the good side, the hall still boasts some of the best acoustics around. On the bad, the bench seats are just as uncomfortable as ever. But if the show is good, you probably won't even notice.

Country Music Hall of Fame

The Country Music Hall of Fame (222 5th Ave. S., 615/416-2100, www.countrymusic-halloffame.com) hosts concerts, readings, and musical discussions regularly in an auditorium located inside the hall. These daytime events are often aimed at highlighting one type of country music or another, but sometimes you'll find big names playing. Admission is free with your paid admission to the hall, so it is a good idea to plan your trip to the hall on a day when there's a concert scheduled (separate admission to concerts is not available). Check the website for a listing of upcoming events.

◖ The Bluebird Cafe

For a certain type of music fan, the Bluebird Cafe (4104 Hillsboro Pike, 615/383-1461, www.bluebirdcafe.com, cover varies) has a whole lot going for it. It is intimate and homey. It books some of the best up-and-coming country and acoustic acts in the business. Its shows start as early as 6:30 P.M. There's no smoking, no talking during the acts, and virtually none of the usual bar pick-up scene. In short, the Bluebird is a place where music comes first, and everything else is a far second.

Opened in 1982 by Amy Kurland, the Bluebird started out as a casual restaurant with live music. It's located next to a dry cleaners in a nondescript shopping mall a few miles south of Hillsboro Village. Over the years, it has evolved into a destination for music lovers who appreciate its no-nonsense take on live music, and who hope that they just might stumble in on the next big thing. The Bluebird is famous as an early venue for the then-unknown Garth Brooks, but its stage has also hosted the likes of Emmylou Harris, Kathy Mattea, Gillian Welch, Trisha Yearwood, and Steve Earle, among many more.

The Bluebird Cafe hosts intimate concerts and open mics.

The Bluebird opens every night of the week, and most evenings the entertainment starts at 6:30 P.M. Cover is usually under $10. There is no cover charge and no reservations accepted for the shows on Sunday, songwriters' night, or Monday, open-mic night, but guests should arrive by 5:30 P.M. to get one of the first-come, first-served seats. There are only 21 tables and a few additional seats at the bar, so you have to be on your toes to get a spot in the house. For shows on Friday and Saturday nights, the Bluebird takes reservations the Monday of that week noon–5 P.M. Be advised that many weeks the shows sell out in a mere half hour, so keep hitting that redial button! Reservations for Tuesday–Thursday shows are available a week ahead 11 A.M.–5 P.M. You can also make reservations online. There is a $7 minimum per seat at all shows, so come hungry or thirsty. The food is standard bar fare, nothing more and nothing less. No outside drinks are allowed.

Once you've successfully navigated the rules of getting a seat at the Bluebird, sit back and enjoy some fine live music. Nashville is the city where anybody can become a somebody, and it's places like the Bluebird that make that happen. Be a part of it.

Clubs

If there is one false assumption that many people have about Nashville, it is that this is a strictly country town. In fact, Nashville has a vibrant rock 'n' roll music scene, plus good blues and jazz. So in a city where country music rubs shoulders with great rock, blues, and Americana, most live music venues refuse to be pigeonholed.

Venues here are categorized by their predominant music type, but keep in mind that variety is the name of the game. Most bars and clubs charge a cover when there is a band or performer, while songwriter nights and open mics are usually free.

COUNTRY

Nashville's most colorful country music establishments are the honky-tonks that line Broadway. Once places where country boys and girls would come to shake a leg or meet a beau, these all-day, all-night bars and music clubs now cater to visitors. **Tootsie's Orchid Lounge** (422 Broadway, 615/726-0463, no cover) is painted purple and exudes classic country every day of the week beginning as early as 10 A.M. Three doors down from Tootsie's is **Robert's Western World** (416 Broadway, 615/244-9552, no cover), voted the city's best honky-tonk. Originally a store selling boots, cowboy hats, and other country music regalia, Roberts morphed into a bar and nightclub with a good gift shop. Another choice is **The Stage** (412 Broadway, 615/726-0504, no cover), with a large dance floor and music seven nights a week.

After the Opry moved to Music Valley in the late 1970s, taking with it the customers who kept Broadway businesses afloat, the street's honky-tonks subsisted first on local bar flies and later on the tourist trade. Whether you're looking for a place to drown your sorrows or kick off a night on the town, Broadway's honky-tonks are a good place to go.

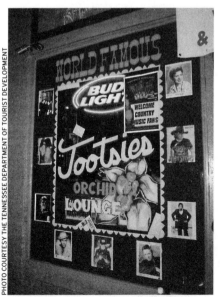

Tootsie's Orchid Lounge on Broadway is Nashville's most famous honky-tonk.

Probably the most popular country music nightclub downtown, the **Wildhorse Saloon** (120 2nd Ave. N., 615/902-8200, www.wildhorsesaloon.com, cover varies) is a boot-scootin' and beer-drinking place to see and be seen. When the Wildhorse opened in 1994, promoters drove a herd of cattle through the streets of downtown Nashville. Today, the Wildhorse is still a place where a good show and a good time are the top priorities. The huge dance floor is often packed with cowboys and cowgirls line dancing to the greatest hits of the country music genre. Dance lessons are offered every day (Mon.–Thurs. 6:30–8:30 P.M., Fri. 6–9:30 P.M., Sat. noon–9:30 P.M., Sun. 2–7:30 P.M.). The Wildhorse books big-name acts many nights of the week, including country music, roots rock, and classic rock stars. The Wildhorse opens Thursday through Sunday at 11 A.M., and on Monday at 5 P.M. When there is a show on, doors normally close at 6 P.M. and re-open at 7 P.M. for people with tickets. On other nights the cover charge ranges $4–6. From 10 P.M. on, the Wildhorse is a 21-and-up club.

The city's most popular venue for bluegrass and roots music, **The Station Inn** (402 12th Ave. S., 615/255-3307, cover varies) showcases fine artists every night of the week. This homey and casual club opens nightly at 7 P.M., with music starting about 9 P.M. This is a 21-and-over club, unless you come with a parent or guardian. There is no cover for the Sunday-night bluegrass jam.

The **Douglas Corner Cafe** (2106-A 8th Ave. S., 615/298-1688, cover varies) offers a Tuesday-night open mic, and country acts the rest of the week. It is known as a place where singer-songwriters are discovered, and it is not unlike the Bluebird Cafe in attitude and ambience. An intimate setting, full menu, and good acoustics make this a popular choice for music listening. Several live albums have been recorded here.

The **Nashville Palace** (2400 Music Valley Dr., 615/889-1540, no cover) is a restaurant, nightclub, and dance floor across from the Opryland Hotel. Live music is on tap daily starting at 5 P.M., and talent nights on Tuesday and Wednesday always draw a crowd.

JAZZ AND BLUES

If you need to get that country twang out of your head, a good dose of the blues will do it. **B. B. King Blues Club** (152 2nd Ave. N., 615/256-2727, cover varies) is a good place to start for a night of the blues. The club is a satellite of King's original Beale Street club, and it books live blues every night. The cover charge is usually under $10, unless B. B. King himself is making one of his rare appearances.

In Printer's Alley, the **Bourbon Street Blues and Boogie Bar** (220 Printer's Alley, 615/242-5867, cover varies) is a hole-in-the-wall nightclub that specializes in New Orleans–style jazz and blues.

A fine dining restaurant next door to Green Hills Mall, **F. Scott's** (2210 Crestmore Rd., 615/269-5861, no cover) is also the city's premier venue for live jazz. The music goes well with the restaurant's art deco appeal. Come for dinner or for a few drinks at the bar while you listen in. Although there's no cover at the door, there is a two-drink minimum if you're not dining.

ECLECTIC

Clubs listed here may book a rock band one night and folk the next. Always check the free weekly *Nashville Scene* for the latest entertainment listings.

12th and Porter (114 12th Ave. S., 615/254-7250, cover varies) is a favorite venue for live music in the city. Second only to the Ryman in popularity, 12th and Porter books all kinds of acts. They are a popular choice for music-label showcases, and legendary performers have been known to stage impromptu shows here. Spacious and offering a full menu, including good Mexican food, 12th and Porter is a great hangout and place to hear live music.

The **Exit/In** (2208 Elliston Pl., 615/321-3340, cover varies) has been a favorite rock music venue for years, although it also books alternative country, blues, and reggae. Located on Elliston Place, the club is convenient to Vanderbilt and downtown.

Coffee shop by day, bar and live music venue by night, **Café Coco** (210 Louise Ave., 615/321-2626, cover varies) in Elliston Place is the best of both worlds. Monday is songwriter's night, Tuesday is open-mic poetry, and Thursday is open-mic music. Jazz and rock bands play other nights, when the cover ranges $2–5.

The Basement (1604 8th Ave. S., 615/254-8006, www.thebasementnashville.com, cover varies) calls itself a cellar full of noise, but it's a good kind of noise. Indie rock is the most common art form here, but they book other types of acts too. The Basement's New Faces Night on Tuesday is a popular place to hear singer-songwriters. Admission is 21 and over, unless accompanied by a parent or guardian. There is a full bar and light menu. Note that inside the club is totally smoke-free; there is an outdoor smoking porch. The brick walls and subterranean feel give the Basement its cool atmosphere. Park behind the club and on side streets.

Located in an old warehouse that has housed a flour mill, jam factory, and country music concert hall, **Cannery Row** (One Cannery Row, 615/251-3020, www.mercy-lounge.com, cover varies) and its derivative **Mercy Lounge** are two cool venues for live music. Cannery Row is a large, somewhat cavernous space with lots of nice cherry-red touches, hardwood floors, and a shiny red bar. It can hold up to 1,000 people. The Mercy Lounge upstairs is a bit more intimate, with a capacity of up to 500 people. The Mercy Lounge hosts 8 off 8th on Monday nights, an open mic where eight different bands get to perform three songs. Both venues book rock, country, soul, and all sorts of other acts. It is located off 8th Avenue South.

A music venue designed by performers, **The Rutledge** (410 4th Ave. S., 615/782-6858, www.therutledgelmv.com, cover varies) has some of the most ear-pleasing acoustics in the city. An intimate venue—it seats only 250—the Rutledge books a wide variety of acts, hosts industry events, and even puts on tribute shows now and then. It is a smoke-free club and serves a limited food menu.

3rd and Lindsley (818 3rd Ave. S., 615/259-

9891, www.3rdandlindsley.com, cover varies) is a neighborhood bar and grill that showcases rock, alternative, progressive, Americana, soul, and R&B music. Over the years they have developed a reputation for booking good blues acts. They serve a full lunch and dinner menu, the bar is well-stocked, and the club offers a great atmosphere and sound quality. Smoking is allowed.

Over in East Nashville, the **French Quarter Cafe** (823 Woodland St., 615/227-3100, cover varies) offers a Thursday night in-the-round songwriter's night. Weekends will find blues, rock, and soul musicians on the stage at this New Orleans–style nightclub. Dine on spicy po-boys, muffaletta, or other Cajun specialties while you enjoy a night out.

CONCERT SERIES

Dyer Observatory (1000 Oman Dr., 615/373-4897, www.dyer.vanderbilt.edu), a working space observatory operated by Vanderbilt University, has emerged as a popular venue for music, thanks to two ongoing concert series. **Music on the Mountain,** with Blair School of Music, and **Bluebird on the Mountain,** with the Bluebird Cafe, bring live music to this dramatic and one-of-a-kind spot. Imagine a night of fine music enjoyed under the stars, with the fresh air and the atmosphere of the forest all around you.

Every October the Grand Ole Opry celebrates its birthday with **Opry Month,** four weeks of star-studded performances, including several at the Opry's original home, the Ryman Auditorium. Get your tickets early, since these shows are always popular.

Also taking place on Thursday nights in the summer, **Bluegrass Nights at the Ryman** is a concert series that features some of the best pickers in the country. Starting in June and ending in July, this Ryman Auditorium series is always popular.

For a laid-back evening in a one-of-a-kind setting, check out the Tennessee Jazz and Blues Society's concert series **Jazz on the Lawn** (www.jazzblues.org). On Sunday evenings from May to October, jazz and blues artists take the stage on the lawns of some of Nashville's most historic homes, including the Hermitage, Belle Meade, and Cheekwood. Bring your own picnic and blanket.

BARS

Bar-hopping is best enjoyed downtown, where there is the greatest concentration of nightclubs, restaurants, and bars. Even on weeknights, the District, which lies along lower Broadway and its side streets, is crowded with people dressed in designer cowboy boots and fringed shirts. This is the official entertainment district of Nashville, and it is well-patrolled by police and cruisers alike.

Outside of the District, there are several other enclaves of nightlife that cater more to residents than visitors.

Nashville won't issue a liquor license unless the establishment also serves food, so all of the bars listed below double as restaurants.

The District

The honky-tonks along Broadway, Wildhorse Saloon, and B. B. King Blues Clubs are several of the most popular nightclubs in the District. Right next to the Wildhorse Saloon in the heart of the District, **Coyote Ugly** (154 2nd Ave. N., 615/254-8459, www.coyoteugly.com) draws a youthful, raucous crowd. Drinking beer and making friends are the two primary pursuits here, and for many people, there's no better place to do either.

Memorabilia of Nashville's past adorns the walls at **Legends Corner** (428 Broadway, 615/248-6334), a popular club for live music and rollicking crowds. There is never a cover, but be sure to put in a few bucks when they pass the hat for the performer.

Farther afield, but still downtown, you'll find one of the city's best beer bars. Behind the Union Station Hotel on the west side of downtown, the **Flying Saucer** (1001 Broadway, 615/259-7468) has one of the best selections of beer in town. Monday is pint night, when you can get $2.50 pints of just about any of the beers on the wall.

Duck into **The Beer Sellar** (107 Church St.,

615/254-9464) to experience its "50 draughts, 150 bottles and 1 bitching jukebox." Located within walking distance of downtown, this is a cozy bar for conversation and fun.

Another popular brewpub is **Big River Grille and Brewing Works** (111 Broadway, 615/251-4677), an imposing bar and restaurant in the heart of the District. They serve food as well as boutique beers from around the world.

Printer's Alley

This narrow patch of downtown, located in between 3rd and 4th Avenues off Church Street, is home to a half-dozen nightclubs and bars, many that cultivate a seedy reputation. While reality may be a bit more tame, it is still a popular place to let loose. Elaborate wrought-iron balconies and the cobblestone underfoot evoke Bourbon Street, a parallel that seems to suit the place. Bars here include **Bourbon Street Blues and Boogie Bar** (220 Printer's Alley, 615/242-5867) and **Fiddle and Steel** (201 Printer's Alley, 615/251-9002). Printer's Alley also has a karaoke bar and one of the city's most storied adult-entertainment bars.

Midtown

Elliston Place is home to several live music clubs plus a few neighborhood bars. The Exit/In and The End have live bands most nights of the week. You can play a game of pool at **Elliston's Pool Place Hall** (2200 Elliston Pl., 615/320-9441). This is a back-to-the-basics hangout where good drinks, good pool, and good people make for a good night out. **The Gold Rush** (2205 Elliston Pl., 615/321-1160) is a popular late-night mellow hangout. Finally, **Sherlock Holmes' Pub** (2206 Elliston Pl., 615/327-1047), which models itself as an old-fashioned English pub, has fish-and-chips and pints of beer.

Also an upscale restaurant, **Virago** (1811 Division St., 615/320-5149) in Music Row is a trendy bar and late-night pit stop. The S-shaped bar is the perfect place to order a martini and imagine you're in a big city.

Boscos (1805 21st Ave. S., 615/385-0050)

calls itself a beer-lover's restaurant. While food is important here, it is Boscos' reputation for good beer that keeps patrons coming back. Stake out a front window seat to people-watch in trendy Hillsboro Village while you drink your beer.

Also in Hillsboro Village, **Cabana** (1910 Belcourt Ave., 615/577-2262) is a popular place to people-watch and unwind. It is a bar/restaurant/late-night hangout that attracts a youthful and well-dressed crowd. Lounge at the bar or in the expansive backyard. Choose from dozens of beers, wines, and some excellent martinis.

In the Green Hills area, **The Greenhouse** (2211 Bandywood Dr., 615/385-3357) offers specialty drinks, beers, and lots of hanging plants. To find it, look for the Green Hills Kroger and take a left. A few doors down, **The Box Seat** (2221 Bandywood Dr., 615/383-8018) is a bona fide sports bar with televisions in every direction.

South Street Original Crab Shack and Authentic Dive Bar (907 20th Ave. S., 615/320-5555) is an institution, serving Cajun specialties and a relaxed atmosphere. Head upstairs to the open-air Treehouse, perfect for a warm Nashville night.

Broadway Brewhouse (1900 Broadway, 615/340-0089) has more than 70 different beers on tap and 100 more in coolers.

East Nashville

Edgefield Sports Bar and Grille (921 Woodland St., 615/228-6422) is a no-frills watering hole that caters to East Nashville residents.

The Family Wash (2038 Greenwood Ave., 615/226-6070) is a live music listening room where people come for a pint of beer and food too. It's also a neighborhood joint for the up-and-coming East Nashville community.

For a fun, retro vibe and a dance floor that gets hopping most nights of the week, grab a table at the **Alleycat Lounge** (1008-B Woodland St., 615/262-5888).

You might think you're in Austin at the **Rosepepper Cantina** (1907 Eastland Ave., 615/227-4777), a Mexican restaurant and bar.

Choose from 30 different variations on the margarita, and enjoy the house band on weekend nights.

12 South

The up-and-coming neighborhood on 12th Avenue South is attracting new residents and businesses. Here you can enjoy a martini at **Mirror** (2317 12th Ave. S., 615/383-8330), a Miami Beach–inspired restaurant and bar. Enjoy the tapas menu while you sip your drink and people-watch.

Snag a seat on the crowded patio outside **Mafiaoza's Pizzeria and Neighborhood Pub** (2400 12th Ave. S., 615/269-4646, www.mafiaozas.com), a popular neighborhood hangout known for its top-notch pizza.

For something a little different, head to **Rumors Wine and Art Bar** (2304 12th Ave. S., 615/292-9400), a homey wine bar and art gallery. Good for wine lovers and aspiring wine lovers alike, this is a popular place for residents of the trendy 12 South district to get together. Rumors has a satellite location in East Nashville, at 112 Woodland Street (615/262-5346).

GAY AND LESBIAN NIGHTLIFE

You don't have to be gay to enjoy **Tribe** (1517-A Church St., 615/329-2912), but it helps to be beautiful, or at least well-dressed. The dance floor here is one of the best in the city, and the atmosphere is hip. Martinis and other specialty drinks are the poison of choice at this standard-setting club, which stays open until the wee hours.

Right next door to Tribe is **Play** (1519 Church St., 615/322-9627), the city's newest gay club, with drag shows and performances by adult-film stars.

The Chute Complex (2535 Franklin Rd., 615/297-4571) has karaoke, drag shows, and a dance floor. It caters to gay men.

Women outnumber men at the **Lipstick Lounge** (1400 Woodland St., 615/226-6343), a cool yet homey club in East Nashville. Live music, pool, and great food attract a crowd nearly every night.

For a low-key evening of pool or a happy hour stop before dinner, **TRAX** (1501 2nd Ave. S., 615/742-8856) is the place to go. The patio is a nice place to sit in warm weather. There is wireless Internet and big-screen televisions.

Outloud Cafe (1707 Church St., 615/329-8006) is a casual restaurant, coffee shop, and low-key venue for entertainment, catering to the gay and lesbian crowd. Thursday is movie night, there are monthly art exhibits, and game night is Monday beginning at 7 P.M.

COMEDY

Nashville's only comedy club is **Zanies** (2025 8th Ave. S., 615/269-0221), where you can hear stand-up comics every weekend and some weeknights.

THE ARTS

Before Nashville was Music City, it was the Athens of the South, a city renowned for its cultural, academic, and artistic life. Universities, museums, and public arts facilities created an environment for artistic expression unparalleled by any other Southern city.

These days, most people think that country music is Nashville's only art form. But the truth is that Nashville offers far more than honky-tonks and the Opry. It has an opera company of its own, not to mention an award-winning symphony, buoyant arts scene, and ample opportunities to sample contemporary and classic music, film, and theater.

Theater

The **Tennessee Repertory Theatre** (505 Deaderick St., 615/782-4000, www.tennesseerep.org) is Tennessee's largest professional theater company. It stages five big-name shows and three off-Broadway productions annually. The Rep performs in the Tennessee Performing Arts Center, located in the James K. Polk Cultural Center in downtown Nashville. This is the same building that houses the Tennessee State Museum, plus the Nashville Opera Association and the Nashville Ballet. Some of their productions have included *The Crucible, I Hate Hamlet,* and *Doubt.* The season runs from October to May.

FAMOUS NASHVILLIANS

Nashville is used to celebrity, what with all the country music stars around. But it's not just musicians who call, or called, Nashville home:

"Jefferson Street Joe" Gilliam, one of the first African-American quarterbacks in the National Football League, played his college ball at Tennessee State University. The former quarterback for the Pittsburgh Steelers died in 2000 in his hometown of Nashville, five days before his 50th birthday.

Madison Smartt Bell was born and raised in Nashville. The novelist's works include *All Souls Rising, Ten Indians,* and *The Year of Silence.*

Oprah Winfrey was raised in Nashville by her father, Vernon. In her second year at Tennessee State University she was hired as Nashville's first female and first African-American TV news anchor on WTVF-TV.

Julian Bond, civil rights activist, political activist, and the chairman of the NAACP, was born in Nashville and lived here until he was five years old.

Bobby Jones, host of BET's Bobby Jones Gospel, was once a professor at Tennessee State University. The program is the longest-running show on cable television and is taped in Nashville.

Red Grooms was born and raised in Nashville. Grooms is a prominent modern American artist, whose pop art depicts frenetic scenes of urban life.

Al Gore Jr., though born in Washington, D.C., and raised in Carthage, Tennessee, is closely associated with Nashville. After the Vietnam War he attended Vanderbilt University for one year and then spent five years as a reporter for the *Tennessean.* The former U.S. vice president and his wife, Tipper, have had a home in Nashville for many decades.

Artists' Cooperative Theatre (615/726-2281, www.act1online.com) is an organization dedicated to bringing theatrical gems, both classic and modern, to Nashville audiences. Founded in 1989, ACT 1, as it is called, has presented productions of more than 90 of the world's greatest plays. Each year the theater puts on four or five productions. ACT 1 performs at the Darkhorse Theater at 4610 Charlotte Avenue.

New theatrical works are given the spotlight by the **Actors Bridge Ensemble** (1312 Adams St., 615/341-0300, www.actorsbridge. org), a theater company for new and seasoned actors. The Ensemble brings provocative and new plays to Nashville, often performing at the Belmont Black Box Theater in midtown.

Circle Players (www.circleplayers.net) is the oldest nonprofit, all-volunteer arts association in Nashville. As a community theater, all actors, stagehands, directors, and other helpers are volunteers. The company stages four or five performances every year at a variety of theater locations around the city. Performances include classic theater, plus stage adaptations of popular cinema and literature.

Nashville's leading experimental theater group is the **People's Branch Theatre** (615/254-0008, www.peoplesbranch.org). Founded in 2000, the group brings together local actors to produce bold and innovative professional theater. They perform at the Belcourt Theatre in Hillsboro Village.

Children's Theater

Nashville Children's Theatre (724 2nd Ave. S., 615/254-9103, www.nashvillechildrens-theatre.org) is the oldest children's theater company in the United States. During the school year, the theater puts on plays for children from preschool to elementary-school age in its colorful theater. In the summer there are drama classes for youngsters.

Teenagers own and operate the **Real Life Players,** a stalwart theater company that produces original plays written by Nashville teens. Profits are donated to teen-related community organizations. Plays are performed at the

Darkhorse Theater at 4610 Charlotte Avenue. Call the theater at 615/297-7113 to find out when the next Real Life performance will be held.

Don't miss the **Marionette Shows at the Nashville Public Library** (615 Church St., 615/862-5800). Using marionettes from the collection of former library puppeteer Tom Tichenor, plus others acquired from Chicago's Peekabo Puppet Productions, the library's children's room staff put on excellent one-of-a-kind family entertainment.

Music

The **Nashville Symphony Orchestra** (One Symphony Place, 615/687-6400, www.nashvillesymphony.org) is now housed in the Schermerhorn Symphony Center next to the Country Music Hall of Fame. Nominated for four Grammies and selling more recordings than any other American orchestra, the symphony is a source of pride for Music City. Costa Rican conductor Giancarlo Guerrero will begin his tenure as music director in 2009.

The symphony puts on more than 200 performances each year, including classical, pops, and children's concerts. Its season spans September to May. Buying tickets online is a breeze, especially since you can easily choose where you want to sit. There is free parking for symphony-goers in the Sun Trust parking garage on the corner of 4th Avenue and Commerce Street.

During the summer, the symphony plays its **Centennial Park Concert Series.** Come to the Centennial Park band shell to hear free big-band, ballroom, and classical concerts.

The **Blair School of Music** (2400 Blakemore Ave., 615/322-7651) presents student, faculty, and visiting artist recitals frequently during the school year. Vanderbilt University's music school, Blair addresses music through academic, pedagogical, and performing activities.

Listen to new works by American composers performed by the **Nashville Chamber Orchestra** (615/322-1226, www.nco.org). The orchestra's concerts include masterpieces and new works commissioned by the chamber orchestra, many of which fuse tradition with new genres, including jazz, Celtic, Latin, and world music.

Opera

Middle Tennessee's only opera association, the **Nashville Opera Association** (www.nashvilleopera.org) puts on an average of four mainstage performances per season (October–April) and does a six-week tour to area schools. They perform at the Tennessee Performing Arts Center at 505 Deaderick Street.

Ballet

Founded in 1981 as a civic dance company, the **Nashville Ballet** (www.nashvilleballet.com) became a professional dance company in 1986. Entertaining more than 40,000 patrons each year, the ballet performs both classical and contemporary pieces at the Tennessee Performing Arts Center at 505 Deaderick Street.

Dinner Theater

Chaffin's Barn Dinner Theatre (8204 Hwy. 100, 615/646-9977, www.dinnertheatre.com, $33–50) was Nashville's first professional theater and continues to put on popular Broadway-style plays for dinner patrons. If mystery is more your style, have dinner at **Miss Marple's Mystery Dinner Theatre** (135 2nd Ave. N., 615/242-8000, www.missmarples.com, $50), where you and your friends try to guess who done it.

Cinemas

Once the home of the Grand Ole Opry, the **Belcourt Theatre** (2102 Belcourt Ave., 615/383-9140, www.belcourt.org) is Nashville's best venue for independent films. Built in 1925 as a silent movie house, the Belcourt now screens a refreshing variety of independent and unusual films.

More mainstream arty flicks are shown at the **Regal Cinemas Green Hills** (3815 Green Hills Village, 615/269-5910). Mainstream multiplex cinemas can be found on the outskirts of town in nearly every direction.

FAN FAIR

Like country music itself, the annual event known as Fan Fair has evolved from a down-home meet-and-greet to large-scale musical theater.

Fan Fair began in 1972 as a convention for music fans. Each year, the event grew as more and more people wanted to meet their country idols in person. Fans bought tickets months in advance, camped out at the state fairgrounds, and yearned to see, touch, and speak with the stars. Fan Fair delivered. Stars endured marathon autograph sessions – Garth Brooks famously spent 23 hours signing autographs without a bathroom break – and they performed to crowds of their most dedicated fans.

But country music's remarkable boom of the 1990s was the end of that kind of Fan Fair – the music simply outgrew the event. Country music was no longer the step-child of the recording industry; it was corporate, and it was big business. Fans, politicians, and industry representatives tangled over the future of Fan Fair. One plan to move Fan Fair to the Nashville Superspeedway in Lebanon was nixed because it would take the event out of Nashville.

In the end, the CMA (Country Music Association) Music Festival replaced Fan Fair in 2000. With venues at Riverfront Park and LP Field, there is still plenty of music. Stars perform day and night. The autograph sessions continue in the Nashville Convention Center, but the artists you'll find here are the unknowns and up-and-comings. You need an invitation to meet and greet the stars.

The rebirth of Fan Fair as the CMA Music Festival still attracts criticism, especially from those who remember the glory days of the old Fan Fair. But today's fans delight in the modern event, and even some of the critics are coming around.

EVENTS
February

The second week of February is **Antiques Week** in Nashville. During this period, four separate antiques events top the bill. At the Tailgate Antique Show at the Fiddler's Inn Hotel in Music Valley, antiques dealers set up their shops in hotel rooms and parking spaces. A similar set-up exists at the Radisson Hotel Opryland for the Music Valley Antiques Market. The biggest sale is at the Gaylord Opryland Hotel and Convention Center. The final event for Antiques Week is the upscale Antiques and Garden Show of Nashville, which features antique dealers, exhibition gardens, and lectures at the Nashville Convention Center.

April

Nashville celebrates the coming of spring in a big way. **Awesome April** (www.visitmusiccity.com) is the name that encompasses the half dozen or more big events that take place during this month, one of the most pleasant on the city's weather calendar.

The **Country Music Television Music Awards** (www.cmt.com) was country music's first fan-voted awards show. Founded in 2002, the show lets fans participate in both the first and final rounds of voting. The show is broadcast live on television from Nashville, usually from the Curb Event Center at Belmont University.

Gospel music hosts its annual awards night in April too. The **Gospel Music Association Dove Awards** (www.gospelmusic.org) is billed as gospel music's biggest night. The celebration takes place at the Grand Ole Opry House in Music Valley, and is preceded by Gospel Music Week at the Nashville Convention Center, part trade show and part fan fair.

Film lovers throughout Tennessee look forward to the **Nashville Film Festival** (www.nashvillefilmfestival.org) held every April at the Green Hills Cinema 16. The film festival was founded in 1969 as the Sinking Creek Film Celebration. These days, upwards of 20,000 people attend the weeklong event, which includes film screenings, industry panels, and lots of parties.

Tin Pan South (www.tinpansouth.com) is an annual celebration of songs and songwriting organized by the Nashville Songwriters Association International. The event features five nights of performances by some of the best singers and songwriters around. Shows are held in 10 different intimate venues around the city, presenting music fans with the tough choice of where to go each night.

The **Country Music Marathon** (www.cmmarathon.com) takes place every April. More than 15,000 professional and amateur runners take part, and tens of thousands more come out for the live music and cheer squads that line the racecourse. The post-race concert usually boasts nationally known country music artists.

May

Held in Centennial Park, the **Tennessee Crafts Fair** (www.tennesseecrafts.org) showcases the work of more than 180 different fine craftsmen and women. More than 45,000 people come to the three-day event every year, which also includes craft demonstrations, a food fair, and entertainment. The fair repeats in September.

For something a little different, plan to attend the **Running of the Iroquois Steeplechase** (www.iroquoissteeplechase.org) at Percy Warner Park. Taking place on the second Saturday of May, the race is the nation's oldest continuously run weight-for-age steeplechase in the country. Fans in sundresses or suspenders and hats enjoy watching some of the top horses in the country navigate the race course. You can pay $15 general admission to sit on the hillside overlooking the stadium. Pack a blanket, food, and drinks, and you'll have an excellent day. Various tailgating tickets are available and are priced according to how good the view is from the parking spot. If you want to tailgate, you need to buy tickets well in advance.

Taking place every weekend in May, the **Tennessee Renaissance Festival** (www.tnrenfest.com) celebrates all things medieval. Come to watch jousting matches, hear 16th-century comedy, or buy capes and swords. The festival takes place off Highway 96 between Franklin and Murfreesboro, about 25 minutes' drive south from Nashville.

June

What was once called Fan Fair, and is now called the **Country Music Association Music Festival** (www.cmafest.com), is a four-day music mega-show in downtown Nashville. The stage at Waterfront Park along the Cumberland River is occupied by day with some of the top names in country music. At night the hordes move to LP Field across the river to hear a different show every night. Four-day passes, which cost between $80 and $300 per person, also give you access to the exhibit hall, where you can get autographs and meet up-and-coming country music artists. This is Nashville's biggest event of the year, and you are wise to buy your tickets and book your hotel early. Get a room downtown so you don't need a car; parking and traffic is a nightmare during the festival.

Early June sees Nashville's gay, lesbian, bisexual, and transgender community show its colors at the **Nashville Pride Festival** (www.nashvillepride.org), a one-day event at Centennial Park.

July

Independence Day (www.visitmusiccity.com) is celebrated in a big way with fireworks and a riverfront concert that's broadcast live on television. The event is free and attracts upwards of 100,000 people every year.

The **Music City Brewer's Festival** (www.musiccitybrewersfest.com) is a one-day event on the lawn behind the Hilton Hotel downtown. Come to taste local brews, learn about making your own beer, and enjoy good food and live music. Tickets are required, and the event often sells out.

August

The **East Nashville Tomato Art Festival** (www.tomatoartfest.com) is a tongue-in-cheek celebration of tomatoes and the hip, artsy vibe of East Nashville. Events include a parade of tomatoes, the "Most Beautiful Tomato Pageant," biggest and smallest tomato contests, tomato toss, and Bloody Mary taste-off. The festival usually takes place on the second Saturday of August.

September

The Belle Meade Plantation (www.bellemeadeplantation.org) hosts its biggest fundraising event of the year, **Fall Fest,** every September. The two-day festival features antiques, arts and crafts, live music, and children's activities.

Nashville's annual **Greek Festival** (615/333-1047) is hosted by the Holy Trinity Greek Orthodox Church. Nashville residents flock here for homemade Greek food and entertainment, which includes dancing and tours of the historic cathedral.

The **John Merritt Classic** (www.johnmerrittclassic.com) held over Labor Day starts with fashion shows and concerts and culminates with a football contest between the Tennessee State University Tigers and another historically black collegiate football team. The annual showdown is named for legendary former TSU football coach John Ayers Merritt.

The **Music City Jazz and Blues Festival (JAMS)** (www.nbl4u.com) over Labor Day is a two-day festival featuring jazz, blues, soul, R&B, and reggae performers. It is held at Riverfront Park along the Cumberland.

October

The **Southern Festival of Books** is held during the second full weekend of October on Legislative Plaza in downtown Nashville. Featuring book readings, autograph sessions, and discussions, the festival is a must for book lovers. It has activities for children, too. The festival is organized by Humanities Tennessee (www.tn-humanities.org).

Oktoberfest (www.nashvilleoktoberfest.com) is a Nashville tradition. Held in historic Germantown north of the Bicentennial Mall, this weekend festival is enhanced by its setting in what was once Nashville's German enclave. The events include a walk-run, church services, and a street fair with German music, food, and

other entertainment. Oktoberfest usually takes place in mid-October.

Vanderbilt's Scarritt-Bennett Center hosts the **Celebration of Cultures** (www.celebrationofcultures.org) every October in Centennial Park. This international festival features food and music from around the world.

November

Beginning in November and continuing through the new year, several Nashville institutions put up special holiday decorations. Belmont University, Travellers Rest Plantation, the Hermitage, and Belle Meade all celebrate the holiday season with special decorative flair.

December

The **Music City Bowl** (www.musiccitybowl.com) pits a Southeastern Conference team against a Big Ten rival. This nationally televised football game is held at LP Field.

SHOPPING

You'll find many good reasons to shop in Nashville. Who can pass up Western wear in Music City? Fine boutiques cater to the well-heeled in tony West End. Malls in the suburbs offer upscale department stores or outlet bargains. And downtown you'll find unique art and gifts.

One of the best all-around shopping districts is **Hillsboro Village,** the commercial district that borders Vanderbilt University in midtown. Upscale clothing stores, used books, and trendy housewares are just a few of the things you'll find in this neighborhood, best explored on foot.

Music

The Texas Troubadour, Ernest Tubb, founded his famous record store on Broadway in 1947. **Ernest Tubb's Record Shop** (417 Broadway, 615/255-7503) remains an excellent source of classic and modern country music recordings, as well as DVDs, books, clothing, and souvenirs. At the back of the shop you can see the stage where Ernest Tubb's Midnite Jamboree was recorded and aired after the Grand Ole

Opry on Saturday nights. The Jamboree still airs, but it's recorded at the Texas Troubadour Theatre in Music Valley.

For new and used CDs, DVDs, and vinyl, go to **Grimey's** (1604 8th Ave. S., 615/254-4801). Here you'll find a wide selection of not just country, but rock, folk, blues, R&B, and other genres. The staff are knowledgeable and friendly.

If you want to make your own music, head to **Gruhn Guitars** (400 Broadway, 615/256-2033), a guitar shop with one of the best reputations in the music world. Founded by guitar expert George Gruhn, the shop is considered by some the best vintage guitar shop in the world. Shiny guitars, banjos, mandolins, and fiddles looks like candy hung up on the walls of the Broadway storefront that serves both up-and-coming and established Nashville musicians.

Nashville's other guitar shop is the **Gibson Bluegrass Showcase** (Opry Mills, 615/514-2233). Part retail outlet, part live music venue, the Gibson store celebrates both the instruments and the sound of bluegrass music. You can buy fiddles, mandolins, Dobros, or guitars, and they will ship all over the world.

If country music is just one of many musical interests, head to **The Great Escape** (1925 Broadway, 615/327-0646). This record and comic book shop was founded in 1977, and continues to offer a pleasing array of used CDs, records, and cassettes for music fans. The location near Vanderbilt attracts a youthful clientele.

Western Wear

No city is better endowed with places to buy Western-style wear. The best selection is found in shops along Broadway in downtown Nashville, where you'll find hats, boots, shirts, belts, jeans, and everything else you'll need to look the part. Opry Mills, the mall next to the Grand Ole Opry, also has a good selection of Western wear.

Trail West (312 Broadway, 615/251-1711) is a one-stop shop for country clothes. **Boot Country** (304 Broadway, 615/259-1691) specializes in all styles and sizes of cowboy boots.

Music-industry men and women get dressed at **flavour** (1522-B Demonbreun, 615/254-2064), a hip clothing store on Music Row. Come here for stylish denim, cowboy boots, plus casual and dressy wear for ladies and gents. This is not your daddy's boot store; this is country music chic.

The name says it all at **Manuel Exclusive Clothier** (1922 Broadway, 615/321-5444), a clothing shop where the cowboy shirts start at $750 and jackets at over $2,000.

Even without a ton of cash you can outfit yourself in some of the best Western designs at **Katy K Designs Ranch Dressing** (2407 12th Ave. S., 615/297-4242). This is the showplace of designer Katy K's unique clothing line, which has been worn by the likes of Loretta Lynn and BR549. Ranch Dressing has a well-curated selection of vintage goods, plus clothing from other designers' lines. To find the shop, look for the giant cowgirl on the facade of an otherwise nondescript office building.

Clothing

Ginette's Boutique (2420 Elliston Pl., 615/327-1440) offers the latest fashions in women's clothes, handbags, and accessories at non-runway prices.

With two locations, one in Hillsboro Village and one downtown at 305 Church Street, **Fire Finch** (615/942-5271) is known for trendy jewelry and accessories. Its downtown location also has a few home decor items as well.

A relative newcomer on the Nashville clothing scene, **Nashville Clothing Company** (2922 West End Blvd., 615/577-5346) sells stylish men's and women's clothes and shoes. This includes a wide selection of funny T-shirts, purses, and bags.

Men can be outfitted from toe to top hat at **J. Michael's Clothiers** (2525 West End Ave., 615/321-0686). An old-fashioned clothing store that specializes in one-on-one advice, J. Michael's is famous for its personal touch; in addition to selling off-the-rack name brand they tailor to suit. Whether you're just starting a new career or looking for a special-occasion outfit, you'll find what you need at J. Michael's.

Art

While not exactly a gallery, **Hatch Show Print** (316 Broadway, 615/256-2805) is one of Nashville's best-known places to buy art. Hatch has been making colorful posters for decades, and their letterpress style is now one of the trendiest looks in modern design. They continue to design and print handouts, posters, and T-shirts for local and national customers. Visitors to the shop can gaze at the cavernous warehouse operation, and buy small or large samples of their work, including reproductions of classic country music concert posters. This is a great place to find a special souvenir of your trip to Nashville.

At **All Fired Up** (21st Ave. S., 615/463-8887), choose a piece of unfinished pottery for between $5 and $50, then pay an additional $6 "painting fee," and choose from hundreds of different paints and glazes to finish your piece. This is a great way to spend a rainy afternoon or have fun with a date.

Transplanted New Yorkers Theo Antoniadis and Veta Cicolello opened **Ovvio Arte** (42 S. Chestnut St., 615/256-8756, www.ovvioarte. com) in 2008. This art gallery and performance space is a venue for the unexpected. It offers regular theater, dramatic readings, and art shows.

The Tennessee Artists Guild operates **TAG Gallery** (83 Arcade, 615/429-7708, www. tagartgallery.com), one of the best galleries in Nashville. Founded in 2000, the TAG specializes in selling affordable art to up-and-coming collectors. They offer a regular diet of unique shows.

Garage Mahal (1106 Woodland St., 615/226-2070), also known as the Art and Invention Gallery, is an East Nashville institution. Proprietors Meg and Bret MacFayden put on between five and six shows each year, including their signature Tomato Art Show, part of the annual Tomato Art Festival.

Also in East Nashville, **Plowhaus** (211 S. 17th St., 615/349-3777) is an artists' co-op with a gallery and lots of community outreach activities.

Home Decor

Find fine crystal, tableware, jewelry, and other upscale housewares at **AshBlue** (4231 Harding Rd., 615/383-4882). This sophisticated shop is perfect for bridal registries, housewarming gifts, or that special touch for your home or office.

Natural soaps, hand-crafted fragrances, and soy candles are just a few of the things you will find at **Green Pergola Aromatherapy and Soap Company** (223 Donelson Pk., 615/889-0044). One of the best things about the store, however, is its unique partnership with two other businesses. **Teas for Two** sells loose tea and **One 2 Yoga Studio** offers one-on-one and group yoga instruction. You can also buy a hot or cold cup of tea to drink while you enjoy the relaxing atmosphere of the store.

Modern home furnishings, large and small, are what draws shoppers to **Mad Mod** (162 8th Ave. N., 615/244-6807). A complete line of bamboo textiles, local art, and trendy furniture make this a popular stop for the downtown condo set.

Books

Nashville has several good bookstores, and at least one is bound to suit your taste. **Bookman Bookwoman Used Books** (1713 21st Ave. S., 615/383-6555), in the trendy Hillsboro neighborhood, is chock-a-block with used books, including cheap paperbacks and rare must-haves. **Elder's Books** (2115 Elliston Pl., 615/327-1867), close to Vanderbilt and Centennial Park, is a book-lover's bookstore. The store is packed with books, but not just any books. The collection is carefully chosen and includes many signed and first editions. Elder's has an excellent collection of books about Nashville, Tennessee, the Civil War, and the South, as well as lots of other topics. Be warned that this is a store for book-loving adults, not their children. Noisy or misbehaving children are not tolerated.

For new books, head to **Davis-Kidd Booksellers** (Green Hills Mall, 615/385-2645), a Nashville-based independent bookseller with locations throughout Tennessee. Davis-Kidd puts on a number of literary events, such as book signings, discussions, and readings.

Outloud! Books and Gifts (1701 Church St., 615/329-8006) specializes in books, videos, music, and gifts with a gay or lesbian theme. There is an adjoining café, special events, and comfortable couches for relaxing.

The newest addition to the Nashville book scene is **McKays** (5708 Charlotte Pike, 615/353-2595), which sells used books, CDs, and DVDs. A Knoxville institution for years, McKays moved to Music City in 2007. Calling itself a "free enterprise library," McKays encourages readers to return books for store credit after they've read them.

Antiques

Near 100 Oaks Mall in South Nashville you'll find Nashville's largest and most popular antiques mall. **Gaslamp Antique and Decorating Mall** (100 Powell Ave., 615/297-2224, www.gaslampantiques.com) is squeezed between a Staples and Home Depot. It has more than 150 vendors and a great selection of all types of antiques.

For something closer to town, head to **Eighth Avenue Antiques Mall** (2015 8th Ave. S., 615/279-9922) or **Wonders on Woodland** (1110 Woodland St., 615/226-5300) in East Nashville.

Malls

The finest shopping mall in Nashville is the **Mall at Green Hills,** an indoor mall located about 15 minutes' drive south from downtown Nashville along Hillsboro Road. Stores include Macy's, Dillard's, Tiffany & Co., and Davis-Kidd Booksellers. The mall has spawned additional shopping opportunities nearby, so this is a good place to head if you're in need of just about anything. Call the mall concierge (615/298-5478, ext. 22) to find out if your favorite store is there.

Farther south of Nashville, at the Moore's Lane exit off I-65, is **Cool Springs Galleria** (1800 Galleria Blvd., 615/731-6255, www.coolspringsgalleria.com), the newest mall in the area. Four major department stores

anchor the mall, which includes 100 specialty shops. The mall is surrounded by acres more of drive-up shopping centers and restaurants.

Heading west from town on Highway 70, you'll run into **Bellevue Center** (7620 U.S. 70, 615/646-8690, www.bellevuecenter.com), where you'll find Dillard's, Sears, Hecht's, and more than 115 specialty shops. Many Nashvillians consider this the city's best mall.

Outlet Malls

Some Nashville residents look down their nose at **Opry Mills** (433 Opry Mills Dr., 615/514-1000), the discount mall in Music Valley that sits across the street from the Grand Ole Opry. Indeed, if upscale shopping is your thing, don't come here. But if good deals on name-brand merchandise appeal to you, Opry Mills is the mall for you. Brands include Corning, Levi's, Banana Republic, American Eagle Outfitters, Barnes & Noble, Gap, and Off Fifth. There is also a 20-screen movie theater, IMAX, and Bass Pro Shop with all sorts of outdoor equipment.

A bit farther down the highway in Lebanon, about 30 miles east of Nashville on I-40, **Prime Outlets** (800/617-2588) features name-brand outlet stores. Brands include Polo Ralph Lauren, Coach, Tommy Hilfiger, and Ann Taylor. To get to Prime Outlets, take I-40 east from Nashville and get off at exit 238.

Flea Markets

Nashville's largest flea market takes place on the fourth weekend of every month at the Tennessee State Fairgrounds. The **Tennessee State Fairgrounds Flea Market** (615/862-5016, www.tennesseestatefair.org) is a bargain-lover's dream, with thousands of sellers peddling clothes, crafts, and all sorts of vintage and used housewares. The fairgrounds are located on 4th Avenue, south of downtown.

The **Nashville Farmer's Market** next to the Bicentennial Mall downtown has a flea market on weekends.

Sports and Recreation

Nashville has good parks, numerous sports teams, and nice weather to enjoy both.

PARKS
Centennial Park

Nashville's best city park, Centennial is best-known as home of the Parthenon. It is also a pleasant place to relax. A small lake provides a habitat for ducks and other water creatures; paved walking trails are popular for walking during nice weather. The park hosts numerous events during the year, including Shakespeare in the Park.

Radnor Lake State Natural Area

Just seven miles southwest of downtown Nashville, Radnor Lake State Natural Area (Otter Creek Rd., 615/373-3467) provides a natural escape for visitors and residents of the city. Eighty-five acre Radnor Lake was created in 1914 by the Louisville and Nashville Railroad Company, which impounded Otter Creek to do so. The lake was to provide water for the railroad's steam engines. By the 1940s, the railroad's use of the lake ended and 20 years later the area was threatened by development. Local residents, including the Tennessee Ornithological Society, successfully rallied against development and Radnor Lake State Natural Area was established in 1973.

There are six miles of hiking trails around the lake, and Otter Creek Road, which is closed to vehicular traffic, is open to bicycles and walkers. A nature museum at the visitors center describes some of the 240 species of birds and hundreds of species of plants and animals that live at Radnor. The visitors center is open Sunday–Thursday 9 A.M.–4 P.M. and Friday–Saturday 8 A.M.–4 P.M.

Radnor is well-used and well-loved by Nashvillians, and for good reason. Very few American cities have such a large and pristine natural area so close to the urban center.

Edwin and Percy Warner Parks

The largest city parks in Tennessee, Edwin and Percy Warner Parks (Hwy. 100) are a 2,600-acre oasis of forest, fields, and quiet pathways located just nine miles southwest from downtown Nashville. Nashvillians come here to walk, jog, ride bikes and horses, and much more. The parks have scenic drives, picnic facilities, playgrounds, cross-country running trails, an equestrian center, bridle trails, a model-airplane field, and athletic fields. Percy Warner Park is also home to the Harpeth Hills Golf Course, and Edwin Percy Park has a nature center that provides year-round environmental education. The nature center also hands out maps and other information about the park.

Warner Parks hosts the annual Iroquois Steeplechase Horse Race in May. A 10-mile bridle path is open to horseback riding year-round. Visit the park's Equestrian Center (2500 Old Hickory Blvd.) for more information.

J. Percy Priest Lake

J. Percy Priest Lake was created in the mid-1960s when the Army Corps of Engineers dammed Stones River east of Nashville. The lake is a favorite destination for fishing, boating, swimming, and picnicking.

J. Percy Priest Lake sprawls over 14,200 acres. Access is provided through more than a dozen different parks and access areas on all sides of the lake. Many of these areas bear the names of communities that were inundated when the lake was created.

The lake's main visitors center, operated by the Army Corps of Engineers, is located at the site of the dam that created the lake. The visitors center is located on Bell Road at exit 219 off I-40 heading east from downtown Nashville. There you will find a lake overlook and one of four marinas on the lake.

In addition to access areas managed by the Corps of Engineers, Nashville operates **Hamilton Creek Park** on the western shore of the lake. The State of Tennessee operates **Long Hunter State Park** on the eastern shore.

There are several hiking trails around the lake. The **Three Hickories Nature Trail** is an easy 1.6-mile trail found in the Cook Recreational Area. **Anderson Road Fitness Trail** is a paved one-mile trail that travels through woodlands and along the lake.

For a long hike, or for horseback riding, go to the **Twin Forks Horse Trail,** an 18-mile trail located in the East Fork Recreation Area on the southwestern shore of the lake. Within Long Hunter State Park there are three hiking trails, including a nature loop trail and the mile-long Deer Trail leaving from the visitors center.

Boating, fishing, and watersports are among the most popular activities on J. Percy Priest Lake. Launch ramps are found in Long Hunter State Park and at several marinas around the lake. Elm Hill Marina (3361 Bell Rd., 615/889-5363, www.elmhillmarina.com) is the marina closest to downtown Nashville.

The Corps of Engineers operates three day-use swim areas that have sand beaches, bathrooms, and other amenities for a day in the water. These swim areas are located at Anderson Road, Cook Campground, and Seven Points Campground. There is a $4 per-vehicle fee at Anderson and Cook. There is swimming at Long Hunter State Park's Bryant Grove as well.

GOLF

Nashville operates seven public golf courses in the city. Many of these are in parks and offer excellent golf in beautiful settings. You can find details about all city courses at www.nashville. gov/parks/golf/golf.htm. Most courses are open year-round; call ahead for operating hours and to reserve a tee time.

Harpeth Hills Golf Course (2424 Old Hickory Blvd., 615/862-8493) is a par-72 course built in 1965 and renovated in 1991. It is located in Percy Warner Park, and is considered one of Tennessee's best public golf courses. Green fees are $23 on weekdays and $25 on weekends.

Percy Warner Park is home of **Percy Warner Golf Course,** a nine-hole course good for beginner golfers, available on a walk-in basis only.

Probably the most-used public golf course in Nashville, **McCabe Golf Course** (615/862-8491) is located in West Nashville near Sylvan Park. McCabe consists of a par-70 18-hole course and 9-hole course. Upgrades have introduced new green complexes and tee complexes. Green fees are $20 on weekdays and $22 on weekends.

The oldest city golf course in Nashville is **Shelby Golf Course** (615/862-8474), located in Shelby Park in East Nashville. Shelby is a short course with small mounded greens that places a premium on accuracy. Green fees are $16.

Situated on the Cumberland River in North Nashville, **Ted Rhodes Golf Course** (615/862-8463) is scenic, and pleasant to walk. Built in 1953 as a nine-hole course, Ted Rhodes was expanded to 18 holes in 1992. It is par 72. Green fees are $20 on weekdays and $22 on weekends.

Located near Music Valley in Donelson, **Two Rivers Golf Course** (615/889-2675) offers a challenging course for golfers of all skill levels. A bonus is the view of the Nashville skyline at the eighth hole. Greens fees are $20 on weekdays and $22 on weekends.

There are many privately owned golf courses in Nashville, some of which are open to the public. **Gaylord Springs** (18 Springhouse Ln., 615/458-1730), located next to the Gaylord Opryland Hotel in Music Valley, is a par-72 18-hole course built in 1990. Greens fees are $50–90. **Nashboro Golf Club** (1101 Nashboro Blvd., 615/367-2311) offers a par-72 18-hole course with fees between $27 and $41. **Hillwood Country Club** (6201 Hickory Valley Rd., 615/352-5600) is a par-72 6,903-yard course built in 1955. Greens fees are around $85.

BIKING

The first destination for bikers around Nashville is the **Natchez Trace Parkway** (www.nps.gov/natr), a two-lane 444-mile blacktop scenic drive that originates in Nashville and journeys south through Tennessee and Mississippi countryside, eventually terminating in Natchez, Mississippi. The parkway is closed to commercial traffic and the speed limit is strictly enforced, making it popular for biking.

Biking the Trace can be an afternoon outing or a weeklong adventure. The National Park Service maintains three campgrounds along the Trace, plus five bicyclist-only campsites with more modest amenities. The northernmost bike campsite is located at the intersection of the Trace and Highway 50, about 36 miles south of Nashville.

When biking on the Trace, ride in a single-file line and always wear reflective clothing and a helmet. Pack food and water, and carry a cell phone, ID, and emergency information.

Short paved trails good for biking can be found at Radnor Lake State Natural Area, Warner Parks, and in any of Nashville's greenways, including those at Shelby Bottoms along the Cumberland River.

Nashville's only dedicated mountain bike trail is at **Hamilton Creek Park** (www.hamcreek.com) on J. Percy Priest Lake, on the east side of the Nashville airport. This 10-mile bike trail consists of an eastern trail better for beginning bikers and a western trail for advanced bikers. The two trails meet at a tunnel that crosses Bell Road.

Bike Shops

There are several good bike shops in Nashville. If you need bike gear, repairs, or advice, check out **Cumberland Transport** (2807 West End Ave., 615/321-4069), **Nashville Bicycle Company** (2817 West End Ave., 615/321-5510), or **Trace Bikes** (8400 Hwy. 100, 615/646-2485), located next to the Loveless Café near the Natchez Trace Parkway.

Resources

If you're looking for the inside scoop on biking around Nashville and recommended routes in the surrounding countryside, check out www.nashvillecyclist.com, an online community of bikers.

The **Harpeth Bike Club** (www.harpethbikeclub.com) is Nashville's largest bike club. It organizes weekend and weekday group rides from April to October, plus races and social events where you can meet other bike enthusiasts.

TENNIS

The **Centennial Sportsplex** (222 25th Ave. N., 615/862-8480, www.sportsplextennis.com) has 15 lighted outdoor tennis courts and four indoor courts, as well as a ball machine, pro shop, and concession stand. The center is open seven days a week; specific hours vary by season. Indoor court rental fees are $18 per hour; courts may be booked up to three days in advance. Outdoor courts are available for $3 per hour per person and they can be reserved up to six days in advance.

The Sportsplex organizes numerous tennis tournaments, leagues, and classes during the year. Call or stop by for details.

SWIMMING

The city's biggest pool is found at the **Centennial Sportsplex Aquatic Center** (222 25th Ave. N., 615/862-8480, www.centennialsportsplex.com, Mon.–Thurs. 5:30 A.M.–7:50 P.M., Fri. 5:30 A.M.–5:50 P.M., Sat. 9 A.M.–4:50 P.M., adults $6, children under 13, military, disabled, seniors, and students $5, children 4 and under free). The center, located near Centennial Park in midtown, has both a large lap pool and a small play pool. Various swim classes are offered; call for a schedule.

Take the kids to **Wave Country** (2320 Two Rivers Pkwy., 615/885-1052, daily 10 A.M.–6 P.M., adults $8, children under 12 $7, children under 4 free), a waterpark with exciting slides, wave pool, and sand volleyball courts. Wave Country is managed by the city parks commission, and is open from Memorial Day to Labor Day.

A great destination for swimming and watersports is **Nashville Shores** (4001 Bell Rd., Hermitage, 615/889-7050, www.nashvilleshores.com, Mon.–Sat. 10 A.M.–6 P.M., Sun. 11 A.M.–6 P.M.). Here you'll find miles of sandy beaches along the shore of J. Percy

Priest Lake, pools, waterslides, and watersports. Admission includes the opportunity to take a 45-minute lake cruise. Admission rates are based on height; 48 inches and taller pay $22, shorter than that $17. Children two years and under are free. General admission is half-price after 3 P.M. Nashville Shores is open from Memorial Day to Labor Day.

GYMS

The City of Nashville operates a fitness center in the **Centennial Sportsplex** (222 25th Ave. N., 615/862-8480, www.centennialsportsplex.com, Mon.–Thurs. 5:30 A.M.–8 P.M., Fri. 5:30 A.M.–6 P.M., Sat. 9 A.M.–5 P.M., adults $6, children under 13, military, disabled, seniors, and students $5, children 4 and under free). The fitness center has modern cardiovascular and weight-lifting machines. Fitness classes are also offered.

The Sportsplex also has two pools, tennis courts, and an ice rink. The ice rink offers public skate periods every week, with more during the winter months and holiday season.

SPECTATOR SPORTS
Football

You simply cannot miss 68,000-seat LP Field, home of the **Tennessee Titans** (460 Great Circle Rd., 615/565-4000, www.titansonline.com). The stadium, which was finished in 1999, towers on the east bank of the Cumberland River, directly opposite downtown. Since their move to the stadium in 1999, the Titans have sold out each and every home game. They play from September to December.

Tickets sell out early—often months in advance. If you want to see a game on short notice, your best bet is a program where season ticket–holders can sell their seats to games they don't want to attend.

For an altogether different football experience, catch a home game of the **Nashville Dream** (615/907-6617, www.nashville-dream.com) at Glencliff High School. The Nashville Dream is a women's football team and a member of the National Women's

Football Association. The season runs from April to July.

Finally, the most unique brand of football played in Nashville is Australian rules. The **Nashville Kangaroos** (www.nashvillekangaroos.org) were founded in 1997 and were one of the first Australian football teams in the United States. The "Roos" play at Elmington Park (3500 West End Ave.), and sometimes practice with Vanderbilt's own Aussie rules squad. One of the missions of the club is to promote cultural understanding and exchange, so the social calendar can be just as grueling as the sports one. The Roos also sponsor a women's netball team.

Racing

The **Nashville Superspeedway** (4847-F McGreary Rd., Lebanon, 615/547-7223, www.nashvillesuperspeedway.com) is a 1.33-mile course that hosts Indy Racing League, NASCAR Craftsman Trucks, and two NASCAR Busch Series races. Seating up to 150,000 fans, Nashville Superspeedway has been drawing capacity crowds since it opened in 2001. The Superspeedway is located in Lebanon, Tennessee, about 30 minutes' drive east of town.

Baseball

What a fine name for a minor-league baseball team! The **Nashville Sounds** (534 Chestnut St., 615/242-4371, www.nashvillesounds.com) are a AAA affiliate of the Milwaukee Brewers, and they play about 30 home games a year from June to October. Before the 2008 season opener, the team invested $1 million in stopgap improvements to the aging Greer Stadium, their home in south Nashville. The remedial works were intended to keep the stadium running only for the next few years, and Sounds officials have said that they will need a new stadium soon.

Tickets are $10 for reserved seats or $6 general admission.

Soccer

Nashville's professional soccer team, the

Metros (Ezell Park, 5135 Harding Pl., 615/832-5678, www.nashvillemetrosoccer.com), play just south of Nashville International Airport. Founded in 1989, the Metros have endured a half-dozen name, field, and league changes. They have survived thanks to the dogged support of soccer fans in the city.

The Metros are a member of the United Soccer League's Premier Development League, and the season runs from May to July. They play other teams from the southeastern United States. Single-game tickets are $7 for adults and $4 for youths.

Ice Hockey

Nashville celebrated the 10th anniversary of its National Hockey League franchise, the **Predators** (501 Broadway, http://predators.nhl.com), in 2008. It was a sweet victory for fans, who fought to keep the team in the city in the face of lackluster support from the community. The Predators play in the 20,000-seat Sommet Center, also called the Nashville Arena, located on Broadway in the heart of downtown. The regular season begins in October and ends in early April. Single-game tickets start at $17 and can cost as much as $150.

College Sports

In addition to Nashville's smorgasbord of professional and semi-professional sports teams, the city's colleges provide lots of good spectator sports. Vanderbilt plays football, men's and women's basketball, and baseball in the Southeastern Conference. Tennessee State University and Belmont University play Division 1-A basketball, and Lipscomb University is a member of the Atlantic Sun Division.

Accommodations

Nashville has more than 32,000 hotel rooms. Accommodations range from historic downtown hotels to standard motels. Some of the city's most distinctive accommodations are in bed-and-breakfast inns in Hillsboro and East Nashville.

Downtown has the most appealing and convenient hotels. More budget-friendly options are found in midtown and Music Valley.

BROADWAY AND THE DISTRICT

Hotels in this neighborhood are as close as you can get to attractions including the Country Music Hall of Fame and Broadway honky-tonks.

$150-200

Located across Broadway from the Frist Center for the Visual Arts, **Holiday Inn Express Nashville-Downtown** (902 Broadway, 615/244-0150, $150) offers a comfortable compromise between value and location. There is an on-site fitness room, free wireless Internet, a business center, and a guest laundry. Guest rooms have desks, coffeemakers, and two telephones. Suites ($250) have refrigerators and microwave ovens. All guests enjoy free continental breakfast. On-site parking is available for $14 a day. The Holiday Inn is located about five blocks away from lower Broadway.

Over $200

Nashville's most notable downtown hotel is ❰ **Union Station** (1001 Broadway, 615/726-1001, $160–270), a 125-room Wyndham Hotel located in what was once the city's main train station. Distinctions include magnificent iron work and molding, and an impressive marble-floored great hall that greets guests. High ceilings and lofty interior balconies make this one of Nashville's great old buildings, and hotel guests get to make it their home away from home. Union Station is a fine hotel, with amenities like free turn-down service, a fitness center, wireless Internet, plasma televisions, complimentary morning newspapers, and room service. Rooms have cathedral ceilings, stylish furnishings, and a subtle art deco touch. The bathrooms have soaking tubs, walk-in showers, and expansive marble vanities. You can choose from a standard room with one double bed or a premium room with a king-sized bed or two double beds. Four suites are also available.

The all-suite 🍷 **Hilton Nashville Downtown** (121 4th Ave. S., 615/620-1000, www.nashvillehilton.com, $170–240) is next door to the Country Music Hall of Fame, Broadway's honky-tonks, and the home of the Nashville Symphony. It's also across the street from the Nashville Convention Center. All of the hotel's 330 suites have two distinct rooms—a living room with sofa, cable television, microwave oven, refrigerator, and coffee-maker, and a bedroom with one or two beds. The rooms are appointed with modern, stylish furniture and amenities. An indoor pool, workout room, valet parking, and two award-winning restaurants round out the hotel's amenities. The Hilton's combination of luxury and location make it one of the best choices for travelers to Nashville.

The **Renaissance Hotel** (611 Commerce St., 615/255-8400, $290–310) is connected to the Nashville Convention Center by a raised and covered walkway. Located one block north of Broadway, it stands 25 stories, providing impressive views of the city below. The Renaissance's 646 rooms offer web TV, hairdryers and ironing boards, crisp linens, coffeemakers, and business services. For an additional $12 daily, guests can enjoy high-speed wired Internet access and unlimited local and U.S. long-distance calls. The fitness center is next door to an indoor heated swimming pool, whirlpool, and sauna.

DOWNTOWN

Downtown hotels are convenient to downtown businesses and government offices, and a short walk from tourist attractions along Broadway.

Over $200

The last of a dying breed of downtown hotels, the 🍷 **Hermitage Hotel** (231 6th Ave., 615/244-3121, www.thehermitagehotel.com,

$300–800) has been the first choice for travelers to downtown Nashville for almost 100 years. The 123-room hotel was commissioned by prominent Nashville citizens and opened for business in 1910, quickly becoming the favorite gathering place for the city's elite. Prominent figures including Al Capone, Gene Autry, and seven U.S. presidents have stayed at the Hermitage. In modern times, its roll call includes some of country music's biggest names. You don't have to be famous to stay at the Hermitage, but having plenty of cash will help your cause. Rooms start at $300 a night, but check for last-minute specials on its website when rates will dip to $200. Guests enjoy top-of-the-line amenities, including 24-hour room service, pet walking, valet parking, and laundry services. Rooms are furnished in an opulent style befitting a luxury urban hotel, and have CD/DVD players, refreshment centers, marble baths, and high-speed wireless Internet access. Many rooms have lovely views of the Capitol and city.

Courtyard by Marriot (179 4th Ave. N., 615/256-0900, $200–250) is a 181-room renovated hotel set in a century-old downtown high-rise. It is located right next to Printer's Alley, and is set midway between the downtown business district and Broadway's entertainment attractions. Guest rooms are tastefully decorated, with web TV, wired Internet access, coffeemakers, ironing boards, cable TV, voice mail, and super-comfortable beds. There are two restaurants on-site, and guests can take advantage of valet parking for $20 a day.

Located just steps from the Tennessee State Capitol and near dozens of downtown office buildings, the **Doubletree Hotel Nashville** (315 4th Ave. N., 615/244-8200, $190–250) is a popular choice for business travelers. Rooms are spacious and bright, and even basic rooms have a comfortable desk and chair, coffeemaker, free Internet access, voice mail, and ironing boards. The hotel boasts a beautiful indoor swimming pool, business center, above-average fitness center, and on-site restaurant and coffee shop. Parking at the Doubletree is valet only and costs $20 per day.

The **Sheraton Downtown Nashville** (623 Union St., 615/259-2000, $200–270) is a city landmark. The 476-room hotel stands tall above neighboring buildings, providing most guest rooms with views of the city below. Located in the middle of Nashville's bustling downtown business district, it is another good option for business travelers. The hotel is 100 percent smoke-free, and has a fitness room, business center, indoor pool, and laundry and concierge services. Internet access and on-site parking is available for an additional fee.

MIDTOWN

Midtown hotels are near Music Row, Vanderbilt and Belmont Universities, and the entertainment, dining, and shopping attractions of Hillsboro Village.

Under $100

One of two hostels in Nashville, **Music City Hostel** (1809 Patterson St., 615/692-1277, www.musiccityhostel.com, $25) is located among doctor's offices and commercial buildings in between downtown Nashville and Elliston Place. The low-slung '70s-style building looks like nothing much on the outside, but inside it is cheerful, welcoming, and a comfortable home base for budget travelers. Music City Hostel offers the usual dorm-style bunk-bed accommodations, as well as a handful of private apartments, which rent for $75–85 a night. You can also have a private bedroom with private bath plus shared kitchen and common room for $60 a night. Common areas include a large kitchen, dining room, reading room, cable TV room, computer with Internet access, and a coin laundry. The entire facility is smoke-free. Parking is free, and the hostel is within walking distance of restaurants, a bus stop, car rental agency, post office, and hospitals. It would be a hike to get downtown on foot from here.

$100-150

Best Western Music Row (1407 Division St., 615/242-1631, $90–110) is a no-nonsense motel with an outdoor pool, free continental breakfast, Internet access, and indoor corridors. Rooms have cable TV, AM/FM alarm clocks, and coffeemakers. Pets are allowed for $10 a day, and parking is free. The 75-room hotel is located a few steps away from the Music Row traffic circle and nearby restaurants.

Located near Elliston Place and Vanderbilt University, **Guesthouse Inn and Suites** (1909 Hayes St., 615/329-1000, $109) offers a free shuttle to nearby hospitals, including Baptist Hospital, Vanderbilt Medical Center, and the Veterans Administration Hospital. All rooms have microwave ovens, refrigerators, and coffeemakers, and guests enjoy free breakfast including made-to-order waffles. Suites ($140) include a sleeper couch. Rooms are typical motel-style, with two double beds or a single king-sized bed. The property is convenient to Hillsboro Village, Music Row, and Centennial Park.

Come home to **Hillsboro House** (1933 20th Ave. S., 615/292-5501, www.visitnashville.net, $130–175), a restored Victorian buttercup cottage in a quiet residential neighborhood near Vanderbilt, Hillsboro Village, and Belmont University. The bed-and-breakfast offers three mini-suites, each with a private bathroom and telephone. Rooms have comfortable feather beds, antique furniture, and touches of home. Guests are invited to lounge in an upstairs library. There is free wireless Internet access for guests, and the full breakfast includes homemade breads.

Another bed-and-breakfast choice in this part of the city is **1501 Linden House Bed and Breakfast** (1501 Linden Ave., 615/298-2701, www.nashville-bed-breakfast.com, $110–165). This cheerful yellow-brick home on a corner lot has three guest rooms, each with stylish furniture and hardwood floors; one room has a private whirlpool and another has a fireplace.

Over $200

For luxurious accommodations near Vanderbilt, choose █ **Loews Vanderbilt Plaza** (2100 West End Ave., 615/320-1700, $260–310), a 340-room hotel on West End Avenue close to Centennial Park and Hillsboro Village. Loews boasts 24-hour room service, luxurious sheets, towels, and robes, natural soaps, and spacious bathrooms. Guests enjoy top-of-the-line coffee and tea kettles, evening turn-down service, and free high-speed Internet access. Many rooms have views of the Nashville skyline; premium rooms provide guests with access to the concierge lounge, with continental breakfast and evening hors d'oeuvres and a cash bar. All guests can enjoy a fine fitness room, spa, art gallery, and gift shop.

You can't get closer to Vanderbilt University than the **Marriott Nashville Vanderbilt** (2555 West End Ave., 615/321-1300, $180–300). Set on the northern end of the university campus, the Marriott has 301 guest rooms, six suites, and meeting space. It is located across West End Avenue from Centennial Park, home of the Parthenon, and a few steps from Vanderbilt's football stadium. There is an indoor pool, full-service restaurant, deli, concierge lounge, ATM, and business center.

EAST NASHVILLE

While it does not have many attractions, there are a few good reasons to stay in East Nashville. For football fans, this part of the city is close to the Tennessee Titans' stadium. Others will enjoy bed-and-breakfasts in Edgefield, a cool, laid-back, and diverse residential neighborhood. Good dining abounds, and downtown is a short drive or walk across the Cumberland River.

Under $100

Located on the east bank of the Cumberland River, **Days Inn at the Stadium** (211 N. 1st St., 615/254-1551, $75–100) is near LP Field, where the Tennessee Titans play. The hotel's 180 rooms have clock-radios, cable TV, and wireless Internet. Some have nice views of the Nashville skyline. Guests enjoy access to a fitness room, indoor pool, and laundry facilities, plus free breakfast. There is a bar and restaurant inside the hotel. While not within easy walking distance of downtown Nashville, the Days Inn is just across the river from the city's premier attractions. Free parking is a plus.

$100-150

Carole's Yellow Cottage (801 Fatherland St., 615/226-2952, $100–125) is a bed-and-breakfast offering two comfortable guest rooms. The decor is not as fussy as many bed-and-breakfasts, and the atmosphere is homey and low-key. Rooms have a private bathroom, and guests can relax in a library with a TV/VCR. Breakfasts are homemade and feature organic foods when available.

The Big Bungalow (618 Fatherland St., 615/256-8375, www.thebigbungalow.com, $110–160), a Craftsman-style early-1900s townhouse, offers three guest rooms, each with its own private bath and television. Guests have shared access to a computer, microwave, and refrigerator. Common areas are comfortable and stylish, with tasteful decor and hardwood floors. Hostess Ellen Warshaw prepares breakfast for her guests and sometimes hosts in-the-round concerts in her living room. She is also a licensed masseuse. This is a pet-free, non-smoking facility; children over 10 years are welcome. The bed-and-breakfast is located about seven blocks from the Shelby Street Pedestrian Bridge that takes you to the heart of the District.

$150-200

The East Park Inn (822 Boscoble St., 615/226-8691, $155) is a brightly painted Queen Anne–style bed-and-breakfast in Edgefield, on the east bank of the Cumberland River. Two guest suites offer private bathrooms and elegant furnishings. Guests also enjoy a relaxing terrace and garden, comfortable common rooms, and delicious breakfasts of fresh fruit, breads, quiche, waffles, and fresh-squeezed orange juice, served by host Brooks Parker. Afternoon tea or wine is served on the front porch, which enjoys a pleasant view of the Nashville skyline. The inn is located 10 blocks from downtown Nashville, and three blocks from coffee shops and restaurants.

You'll be happy to call **Top O'Woodland** (1603 Woodland St., 888/288-368, www.topofwoodland.com, $160) home during your stay in Nashville. This redbrick home on a corner lot is distinctive and beautiful. Features include a spacious wraparound front porch, original stained-glass windows, a turret, a baby grand Steinway piano, and lots of period and original antiques. The bed-and-breakfast is within five blocks of restaurants and pubs, and a short drive over the Cumberland to downtown Nashville. Guests can choose to stay in the master suite, with a king-sized four-poster bed, working fireplace, private bath, and private entrance, or in Mr. Green's Cottage, a detached cottage with kitchenette that can sleep up to six people. The home has wireless high-speed Internet access, and a generous continental breakfast is served at your convenience. Hostess Belinda Leslie is a chaplain and a certified wedding and event planner, and Top O'Woodland is a beautiful place for an old-fashioned wedding or quiet elopement.

MUSIC VALLEY

There are a dozen or more chain hotels in Music Valley, all close to restaurants and a short drive from the Grand Ole Opry and Opry Mills mall. Nashville's most famous hotel, Opryland, is luxurious and within walking distance of the Opry.

These hotels tend to provide more for your money than downtown digs, but they are a 10- to-15-minute drive to the city center.

Under $100

If you're looking for a clean, comfortable room and friendly welcome, look no farther than the ◖ **Fiddler's Inn** (2410 Music Valley Dr., 615/885-1440, www.fiddlers-inn.com, $60–75). This 204-room no-frills hotel offers a solid Tennessee welcome to its guests, who come in droves to see the Opry and enjoy other Music Valley attractions. It's right next to a Cracker Barrel restaurant and there's plenty of parking for cars and tour buses. Guests enjoy cable TV, free coffee and pastries in the morning, an outdoor pool, and a gift shop stocked with Nashville souvenirs.

The all-suite **Best Western Suites near Opryland** (201 Music City Cir., 615/902-9940, $70–80) is a comfortable compromise between the luxury of the Opryland Hotel and the affordability of a motel. Each of the hotel's 100 suites has a couch, desk, high-speed Internet access, coffee- and tea-maker, microwave, ironing board, and refrigerator. Rooms with whirlpools tubs are available for about $80 more per night. Guests enjoy an on-site fitness room, 24-hour business center, outdoor pool, free continental breakfast, and weekday newspaper. The Best Western is located along a strip of motels and restaurants about one mile from the Grand Ole Opry and other Opryland attractions.

Located about two miles from the Opryland, **Comfort Inn Opryland Area** (2516 Music Valley Dr., 615/889-0086, $70–75) offers 121 clean, comfortable guest rooms with cable TV, wireless Internet, ironing board, hair dryer, and free daily newspaper. There is free outdoor parking, and interior corridors.

$100-150

Guests at the **Courtyard by Marriott Opryland** (125 Music City Cir., 615/882-9133, $140–150) enjoy refurbished rooms with soft beds, wireless Internet, coffeemakers, ironing boards, and refrigerators. The on-site restaurant serves breakfast, and business rooms come with a desk, dataport, voice mail, and speakerphone.

Over $200

The **Gaylord Opryland Hotel** (2800 Opryland Dr., 615/889-1000, $240–310) feels like a cruise ship on land. This 2,881-room luxury hotel and convention center is built around a nine-acre indoor garden. Glass atriums invite sunlight, and miles of footpaths invite you to explore the climate-controlled gardens. Highlights include a 40-foot waterfall and flatboats that float along a river.

Set among the gardens are dozens of different restaurants and cafés, ranging from casual buffets to elegant steakhouses. A few shops are sprinkled in, but it has not yet totally morphed into a mall. Hundreds of room balconies overlook the gardens, providing some guests with views of the well-kept greenery, even in winter. If you stay, choose between a "traditional view" looking outside the hotel, or an "atrium view" for about $60 more per night.

The property has a full-service salon and fitness center, on-site child care and "kid's resort," and a car rental agency. You can walk to Opry Mills mall and the Grand Ole Opry from the hotel or take the free shuttle. Guest rooms are luxurious and feature coffee- and tea-makers; two telephones; wireless Internet access; pay-per-view movies, games, and music; daily national newspapers; and other usual amenities. You can add a refrigerator for a one-time $20 fee, and you get up to 20 minutes of local calls free per day. Guests can buy one-time or daily passes on the downtown shuttle for about $15 a day, and the airport shuttle costs $35 round-trip.

While room rates at the Opryland are steep, the hotel offers attractive packages that add on other Gaylord-owned attractions and properties. These often include tickets to the Grand Ole Opry, a ride on the General Jackson Showboat, trips into Nashville to visit the Ryman Auditorium or the Wildhorse Saloon, and extras like spa visits and golf games at the hotel. Many of these packages are a good deal for travelers who want to pay one price for their whole vacation.

AIRPORT
Under $100

The **Alexis Inn and Suites Nashville Airport** (600 Ermac Dr., 615/889-4466, www.nashvillealexishotel.com, $60–70) is a comfortable and convenient place to stay near the airport. Rooms have all the usual amenities, plus guests get free popcorn in the lobby, a free airport shuttle daily between 7 A.M. and 9 P.M., and a business center. All rooms have refrigerators, and most have microwaves. There is a free continental breakfast. Suites cost $80–100 per night.

$100-150

Drury Inns and Suites (555 Donelson Pike, 615/902-0400, $100–130) offers guests an appealing array of extras, including a free hot breakfast, free evening beverages and snacks, a free airport shuttle, 60 minutes of free long-distance calls, and $7 daily park-and-fly parking. There is both an indoor and outdoor pool and a fitness center. Drury Inn is about two miles north of the airport and five miles south of Music Valley.

Hotel Preston (733 Briley Pkwy., 615/361-5900, www.hotelpreston.com, $110–140) is a boutique hotel near the airport. Youthful energy, modern decor, and up-to-date rooms set this property apart from the crowd. Rooms are stocked with Tazo tea and Starbucks coffee and there's and a 24-hour fitness center. The "You-Want-It-You-Got-It" button in each room beckons the 24-hour room service, and whimsical extras including a lava lamp, pet fish, and art kit are available by request when you check in. High-speed Internet is an add-on extra. Naughty packages—like the "Ooey Gooey Night Out" couple's getaway with late checkout, wine, and whipped cream on request—prove that this isn't your parents' motel, though the hotel caters equally to business travelers with meeting rooms and a business center. Two restaurants, including a bar and nightclub, provide food and entertainment.

SOUTH OF NASHVILLE
Under $100

Nashville's second hostel is located a half-hour drive south of the city in Brentwood. **Country Hostel Nashville** (9900 Maxwell Ln., 615/578-7207, www.countryhostelnashville.com, $22) is indeed semi-rural, and guests can enjoy bike riding (the hostel rents bikes) or sitting out on the comfortable deck. The hostel has free wireless Internet, a barbecue, and a spacious kitchen. It is non-smoking inside and air-conditioned in summer. Accommodations are divided into male and female dorm-style rooms with bunk beds and clean sheets. Towels and linens are provided, and the hostel will pick you up from the airport or bus station for an additional fee.

This hostel is also convenient to attractions in Franklin, Tennessee, and close to malls, shopping, and dining. You need a car to explore any of these areas, however.

Food

You can eat in a different restaurant each day in Nashville and never get bored. Southern cooking stars at meat-and-three diners and barbecue joints, fine dining restaurants cater to the well-heeled, and ethnic eateries reflect the city's diversity.

The Arcade

One of two downtown food destinations, the Arcade is an old outdoor shopping mall that lies between 4th and 5th Avenues. The ground floor of the Arcade is full of hole-in-the-wall restaurants that cater to the downtown lunchtime crowd with quick, cheap eats. Upstairs are professional offices and a few galleries.

Katie's Meat & Three (10 Arcade, 615/256-1055) has four different meat specials daily, which you can get with sides like turnip greens, mashed potatoes, and white beans. A meat-and-three plate costs $7; order your choice of four sides for $5. **The Greek Touch** (13 Arcade, 615/259-9493) has gyro, sausage, veggie, and chicken divine sandwiches, platters, and salads, all for under $6. There are also several sandwich shops, a pizza parlor, and a Chinese restaurant.

Most restaurants at the Arcade have some seating inside, or you can sit outside and watch the world go by around you. The outdoor experience is made slightly less enjoyable by the presence of smokers who have been forbidden to enter many eateries.

Nashville Farmer's Market

Organizers of the Nashville Farmer's Market have hit upon a good thing. The outdoor components of the market include a farm shed with fresh produce year-round and a flea market with arts and crafts on weekends. The interior of the market is a food court with choices ranging from Southern specialties to Caribbean cuisine. **Swett's** (900 8th Ave. N., 615/742-9699), a popular soul food restaurant, has an outpost here. **Jamaicaway** (900 8th Ave. N., 615/255-5920) serves oxtail, steamed fish, and Jamaican patties. There are also Mexican, Chinese, and Greek choices, as well as a super salad bar. The food court is open daily 9 A.M.–5 P.M.

DINERS AND COFFEE SHOPS
Downtown

Provence (601 Church St., 615/664-1150, Mon.–Fri. 7 A.M.–6 P.M., Sat. 8 A.M.–5 P.M., $5–12), located inside the Nashville Public Library, serves excellent European-style pastries, breads, and salads, as well as coffee. Provence's signature sandwiches include creamy chicken salad and turkey-and-brie. Or you can try a sampler of the café's salads, including roasted-vegetable salad, parmesan potato salad, or creamy penne pasta. Save room for a decadent pastry, or at least a cookie, which come in varieties like raspberry hazelnut, chocolate espresso, and ginger molasses. For breakfast, nothing beats a buttery croissant spread with jam. Provence also has locations at 1600 Division Street at Roundabout Plaza; at 315 Deaderick Street in the AmSouth Building downtown; and in Hillsboro at 1705 21st Avenue South.

For homemade salads, wraps, and sandwiches, follow the crowds of downtown office workers to the **Frist Center Cafe** (919 Broadway, 616/244-3340, Mon.–Wed. and Sat. 10 A.M.–5:30 P.M., Thurs.–Fri. 10 A.M.–9 P.M., Sun. noon–5 P.M., $5–8), located at the rear of the Frist Center for the Arts. Sandwiches are available whole or half, and you can add a soup, salad, or fries for a well-rounded lunch. The café has daily hot lunch entrées, plus a case of tempting desserts.

Midtown

When Nashvillians are in the mood for a hearty deli sandwich, they head to **Noshville** (1918 Broadway, 615/329-6674, Mon. 6:30 A.M.–2:30 P.M., Tues.–Thurs. 6:30 A.M.–9 P.M., Fri. 6:30 A.M.–10:30 P.M., Sat. 7:30 A.M.–10:30 P.M., Sun. 7:30 A.M.–9 P.M., $7–12), which is as close to a genuine New York delicatessen as you'll find in this town. Lox and bagels, oatmeal, and a variety of egg dishes are popular at breakfast.

At lunch and supper choose from a variety of sandwiches, all served double-stacked, which means it's really more than any one person should eat. To find Noshville, look for the miniature statue of Lady Liberty on the roof. There is a second location in Green Hills at 4014 Hillsboro Circle, 615/269-3535.

The hype surrounding Nashville's favorite breakfast restaurant, the **Pancake Pantry** (1796 21st Ave. S., 615/383-9333, Mon.–Fri. 6 A.M.–3 P.M., Sat.–Sun. 6 A.M.–4 P.M., $6–14) is deserved. Founded in 1961 and still family-owned, the Pantry serves the best pancakes in the city, and probably the state. Owner David Baldwin says that the secret is in the ingredients, which are fresh and homemade. Many of the flours come from Tennessee, and the syrup is made right at the restaurant. The Pantry proves that a pancake can be much more than plain. The menu offers no less than 21 varieties, and that doesn't include the waffles. Try the fluffy buckwheat cakes, savory cornmeal cakes, sweet blintzes, or the old standby buttermilk pancakes. And if you decide to order eggs instead, the good news is that most of the other breakfast platters on offer come with a short stack of pancakes too. To its credit, the Pantry offers no-yolk omelets for the health-conscious, and it's very kid-friendly as well.

The Pantry also serves lunch, which is limited to sandwiches, salads, and soups. Beware that on many weekend mornings, and some weekdays, the line for a seat at the Pantry goes out the door.

In today's retro-happy world, it isn't too hard to find an old-fashioned soda shop. But how many of them are the real thing? **Elliston Place Soda Shop** (2111 Elliston Pl., 615/327-1090, Mon.–Fri. 7 A.M.–7 P.M., Sat. 7 A.M.–5 P.M., $5–9), near Centennial Park and Vanderbilt, is one of these rare holdovers from the past, and it's proud of it. The black-and-white tile floors, lunch counter, and Purity Milk advertisements may have been here for decades, but the food is consistently fresh and good. Choose between a sandwich or a plate lunch, but be sure to save room for a classic milkshake or slice of hot pie with ice cream on top. Yum!

Nashville's original coffee shop, **Bongo Java** (2007 Belmont Blvd., 615/385-5282, Mon.–Fri. 7 A.M.–11 P.M., Sat.–Sun. 8 A.M.–11 P.M.) is just as popular as ever. Located near Belmont University, Bongo, as its frequent patrons call it, is regularly full of students chatting, texting, and surfing the Internet thanks to free wireless Internet. Set in an old house with a huge front porch, Bongo feels homey and welcoming, and a bit more on the hippie side than other Nashville coffee shops. Nonetheless, expect the latest in coffee drinks, premium salads, and sandwiches. Breakfast, including Bongo French toast, is served all day. There is a bulletin board, a good place to find and seek roommates or apartments.

Voted Nashville's favorite coffee shop, **Fido** (1812 21st Ave. S., 615/777-3436, Mon.–Fri. 7 A.M.–11 P.M., Sat. 8 A.M.–midnight, Sun. 8 A.M.–11 P.M.) near Vanderbilt is a place to see and be seen. Take a seat along the front plate-glass windows to watch the pretty people as they stroll between the Sunset Grill and Posh, one of Nashville's most upscale clothing boutiques. Fido's is a tad dark, with sleek furnishings and rock music playing. It is not unfriendly, but has a harder edge than Bongo Java. In addition to coffee, sandwiches, salads, and baked goods are also on the menu.

Said to have the best burger in Nashville, **Rotier's** (2413 Elliston Pl., 615/327-9892, Mon.–Fri. 10:30 A.M.–10 P.M., Sat. 9 A.M.–10 P.M., $5–12) is also a respected meat-and-three diner. Choose from classic sandwiches or comfort-food dinners. The Saturday breakfast will fuel you all day long. Ask about the milkshake, a city favorite that appears nowhere on the menu.

Dessert takes center stage at **Bobbie's Dairy Dip** (5301 Charlotte Ave., 615/292-2112, Mon.–Thurs. 11 A.M.–9 P.M., Fri.–Sat. 11 A.M.–10 P.M., Sun. noon–9 P.M., $4–7). The cheeseburgers and chili dogs are the comfort food you've dreamed of, and you can finish off with soft-serve ice cream, dipped cones, sundaes, and banana splits. Bobbie's closes during the winter months; call ahead to confirm they're open.

East Nashville

The most creative deli in Nashville is **Mitchell's Delicatessen** (1402 McGavock Pk., 615/262-9862, Tues.–Sat. 7 A.M.–7 P.M., Sun. 7 A.M.–4 P.M., $5–9). Order the roasted lamb and raita; a Vietnamese-style creation with pork, liver pate, and veggies; or a BLT fit for a king. Breakfast is served until 11 A.M., and there is also a daily menu of soups and hot plate specials. Stop here for top-notch bread, cheese, and meats for your own sandwiches, too.

South Nashville

Aurora Bakery and Cafe (3725 Nolensville Pike, 615/837-1993, Mon.–Sat. 7 A.M.–8 P.M., $5–6) offers one of the most cheerful welcomes among Nashville eateries. The café is clean, bright, and full of the smell of fresh baked goods. Come here to buy loaves of fresh white bread, or to sample one of the dozens of types of pastries, cookies, and cakes, many of them traditional Hispanic recipes. Specialties include empanadas and *tres leche* cake.

SOUTHERN SPECIALTIES
Downtown

Run, don't walk, to ◖ **Arnold's Country Kitchen** (605 8th Ave. S., 615/256-4455, Mon.–Fri. 10:30 A.M.–2:45 P.M., $7–10) for some of the best Southern cooking in town. Set in a red cinder-block building on the southern outskirts of downtown, Arnold's a food-lover's dream. No haute or fusion cuisine here—this is real food! It's set up cafeteria style, so start out by grabbing a tray while you peer at the wonders before you: chocolate pie, congealed salad (that's Jell-O to those who don't know), juicy sliced tomatoes, turnip greens, mashed potatoes, squash casserole, macaroni and cheese—and that's just the "vegetables." Choose a vegetable plate, with either three or four vegetables, or a meat-and-three for just about a buck more. Common meat dishes include ham, baked chicken, fried fish, and beef tips. All meals come with your choice of pillowy yeast rolls or cornbread. The full lunch, plus a drink, will run you under

$10. As you leave, full and happy, the only question on your mind will be, When can I come back?

Midtown

One of Nashville's most beloved meat-and-threes is **Swett's** (2725 Clifton Ave., 615/329-4418, daily 11 A.M.–8 P.M., $7–10), family owned and operated since 1954. People come from all over the city to eat at this North Nashville institution, which combines soul food and Southern cooking with great results. The food here is homemade and authentic, down to the real mashed potatoes, the vinegary greens, and the yeast rolls. Swett's is set up cafeteria style. Start by grabbing dessert—the pies are excellent—and then you move on to the good stuff: Country-fried steak, pork chops, meatloaf, fried catfish, and ham are a few of the usual suspects. A standard plate comes with one meat, two sides, and a serving of either yeast roll or cornbread, but you can add more sides if you like. Draw your own iced tea—sweet or unsweet—at the end and then find a seat, if you can.

North Nashville

Nashville's most sublime food experience is not to be found in a fine restaurant or even at a standard meat-and-three cafeteria. The food that you'll still be dreaming about when you get home is found at ◖ **Prince's Hot Chicken Shack** (123 Ewing Dr., 615/226-9442, Tues.–Thurs. noon–10 P.M., Fri.–Sat. 2 P.M.–1 A.M., $4–6) in North Nashville. Hot chicken is skillet-fried chicken that is also spicy, and you can find hot chicken outlets in Nashville, Memphis, and a few other Southern cities. But no hot chicken shop does it quite as well as Prince's, where the hot chicken comes in three varieties: mild, hot, and extra-hot. Most uninitiated will find the mild variety pretty darn spicy, so beware. It is served with slices of white bread—perfect for soaking up that spicy chicken juice—and pickles. You can add a cup of creamy potato salad, coleslaw, or baked beans if you like. When you walk into Prince's, head to the back where you'll place your order

a typical meat-and-three plate lunch, as served at Swett's

at the window, pay, and be given a number. Then take a seat—if you can find one—while you wait for your food. You can order to go or eat in. Your food is made to order, and Prince's is very popular, so the wait often exceeds 30 minutes. Have heart though—Prince's chicken is worth the wait.

West End
For a refined Southern food experience there's **Martha's at the Plantation** (5025 Harding Rd., 615/353-2828, daily 11 A.M.–2 P.M., $9–15), a sunny family-friendly café located above the gift shop at Belle Meade Plantation. Proprietor Martha Stamps offers favorites like chicken croquettes, fried chicken, and fried catfish sandwiches. Salads include cornmeal-crusted oysters on a bed of romaine, and popular side dishes are squash casserole, baked cheese grits, and spicy kale. For your main dish, try the boneless pork chop with cranberry glaze or a patty melt on sourdough toast. Her chicken and tuna salad sandwiches are also consistently good. Kids can choose from

favorites including macaroni and cheese and peanut butter and jelly sandwiches.

West of Nashville
The **Loveless Cafe** (8400 Hwy. 100, 615/646-9700, daily 7 A.M.–9 P.M., $7–13) is an institution, and some may argue it's a state of mind. But this little café-that-could is increasingly a destination too, for visitors not just to Nashville but the entire heartland of Tennessee. The Loveless got its start in 1951 when Lon and Annie Loveless started to serve good country cooking to travelers on Highway 100. Over the years the restaurant changed hands, but Annie's biscuit recipe remained the same, and it was the biscuits that kept Nashvillians, including many famous ones, coming back for more. In 1982 then owner George McCabe started the Hams & Jams mail-order business, and in 2003 the Loveless underwent a major renovation that expanded the kitchen and dining rooms and added additional shops in the rear. The food at the Loveless is good, no doubt about it. The biscuits are fluffy and buttery,

© SUSANNA HENIGHAN POTTER

The Loveless Cafe is a culinary landmark.

the ham salty, and the eggs, bacon, and sausage will hit the spot. The supper and lunch menu has expanded to include Southern standards like fried catfish and chicken, pit-cooked pork barbecue, pork chops, and meatloaf, as well as a few salads. The prices are a bit on the high side—a basic plate of bacon and eggs will run you at least $9—but a destination restaurant can do that. Parties of four or more can choose the family-style breakfast, which offers all the fruit, bacon, sausage, fries, gravy, eggs, biscuits, and preserves you can eat for $11 per adult and $6 per child. The Loveless is located about 20 miles from downtown Nashville; plan on a 30-minute drive out Highway 100. Once you get out of the clutter of West End, it's a pretty trip.

BARBECUE
Downtown

Thousands of tourists can't be wrong; **Jack's Bar-B-Que** (416 Broadway, 615/254-5715, Mon.–Thurs. 10:30 A.M.–9 P.M., Fri.–Sat. 10:30 A.M.–10 P.M., Sun. noon–6 P.M., $4–13)

is a great place to grab a bite on Broadway. Choose from barbecue pork shoulder, brisket, turkey, ribs, or sausage, and pair it with classic Southern sides like green beans, macaroni and cheese, and fried apples. Jack's serves five types of barbecue sauce, including classic Tennessee, Texas, and Kansas City. Most diners opt for a plate of one meat, two vegetables, and bread for $8–9, but if you're really hungry go for the three-meat platter for $13. Adding to the appeal of the good, affordable food is the fact that Jack's service is fast and friendly.

Midtown

Near Centennial Park and Vanderbilt, **Hog Heaven** (115 27th Ave. N., 615/329-1234, Mon.–Sat. 10 A.M.–7 P.M., $5–10) is a small yet well-known landmark for barbecue. Pulled-pork sandwiches and beef brisket are among the most popular at this mostly take-out eatery.

East Nashville

Family-operated **Dee's Q** (1000 Riverside Dr., 615/227-0024, Mon.–Thurs. 11 A.M.–9 P.M.,

Fri.–Sat. 11 A.M.–10 P.M., Sun. 11 A.M.–7 P.M., $2.50–10) serves up Memphis-style barbecue dry ribs, brisket, turkey, and chicken. He smokes his meats over hickory fire right next door to the open-air seating area. Call for winter hours.

South Nashville

Tucked on Nolensville Pike, the land of ethnic eateries, is one of Nashville's best barbecue houses. **Martin's Bar-B-Que Joint** (7215 Nolensville Pike, 615/776-1856, Tues.–Sat. 11 A.M.–8 P.M., $3.50–20.50) has pulled pork, barbecue spareribs, smoked wings, and beef brisket, plus all the side dishes you could want: coleslaw, green beans, potato salad, and the best corncakes this side of town. You can also order burgers and a mean catfish po-boy. Martin's is located inside the Nolensville city limits, about 30 minutes' drive south from downtown Nashville.

STEAKHOUSES
Downtown

Most everything about **Demos' Steak and Spaghetti House** (300 Commerce St., 615/256-4655, daily 11 A.M.–11 P.M., $6–15) is upscale except the price. Just as the name suggests, Demos' specializes in steaks and spaghetti, and it has earned a reputation among Nashville residents for quality food and good value. Choose from hamburger steak, rib eye, or sirloin, or try one of the 12 different spaghetti dinners, including seafood sauce and browned butter with garlic. The portions are more than generous, pleasing to the biggest appetites. The original Demos' is in Murfreesboro, and there are other locations in Lebanon and Hendersonville.

Midtown

◖ **Jimmy Kelly's** (217 Louise Ave., 615/329-4349, Mon.–Sat. 5 P.M.–midnight, $12–36) is a family-run old-school steakhouse. Set in an old Victorian mansion a few blocks from Centennial Park and Vanderbilt, Jimmy Kelly's has been operated by the Kelly family since 1934. During its lifetime, food fads have come and gone, but Jimmy Kelly's has

continued to serve excellent steaks and other grill foods. Dinner begins with irresistible corn cakes, and continues with classic appetizers like crab cakes or fried calamari. Entrée choices include a half-dozen different steaks, lamb, grilled chicken, and seafood, including the best blackened catfish in the city. Jimmy Kelly's offers low lighting, wood paneling, and attentive, but not fussy, service. Tables are set throughout what were once parlors, bedrooms, and porches in the old home, giving diners a feeling of homey intimacy.

CONTEMPORARY
Downtown

The thoughtful menu, careful preparations, and intimate atmosphere at the ◖ **Mad Platter** (1239 6th Ave. N., 615/242-2563, Mon.–Fri. 10 A.M.–2 P.M., Wed.–Sat. 5:30–11 P.M., Sun. 5–11 P.M., $18–29) have made it one of Nashville's favorite "nice" restaurants for years. Located among restored townhouses in the tiny Germantown neighborhood just north of the Bicentennial Mall, the Mad Platter is the work of Craig and Marcia Jervis, two chefs who met while catering the mid-1980s Michael Jackson's Victory tour. The Jervises married and opened the Mad Hatter, where they demonstrate their love for food, and each other, every day. Signature entrées include the Mad Platter rack of lamb, which is tender and juicy, and the porcini-dusted shrimp. For a special occasion, or just to enjoy one of the city's best dining deals, choose the five-course special. Add $20 to your favorite entrée and you'll get soup, appetizer, salad, and dessert, too. Talk about a meal to remember! Lunch features sandwiches, pasta, and salads for $7–13. The chicken salad is sweet and tangy, and comes with fresh banana bread. Reservations are advisable at dinner; for lunch, come early to head off the business crowd.

Rub elbows with legislators, lobbyists, and other members of the jet set at the **Capitol Grill** (23 6th Ave. N., 615/345-7116, daily 6:30 A.M.–2 P.M. and 5:30–10 P.M., $16–47). Located in the ground floor of the elegant Hermitage Hotel and set a stone's throw from the Tennessee State Capitol, this is the sort of restaurant where marriages are proposed and deals are done. The menu is fine dining at its best: choice cuts of meat prepared with exacting care. Dinner features rack of elk, sea bass, and pork chops; the provenience of each is noted on the menu. The lunch menu is more modest, including the Capitol Grill burger, a grilled pimento cheese sandwich, and meat entrées for $11–18. The business lunch offers a lunch entrée and your choice of soup or salad for $20. Breakfast ($4–16) may be the most decadent of all, with cinnamon-swirl French toast, eggs Benedict, lobster and shirred eggs, and an array of fresh pastries and fruit. The Sunday Brunch features the best of the grill's lunch and breakfast menus, and is consistently popular.

Adjacent to the Capitol Grill is the Oak Bar, a wood-paneled and intimate bar for pre- or post-dinner drinks and conversation.

Midtown

Restaurant Zola (3001 West End Ave., 615/320-7778, Mon.–Thurs. 5:30–10 P.M., Fri.–Sat. 5:30–11 P.M., $16–30) is consistently among Nashville's favorite restaurants for romance, special occasions, and its menu. Located in a strip mall in the city's upscale West End, Restaurant Zola wows with its intriguing fusion of Mediterranean and Southern cuisine and superb wine list. Fresh seafood, top-grade meats, and vegetarian entrées that are much more than an afterthought define the menu. Zola's paella and the lobster omelet headline the seafood menu; pork tenderloin and grilled venison highlight the meats, and the signature vegetable tower will make even meat-eaters smile. Be sure to save room for some of the best desserts in town.

◖**F. Scott's** (2210 Crestmore Rd., 615/269-5861, Mon.–Thurs. 5:30–10 P.M., Fri.–Sat. 5:30–11 P.M., Sun. 5:30–9 P.M., $26–38) is an upscale restaurant and jazz bar with one of the best wine lists in Nashville. Diners are ushered into a black-and-white-tiled dining room, where the sounds of live jazz from the adjacent

listening room follow them. Enjoy a relaxed meal with wine pairings and great conversation. Food at F. Scott's is meant to be savored. Appetizers include rabbit tart, or pancetta and scallops with caviar, and entrées might be pan-seared seafood, dressed-up shepherd's pie, and grilled beef tenderloin. Save room for dessert: homemade ice cream, coconut cake, or a cheese plate paired with the perfect dessert wine.

A favorite for Music Row power lunches, special occasions, and late-night bar food, **Sunset Grill** (2001 Belcourt Ave., 615/386-3663, $11–30) serves lunch Tuesday–Friday 11 A.M.–3 P.M., dinner nightly 5–11 P.M., and late-night Monday–Saturday until 1:30 A.M. Dinner favorites include Voodoo Pasta, a spicy pasta dish with shrimp and andouille sausage, and the grilled beef tenderloin. At lunch, when most choices clock in at under $12, you can order salads, sandwiches, and pasta. The Cobb salad and chicken-salad sandwiches are always popular. Food here is prepared with care, often using organic and locally produced ingredients. The outdoor patio is popular during warm weather, and it is a great place to people-watch.

East Nashville

The Family Wash (2038 Greenwood Ave., 615/226-6070, Tues.–Sat. 6 P.M.–midnight, $9–15) is a live music listening room that serves good food at surprisingly low cost. Where else can you get a well-cooked steak for just $14? Choose from baked mac and cheese, the killer meat or vegetarian shepherd's pie, or roasted salmon and jasmine rice. Pizzas and the flank steak sandwich are always good. Reservations are accepted, and a good idea, especially when a popular musician is on the stage. The Wash, located in an old laundry, books up-and-coming singer-songwriters, and when the music is on, the conversation stops. This is a restaurant with a lot of energy and a little attitude.

ETHNIC CUISINE
Downtown

There are several Greek restaurants amid Nashville's office towers and State buildings.

One of the best is **Santorini** (210 4th Ave., 615/254-4524, Mon.–Fri. 10:30 A.M.–3 P.M., $3.50–5.75). Choose from falafel, gyro, chicken, or spinach pie, served as a plate (with rice, salad, and pita), salad (with pita, tabouli, and salad), or meal (with fries). The food is fresh and well prepared, and the premises are neat and clean.

Located in the downtown Arcade, **House of Pizza** (15 Arcade, 615/242-7144, Mon.–Fri. 10 A.M.–6 P.M., Sat. 11 A.M.–4:30 P.M.) serves up thick- and thin-crust varieties, massive stromboli, mighty lasagna, and huge meatball subs. The restaurant is small; eating in can be a challenge, especially since Nashvillians flock here for the best pizza in town.

Midtown

The venerable **International Market and Restaurant** (2010 Belmont Blvd., 615/297-4453, daily 10:30 A.M.–9 P.M., $4–10) near Belmont University and Hillsboro Village may well be the best choice for a cheap lunch in Nashville. The cafeteria serves lots of vegetable, noodle, and rice dishes, many of them Thai in origin, at prices that seem not to have risen much since the restaurant was established in 1975. If you want to splurge, order a "from the kitchen" special of pad thai or another dish, which will be made from scratch just for you.

For the best Italian food in Nashville, head west to the neighborhood of Sylvan Park, where you'll find **Caffe Nonna** (4427 Murphy Rd., 615/463-0133, Tues.–Fri. 11 A.M.–2 P.M., Mon.–Thurs. 5–9 P.M., Fri.–Sat. 5–10 P.M., $12–21). Inspired by chef Daniel Maggipinto's own Nonna (grandmother), the café serves rustic Italian fare. Appetizers include salads and bruschetta and entrées include the divine Lasagne Nonna, made with butternut squash, ricotta cheese, spinach, and sage. One of the best deals is the mix-and-match pasta; choose your own pasta and sauce for $10 at lunch and $12 at dinner. The lunch menu offers a dozen different sandwiches, including basil chicken salad and Italian-fried tilapia, for under $10. The

service at Caffe Nonna is friendly and attentive, and the atmosphere is cozy.

Located just west of the Kroger food store and on the opposite side of the street, K&S World Market on Charlotte Avenue, the second in a chain whose original location is on Nolensville Pike, will keep any foodie happy for hours with its obscure and unusual food items. In the same shopping center you'll find Nashvillians' favorite Vietnamese restaurant, **Kien Giang** (5825 Charlotte Ave., 615/353-1250, Tues.–Fri. 11 A.M.–9 P.M., Sat.–Sun. 10 A.M.–9 P.M., $4–12).

Drive a bit farther out to find **La Hispana Panaderia** (6208 Charlotte Pike, 615/352-3798, daily 6 A.M.–9 P.M.), whose bread and pastries are as good as the finest European bakery but at a fraction of the cost.

One of Nashville's oldest Indian restaurants, **Shalimar** (3711 Hillsboro Rd., 615/269-8577, Mon.–Sat. 11 A.M.–10 P.M., $11–17) offers fine food and efficient service. The $11 lunch combo of entrée, rice, naan, salad, and a drink is popular, along with the Saturday lunch buffet. At dinner, Shalimar takes on a slightly more elegant cast with vegetarian, chicken, lamb, and seafood entrées in popular preparations including masala, biryani, tikka, saag, or korma. Shalimar is a few blocks away from the Green Hills Mall.

South Nashville

Chosen by Nashvillians as the best Mexican restaurant in a very crowded field, **La Hacienda Taqueria** (2615 Nolensville Pike, 615/256-6142, Mon.–Thurs. 10 A.M.–9 P.M., Fri. 10 A.M.–10 P.M., Sat. 9 A.M.–10 A.M., Sun. 9 A.M.–9 P.M., $2–14) is located within a colorful storefront on Nolensville Pike, Nashville's most ethnically diverse thoroughfare. The menu offers a dizzying array of choices—tacos, enchiladas, tamales, burritos, quesadillas, and *tortas,* just to name a few. Most come with your choice of chicken, chorizo, tripe, pork, or steak filling, and many have an authenticity often missing from Mexican restaurant fare. Combination platters, which offer three items plus rice and beans, are a good way to sample the options if you aren't sure what to order.

If you aren't in the mood for Mexican, just drive a bit farther along Nolensville Pike for other choices. Among them is **Dunya Kebob** (2521 Nolensville Pike, 615/242-6664, Mon.–Thurs. 11 A.M.–9:30 P.M., Fri.–Sat. 11 A.M.–10:30 P.M., Sun. noon–9:30 P.M., $5–10), which offers chicken, lamb, beef, and seafood kebobs and gyro sandwiches.

Not far from Nolensville, you'll find two more international favorites in the same shopping center on Trousdale Drive. **Back to Cuba** (4683 Trousdale Dr., 615/837-6711, Tues.–Sat. 11 A.M.–9 P.M., $8–12) serves traditional Cuban favorites: Grilled sandwiches of pork, ham, cheese, and pickle are a popular choice at lunchtime. For dinner, try the roast pork or grilled shrimp and don't skip the lacy fried plantains and spicy black beans.

For homemade Italian fare, go to **Mama Mia's** (4501 Trousdale Dr., 615/331-7207, Mon.–Fri. 11 A.M.–2 P.M., Mon.–Sat. 5–10 P.M., $7–16), which offers lasagna, ravioli, chicken, veal, and seafood dishes. Bring your own wine.

MARKETS

For fresh fruits, vegetables, preserves, and honey, go to the **Nashville Farmer's Market** held daily in the large covered building between 8th Avenue and the Bicentennial Mall. Many of the goods for sale here are home-

© SUSANNA HENIGHAN POTTER

Fresh vegetables are on sale at the Nashville Farmer's Market on 8th Avenue.

grown at farms near Nashville; to be sure, ask whether you're getting Tennessee products.

There is an abundance of traditional grocery stores around Nashville. Common chains are Kroger, Publix, and H. G. Hill. Drive out any of the main corridors into the city and you will quickly find a grocery store. There is a Trader Joe's, which specializes in organic and specialty items, in Green Hills, just south of the Green Hills Mall.

Information and Services

INFORMATION
Visitors Centers

The main visitors center (615/259-4747, Mon.–Sat. 8 A.M.–5 P.M., Sun. 10 A.M.–5 P.M.) is located at the corner of 5th Avenue and Broadway, inside the Nashville Arena. Here you can pick up brochures, get a free map, and find answers to just about any question. It is open late when there is an event at the Nashville Arena.

There is another visitors center a few blocks uptown at 1 Nashville Place (615/259-4730, Mon.–Fri. 8 A.M.–5 P.M.).

Maps

Visitors centers offer a free hand-out map of downtown and an area map that shows major thoroughfares. This will be sufficient for many travelers. However, if you plan to do a lot of driving or off-the-beaten-track exploring, pick up a city map such as those published by Rand McNally or AAA. Detailed maps may be purchased from local drugstores and bookstores. Save time by buying a map before you arrive.

Media
NEWSPAPERS

Nashville's daily morning broadsheet is the *Tennessean* (www.tennessean.com). Published under various names since 1812, the *Tennessean* offers what every big-city newspaper does: local, regional, and national news, plus lots more. The paper's entertainment insert is published with the Friday newspaper. The newspaper is available all over town for 50 cents on weekdays and Saturdays, $1.75 on Sundays.

The *City Paper* (www.nashvillecitypaper.com) is a free twice-weekly tabloid with a strong website that specializes in local news, sports, and events. It offers an alternative viewpoint to that of the *Tennessean* and makes a good, compact read for locals and visitors. You can pick up *City Paper* in dozens of downtown locations.

The *Nashville Scene* is a fat tabloid-sized alternative weekly that balances its coverage of the local arts, music, and social scene with some political and local news coverage. This is a good go-to choice to understand what's going on in the city. *All the Rage,* owned by the *Tennessean,* is also published on Thursdays and focuses solely on entertainment and events.

Nashville Music Guide (www.nashvillemusicguide.com) is a free tabloid published twice a month. It covers the local music scene and music-industry news.

In addition, the *Nashville Business Journal* (615/248-2222, $1) is a weekly business publication covering industry, commerce, and finance. It is distributed on Mondays. *Nashville Pride* (615/292-9150, $0.50) covers African-American news and is distributed on Fridays.

Also published by the *Tennessean, Nashville Lifestyles* is a monthly magazine with local celebrity profiles, home and garden tips, event information, and advertising. You can pick it up at newsstands throughout the city.

American Songwriter Magazine (1303 16th Ave. S., 615/321-6069, www.americansongwriter.com) is a bimonthly magazine devoted to the art of songwriting. It has been published in Nashville since 1984.

RADIO

The Nashville dial is chock-a-block with the usual commercial radio prospects. There are a few radio stations worth mentioning, however. **WSM 650 AM** is the legendary radio station that started it all when it put a fiddler on the air in 1925. Still airing the Grand Ole Opry after all these years, WSM plays country music at other times.

Nashville Public Radio is **WPLN 90.3 FM.** Tune in here for classical music and National Public Radio news. **WPLN 1430 AM** is a companion station with all-day news and talk, including BBC broadcasts. Nashville's only community radio station is **Radio Free Nashville** (98.9 FM, www.radiofreenashville.org). While its signal only reaches a small part of the city now, Radio Free Nashville is looking to expand its reach as soon as it raises the necessary funds.

WKDA 900 AM is Nashville's Spanish-language radio station. **WAMB 1160 AM** plays big-band music, and **WNAH 1360 AM** plays old-fashioned Southern gospel.

Several Nashville universities liven up the radio dial. Fisk's **WFSK 88.1 FM** plays jazz. Middle Tennessee State University has **WMTS 88.3 FM,** the student-run station, and **WMOT 89.5 FM,** a jazz station. Vanderbilt University's student radio station is **WRVU 91.1 FM.**

TELEVISION
Nashville's network affiliates offer local news morning and night. These include **WKRN** (Channel 2 ABC), **WSMV** (Channel 4 NBC), **WTVF** (Channel 5 CBS), and **WZTV** (Channel 17 FOX).

The local public-television station is **WNPT** (Channel 8 PBS).

Remember that since Nashville is in the Central time zone, most nationally televised programs air one hour earlier than they do on the East Coast.

SERVICES
Internet
You can go online free at the **Nashville Public Library** (615 Church St., 615/862-5800). There is free wireless access at the visitors center located at 5th and Broadway.

Postal Service
Mail a letter or buy stamps from the down-town post offices at 901 Broadway and 1718 Church Street. Both are open Monday–Friday 8:30 A.M.–5 P.M. There is also a post office in the downtown Arcade.

Emergency Services
Dial 911 for police, fire, or ambulance in an emergency. For help with a traffic accident, call the Tennessee Highway Patrol at 615/741-2060. The Davidson County Rescue Squad can be summoned by calling 615/226-0462.

Libraries
Nashville's downtown library is the crown jewel of its library system. The **Nashville Public Library** (615 Church St., 615/862-5800, www.library.nashville.org, Mon.–Fri. 9 A.M.–8 P.M., Fri. 9 A.M.–6 P.M., Sat. 9 A.M.–5 P.M., Sun. 2–5 P.M.) opened in 2001, replacing an older library that had served the city since 1965. The new library is dynamic and busy serving its community. There are story hours, children's programs, art exhibits, a local history collection, and meeting rooms. Visitors to the city will find the public Internet access and wireless Internet network most useful. There is a nice courtyard inside the library where people eat lunch, relax, and enjoy occasional concerts.

If you are visiting the library, you can park in the Nashville Public Library Parking Garage. Enter on 6th or 7th Avenues between Church and Commerce Streets. The first hour of library parking is free, and the daily maximum is $6. Be sure to validate your ticket at the security desk as you enter the library.

Getting There and Around

GETTING THERE
By Air
Nashville International Airport (BNA; 615/275-1675, www.nashintl.com) is located eight miles east of the city center. To get downtown from the airport, head west on I-40; it's a short 15-minute drive. One-way taxi fare from the airport to most hotels is $22.

AIRPORT SHUTTLE
ShuttleMax (615/361-6184 or 888/500-7629, www.shuttlemax.net) provides regular shuttle service from the airport to hotels in Brentwood, Franklin, and the Opryland area. One-way fare is between $11 and $30, depending on the location of your hotel. Round-trip is between $20 and $50. Reservations are highly recommended.

Gray Line Transportation (615/883-5555, www.graylinenashville.com) offers regular shuttle service from the airport to downtown, West End, and Music Valley hotels. The shuttle departs from the airport every 15–20 minutes between 5 A.M. and 11 P.M.; reservations are not required. Call ahead to book your hotel pick-up. Fare is $11 one-way and $18 round-trip.

By Car

Driving is the most popular way to get to Nashville. The city is 250 miles from Atlanta, 330 miles from St. Louis, 400 miles from Charlotte, 550 miles from New Orleans, and 670 miles from Washington, D.C.

No less than three major interstate highways converge in Nashville. I-40 runs east–west, connecting Nashville with Knoxville and Memphis. I-65 runs north–south, and connects the city with Louisville, Kentucky, and Birmingham, Alabama. I-24 travels at a southeastern angle down to the city, connecting it with the cities of Clarkesville and St. Louis in the north, and Chattanooga and Atlanta in the south.

By Bus

Greyhound (800/231-2222, www.greyhound.com) serves Nashville with bus service to the city from Memphis, Jackson, Chattanooga, and Knoxville, Tennessee, as well as Paducah and Bowling Green, Kentucky. The Greyhound station (200 8th Ave. S., 615/255-3556) is on the southern end of downtown Nashville.

Expect to pay about $40 for a one-way ticket from Memphis to Nashville.

GETTING AROUND
Driving

The best way to get around Nashville is by car. Although visitors staying downtown will be able to find plenty to do and places to eat all within walking distance, many of the best attractions are located outside of the city center. So unless your stay is but a few days, it is best to bring or rent a car to get around.

If you don't bring your own, a dozen different major rental agencies have a fleet of cars, trucks, and SUVs at the airport. Agencies include **Alamo** (615/361-7467, www.alamo.com), **Avis** (615/361-1212, www.avis.com), and **Hertz** (615/361-3131, www.hertz.com). For the best rates, use an online travel search tool, such as Expedia (www.expedia.com) or Travelocity (www.travelocity.com), and book the car early, along with your airline tickets.

NAVIGATING NASHVILLE

Nashville is quite easy to navigate. I-65 and I-24 create a tight inner beltway that encircles the heart of the city. I-440 is an outer beltway that circles the southern half of the city. Briley Parkway, shown on maps as Highway 155, is a limited-access highway that circles the northern outskirts of the city.

City residents use the interstates not just for long journeys but for short cross-town jaunts as well. Most businesses give directions according to the closest interstate exit.

Non-interstate thoroughfares emanate out from Nashville like spokes in a wheel. Many are named for the communities that they eventually run into. Murfreesboro Pike runs southeast from the city; Hillsboro Pike (Rte. 431) starts out as 21st Avenue South and takes you to Hillsboro Village and Green Hills. Broadway becomes West End Avenue and takes you directly to Belle Meade and, eventually, the Loveless Café. It does not take long to realize that roads in Nashville have a bad habit of changing names all of a sudden, so be prepared and check the map to avoid getting too confused.

For real-time traffic advisories and road construction closures, dial 511 from any touchtone phone, or go to www.tn511.com.

PARKING

There is metered parking on most downtown streets, but some have prohibited-parking signs effective during morning and afternoon rush hours. Always read the fine print carefully.

There is plenty of off-street parking in lots and garages. Expect to pay about $10 a day for garage parking. Meters are free after noon on Saturday, and on Sunday and holidays.

Public Transportation

Nashville's **Metropolitan Transit Authority** operates city buses. Pick up a map and schedule from either of the two downtown visitors centers, or online at www.nashvillemta.org.

Few tourists ride the buses because they can be difficult to understand if you're new to the city, and because they are not the most efficient use of your time. One route that is helpful, however, is the Opry Mills Express that travels from downtown Nashville to Music Valley, home of the Grand Ole Opry, Opryland Hotel, and Opry Mills, a shopping mall. The Opry Mills Express departs the Nashville Arena 13 times a day on weekdays. Fare is $1.75 one way; $0.60 for senior citizens. You can pick up a detailed route timetable from either of the two downtown visitors centers.

On Tennessee Titans' game days, the MTA offers its End Zone Express. Park at either Greer Stadium (where the Nashville Sounds play) or the State employee lot at 4th Avenue North and Harrison, and for just $6 you get shuttled straight to LP Field.

COMMUTER RAIL

In 2006 Nashville debuted the **Music City Star Rail** (501 Union St., 615/862-8833, www.musiccitystar.org), a commuter rail system designed to ease congestion around the city. With service Monday through Friday, three morning trains and three afternoon trains connect Donelson, Hermitage, Mt. Juliet, and Lebanon to downtown Nashville. More routes are planned for the future.

One-way tickets can be purchased for $5 each from vending machines at any of the stations. You can pre-purchase single-trip tickets, 10-trip packs, and monthly passes at the Regional Transportation Authority Office at 501 Union Street Monday–Friday 10 A.M.–2 P.M. For a complete list of ticket outlets, contact the railway.

Taxis

Licensed taxicabs will have an orange driver permit, usually displayed on the visor or dashboard.

Several good cab companies are **Allied Cab Company** (615/244-7433 or 625/320-9083), **Checker Cab** (615/256-7000), **Music City Taxi Inc.** (615/262-0451, www.musiccitytaxi.com), and **United Cab** (615/228-6969).

If cruising around in a stretch limo is more your style, call **Basic Black Limo** (615/430-8157, www.basicblacklimo.net). The rate is $125 per hour on Saturday nights; the limo seats up to 14 passengers.

OUTSIDE NASHVILLE

The countryside surrounding Nashville invites exploration. The scenes are familiar: winding country roads, cutting through horse pasture; perfectly fried chicken, served with the nonchalance of someone who knows just how good it is; and charming old railroad towns, where the trains still run.

But there are other attractions that just might surprise you: an 1850s homestead, a celebration dedicated to the lowly mule, and some of the best shopping in the whole state of Tennessee. The heartland of Tennessee is a landscape of natural beauty, notable history, and some outstanding stories that will captivate its visitors.

PLANNING YOUR TIME

Franklin may be one of the most popular daytrip destinations from Nashville. It is close—a mere 20 miles down the interstate—but a world apart. The historic Carnton Plantation is the best place to learn about the Battle of Franklin; downtown Franklin is the best place to shop.

The best-known excursion from Nashville is Lynchburg, where Jack Daniel's Tennessee Whisky is made. But the best distillery tour is at the George Dickel Distillery a few miles up the road and light years apart. There are no tour buses, just the fresh country air of Cascade Hollow. On your way, stop at the charming railroad towns of Bell Buckle and Wartrace for shopping, sightseeing, and good country cooking.

Go to Land Between the Lakes for outdoor adventure and to see The Homeplace, a living-history museum that depicts frontier life in

PHOTO COURTESY THE TENNESSEE DEPARTMENT OF TOURIST DEVELOPMENT

HIGHLIGHTS

◖ Carnton Plantation: Let your imagination live at this mansion, which served as a Confederate field hospital during the Battle of Franklin. It is the setting of the novel *The Widow of the South* (page 98).

◖ George Dickel Distillery: Tennessee whiskey is world-famous, but you can beat the crowds at this lesser-known distillery in beautiful Cascade Hollow (page 109).

◖ Tennessee Museum of Early Farm Life: Celebrate the ingenuity and relentless work ethic of generations gone at this museum in Spring Hill (page 119).

◖ Ancestral Home of James Knox Polk: Boost your James K. Polk IQ at the only surviving home – besides the White House – where he lived (page 121).

◖ The Homeplace: Located in beautiful Land Between the Lakes, this living-history museum depicts the farmer's way of life at the mid-point of the 19th century (page 124).

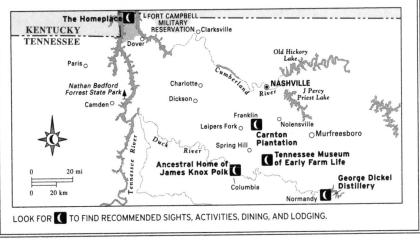

LOOK FOR ◖ TO FIND RECOMMENDED SIGHTS, ACTIVITIES, DINING, AND LODGING.

Tennessee. Or take a drive down the Natchez Trace Parkway. Say yes to inviting detours to towns like Leiper's Fork and Spring Hill, where you can visit the Tennessee Museum of Early Farm Life. Brush up on your presidential history in Columbia at the Ancestral Home of James Knox Polk, the eleventh president of the United States.

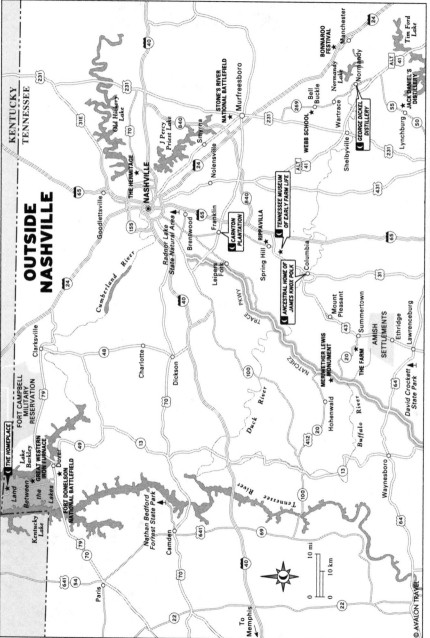

© AVALON TRAVEL

Franklin

Located a mere 20 miles south of Nashville, Franklin is one of the most picturesque small towns in Tennessee. It has preserved its Civil War heritage and is emerging as one of the state's best destinations for shopping.

SIGHTS

Contained within four square blocks, downtown Franklin consists of residential streets with old and carefully restored homes. The business district runs along West Main Street and includes professional offices, restaurants, and boutiques. The center of town is a traffic circle, crowned by a simple white Confederate monument. The circle is fronted by banks, more offices, and the 1859 Williamson County courthouse.

The best way to explore downtown Franklin is on foot. Free parking is available along the streets or in two public lots, one on 2nd Avenue and one on 4th Avenue. Pick up a printed walking-tour guide from the visitors center on East Main Street.

Guided walking tours of Franklin are offered by **Franklin on Foot** (615/400-3808, www.franklinonfoot.com). The classic Franklin tour provides an overview of the history of the town and its buildings. The Widow of the South Tour is combined with admission to the Carnton Plantation and is a must for lovers of that popular novel. Other tours include a children's tour and haunted Franklin tour. Tours cost between $5 and $18 per person.

McLemore House

Five generations of the McLemore family lived in the white clapboard home at the corner of Glass Street and 11th Avenue in downtown Franklin. McLemore House was built in 1880 by Harvey McLemore, a former slave and farmer. Inside, a small museum has been created that documents the story of African Americans in Williamson County.

McLemore House is open by appointment only. Contact Mary Mills at 615/794-2270 or the Convention and Visitors Bureau to arrange a tour.

◖ Carnton Plantation

When Robert Hicks's novel *The Widow of the South* became a bestseller in 2005, the staff at the Carnton Plantation (1345 Carnton Ln., 615/794-0903, www.carnton.org, Mon.–Sat. 9 A.M.–5 P.M., Sun. 1–5 P.M., $3–8) noticed an uptick in the number of visitors. The novel is a fictionalized account of Carrie McGavock and how her home, the Carnton Plantation, became a Confederate hospital during the Battle of Franklin in the Civil War.

The Carnton mansion was built in 1826 by Randal McGavock, a former Nashville mayor and prominent lawyer and businessman. Randal had died by the time of the Civil War, and it was his son, John, and John's wife, Carrie, who witnessed the bloody Battle of Franklin on November 30, 1864.

The Carnton Plantation in Franklin was made famous by the novel *The Widow of the South*.

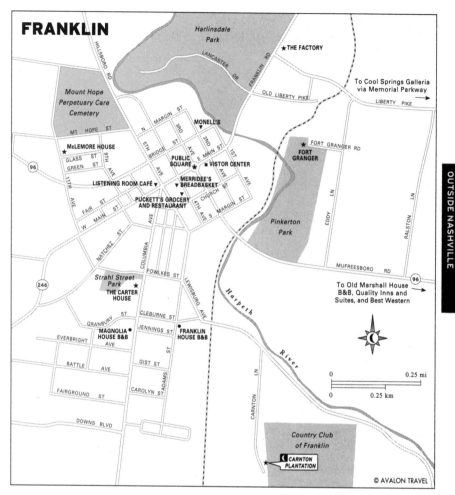

FRANKLIN

Located behind the Confederate line, the Carnton Plantation became a hospital for hundreds of injured and dying Confederate soldiers. As late as six months after the battle, the McGavock home remained a refuge for recovering veterans.

In the years that followed the battle, the McGavocks raised money, donating much of it themselves, to construct a cemetery for the Confederate dead, and donated two acres of land to the cause.

Visitors to the Carnton Plantation can pay full price for a guided tour of the mansion and self-guided tour of the grounds, which include a smokehouse, slave house, and garden. You can also pay $3 for the self-guided tour of the grounds. There is no admission charged to visit the cemetery.

Fort Granger

An unsung attraction, Fort Granger is a lovely and interesting place to spend an hour or so.

THE SOUTH'S LAST STAND

In the waning days of the Confederacy, its president, Jefferson Davis, met with his commanders to plan strategy. It was September 1864, and the Federals were pushing southward in Virginia and Georgia.

The plan that Davis and his commanders, including Gen. John Bell Hood, agreed was a daring march northward through Middle Tennessee. It was hoped that Gen. Hood's Army of the Tennessee would draw Federal forces away from the battles elsewhere and that they would eventually be repelled from the South entirely.

The last-ditch plan failed, and cost the Confederacy some 13,500 lives. The battles of Spring Hill, Franklin, and Nashville were major blows to the Southern cause and its last losing stratagem.

an unidentified Confederate soldier

COURTESY OF LIBRARY OF CONGRESS

SPRING HILL

On November 29, 1864, Gen. John M. Schofield and his federal troops were stationed in Columbia. Moving northward, Hood went around Columbia and headed towards Spring Hill. From here, Hood could either have marched to Nashville ahead of the Federals or returned to Columbia and attacked them from the rear. It was a promising position.

But the opportunity was squandered when the Confederates camped just short of a critical road northward. Schofield, who suspected Hood's strategy and realized his grave error, moved his men in the dead of night and marched them safely northward, passing within "talking distance" of the encamped Southern army.

Explanations for Hood's mistake suggest that he was not himself on that day. He was probably in tremendous physical pain from earlier war injuries (Hood had already lost the use of his left arm and had his right leg amputated below the hip), and was probably taking opium. He may also have been drunk. If walls could talk, the ones at Oaklawn on Denning Lane in Spring Hill, an 1835 mansion that served as the Confederate headquarters, would have a tale to tell.

Built between 1862 and 1863 by Union forces, the earthenwork fort is set on a bluff overlooking the Harpeth River just south of downtown Franklin. The fort was the largest fortification in the area built by Captain W. E. Merrill during the Federal occupation of Franklin. It saw action twice in 1863 and also in 1864 during the Battle of Franklin.

Many features of the fort remain intact for today's visitors. You can walk around portions of the breastworks. The interior of the fort is now a grassy field, perfect for a summer picnic or game of catch. An overlook at one end of the fort provides an unmatched view of the surrounding countryside.

You can reach Fort Granger two ways. One is along a short but steep trail departing Pinkerton Park on Murfreesboro Road east of town. Or you can drive straight to the fort by heading out of town on East Main Street. Turn right onto Liberty Pike, right onto Eddy Lane, and, finally, right again onto Fort Granger Drive.

The fort, which is maintained by the City of Franklin, is open during daylight hours only. While there is no office or visitors center at the

Whatever the cause, on the morning of November 30, when Hood realized what had happened, he resolved to battle the Federals in Franklin. Fueled by shame and desperation, Hood ordered the charge at the Battle of Franklin, one of the South's bloodiest defeats of the war.

FRANKLIN

By the time Hood and his army reached Franklin on November 30, 1864, the general was frustrated and the men exhausted. The missed opportunity at Spring Hill stung, but worse was yet to come.

Ignoring the advice of his commanders, including Nathan Bedford Forrest and Benjamin Franklin Cheatham, Hood ordered a full frontal attack on the federal line around Franklin. Unlike many other battles of the Civil War, the troops at Franklin had a full view at each other. There were some 23,000 Federal soldiers on one side, and 20,000 Confederates on the other. At about 4 P.M. on the last day of November, 1864, 18 brigades of Confederate soldiers, many of them from Tennessee, marched towards the Federal line. With the rebel yell that made them famous, the attack had begun. It was like sending soldiers to the slaughter.

It was a bloody and fierce battle. Even those commanders and soldiers on the Confederate side who had doubts about the battle strategy fought bravely and often to the death. The hand-to-hand combat around the Carter House near downtown Franklin was some of the fiercest of the battle. One Federal soldier said that the fighting was in such close quarters that "even the poorest marksman could not fail to hit a human target."

The Confederate assault failed. The fighting ended around 9 P.M. and overnight Federal Gen. John M. Schofield and all his soldiers who could walk marched to Nashville. They left their dead on the battlefield. Two weeks later, they defeated Hood's army again during the Battle of Nashville.

The death toll at Franklin was staggering. Some 7,000 Confederate were killed, wounded, or captured in just five hours of battle. The Federals lost 2,500 men. Many injured warriors died on the battlefield overnight, when temperatures dropped below freezing.

The townspeople of Franklin were left to tend to the wounded on both sides of the battle. Nearly every home in the city became a makeshift hospital. The most famous of these was the Carnton Plantation, where visitors today can still see blood stains on the floor, left by injured and dying soldiers.

In 1866, John and Carrie McGavock established a Confederate cemetery on the grounds of Carnton. It holds 1,500 graves, making it the largest private military cemetery in the nation. Carrie kept a careful record of the men who were buried there, and her cemetery book was used by thousands of people who came to Franklin to mourn loved ones who died there.

fort, you may contact Franklin's parks department (615/794-2103) for more information.

The Carter House

Some of the fiercest fighting in the Battle of Franklin took place around the farm and house belonging to the Carter family on the outskirts of town. The family took refuge in the basement while Union and Confederate soldiers fought hand to hand right above them. Today, the Carter House (1140 Columbia Ave., 615/791-1861, www. carter-house.org, Mon.–Sat. 9 A.M.–5 P.M., Sun. 1–5 P.M., adults $8, seniors $7, children 7–13 $4) is the best place to come for a detailed examination of the battle and the profound human toll that it exacted on both sides.

You will see hundreds of bullet holes, which help to illustrate the ferocity of the fight. Guides describe some of the worst moments of the battle, and bring to life a few of the people who fought it. The house also holds a museum of Civil War uniforms and memorabilia, including photographs and short biographies of many of the men who were killed in Franklin. There is also a video about the battle, which shows scenes from a reenactment.

ENTERTAINMENT
Theater
The **Boiler Room Theatre** (The Factory, 615/794-7744, www.boilerroomtheatre.com) is a professional theater company that performs seven or eight productions each year. Shows take place in a 120-seat theater in building six at the Factory (see *Shopping*), and range from light-hearted musical theater to dramas. The theater's season runs year-round.

Live Music
The **Listening Room Cafe** (500 W. Main St., 615/591-5725) hosts in-the-round and other intimate concerts several nights a week. Songwriters and musicians from Nashville frequently head down here for a night's show, which typically begins around 7 P.M.

SHOPPING
In many respects, shopping is Franklin's greatest attraction. Trendy downtown shops, the unique environment of the Factory, and proximity to a major mall make this a destination for shoppers. It is also one of Tennessee's most popular antiques shopping destinations.

Antiques
Franklin declares itself "the new antiques capital of Tennessee." Indeed, antiquing is one of the most popular pursuits of Franklin's visitors, and at least two dozen antiques shops serve to quench the thirst for something old. The town's antiques district is huddled around the corner of Margin Street and 2nd Avenue. Here you'll find no less than six major antiques stores. Other shops are found along Main Street in the downtown shopping district.

The best place to start antiquing is the **Franklin Antique Mall** (251 2nd Ave. S., 615/790-8593), located in the town's old ice house. The mall is a maze of rooms, each with different goods on offer. Possibilities include books, dishware, quilts, furniture, knick-knacks, and housewares. You can also follow 5th Avenue about two blocks south of downtown to find **Country Charm Antique Mall** (301 Lewisburg Ave., 615/790-8998),

whose three buildings house a vast array of furniture, quilts, glassware, china, and home decor.

Just outside the Franklin Antique Mall are at least five other antiques shops to roam through, including **J. J. Ashley's** (125 S. Margin St., 615/791-0011), which specializes in French and English Country accessories, as well as European furniture. **Scarlett Scales Antiques** (212 S. Margin St., 615/791-4097), located in a 1900s shotgun house, has American country furnishings, accessories, and architectural elements arriving daily.

Downtown
Retail is alive and well in Franklin's downtown. West Main Street is the epicenter of the shopping district, although you will find stores scattered around other parts of downtown as well. Home decor, classy antiques, trendy clothes, and specialty items like candles, tea, and gardening supplies are just a few of the things you'll find in downtown Franklin.

Most shops in downtown Franklin are open by 10 A.M. and many stay open until the evening to catch late-afternoon visitors. You can easily navigate the downtown shopping district on foot, although you may need to stow your parcels in the car now and then.

Bink's Outfitters (421 Main St., 615/599-8777) sells outdoor clothing and equipment. Stylish ladies' apparel and accessories are sold at **Chico's** (348 Main St., 615/599-8471). Go to **ENJOUE** (400 Main St., 615/599-8177) for funky fashions and trendy styles.

The city's best bookstore is **Landmark Booksellers** (114 E. Main St., 615/791-6400), found on the other side of the town square. They have a wide selection of used and new books, including many regional titles. It is friendly and welcoming, with fresh coffee for sale in the mornings.

Franklin Tea Merchant (430 Main St., 615/794-6311) has a wide selection of loose tea and various tea accessories. Toys old and new are on sale at **Main Street Toy Co.** (412 Main St., 615/790-4869). For the best in paper, wrappings, and stationery, go to **Rock Paper**

Scissors (317 Main St., 615/791-0150). **Heart and Hands** (418 Main St., 615/794-2537) is one of several shops specializing in crafts and home decor.

The Factory

Franklin's most unique retail center is the Factory (230 Franklin Rd., 615/791-1777, www.factoryatfranklin.com). A 250,000-square-foot complex of 11 different old industrial buildings, the Factory once housed stove factories and a textile mill. In the mid-1990s, Calvin Lehew bought the dilapidated eyesore and began the lengthy process of restoring the buildings and converting them to a space for galleries, retail shops, restaurants, and other businesses.

Today, the Factory is a vibrant commercial center for the city of Franklin. It houses a refreshing array of local independent retailers, including galleries, salons, candy shops, and a pet boutique. **The Little Cottage** (615/794-1405) sells children's fashions. Quilting supplies and fabric are the mainstays at **The Smocking Loft** (615/794-6226).

There are also 11 different studios and learning centers, including the **Viking Store** (615/599-9617), which offers cooking demonstrations and classes; **Creation Station** (615/791-9192), where you can practice scrapbooking; and **Arts for Life** (615/995-2778), which offers art classes and music lessons. There are also talent agencies and a Taekwondo academy.

In addition to retail and learning centers, the Factory has four restaurants and a fish market.

Cool Springs Galleria

Cool Springs Galleria (1800 Galleria Blvd., Cool Springs, 615/771-2128, www.coolspringsgalleria.com) is a mall with 165 specialty stores, 5 major department stores, 20 restaurants, and a 500-seat food court. It is located a few miles north of Franklin, convenient to I-65. Shops include Zales, Wild Oats, Talbots, Pier 1, Pottery Barn, Macy's, JC Penney, and Eddie Bauer. The mall is found at exits 68B and 69 on I-65.

ACCOMMODATIONS
Under $100

Several chain motels surround the interstate near Franklin. Closest to town are the 89-room **Quality Inns and Suites** (1307 Murfreesboro Rd., 615/794-7591, $65–110) and the 142-room **Best Western** (1308 Murfreesboro Rd., 615/790-0570, $55–70). Both offer wireless Internet, free continental breakfast, and an outdoor pool.

$100-150

The **Magnolia House Bed and Breakfast** (1317 Columbia Ave., 615/794-8178, www.bbonline.com/tn/magnolia, $100–120) is less than a mile from downtown Franklin, near the Carter House. A large magnolia tree shades the early 20th-century Craftsman home. There are four carpeted guest rooms, each with a private bath. Three house queen-sized beds; the fourth has two twin beds. Common areas include a polished sitting room, cozy den, and sunroom that looks out on the quiet residential neighborhood. Hosts Jimmy and Robbie Smithson welcome guests and prepare homemade breakfast according to your preferences.

Also less than a mile from downtown, **Franklin House Bed and Breakfast** (304 Stewart St., 615/791-9895, www.bbonline.com/tn/franklinhouse, $125) has two queen-sized guest accommodations located upstairs in the 100-year-old farmhouse. Common areas include a gracious wraparound porch. Breakfast of homemade bread, breakfast casseroles, and other favorites is served in the spacious dining room.

 Old Marshall House Bed and Breakfast (1030 John Williams Rd., 615/791-1455, www.oldmarshallhouse.com, $120–170) is the best bed-and-breakfast in the Franklin area. The 19th-century farmhouse located about five miles east of the city has three bedrooms plus a unique log cabin on the grounds. King-sized guest rooms feature handmade quilts, large bathrooms, fireplaces, and private sitting areas. The queen-sized guest room, the most modestly priced, also has a private bathroom and its own cable TV and DVD player. Outside is a restored 1850s log cabin that has been carefully converted into a perfect overnight retreat. Guests enjoy a living room made cozy by a cast-iron gas stove, modern bathroom with a claw-foot tub, and king-sized sleeping loft. The cabin has a microwave, coffee-maker, and refrigerator and rents for $170 a night.

Weather permitting, breakfast is served on a terrace overlooking the five-acre yard. Dishes include French toast, fruit compote, and hashbrown quiche. The property is equipped with wireless Internet, and owners Glen and Ursula Houghton are friendly, knowledgeable, and seasoned hosts.

FOOD
Downtown

Think country buffet, and then think ten times better. ⟨ **Monell's** (108 Bridge St., 615/790-6993, Mon.–Fri. 10:30 A.M.–2 P.M., Tues.–Sat. 5–8:30 P.M., Sat. 8:30 A.M.–1 P.M., Sun. 8:30 A.M.–4 P.M., $13–20) does fine Southern cooking, served all-you-can-eat family style. Come in and you'll be seated at a long table with other diners. If you feel weird about that, well, get over it and just remember to pass the dishes to the left. Chances are you'll wind up enjoying the unexpected company. The tables at Monell's sag with good food. When you're seated you'll already find cold cucumber salad, coleslaw, and iced tea on the table. Soon after, the server will bring out plate after plate of more temptations: savory greens, fluffy biscuits, cheesy potato casserole, golden skillet-fried chicken, and much more. Each lunch or dinner they offer three different main-course meats, including things like chicken and dumplings, skillet-fried chicken, pot roast, pork chops, and meatloaf. The main dishes are accompanied by traditional country sides. Dessert may be banana pudding, fruit cobbler, or some other sweet specialty. For breakfast, expect smoked sausage, bacon, country ham, pancakes, hash browns, grits, and—if you can imagine it—more. Monell's is a great choice for those who love country cooking, for the uninitiated who want to try it out, and for all those in between.

The best choice for baked goods, coffee, and light fare, including soups, salads, and sandwiches, is **Merridee's Breadbasket** (110 4th Ave., 615/790-3755, Mon.–Sat. 7 A.M.–5 P.M., $3–7). Merridee grew up in Minnesota and learned baking from her mother, a Swede. When Merridee married Tom McCray and moved to Middle Tennessee in 1973, she kept up the baking traditions she had learned as a child. In 1984, she opened Merridee's Breadbasket in Franklin. Merridee McCray died in 1994, but her restaurant remains one of Franklin's most popular. Come in for omelets, scrambled eggs, or sweet bread and fruit in the morning. At lunch choose from the daily soup, casserole, or quiche, or order a cold or grilled sandwich. Merridee's also bakes fresh bread daily; take home a loaf of the always-popular Viking bread. Merridee's attracts a variety of people—students, businesspeople, and families out on the town. The creaky wood floors and comfortable seating make it a pleasant and relaxing place to refuel.

Puckett's Grocery and Restaurant (120 4th Ave. S., 615/794-5527), the Leiper's Fork institution, has expanded with a second location in Franklin. The Franklin shop offers traditional breakfasts with eggs, bacon, country ham, and biscuits and plate lunches in the day. In the evening, order up a handmade burger (the locals swear that they're the best in town), a Southern dinner of fried catfish, or traditional steak, chicken, or fish entrée. For vegetarians, they offer a veggie burger or a vegetable plate, as well as salads. The food is well prepared and the service friendly, and there's almost always a crowd.

Award-winning and always popular, ⟨ **Saffire** (The Factory, 615/599-4995, Tues.–Sun., $14–35) serves lunch 11 A.M.–3 P.M. and dinner beginning at 5 P.M. Using primarily organic and biodynamic ingredients, Saffire's menu sparkles with unique dishes. Try the tender and flavorful Cuban roasted pork appetizer plate, or a simple salad of heirloom tomatoes. Entrées include upscale dishes like prime rib and ahi tuna. Their fried chicken is dusted with Panko flakes, topped with country ham gravy, and served with luscious macaroni and cheese. Saffire has an extensive wine and cocktail list, including organic choices. Take $4 off signature cocktails during happy hour (5–6 P.M.) and on Tuesday night most bottles of wine go for half-price. The lunch menu is casual, featuring sandwiches, salads, and lunch-sized entrées. Or choose the "green plate" daily special, featuring local and organic ingredients. There is also a midday kid's menu with favorites like grilled cheese and chicken bites.

Set within an old warehouse, Saffire's dining room is spacious with exposed brick and beams. The kitchen opens out onto the dining room, so you can watch the cooks work. With live music many nights, Saffire is a fine choice for excellent food in a pleasant and exciting environment.

Farmer's Market

The Franklin Farmer's Market takes place at the rear of the Factory on Saturday mornings during spring, summer, and fall 8 A.M.–noon. This is one of the finest small-town farmer's markets in the state, featuring a wide variety of fruit and vegetable growers, and cheese, milk, and meat sellers, as well as craftspersons and live music.

INFORMATION

The **Williamson County Convention and Visitors Bureau** (615/791-7554 or 866/253-9207, www.visitwilliamson.com) publishes guides and maintains a website about Franklin and the surrounding area. They also operate the **Williamson County Visitor Center** (209 E. Main St., 615/591-8514, Mon.–Fri. 9 A.M.–4 P.M., Sat. 10 A.M.–3 P.M., Sun. noon–3 P.M.).

Walking Horse Country

The territory directly south of Nashville is Tennessee Walking Horse Country. The high-stepping, smooth-riding Tennessee Walking Horse is bred on horse farms that dot the landscape.

The attractions are more than horses, however. The town of Bell Buckle is a charming pit stop for country cooking and antiques shopping and Wartrace has a lovely old-fashioned railroad hotel. For the best distillery tour in Tennessee, head to the George Dickel Distillery near Normandy; for the most popular, press on to Lynchburg and the Jack Daniel's Distillery.

BELL BUCKLE

A tiny town nestled in the northern reaches of the Walking Horse region, Bell Buckle is a charming place to visit. Once a railroad town, Bell Buckle has successfully become a destination for antiques shopping, arts and crafts, small-town hospitality, and country cooking. The town's single commercial street faces the old railroad tracks; handsome old homes—some of them bed-and-breakfast inns—spread out along quiet residential streets.

What makes Bell Buckle so appealing is the sense of humor that permeates just about everything that happens here. T-shirts for sale on the main street proclaim "Tokyo, Paris, New York, Bell Buckle," and the town's quirky residents feel free to be themselves. Tennessee's poet laureate, Margaret "Maggie" Britton Vaughn, who operates the Bell Buckle Press and had an office on Main Street for many years, once told an interviewer that William Faulkner "would have killed" for a community with the ambience, and characters, of Bell Buckle.

Bell Buckle's name is derived from the Bell Buckle Creek, named thus because a cow's bell was found hanging in a tree by the creek, attached by a buckle.

The town's annual Moon Pie Festival in June attracts thousands to the small town, and the Webb School Arts and Crafts Festival in October is one of the finest regional arts shows in the state.

Sights

Bell Buckle is noted as the home of the elite and well-regarded **Webb School.** Founded in 1870 and led by William Robert Webb until his death in 1926, Webb School has graduated 10 Rhodes scholars, several governors, attorneys general, and numerous successful academics. The school now has about 300 students in grades 8 through 12 from around the country and the world. While it was all-male for many years of its life, Webb School now admits both male and female students. Its athletic mascot is the "Webb Feet."

The Webb campus is about three blocks north of downtown Bell Buckle. You can visit the main administrative office during regular business hours, where there are photographs and school memorabilia on display.

Events

Bell Buckle's biggest annual event is the **RC and Moon Pie Festival** in mid-June. This weekend event includes country and bluegrass music, Moon Pie games, arts and crafts booths, the crowning of a Moon Pie King and Queen, and a 10-mile run. You can also witness the cutting of the world's largest Moon Pie. In case you're wondering why Bell Buckle has rights to the Moon Pie festival, it's because they asked for it.

The **Webb School Arts and Crafts Festival** brings hundreds of artisans to town. It is one of the finest arts and crafts shows in the region, attracting fine and folk artists from Tennessee and beyond.

Shopping

The single most popular pursuit in Bell Buckle is shopping. Antiques are the main attraction, but arts and crafts are a close second.

The **Bell Buckle Art Gallery** (26 Railroad Sq., 931/389-0004) sells a wide selection of artwork, from pottery and sculpture to paintings. Most pieces here have a fresh, modern appeal.

The Cat's Meow (25 Railroad Sq., 931/389-0064) has purses, totes, linens, throws, and jewelry, plus lots of gifts for babies and new

antique shopping in Bell Buckle

parents. The **Doodle Bug** and **Doodle Bug Too** (Railroad Sq., 931/389-9009) are sister shops that sell jewelry, housewares, gifts, and folk art.

For antiques try the **Bell Buckle Antique Mall** (112 Main St., 931/389-6174) or **Blue Ribbon Antiques** (Railroad Sq., 931/684-2588).

Accommodations

Hostess Ina Mingle runs the **Mingle House Bed and Breakfast** (116 Main St., 931/389-9453, $80–85) in a restored 1898 Victorian home. Rooms are furnished with antiques, and guests can fuel up with a country-style breakfast of eggs, sausage, bacon, and more in the morning.

Food

There's no debate about where to eat in Bell Buckle. The **(C** **Bell Buckle Cafe** (Railroad Sq., 931/389-9693, Mon. 10:30 A.M.–2 P.M., Tues.–Thurs. 10:30 A.M.–8 P.M., Fri.–Sat. 10:30 A.M.–9 P.M., Sun. 11 A.M.–5 P.M., $5–15)

THE TENNESSEE WALKING HORSE

Considered the world's greatest pleasure, trail, and show horse, the Tennessee Walking Horse is the first breed of horse to bear the name of a state. Tennessee Walkers existed for many years before the breed was identified and named; early settlers needed horses that could travel easily and comfortably over rocky and uneven terrain. These early walkers were not trained to show – they were purely utilitarian.

In 1886 a black colt named Black Allan was foaled. He was the result of a cross between a stallion called Allendorf, from the Hambletonian family of trotters, and Maggie Marshall, a Morgan mare. Black Allen was crossed with a Tennessee Pacer, and the modern Tennessee Walking Horse breed was born.

Tennessee Walkers are known for their docile temperament and kind manner. They are also known for their unique running walk –

The Tennessee Walking Horse is a champion show horse.

in which each of the horse's hooves hit the ground separately at regular intervals. In this gait, the animal's front legs rise in an exaggerated step and the horse's head nods in time with the rhythm of its legs.

PHOTO COURTESY OF THE TENN DEPT OF TOURIST DEVELOPMENT

OUTSIDE NASHVILLE

is not only a Bell Buckle institution, it's the only game in town. The menu is Southern, with a few refined touches (like ostrich burger and spinach-strawberry salad) you won't find at most small-town cafés. The menu is also mighty diverse, with seafood, pasta, and sandwiches in addition to the usual plate lunches and dinner entrées. The large dining room fills up quick, especially for lunch, so there's no shame in coming a bit early. The Bell Buckle Cafe takes care of your entertainment needs too. There's always live music on Thursday, Friday, and Saturday night, usually bluegrass or country. Local radio station WLIJ broadcasts a musical variety show from the café on Saturday 1–3 P.M., which is a great reason to come to the café for lunch.

If you managed to pass up homemade dessert at the Bell Buckle Cafe, then head to **Bluebird Antiques and Ice Cream Parlor** (15 Webb Rd., 931/389-6549). Here you'll find a turn-of-the-20th-century soda fountain with hand-dipped ice cream and homemade waffle cones. Come in the morning to see (and smell) them making the cones. Not to be missed.

Information

The **Bell Buckle Chamber of Commerce** (931/389-9663, www.bellbucklechamber.com) publishes brochures, promotes the town, and operates as a clearinghouse for information.

WARTRACE

This tiny railroad town about 10 miles east of Shelbyville is the birthplace of the Tennessee Walking Horse. It was on the grounds of the town's Walking Horse Hotel that Albert Dement trained a $350 plow horse into **Strolling Jim,** the first world grand champion walking horse. Strolling Jim died in 1957; you can visit his grave in the pasture behind the hotel, across the railroad tracks from the town square.

The annual walking horse celebration that now draws a quarter million people to Shelbyville every year started in Wartrace, but got too big for the small town and moved to Shelbyville in 1935.

Accommodations

The **(Walking Horse Hotel** (101 Spring St.,

BONNAROO

Bonnaroo Music and Arts Festival (www. bonnaroo.com) started out in 2002 as a jam band music festival, but diversification has made this summertime mega event a destination for all types of music fans. The 'Roo takes place over four days in June on a rural farm in Manchester. Between 75,000 and 90,000 people come each year.

Bonnaroo has a hippie heart with a slightly hard edge. Place names are Suessian – the music tents are called, from largest to small-

est, What Stage, Which Stage, This Tent, That Tent, and The Other Tent. Activities run the gamut from a Mardi Gras parade to kid's art activities. Of course, it's the music that really draws the crowds: reggae, rock, Americana, jam bands, world, hip-hop, jazz, electronic, folk, gospel, and country. The event is truly a feast for the ears.

In 2007, the Police were reunited at Bonnaroo. In 2008, headliners included Kanye West, Willie Nelson, and Pearl Jam. But quality

PHOTO COURTESY OF THE TENN DEPT OF TOURIST DEVELOPMENT

Bonnaroo Music and Arts Festival

931/389-7030, www.walkinghorsehotel.com) is the best place to stay not only in Wartrace, but for a good distance in any direction. When Joe Peters bought the hotel in 2007 he was intent on paying tribute to his late wife, Chais, who loved the old 1917 hotel. Peters and his family have brought new life to the old hotel by refurbishing the rooms, recruiting beloved chef Bill Hall to run the Strolling Jim Restaurant, and opening the Chais Music Hall, a state-of-the-art venue for all types of music.

Rooms are a fusion of old and new. Classic touches from the hotel's early days have been preserved, but guests can expect the best modern amenities, including flat-screen

televisions, wireless Internet, super-comfortable beds, and good linens.

Another choice in Wartrace is the **Historic Main Street Inn** (207 Main St. E., 931/389-0389, www.historicmainstreetinn.com, $95–115), a bed-and-breakfast located half a block from main street. Each of the five guest rooms are lavishly decorated in a romantic style fitting for the 1906 Queen Anne home. All rooms have a private bath—some have antique claw-footed tubs. Breakfast here is nothing simple or quick; expect choices like homemade fruit crepes, baked apple pancake, or stuffed French toast. Built by a local banker, the home has been operated as a bed-and-breakfast since 1996.

permeates every echelon of the stage. Unknowns and barely-knowns routinely wow audiences. There is a big emphasis on world artists and folk music. A jazz tent provides nightclub ambience, and there's even a comedy tent.

A few things to know about Bonnaroo: First, it's huge. The event takes place on a 700-acre farm, and the list of offerings is seemingly endless: four stages of music, whole villages dedicated to the arts, a 24-hour movie tent, yoga studio, salon, children's activity tents, music-industry showcase, food vendors, and a whole lot more.

Second, Bonnaroo has above-average logistics. Organizers seem to consider everything, including the basics: drinking water, medical care, parking, traffic control, and a general store where you can buy necessities. Food vendors sell Tennessee barbecue, veggie burgers, and just about everything in between. A shuttle service between the Nashville airport and the 'Roo helps minimize traffic. Rules about camping, RVs, re-entry, and security are common-sense and easy to follow.

All that said, you can't turn up with the clothes on your back and expect to have much fun. It's important to pack well: A good camping tent, folding chairs, and water bottles are important. Even if you plan to buy most of your food, at least pack some snacks. There are ATMs at the 'Roo, but lines can be very long, so bringing plenty of cash is also a good idea (but not too much, since you don't want to attract trouble). Also bring garbage bags, sunscreen, and hot-weather, comfortable clothes. Rain renders the farm to mud, so if the weather is iffy – or even if it's not – pack sturdy shoes and a rain coat.

Plenty of Bonnaroo fans take the opportunity to do a lot of drinking and drugs. There are police at the festival, but they don't seem to crack down on every recreational drug user. Beer – including good microbrews – are sold, and consumed generously. That said, getting wasted is not everyone's idea of a good time and if you decide to stay sober, you'll be in good company.

Most people buy a four-day pass to the festival, but day-pass tickets are available too. Four-day passes cost $200 and up; a limited number of reduced-price early-bird tickets go on sale in January each year. Regular tickets go on sale in the spring, after the line-up has been announced.

In 2007, Bonnaroo producers bought most of the farm where the festival is held, saying that they want to improve water lines and roads. They may also start hosting smaller events there during the year.

Food

The **Iron Gait** (106 Fairfield Rd., 931/389-6001, Mon.–Fri. 7 A.M.–2 P.M., Sat. 7 A.M.–7 P.M., Sun. 1–4 P.M., $3–8) serves breakfast, burgers, and meat-and-three dinners. The monster burger is a favorite, as are the plate lunches. Find the Iron Gait just around the corner from Main Street, on the road to Bell Buckle.

For other dining choices, look in Bell Buckle, Normandy, and Shelbyville.

Information

The **Wartrace Chamber of Commerce** (931/389-9999, www.wartracechamber.com) promotes the town.

NORMANDY

Normandy is a tiny one-street town, notable for its position on the railroad and its location amid some of the most beautiful countryside in this part of Tennessee. The rural routes surrounding Normandy are well worth exploring.

George Dickel Distillery

About seven miles south of Wartrace, just outside of the old railroad town of Normandy, is one of the best-kept secrets in this part of Tennessee. The George Dickel Distillery (931/857-3124, Tues.–Sat. 9 A.M.–4 P.M.) makes thousands of gallons of Tennessee sipping whisky every year, and all of it comes from the Dickel distillery

VANNOY STREETER

Self-taught folk artist Vannoy Streeter drew inspiration for his life's work from the elegant stride and unique step of the Tennessee Walking Horse. Born in Wartrace in 1919 and raised on a horse farm, Streeter first displayed his remarkable talent as a child. His family could not afford to buy toy airplanes and cars, so he made them – bending them out of bailing wire.

Streeter was in Wartrace for the first Walking Horse Celebration, and in later years he returned to the event after it moved to Shelbyville. Streeter was proud of the fact that African Americans trained Strolling Jim and many other world-champion walking horses. He created hundreds, if not thousands, of sculpted horses, each with the distinctive high-stepping front leg and each with an African-American rider on the back. Other favorite subjects were performers – he sculpted Tina Turner and Elvis Presley in particular – and vehicles, including big-rig trucks, locomotives, and airplanes.

Streeter made most of his sculptures out of coat-hanger wire; he bought hangers by the hundreds. He did detail work with fine-gauge wire and large-scale work with bracing wire. He worked with regular pliers, wire cutters, and needle-nosed pliers.

Streeter worked on the railroads, and as a lumberyard hand, janitor, and hospital orderly. In 1960 he met and married his wife, Marie, and became father to her six children. He continued to make his wire sculptures, eventually gaining national attention. In 1990 he was a demonstrating artist at the National Black Arts Festival in Atlanta and in 1992 Shelbyville proclaimed Vannoy Streeter Day. His work has been displayed in the White House and at the Tennessee State Museum in Nashville.

Streeter continued to work until his death in 1998, although his productivity declined after his wife's death. His work is sold in folk art galleries in Nashville and other cities, and has been included in African-American and folk art exhibits in Tennessee and elsewhere.

up Cascade Hollow on the Highland Rim of the Cumberland Plateau. (In deference to its connection to scotch, Dickel uses the Scottish spelling for whisky, without the "e.")

It's no secret that the best-known name in whiskey is distilled a few miles down the road in Lynchburg, but the folks at George Dickel don't seem to mind. The Dickel distillery is a smaller operation, and visitors are given a more personalized and detailed look at the operations of the plant. And the setting in the Cascade Hollow is one of the most charming in this part of the state.

George Dickel, a German immigrant, distilled his first bottle of whisky at Cascade Hollow in 1870. Dickel created a unique cold mellowing process, which made his product smoother than others. The distillery still uses Dickel's cold mellowing process, as well as his signature proportions of corn, malt, and rye. The Dickel distillery closed down during Prohibition, only to reopen in the 1950s.

The distillery has changed hands several times over the past 50 years, and it is now owned by Diageo, one of the largest beer, wine, and spirits manufacturers in the world.

Visitors can get a free one-hour tour of the distillery, which takes you through every step in the process. The last tour departs at 3:30 P.M.

To find George Dickel, take Route 269 to Normandy, where you will see signs pointing you to Cascade Hollow Road.

Accommodations

For a high-class country escape, head to the ◖ **Parish Patch Farm and Inn** (1100 Cortner Rd., 931/857-3017, www.parishpatch.com, $80–220), an inn, conference center, and restaurant set in the rural countryside near Normandy. The more than 30 guest rooms are scattered in various buildings on this working farm. They include spacious suites, private cottages, standard-sized bedrooms, and rustic rooms in an old gristmill. The two least expensive rooms share a bath; all other rooms have private bathrooms, televisions, and telephones. Rollaway beds are available. All guests can enjoy the full country breakfast served daily in the inn dining room. Other amenities include a swimming pool, walking trails, a book and video library, hammocks, and lots of countryside to explore. Parish Patch is a working farm, so you can also watch (or join in) on farm chores, pick your own blackberries (in season, of course) or just watch the animals. The Duck River flows through the property, providing opportunities for fishing or canoeing.

Food

The **Cortner Mill Restaurant** (1100 Cortner Rd., 931/857-3018, www.parishpatch.com, Tues.–Sat. 5:30–9 P.M., $16–42) is an upscale country restaurant that serves dinner five nights a week and is often booked for special events. Specialties include Memphis-style dry-rub barbecue ribs, grilled rack of lamb, baked rainbow trout, and frog legs. There is an extensive wine list, and desserts include a flaming bananas foster made tableside. The restaurant hosts special buffets on Easter, Thanksgiving, Christmas, and New Year's Day, and the Champagne Sunday Brunch (Sun. 11:30 A.M.–1:30 P.M.) is a popular treat for locals and visitors.

The restaurant is located in a restored 1825 gristmill and the dining room overlooks the river. It is an elegant choice for a special dinner.

LYNCHBURG

Lynchburg, no longer population 361, has been transformed by the popularity of Jack Daniel's Tennessee Whiskey, which is made a few blocks from the town square. No other small town in Tennessee sees as many visitors, from as many different places, as this one.

Critics may object to the tour buses and crowds, but for now, the town has managed to survive its success with relative grace. It has maintained its small-town feel, and it offers its guests a hospitable and heartfelt welcome.

Lynchburg is centered around the Moore County courthouse, a modest redbrick building. Souvenir shops, restaurants, and a few local businesses line the square. Outside of this, Lynchburg is quiet and residential. The Jack Daniel's Distillery is about three blocks away from the town square; a pleasant footpath connects the two.

Jack Daniel's Distillery

As you drive into Lynchburg, or walk around the town, you might notice some odd-looking grey warehouses peeking out above the treetops. These are barrel houses, where Jack Daniel's Distillery ages its whiskey. Around Moore County there are 74 of these warehouses, and each one holds about one million barrels of whiskey.

Thousands of whiskey drinkers make the pilgrimage every year to Jack Daniel's Distillery (280 Lynchburg Hwy., aka Hwy. 55, 931/759-4221, www.jackdaniels.com, daily 9 A.M.–4:30 P.M., free) to see how Jack Daniel's is made. And what they find is that, aside from

the Lynchburg town square

the use of electricity, computers, and the sheer scale of the operation, things have not changed too much since 1866 when Jack Daniel registered his whiskey still at the mouth of Cave Spring near Lynchburg.

Jack Daniel was an interesting man. He stood just 5 feet, 2 inches tall and liked to wear three-piece suits. He was introduced to the whiskey business by a Lutheran lay preacher named Dan Call, who sold the distillery to Daniel shortly after the Civil War. In 1866, Daniel had the foresight to register his distillery with the federal government, making his the oldest registered distillery in the United States. He never married and had no known children.

Daniel died of gangrene in 1911. He got it from kicking a metal safe in frustration after he couldn't get it open, and breaking his toe. After Daniel died, the distillery passed to his nephew, Lem Motlow. The distillery remained in the Motlow family until it was sold in 1957 to the Brown-Forman Corporation of Louisville, Kentucky.

The one-hour tour of the distillery begins with a video about the master distillers—Jack Daniel's has had seven in its lifetime—who are the final authority on all facets of the product. You then board a bus that takes you up to the far side of the distillery, and from here you'll walk back to the visitors center, stopping frequently to be told about the key steps in the process. The highlight of the tour for some is seeing Cave Spring, where the distillery gets its iron-free spring water. Others enjoy taking a potent whiff of the sour mash and the mellowing whiskey.

The tour ends back at the visitors center where you are served free lemonade and coffee. Moore County, where Lynchburg is located, is a dry county and for 86 years the irony was that Jack Daniel's could not sell any of its whiskey at the distillery. In 1995, however, the county approved a special exemption that allows the distillery to sell souvenir bottles of whiskey at its visitors center. That is all they sell, however; you have to buy other Jack Daniel's merchandise at one of the gift shops in town.

A statue of Jack Daniel stands sentry in front of Cave Spring at the Jack Daniel's Distillery.

Other Sights

A stately two-story brick building on the southwest corner of the square is the **Moore County Jail** (231 Main St., mid-Mar.–Dec. Tues.–Sat. 11 A.M.–3 P.M., free), which served as the sheriff's residence and the county jail until 1990. The building is now a museum and is operated by the local historical society. You can see law-enforcement memorabilia, old newspaper clippings, and vintage clothes. Go upstairs to see the prisoners' cells.

Just down Main Street is the **Tennessee Walking Horse Museum** (Public Sq., 931/759-5747, Tues.–Sat. 9 A.M.–5 P.M., free). The museum was originally located in Shelbyville, but moved to Lynchburg in the early 2000s to take advantage of the bustling tourist trade here.

The Walking Horse Museum displays photographs, trophies, and other memorabilia from walking horse champions. You can admire both show and posed photographs of top horses, and watch a video that explains what makes the walking horse so special. The films include show footage of the breed's distinctive flat walk, fast walk, and canter.

Accommodations

The **Lynchburg Bed and Breakfast** (Mechanic St., 931/759-7158, www.bbonline.com/tn/lynchburg, $70) has been welcoming guests to Lynchburg since 1985. There are two guest rooms; one has a queen-sized bed and one has two twin beds. Each room has a private bathroom and cable TV; a shared telephone and refrigerator are in the hallway between the two rooms. Guests are served a continental breakfast. Accommodations are homey, but not luxurious.

The **Tolley House** (1253 Main St., 931/759-7263, www.tolleyhouse.com, $135–150) is located about a mile from the town square, and is a pleasant country retreat. A handsome antebellum farmhouse once owned by Jack Daniel's master distiller Lem Motlow, the Tolley House provides touches of luxury. Rooms have private baths, television, and wireless Internet access, and are furnished tastefully with antiques. Hosts Frank and Karen Fletcher provide your choice of a full country or light continental breakfast. Discounts are available for stays of two or more nights.

The closest thing to a motel in Lynchburg is the **Lynchburg Country Inn** (423 Majors Blvd., 931/759-5995, www.lynchburgcountryinn.com, $55–65). Its 25 rooms are each furnished with a microwave, refrigerator, and cable TV. There's a pool out back and rocking chairs on the front and back porches. The building is modern, built in 2003, but the decor is pure country.

Food

The most popular place to eat in Lynchburg is **(Miss Mary Bobo's Boarding House** (295 Main St., 931/759-7394, Mon.–Sat. lunch only, $19). Miss Mary's started life as the home of Thomas Roundtree, the founder of Lynchburg. It later became the home of Dr. E. Y. Salmon, a Confederate captain, who maintained an office there and rented out rooms to boarders. In 1908, Lacy Jackson Bobo and his wife, Mary Evans Bobo, bought the house and continued to operate it as a boarding house until the 1980s. Over the years, word of Mary Bobo's legendary home-cooked meals spread and this boarding house became one of the region's best-known eating houses. Today, Miss Mary's is no longer a boarding house, and the restaurant is operated by Miss Lynne Tolley, who has worked hard to keep up the traditions established by Miss Mary. The restaurant is owned by the Jack Daniel's Distillery, and servers are hired from the local community college. A meal at Miss Mary's will easily be the most unique of your trip. On most days there are two seatings—11 A.M. and 1 P.M. Guests should arrive at least 15 minutes early so you can check in, pay, and be assigned to a dining room. When the dinner bell rings, you will be taken to your dining room by a hostess, who stays with you throughout the meal. Everyone sits family-style around a big table. The meal served at Miss Mary's is a traditional Southern dinner. You'll find no less than six side dishes and two meats, plus iced tea (unsweetened), dessert, coffee, and bread. Almost every meal features fried chicken. Side dishes may include green beans, mashed potatoes, fried okra, carrot slaw, and corn bread. Your hostess will make sure that everyone has enough to eat, answer questions about the food, and tell you some stories about the restaurant—if you ask. Be sure to call well ahead to make your reservations. Meals are fully booked weeks and even months in advance, especially during the busy summer months and on Saturdays.

For a more low-key meal, go to the **Bar-B-Que Caboose Cafe** (217 Main St., 931/759-5180, daily 11 A.M.–5 P.M., $7–12). The menu offers pulled-pork barbecue sandwiches, jambalaya,

red beans and rice, and hot dogs. You can also get pizzas. On Friday night (April–October) the restaurant opens for dinner 6:30–8 P.M. and you can get a barbecue plate dinner for $9 while you listen to live music. On Saturday morning from 10 to 11 A.M. a live country music radio show is broadcast from the Caboose Cafe.

There are a handful of other restaurants in Lynchburg, all on the town square. **Elk Coffee** (12 Short St., 931/759-5552, Mon.–Sat. 8 A.M.–5:30 P.M., Sun. noon–5 P.M., $6–12) sells lighter fare, including wraps and salads.

Be forewarned that it is next to impossible to get an evening meal in Lynchburg. By 6 P.M. the place is a ghost town.

The Natchez Trace

The Natchez Trace Parkway cuts a diagonal path through the heartland south of Nashville. The two-lane limited-access highway passes through mostly undeveloped countryside.

Simply driving the Trace is pleasant enough, but short detours to villages and county seats along the way make this a lovely getaway that balances quiet exploration with sights and attractions.

LEIPER'S FORK

Part small town, part yuppified enclave, Leiper's Fork is a pleasant place to spend a few hours. It is located about 15 minutes' drive from Franklin and near milepost 420 on the Natchez Trace Parkway.

Leiper's Fork is a pleasant community. Art galleries and antiques shops line the short main drag. Unusually good food can be found at local restaurants and a laid-back let's-laugh-at-ourselves attitude prevails.

Shopping

Leiper's Fork retailers are open Wednesday–Saturday 10 A.M.–5 P.M. and Sunday 1–5 P.M.

Opening its doors in 2007, **R Place** (4154 Old Hillsboro Rd.) sells the artwork of Anne Goetz, the handmade furniture of Reed Birnie,

and used books curated by Renee Armand. You can also get homemade pie and coffee if you need sustenance while you browse the shop, housed in an old home.

The **Leiper's Creek Gallery** (4144 Old Hillsboro Rd., 615/599-5102) is the finest gallery in town. It shows a wide selection of paintings by local and regional artists and hosts a variety of arts events year-round.

Neena's Primitive Antiques (4158 Old Hillsboro Rd., 615/790-0345) specializes in primitive antiques, linens, home decor items, and leather goods.

Entertainment

Friday night is songwriter night at **Puckett's Grocery** (4142 Old Hillsboro Rd., 615/794-1308, www.puckettsgrocery.com). For $30 you enjoy dressed-up dinner—fresh seafood, poultry, and steak are usually among the options—at 7 P.M. and an in-the-round performance from Nashville singer-songwriters starting at 8:30 P.M. If you prefer, pay $15 for the concert only. Reservations are essential for either, so call ahead. Check the website to find out who is performing.

Jailhouse Industries operates the Leiper's Fork **Lawn Chair Theatre** from May to

PHOTO COURTESY OF THE TENN DEPT OF TOURIST DEVELOPMENT

driving along the Natchez Trace Parkway

September. Bring your lawn chair or blanket and enjoy classic movies and kids' favorites on Friday and Saturday nights. Call 615/477-6799 for more information, or just ask around.

Hiking

The Leiper's Fork District of the Natchez Trace National Scenic Trail runs for 24 miles, starting near milepost 427 and ending at milepost 408, where State Highway 50 crosses the parkway. The trail follows the old Natchez Trace through rural countryside.

The best access point is from Garrison Creek Road, where there is parking, restrooms, and picnic facilities. You can also access the trail from Davis Hollow Road.

Accommodations

Namaste Acres (5436 Leiper's Creek Rd., 615/791-0333, www.bbonline.com/tn/namaste, $120–175) is a unique bed-and-breakfast. Located on a working horse farm, Namaste Acres guests are treated to beautiful farm views and hearty country breakfasts. Three guest suites are decorated with a Western flair: lots of exposed wood, rocking chairs, and woven Indian rugs. Horse owners can board their horses here too. Each suite has a private bathroom, deck, and fireplace, as well as a TV/VCR, telephone, refrigerator, and coffee-maker.

Food

☖ Puckett's Grocery (4142 Old Hillsboro Rd., 615/794-1308, www.puckettsgrocery. com, daily 6 A.M.–6 P.M., $6–25) is home to the heartbeat of Leiper's Fork. An old-time grocery with a small dining room attached, Puckett's serves breakfast, lunch, and dinner to the town faithful and visitors alike. The original country store opened about 1950. In 1998, Andy Marshall bought the store and expanded the restaurant offerings. Solid country breakfasts are the order of the day in the mornings, followed by plate lunches. The pulled pork is a favorite, as is the Puckett Burger. Dinner specials include catfish nights, family nights, and a Saturday-night seafood buffet. Friday night the grocery turns upscale with a supper club and live music. Reservations are essential for Friday night. Puckett's hours vary by the season, so it is best to call ahead, especially for dinner arrangements. A second Puckett's Grocery location in Franklin offers a more varied menu.

For a casual sandwich, decadent pastry, or cup of coffee, head to the **Backyard Cafe** (4150 Old Hillsboro Rd., 615/790-4003, Mon.–Sat. 11 A.M.–3 P.M., Sun. noon–3 P.M.).

THE NATCHEZ TRACE

The first people to travel what is now regarded as the Natchez Trace were probably Choctow and Chickasaw Indians, who made the first footpaths through the region. French and Spanish traders used the 500 miles of intertwining Indian trails that linked the Mississippi port of Natchez to the Cumberland River.

Early white settlers quickly identified the importance of a land route from Natchez to Nashville. In 1801, the Natchez Trace opened as an official post road between the two cities. Boatmen who piloted flatboats from Nashville and other northern cities to Natchez and New Orleans returned along the Trace by foot or horse, often carrying large sums of money. One historian characterized the diverse array of people who used the Trace: "robbers, rugged pioneers, fashionable ladies, shysters, politicians, soldiers, scientists, and men of destiny, such as Aaron Burr, Andrew Jackson and Meriwether Lewis."

The Trace developed a reputation for robberies, and few people traveled its miles alone. Many thieves disguised themselves as Indians, fanning the flames of racial distrust that existed during this period of history. By 1820, more than 20 inns, referred to as "stands," were open. Many were modest – providing food and shelter only.

In 1812, the first steamship arrived at Natchez, Mississippi, marking the beginning of the end of the Trace's prominence. As steamboat

PHOTO COURTESY THE TENNESSEE DEPARTMENT OF TOURIST DEVELOPMENT

The bridge at milepost 438 along the Natchez Trace Parkway is an architectural marvel.

travel became more widespread and affordable, more and more people turned away from the long, laborious, and dangerous overland route along the Trace.

Information

The **Leiper's Fork Merchant's Association** (615/972-2708, www.leipersforkvillage.com) promotes the town, maintains a listing of local businesses, and publishes an annual calendar of events.

SPRING HILL

A small town midway between Franklin and Columbia, Spring Hill is best known by many as the site of a large General Motors automobile factory. To students of

the Civil War, the town is the site of one of the South's greatest missed opportunities of the war. While it is doubtful that a different outcome at Spring Hill would have changed the course of war, it would very likely have saved the many thousands of lives lost at the Battle of Franklin.

Spring Hill is located along U.S. Highway 31. Downtown consists of a few blocks between Beechcroft and Kendron Roads. The town's main street was destroyed by fire and tornado in 1963, leaving only a few remnants

The road's historical importance is evident in the fact that it was not easily forgotten. While it faded from use, the Natchez Trace was remembered. In 1909, the Daughters of the American Revolution in Mississippi started a project to mark the route of the Trace in each county through which it passed. The marker project continued for the next 24 years and eventually caught the attention of Mississippi Rep. Thomas J. Busby, who introduced the first bills in Congress to survey and construct a paved road along the route of the old Natchez Trace.

During the Great Depression, work on the Natchez Trace Parkway began under the Public Works Administration, the Works Project Administration, and the Civilian Conservation Corps. Following the New Deal, construction slowed dramatically and it was not until 1996 that the final leg of the parkway was completed.

The 445-mile parkway follows the general path of the old Natchez Trace; in a few places, they fall in step with each other. Just over 100 miles of the parkway lie within Tennessee. It runs along the Western Highland Rim through Davidson, Williamson, Hickman, Maury, Lewis, and Wayne Counties.

The parkway passes scenic overlooks, historic sites, and quiet pastures. In many places along the route you have the opportunity to walk along the original Trace.

ACCOMMODATIONS AND FOOD
There are no hotels on the parkway. Look for accommodations in nearby cities, including Franklin, Columbia, and Lawrenceburg. The Hampshire-based **Natchez Trace Reservation Service** (800/377-2770, www.bbonline.com/natcheztrace) books bed-and-breakfast inns along the parkway, from Nashville all the way to Natchez. This service is worth considering, especially since many of these inns are located closer to the parkway than motels are.

The closest accommodations to the parkway are three **campgrounds,** one of which lies in Tennessee. The Meriwether Lewis Campground at milepost 385 has 32 sites and a bathhouse. The next campground is Jeff Busby at milepost 193, in Mississippi.

There are no restaurants or food concessions along the parkway. Picnic facilities abound, however, so wise travelers will pack a few sandwiches and avoid traveling off the parkway to eat.

INFORMATION AND SERVICES
The **National Park Service** (800/305-7417, www.nps.gov/natr) publishes a fold-out map and guide to the parkway. The official visitors center for the parkway is in Tupelo, Mississippi. For detailed hiking information, visit the website about the Natchez Trace National Scenic Trail at www.nps.gov/natt.

The only gas station along the parkway is at Jeff Busby, milepost 193, in Mississippi. Fill up your tank before you take off to explore.

of Spring Hill's former charm. To see them, drive up and down the town's side streets, including Murray Hill, Depot, and McLemore Streets. Spring Hill's main attractions are along Highway 31 less than a mile outside of town.

The **Spring Hill Battlefield** (931/486-9037) is a 118-acre park with a one-mile trail that climbs to the top of a hill overlooking the battlefield. Interpretive markers tell the story of Spring Hill. The park is open during daylight hours. To find it, turn east onto Kendron Road and look for the park on the right-hand side of the road, just before the road passes I-65.

Rippavilla
You can tour an 1850s-era mansion at Rippavilla Plantation (5700 Main St., aka Hwy. 31, 931/486-9037, www.rippavilla.org, Tues.–Sat. 9 A.M.–5 P.M., adults $8, seniors $6, children 6–12 $5, children under 6 free), just south of downtown Spring Hill on Highway 31. Rippavilla, originally called Rip-o-villa,

THE FARM

In 1970, hippie spiritual leader Stephen Gaskin and 320 others established a commune in the rural Tennessee countryside near Summertown, Tennessee. Initially governed by beliefs that forbade alcohol and birth control and promoted nonviolence and respect for the environment, the Farm has evolved over the years. While it has loosened some rules, it remains committed to peace, justice, and environmental sustainability.

The Farm has established a number of successful businesses, and it has contributed to its mission for a more peaceful and healthy world. Its businesses include a book publishing company, a soy dairy that manufactures tofu and soy milk, and a yoga studio. Farm books include *The Farm Vegetarian Cookbook* and Ina May Gaskin's works on natural childbirth. Nonprofits on the Farm include Plenty International, an international aid organization, and the Farm School, which provides alternative education for primary through secondary grades.

The Farm is glad to receive visitors. The Ecovillage Training Center puts on workshops and conferences throughout the year, many of them dealing with organic gardening, permaculture, construction, and other sustainable technologies. The Farm also operates a midwifery training center and birthing houses, where women can come to give birth.

About 200 people live at the Farm today. A few have been there since the beginning, but there are also recent transplants. Some work at Farm enterprises, but others have jobs "off the Farm." Farm members become shareholders in the company that owns the Farm land and other assets.

VISITING THE FARM

The Farm is a welcoming and friendly place, where people wave at each other and you can strike up a conversation with just about anybody. The **Welcome Center** (100 Farm Rd., 931/964-3574, www.thefarmcommunity.com) has a museum about the community and sells Farm books, T-shirts, and other products. It is usually open Monday-Friday 1-5 P.M., but it is a good idea to call ahead to confirm; hours are normally cut back from November to March. You can arrange for a tour with a member of the Farm by calling ahead to the welcome center. There are also twice-yearly Farm Experience weekends for people who want to see what Farm living is about.

The **Farm Store** (931/964-4362) is open daily 9 A.M.-7 P.M. and sells organic and natural groceries, household items, vegetarian sandwiches, and drinks.

ACCOMMODATIONS

You can sleep the night at the Farm. The Inn at the Farm is part of the EcoVillage Training Center, and it offers dormitory-style accommodations. Reservations are required, and the inn is sometimes full when there are workshops or conferences underway.

A half-dozen farm residents rent out rooms to visitors, usually for about $35 a night per person. Meals may be available for an additional fee. There is also a campground, where you can pitch your own tent. For more information about staying at the Farm, call the welcome center or go online.

GETTING THERE

The Farm is located off Drake's Lane Road, a few miles west of Summertown along Route 20. Detailed directions and a map are available on the Farm website.

was built in 1851 by wealthy plantation owner Nathaniel Cheairs and his wife, Susan. The story is told that there was a tradition in the Cheairs family for the men to marry women named Sarah, so when Nathaniel told his father that he intended to ask Susan McKissak to marry him, his father offered to pay the young man $5,000 in gold not to. Susan McKissak's father, one of the richest men in the area, heard of this and in reply he offered Cheairs all the bricks and slave labor he needed to build his home.

In the end, Cheairs married Susan and received both the gifts from his father-in-law and the $5,000 from his father—not a bad way to start out in life.

Rippavilla was sold out of the family in the 1920s, and the new owner modernized many of the finishes and also connected what was once a detached smokehouse and kitchen to the main building. Guided tours of the mansion last about 45 minutes and guests may also walk around the property, which includes an 1870s Freedman's School that was moved from another part of the county when it was threatened to be destroyed.

◖ Tennessee Museum of Early Farm Life

For an educational trip back in time, stop at the Tennessee Museum of Early Farm Life (5700 Main St., aka Hwy. 31, 931/381-3686, Fri.–Sat. 9 A.M.–3:30 P.M., adults $3, children and seniors $2), which displays farm, kitchen, and other useful implements used at Tennessee farms and homes in days gone by. Operated by a group of enthusiastic and knowledgeable retired farmers, the museum lovingly preserves plows, cultivators, seeders, wagons, and many other pieces of machinery that helped make a hard life just a bit easier for farmers and their families. You can see machinery and equipment used to make brooms, to make molasses, to sow seeds, to bale hay, and to cure pork. Through the descriptions provided by your tour guide, you begin to understand the ingenuity and inventiveness of these pioneers, as well as the hard work that went into fulfilling their basic needs.

OUTSIDE NASHVILLE

PHOTO COURTESY THE TENNESSEE DEPARTMENT OF TOURIST DEVELOPMENT

Cattle graze along the Natchez Trace Parkway.

AMISH COUNTRY

In 1944, three Amish families moved to Lawrence County. According to some accounts, they came seeking a place where they would not be required to send their children to large, consolidated secondary schools. They also were in search of land where they could farm and make a home.

Over the years the Amish population in Lawrence County has waxed and waned, and estimates put it between 100 and 200 families now. The Amish are known for their conservative dress, rejection of modern technology, including electricity, and their preference to keep to themselves. They are also excellent farmers, craftsmen, and cooks, devout Christians, and peace-lovers. Most of the Amish in this part of Tennessee speak English and Pennsylvania Dutch, and some also know German.

The Amish of Lawrence County live around the tiny town of Ethridge, a few miles north of Lawrenceburg. As you drive through the back roads that criss-cross the Amish area, you will be able to identify the Amish homes because they are old-fashioned farmhouses, without electricity wires, cars, or mechanized farm equipment. You will also notice their fields of corn, peanuts, wheat, oats, tobacco, hay, and oats, and you may see a black horse-drawn buggy – their primary form of transportation.

Many Amish sell goods, ranging from handmade furniture to molasses. As you drive, you will see signs advertising various products for sale. You are welcome to stop by and buy something. Remember that due to their religious beliefs, the Amish do not allow their pictures to be taken. Please respect this fact when you visit them.

If you prefer, you can explore Amish country with a guide on a wagon tour. Such tours are offered by local Lawrence County residents, who are not Amish. Each tour lasts about 90 minutes and will take you to several farms where you can meet the Amish and buy products from them. Tours are provided twice daily Monday–Saturday at 10 A.M. and 3:30 P.M. by the **Amish Country Store** (4011 Hwy. 43 N., 931/829-1621). The rate is $10 for adults. You can also call **Jerry's Amish Buggy and Wagon Tours** (931/629-5055).

If you want to drive through on your own, start in Ethridge and explore the narrow back roads bounded by Highway 43 on the east, State Route 242 on the west, Highway 20 on the north, and U.S. Route 64 on the south. You can pick up a free detailed map of Amish country, with specific farms identified, from the **Lawrence Chamber of Commerce** (1609 Locust Ave., aka Hwy 43, 931/762-4911, www.chamberofcommerce.lawrence.tn.us). You can also buy a map from the **Amish Country Mall** (4011 Hwy 43 N., 931/829-1621) for $3.

A half-dozen stores along Highway 43 just north of Ethridge sell Amish-made goods for those who don't have time to venture into Amish territory themselves. One of the best is **Dutch Country Bakery** (3939 Hwy. 43 N., 931/829-2147, Mon.-Sat. 7 A.M.-5 P.M.), which sells Amish baked goods, cheeses, and bulk goods. It also serves breakfast and lunch daily.

The Amish work Monday through Saturday. Sunday is their Sabbath, the day that they worship and spend time with family. You won't find any Amish farm stands or homes open for business on Sunday.

The museum is open on Friday and Saturday only, but call ahead for an appointment if you'd like to visit on a different day. It is located a few hundred yards behind the Rippavilla Plantation and was once called the Mule Museum, the name that is still reflected on the road sign at Rippavilla.

General Motors Plant

Spring Hill's Saturn automobile plant was re-tooled in 2007 to produce the Chevy Traverse cross-over vehicle. During the retooling and initial phases of production, the plant was closed for tours. To find out the current schedule call the General Motors Spring Hill Tour Office (Hwy. 31, 931/486-3869).

Accommodations

There is a **Best Western** (102 Kedron Pkwy., 931/486-1234, $90–130) in town with an outdoor pool, laundry facility, free full breakfast, fitness room, and business services.

COLUMBIA

Columbia is the seat of Maury County. Founded in 1809 and named for Christopher Columbus, Columbia was the commercial hub for Middle Tennessee's rich plantations. In 1850 it became the third-largest city in Tennessee, behind Nashville and Memphis. A decade later Maury County was the wealthiest county in the whole state. The city's prominence did not survive, however. The economic trauma of the Civil War was largely to blame.

Ⓒ Ancestral Home of James Knox Polk

The United States' eleventh president, James Knox Polk, was born in North Carolina but moved to Middle Tennessee with his family when he was 11 years old. Before moving to town, Polk's family lived for several years on a farm north of Columbia, from where Polk's father ran successful plantations, speculated in land, and was involved in local politics.

The home where James Polk lived as a teenager and young man in Columbia is the only house remaining, besides the White House,

© SUSANNA HENIGHAN POTTER

OUTSIDE NASHVILLE

President James K. Polk's family home in Columbia is now a museum.

where Polk ever lived. It is now the Ancestral Home of James Knox Polk (301–305 W. 7th St., 931/388-2354, www.jameskpolk.com, April–Oct. Mon.–Sat. 9 A.M.–5 P.M., Sun. 1–5 P.M., Nov.–Mar. Mon.–Sat. 9 A.M.–4 P.M., Sun. 1–5 P.M., adults $7, seniors $6, youths 6–18 $5, children under 6 free), and home to a museum about Polk's life and presidency.

The home has a number of furnishings that belonged to President Polk and his wife, Sarah, while they lived at the White House. Other pieces come from Polk Place, the home that the couple planned and built in Nashville following the end of Polk's presidency in 1849. Sadly, Polk died of cholera just five months after leaving office and so had little opportunity to enjoy the home; Sarah Polk lived for another 42 years following her husband's death and she spent them all at Polk Place.

The Polk Home in Columbia was comfortable, but not luxurious, for its time. It was while living here that Polk began his career as a Tennessee lawyer, and eventually won his first seat in the U.S. House of

FIRST MONDAY

Until the widespread mechanization of farming, work animals were indispensable to Tennessee farmers. In many cases, mules were a farmer's most valuable asset – a good pair of mules could make a poor farmer rich.

Mules are a mix of jackass studs and mare horses. They can be either male or female, but most mules are sterile and cannot reproduce.

Mules were more expensive than horses or oxen, and more highly prized. They were said to be stronger, smarter, and more surefooted than other work animals. Their temperament can be stubborn, but some mules are easy and willing to work. For this reason, mule breeders were important, influential, and, often, quite wealthy.

No city in all of Tennessee is more closely associated with mules than Columbia. On the first Monday of April every year, the mule market opened and people flocked to Columbia to buy and sell mules. Other towns, including Lynchburg and Paris, were known for large "First Monday" sales, but Columbia's was the largest.

By 1900, word had spread as far as England about Columbia's First Monday. In that year, the British army sent buyers to Columbia. They bought every available mule and shipped them across the Atlantic to South Africa to aid their army fighting against the Boers.

As farmers adopted tractors and other mechanical farm equipment, mules lost their prominence. In the 1930s, Columbia

PHOTO COURTESY THE TENNESSEE DEPARTMENT OF TOURIST DEVELOPMENT

Mule Day in Columbia

resurrected First Monday and called it Mule Day, but it was foremost a festival, not a functional mule market. After a period of declining interest, the tradition of Mule Day returned in 1974 and has been going strong ever since.

Representatives. He would go on to serve 14 years in the House, four of them as Speaker. He was governor of Tennessee from 1839 to 1841 and defeated Henry Clay, a Whig, to become president in 1845. Polk's presidency was defined by his drive to expand the Union westward, and it was during his term in office that the United States added California, Texas, and Oregon to the territory of the United States.

The Polk Home provides a good introduction to this little-known, but nonetheless important, U.S. president.

Events

Columbia's **Mule Day** (931/381-9557, www. muleday.com) takes place over four days in mid-April. It includes mule sales, mule and donkey seminars, and mule shows and competitions. The highlight is the Mule Day Parade on Saturday morning, when thousands of people crowd to see school bands, mules, and colorful troops parade down the road. There is also live music, storytelling, dancing, gospel singing, and the crowning of the Mule Day Queen. Activities take place at various locations in Columbia, but the heart of Mule Day is the Maury County Park on Lion Parkway.

Accommodations

Columbia has more choices of chain hotels than any other city in Maury County. **Jameson Inn** (715 S. James M. Campbell Blvd., 931/388-3326, $85–90) is a 55-room hotel with all the amenities: complimentary breakfast, fitness center, free wireless Internet, pool, big televisions, movie channels, and ironing boards. Premium rooms add microwaves, refrigerators, and coffee-makers. The inn is located across the street from the Columbia Mall and downtown.

Locally owned, the **Richland Inn** (2405 Hwy. 31, 931/381-4500, www.columbiarichlandinn.com, $70–100) is a 147-room inn with singles, doubles, and suites. There is a continental breakfast and a family restaurant next door.

A host of motels are found around exit 46 on I-65, about 10 miles east of Columbia. They include **Comfort Inn** (1544 Bear Creek Pike, 931/388-2500, $75–100) and **Holiday Inn Express** (1558 Bear Creek Pike, 931/380-1227, $75–120).

For something special, sleep in the Carriage House at 🌾 **Rattle and Snap Plantation** (1522 N. Main St., aka Hwy. 243, Mount Pleasant, 931/379-1700, www.rattleandsnapplantation.com, $250), and you will enjoy your own private tour of one of the state's most famous antebellum homes. The Carriage House is a three-bedroom guesthouse located at the rear of the mansion. It includes two queen-sized bedrooms and a sleeping loft with two twin beds. There is also a kitchen, a sitting room, and a patio where guests can relax and prepare meals. No children are allowed, and smoking is not permitted. There is a two-night minimum stay.

Food

Located on the courthouse square, **Square Market and Cafe** (35 Public Sq., 931/840-3636, Mon.–Thurs. 9 A.M.–2:30 P.M., Fri. 9 A.M.–9 P.M., Sat. 10:30 A.M.–9 P.M., $6–19), serves breakfast and lunch throughout the week, and dinner on Friday and Saturday nights. The weekday menu features salads, sandwiches, and soups. The signature Polk's Roasted Pear Salad of greens, blue cheese, walnuts, and roasted-pear vinaigrette is a favorite for lunch. Heartier appetites can choose hot steamed sandwiches, or the Tennessee Hot Brown, a hot open-faced turkey sandwich topped with white sauce, cheddar cheese, and bacon. The café brews good coffee and the desserts are homemade. Weekend dinner includes entrées like baked salmon with dill caper sauce, spinach-and-garlic ravioli, and Eastern Shore crab cakes. There is live music too.

For country cooking, hearty breakfasts, and plate-lunch specials, head to **Bucky's Family Restaurant** (1102 Carmack Blvd., 931/381-2834, daily 5 A.M.–2 P.M., $4–12).

The best steakhouse in the area, **The Ole Lamplighter Inn** (1000 Riverside Dr., 931/381-3837, Mon.–Sat. 4:30–9 P.M., $10–26) will satisfy the biggest appetite with charbroiled steak, all-you-can-eat soup and salad buffet, bottomless soft drinks, plus seafood and shrimp options. The Lamplighter looks a bit like a log cabin from the outside, and inside it has a low-light tavern feel that hastens relaxation. Come here to enjoy good food at good prices.

Information

The **Middle Tennessee Visitors Bureau** (302 W. 7th St., 931/381-7176 or 888/852-1860, www.antebellum.com) operates a visitors center across the street from the James K. Polk house. The visitors center (931/840-8324) is open Monday–Saturday 9 A.M.–4 P.M.

Land Between the Lakes

The narrow finger of land that lies between the Cumberland and Tennessee Rivers northeast of Clarkesville is a natural wonderland. Comprising 170,000 acres of land and wrapped by 300 miles of undeveloped river shoreline, the Land Between the Lakes National Recreation Area provides unrivaled opportunities to camp, hike, boat, or just simply drive through quiet wilderness. It is the third most-visited park in Tennessee, behind only the Smoky Mountains and Cherokee National Forest.

The area lies between what is now called Kentucky Lake (the Tennessee River) and Lake Barkley (the Cumberland River). At its narrowest point, the distance between these two bodies of water is only one mile. The drive from north to south is 43 miles. About one-third of the park is in Tennessee; the rest is in Kentucky. It is managed by the U.S. Forest Service, an agency of the U.S. Department of Agriculture.

SIGHTS

Driving south-to-north along the main road, or trace, that runs along the middle of the park, you will find the major attractions within Land Between the Lakes.

Great Western Iron Furnace

About 11 miles inside the park is the Great Western Iron Furnace, built by Brian, Newell, and Company in 1854. If you have traveled around this part of Tennessee much, you'll have come to recognize the distinctive shape of the old iron furnaces that dot the landscape in the counties between Nashville and the Tennessee River. Like the Great Western Furnace, these plants were used to create high-quality iron from iron ore deposits in the earth.

The Great Western Furnace operated for less than two years. By 1856 panic over reported slave uprisings and the coming of the Civil War caused the plant to shut down. It would never make iron again.

◖ The Homeplace

Just beyond the furnace is The Homeplace (270/924-2020, www.lbl.org, Mar.–Nov. daily 10 A.M.–5 P.M., $2–5), a living-history museum that re-creates an 1850 farmstead. At the middle of the 19th century, Between the Rivers was home to an iron ore industry and hundreds of farmers. These farmers raised crops and livestock for their own use, as well as to sell where they could. In 1850, about 10,000 people lived in Between the Rivers, including 2,500 slaves and 125 free blacks.

Staff dress up in period clothes and perform the labors that settlers would have done: They sow seeds in the spring, harvest in the summer and fall, and prepare the fields for the next year in the winter. The farm includes a dog trot cabin, where you can see how settlers would have lived, cooked, and slept. Out back there is a small garden, a plot of tobacco, pigs, sheep,

The Homeplace at Land Between the Lakes is a living history museum.

© SUSANNA HENIGHAN POTTER

oxen, and barn. You may see farmers splitting shingles, working oxen, sewing quilts, making candles, or any other of the dozens of tasks that settlers performed on a regular basis.

The Homeplace publishes a schedule that announces when certain activities will take place, such as canning, shearing of sheep, or harvesting tobacco. Even if you come when there is no special program, you will be able to see staff taking on everyday tasks, and you can ask them about any facet of life on the frontier.

Elk and Bison Prairie

Archaeological evidence shows that elk and bison once grazed in Tennessee and Kentucky, including the area between the rivers. Settlers quickly destroyed these herds, however. Both bison and elk were easy to hunt, and they were desirable for their meat and skins. By 1800, bison had been killed off, and about 50 years later elk were gone too.

When Land Between the Lakes was created, elk and bison were reintroduced to the area. The **South Bison Range** across the road from the Homeplace is one of the places where bison now live. The bison herd that roams on about 160 acres here can sometimes be seen from the main road, or from side roads bordering the range.

You can see both bison and elk at the Elk and Bison Prairie, a 700-acre restoration project located near the mid-point of the Land Between the Lakes. In 1996, 39 bison were relocated from the south prairie here, and 29 elk were transported from Canada. Since then, the population of both animals has grown.

Visitors may drive through the range along a one-mile loop. Admission is $5 per vehicle. You are advised to take your time, roll down your windows, and keep your eyes peeled for a sign of the animals. The best time to view elk and bison is in the early morning or late afternoon. At other times of day, you will enjoy the sights and sounds of the grassland.

RECREATION

Promoting outdoor recreation is one of the objectives of Land Between the Lakes. Visitors can enjoy hiking, biking, or horseback riding;

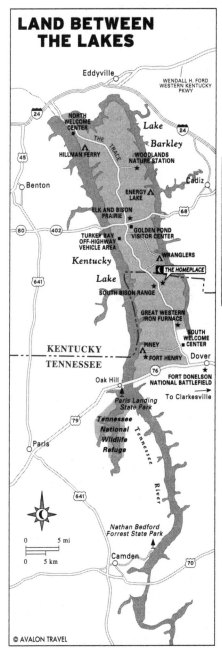

LAND BETWEEN THE LAKES

Eddyville

WENDALL H. FORD WESTERN KENTUCKY PKWY

24

NORTH WELCOME CENTER

Lake

24

45

THE TRACE

HILLMAN FERRY

Barkley

WOODLANDS NATURE STATION

Cadiz

Benton

ENERGY LAKE

68

ELK AND BISON PRAIRIE

80 402

GOLDEN POND VISITOR CENTER

TURKEY BAY OFF-HIGHWAY VEHICLE AREA

WRANGLERS

Kentucky

THE HOMEPLACE

641

Lake

SOUTH BISON RANGE

GREAT WESTERN IRON FURNACE

SOUTH WELCOME CENTER

KENTUCKY

PINEY

TENNESSEE

FORT HENRY Dover

Oak Hill

76

FORT DONELSON NATIONAL BATTLEFIELD

To Clarkesville

Paris Landing State Park

Tennessee National Wildlife Refuge

79

Paris

Tennessee River

641

Nathan Bedford Forrest State Park

0   5 mi

0   5 km

Camden

70

© AVALON TRAVEL

hunting and fishing; and camping. There is even an area specially designated for all-terrain vehicles.

Trails

There are 200 miles of hiking trails in Land Between the Lakes. Some of these are also open for mountain biking and horseback riding.

The **Fort Henry Trails** are a network of 29.3 miles of trails near the southern entrance to the park, some of which follow the shoreline of the Kentucky Lake. The intricate network of trails allows hikers to choose from a three-mile loop to a much longer trek.

Access the trails from the South Welcome Station, or from the Fort Henry Hiking Trails parking area, at the end of Fort Henry Road. These trails criss-cross the grounds once occupied by the Confederate Fort Henry. They are for hikers only.

The **North-South Trail** treks the entire length of the Land Between the Lakes. From start to finish, it is 58.6 miles. Three backcountry camping shelters are available along the way for backpackers. The trail crosses the main road in several locations. Portions of the trail are open to horseback riders. The portion from the Golden Pond Visitor Center to the northern end is also open to mountain bikers.

A detailed map showing all hiking, biking, and horseback trails can be picked up at any of the park visitors centers. You can rent bikes at Hillman Ferry and Piney Campgrounds.

Fishing and Boating

Land Between the Lakes offers excellent fishing. The best season for fishing is spring, from April to June, when fish move to shallow waters to spawn. Crappie, largemouth bass, and a variety of sunfish may be caught at this time.

Summer and fall offer good fishing, while winter is fair. A fishing license from the state in which you will be fishing is required; these may be purchased from businesses outside of the park. Specific size requirements and open dates may be found at any of the visitors centers.

There are 19 different lake access points where you can put in a boat. Canoe rentals are available at the Energy Lake Campground.

Hunting

Controlled hunting is one of the tools that the Forest Service uses to manage populations of wild animals in Land Between the Lakes. Hunting also draws thousands of visitors each year. The annual spring turkey hunt and fall deer hunts are the most popular.

Specific rules govern each hunt, and in many cases hunters must apply in advance for a permit. Hunters must also have a $20 LBL Hunter Use Permit, as well as the applicable state licenses. For details on hunting regulations, call the park at 270/924-2065.

CAMPING

There are nine campgrounds at Land Between the Lakes. All campgrounds have facilities for tent or trailer camping.

Most campgrounds are open from March 1 to November 1 annually. Tent campsites cost $12–13 per night; RV sites range $18–32, depending on whether it has electricity, water, and sewer services.

Reservations are accepted for select campsites at Piney, Energy Lake, Hillman's Ferry, and Wrangler Campgrounds. Reservations are available up to six months in advance; call the National Recreation Reservation Service at 877/444-6777 or go to www.recreation.gov.

Piney Campground

Located on the southern tip of Land Between the Lakes, **◖ Piney Campground** is convenient to visitors arriving from the Tennessee side of the park. Piney has more than 300 campsites: 281 have electricity; 44 have electricity, water, and sewer; and 59 are primitive tent sites.

There are also nine rustic one-bedroom camping shelters with a ceiling fan, table and chairs, electric outlets, and large porch. Sleeping accommodations are one double bed and a bunk bed. Outside there is a picnic table and fire ring. There are no bathrooms; shelter guests use the same bathhouses as other campers. Camp shelters cost $35–37 per night and sleep up to four people.

Piney's amenities include a camp store, bike rental, archery range, playground, swimming beach, boat ramp, and fishing pier.

Energy Lake

Near the mid-point of Land Between the Lakes, **Energy Lake Campground** has tent and trailer campsites, electric sites, and group camp facilities.

Backcountry Camping

Backcountry camping is allowed year-round in Land Between the Lakes. All you need is a backcountry permit and the right gear to enjoy unlimited choices of campsites along the shoreline or in the woodlands.

PRACTICALITIES

There are no restaurants or hotels in Land Between the Lakes. Drive to Dover for food and accommodation other than camping.

The Forest Service maintains a useful website about Land Between the Lakes at www.lbl.org. You can also call 270/924-2000 to request maps and information sheets. The park headquarters is located at the Golden Pond Visitor Center across the Kentucky state line.

When you arrive, stop at the nearest welcome or visitors center for up-to-date advisories and activity schedules. Each of the welcome centers and the visitors center are open daily 9 A.M.–5 P.M.

The **Land Between the Lakes Association** (800/455-5897, www.friendsoflbl.org) organizes volunteer opportunities and publishes a detailed tour guide to the park, which includes historical and natural anecdotes.

FORT DONELSON NATIONAL BATTLEFIELD

On Valentine's Day in 1862, Union forces attacked the confederate Fort Donelson on the banks of the Cumberland River. Fort Donelson National Battlefield (Hwy. 79, 931/232-5706, www.nps.gov/fodo) is now a national park. A visitors center with an exhibit, gift shop,

and information boards is open daily 8 A.M.–4:30 P.M. The 15-minute video does a good job of describing the battle and its importance in the Civil War.

A driving tour takes visitors to Fort Donelson, which overlooks the Cumberland River and may be one of the most picturesque forts in Tennessee. The fort is an earthenwork fort, built by Confederate soldiers and slaves over a period of about seven months.

You are also guided to the **Dover Hotel** (Petty St., 931/232-5706), which was used as the Confederate headquarters during the battle. The hotel, built between 1851 and 1853, is a handsome wood structure and has been restored to look as it did during the battle. It is located a few blocks away from downtown Dover. The hotel is open from noon to 4 P.M. on weekends from Memorial Day to Labor Day.

The **National Cemetery**, established after the war, was built on grounds where escaped slaves lived in a so-called "contraband camp" during the Civil War. The camp was established by the Union army to accommodate slaves who fled behind Union lines during the war. The freedmen and women worked for the Union army, often without pay. It was not until 1853 that the Union army allowed blacks to join as soldiers.

There are more than five miles of hiking trails at Fort Donelson National Battlefield, including the three-mile River Circle Trail and four-mile Donelson Trail. Both hikes begin at the visitors center. Picnic tables are located next to the river near the old fort.

DOVER

A small town set at the southern shore of the Cumberland River, Dover is a major gateway to the Land Between the Lakes. It is also the place where Gen. Ulysses S. Grant earned the nickname "Unconditional Surrender" during the Civil War.

Accommodations

Located right next to Fort Donelson National Cemetery, **[The Riverfront Plantation Inn** (165 Plantation Ln., 931/232-9492, www.riverfrontplantation.com, $85–110) is the best place

UNCONDITIONAL SURRENDER

The Union army won its first major victory of the Civil War at Fort Donelson in 1862. Following unexpected defeats at Manassas and Wilson's Creek in 1861, the Federal victory at Fort Donelson was cause for celebration for supporters of the Union.

The Union forces were attracted to Fort Donelson, and nearby Fort Henry, because of the area's strategic importance. In an age of steamships and river transportation, the Cumberland and Tennessee Rivers were superhighways into the heart of Dixie. Union reconnaissance found that the forts, built hurriedly by the Confederates to protect the rivers, were vulnerable.

Fort Henry fell to a force of Union gunboats on February 6, 1862. The boats bombarded Fort Henry for more than an hour before the fort surrendered. Almost 2,500 Confederate soldiers escaped and fled to Fort Donelson, which had a stronger position.

Meanwhile, Union forces were marching over land to Fort Donelson. By February 13, some 15,000 Union troops had nearly encircled the fort, under the command of Brig. Gen. Ulysses S. Grant. But the Union strategy at Fort Donelson was not land-based alone. On the morning of Valentine's Day, a Union fleet of gunboats attacked Fort Donelson from the Cumberland River. They were not successful, however, due to the fort's protected position. After 90 minutes, the ships retreated.

Despite having repulsed the river attack, Confederate commanders were not optimistic. They knew that the Union army was receiving reinforcements every day and had virtually surrounded Fort Donelson. Confederates feared a siege. So the South's commanders, including Generals John Floyd, Gideon Pillow, and Simon Buckner, decided that their best option was to abandon Fort Donelson and retreat to Nashville, where they could regroup. But in order to retreat, the Confederates had

Fort Donelson is peaceful now; on Valentine's Day, 1862, it was the site of furious fighting.

© SUSANNA HENIGHAN POTTER

to push the Federals back far enough to clear a route of escape.

On February 15, the Confederates attacked, and they won important ground from the Federals. Unfortunately for the South, poor leadership and indecision led to a bad order to retreat, just when they had gained their new ground. Gen. Grant immediately launched a vigorous counter-attack and the Federals retook the ground they had just lost and gained even more.

Seeing the writing on the walls, Southern Generals Floyd and Pillow slipped away overnight, leaving Gen. Buckner in command. A few hundred men under the command of Nathan Bedford Forrest also escaped overnight rather than be taken prisoner. On the morning of February 16, Buckner wrote to Grant asking for the terms of surrender.

In Grant's famous reply, he said no terms other than "unconditional and immediate" surrender would be accepted. Buckner surrendered, and 13,000 Confederate men were taken prisoner. The path to the heart of the Confederacy was now open, and Grant earned a new nickname: "Unconditional Surrender" Grant.

to stay in Dover. A bed-and-breakfast inn with four rooms and a commanding view of the Cumberland River, this is truly a distinctive retreat. Originally built in 1859, the inn was mostly destroyed by fire in 1865. It served as a Union hospital during the Civil War. After the war, the house was rebuilt and remains much the same today.

The inn is a white brick building, graceful and stately above the river. Guest rooms are neat and cozy, and are named after Confederate generals, including Nathan Bedford Forrest and James Longstreet. All have views of the river, and two rooms may be rented together to form a two-bedroom suite. A hearty breakfast is served on the sunny dining porch overlooking the river.

Just west of the entrance to Land Between the Lakes, the **Dover Inn Motel** (1545 Donelson Pkwy., 931/232-5556, $60–70) has both traditional motel rooms and cabins with full kitchens. All rooms have telephones, cable TV, air-conditioning, and coffee makers. They cater to hunters and fishermen who are going to Land Between the Lakes but don't want to camp. There is a swimming pool on the property.

Food

The most elegant dining in Dover is at the **Plantation Inn Dining Room** (165 Plantation Ln., 931/232-9492, Thurs.–Sat. 5–9 P.M., Sun. 10 A.M.–2 P.M., $10–20). Located in a bed-and-breakfast overlooking the Cumberland River, the Plantation Inn serves upscale dinners in its old-fashioned dining room or on the breezy dining porch. Country Cordon Bleu, crab cakes, and cheesy vegetarian pasta are a few of the options on the dinner menu. Entrées are served with your choice of a half-dozen different side dishes, including truffle mashed potatoes and squash casserole. Reservations are recommended, but not essential.

For something entirely different, head to the **B&M Dairy Freeze** (610 Donelson Pkwy., 931/232-5927, daily 10:30 A.M.–7 P.M., $4–8), a casual restaurant with burgers, hot dogs, and ice cream located just west of downtown Dover.

Located downtown, **The Dover Grille** (310 Donelson Pkwy., 931/232-7919, daily 7 A.M.–9 P.M., $5–12) serves burgers, dinner plates, southwestern platters, pasta, and salads.

Several miles east of the town is the **Log Cabin Cafe** (1394 Hwy. 79, 931/232-0220, Mon.–Sat. 6 A.M.–9 P.M., Sun. 6 A.M.–3 P.M., $6–15). The café serves traditional southern food in a log cabin. It is a popular pit stop for workmen; their breakfast will fuel you all day long.

Information

The **Stewart County Chamber of Commerce** (1008 Moore Rd., 931/232-8290, www.stewartcountyvacation.com) provides visitor information.

MEMPHIS

Take away its music, and Memphis would lose its soul. Memphis may owe its existence to the Mississippi River, but it is music that has defined this Southern metropolis. Memphis music started with the spirituals and work songs of poor Mississippi Delta cotton farmers who came to Memphis and created a new sound: the Memphis blues. The blues spawned its own offspring: soul, R&B, country, and, of course, rock 'n' roll as sung by a poor truck driver from Tupelo, Mississippi, named Elvis Presley.

On any given weekend you can still find juke joints where the music flows as freely as the booze, and sitting still is not an option. On Beale Street, music wafts from inside smoky bars out onto the street, inviting you to come inside for a spell. And on Sundays, the sounds of old-fashioned spirituals and new gospel music can be heard at churches throughout the city.

Memphis music is the backbeat of any visit to the city, but by no means the only reason to come. For as rich as Memphis's history is, this is a city that does not live in its past. The past two decades have been ones of rebirth for Memphis, giving new life to the city as a tourist destination. An NBA franchise arrived, the National Civil Rights Museum opened on the grounds of the Lorraine Motel, a fantastic AAA baseball field opened, and Memphis made its mark with films such as *Hustle & Flow, Forty Shades of Blue,* and *Black Snake Moan.* In 2007, more than 9 million people visited Memphis.

While you're here, sustain yourself on the city's world-famous barbecue, its fried chicken and catfish, and its homemade plate lunches.

© SUSANNA HENIGHAN POTTER

HIGHLIGHTS

(Beale Street: The street that gave birth to the Memphis blues celebrates the legacy of this soulful music every night of the week (page 134).

(National Civil Rights Museum: For years the Lorraine Motel represented the tragic assassination of Martin Luther King Jr. Today, it tells the story of the African-American struggle for civil rights, from before the Civil War to the present day (page 137).

(Stax Museum of American Soul Music: Irresistible soul music is what made Stax famous in the 1960s, and it is what makes the Stax museum sweet today. Exhibits bring the work of Otis Redding, the Staple Singers, Isaac Hayes, and more to life (page 147).

(Graceland: The Elvis phenomenon is alive and well. Presley's south Memphis mansion is a testament not only to the King's music, but his fans as well (page 149).

(Elmwood Cemetery: The most surprising attraction in Memphis, Elmwood is the final resting place of dozens of Memphis characters: madames, blues singers, mayors, and pioneers of all types (page 150).

(Barbecue: Tangy, juicy, and just a little sweet, Memphis barbecue at places like the **Cozy Corner** is the stuff of dreams (page 175).

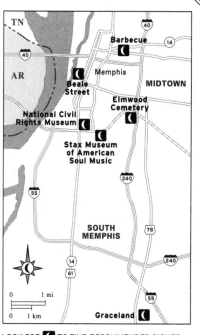

LOOK FOR **(** TO FIND RECOMMENDED SIGHTS, ACTIVITIES, DINING, AND LODGING.

Eating may not be why you come, but it will be why you stay.

Memphis is a city of the South. More than just the largest city in Tennessee, Memphis is the hub city for the entire Mid-South, which stretches from West Tennessee all the way down into Mississippi and Arkansas. As such, the city is a melting pot of cultural, musical, culinary, and economic influences from the entire Mississippi River delta.

PLANNING YOUR TIME

You can knock out Memphis's main attractions in a weekend, but it takes a bit longer to soak up the city's special mojo of music, food, and laid-back attitude. In fact, if you want more than just a taste of Memphis's famous blues, its legendary barbecue, or its rich history, plan to stay a week or longer.

Choose downtown Memphis as your home base. The city center is home to the best bars, restaurants, sports venues, live music clubs, and, of course, Beale Street. Downtown is also the liveliest, and one of the safest, parts of Memphis after the sun sets.

While a lot of Memphis's attractions are downtown, others are located in the eastern and southern stretches of the city. A free shuttle

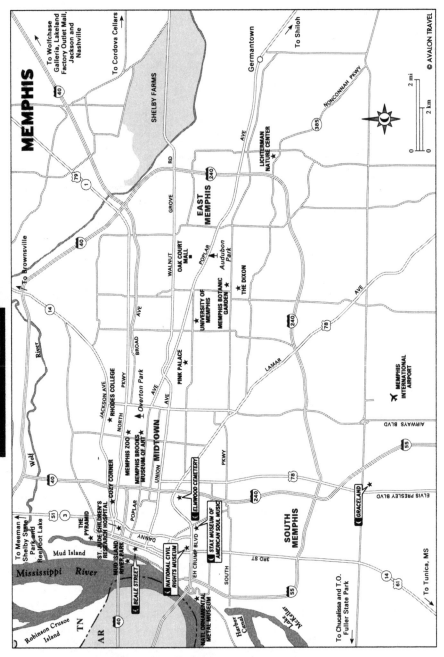

© AVALON TRAVEL

is available to Graceland and Sun Studio from downtown, but for other attractions like the Stax Museum of American Soul Music and the Memphis Brooks Museum of Art, you will need a car or taxi. Take note as well that two of the city's best barbecue joints, as well as its most famous juke joints, are not within walking distance of downtown.

When to Go

Memphis is a city with four seasons. The average temperature in January is 41 degrees, and in July it hits 81 degrees. Summer is certainly the most popular season for visiting—Elvis Week in August sees the most visitors of all—but a Memphis summer is not for the faint of heart.

The best time to visit Memphis is May, when summer is still fresh and mild, and the city puts on its annual Memphis in May celebration. Memphis in May includes the World Championship Barbeque Cooking Contest, the Beale Street Music Festival, and the Memphis International Festival.

Fall is also a good choice. The Memphis Music and Heritage Festival held over Labor Day weekend is a great reason to come to Memphis, and probably the best choice for fans of traditional Memphis music.

But if you can't come when the weather is warm, don't fret. Memphis attractions are open year-round, and the city continues to rock, day in and day out.

ORIENTATION

Memphis perches atop a low bluff overlooking the Mississippi River. The center city district lies, roughly speaking, along the river. Main Street, a pedestrian-only mall (except for the trolleys) runs north–south, while Union, Madison, and Poplar Avenues are main east–west thoroughfares.

While not compact, central Memphis is entirely walkable for people willing to use a little shoe leather. The Main Street trolley makes it easy to see downtown and uptown attractions without a car.

In this book, locations south of Union Avenue are considered **downtown,** while locations north are **uptown.** Downtown's main attraction is Beale Street. Also contained within the downtown district is the area known as **South Main,** a three-block strip along southern Main Street that is home to trendy boutiques, art galleries, restaurants, and condos. South Main is about a 15-minute walk or 5-minute trolley ride from Beale Street.

Another unique neighborhood in the city center is **The Pinch,** located along North Main Street past the I-40 overpass. Originally settled by German immigrants, the Pinch now has restaurants and nightlife. It is also the gateway to residential neighborhoods farther north that are gentrifying.

Restaurants in the Pinch have been categorized as uptown in this book. You can walk to the Pinch, but the best way to get there is to ride the Main Street Trolley.

In 1989, developers created **Harbor Town,** a New Urban community on Mud Island. The concept was to create a city community that offered amenities like schools, gyms, entertainment, and restaurants all within walking distance of each other. It was also designed to promote a sense of community; homes were built close together with short fences, front porches, and small yards, so that residents would use community parks and green spaces.

In 2007, a boutique hotel opened in Harbor Town, putting the area on the accommodations map for the first time. A major draw for Harbor Town is that it is located right across the river from downtown Memphis, but feels like a tight-knit residential community.

Memphis sprawls south, east, and north from the river. Head east from downtown, and you are in **midtown,** a district of strip malls, aging suburbs, and the city's best park and art museum. Poplar Avenue is the main artery of midtown, and a good point of reference when exploring by car (which is really the only way to get around midtown). The city's original suburb, midtown now seems positively urban compared to the sprawling burbs that creep farther eastward every year.

Located within midtown is **Cooper-Young,** a re-developing residential and commercial neighborhood that lies around the intersection of Cooper Street and Young Avenue. Since the 1970s, residents of this neighborhood have fought the tide of urban decay by encouraging investment, good schools, and amenities like parks and restaurants, and generally fostering a sense of pride in the area. The result is a neighborhood where you'll find lots of restaurants, a great used bookstore, record shops, and other attractions that draw the city's young and young-at-heart.

East Memphis is where you will find large shopping malls, major hospitals, the University of Memphis, and lots of traffic jams. There are also a few attractions out here: the Dixon and the Memphis Botanic Gardens among them.

Generally speaking, **north and south Memphis** are the most economically depressed areas of the city. Visitors beat a path to attractions like Graceland and Stax in southern Memphis during the day, but you would be wise to avoid these areas at night unless you are with a local who knows the way around.

Sights

DOWNTOWN

Downtown refers to the area south of Union Avenue in the city center. It is the heart of Memphis's tourist district.

(Beale Street

If you want to delve into the history and character of Memphis music, look no farther for a starting point than Beale Street, home of the blues.

A combination of forces led Beale Street to its place in musical history and popular culture. Named in the 1840s after a war hero, Beale Street was originally part of South Memphis, a separate city that rivaled Memphis during the 1840s.

Beginning in the 1850s, and continuing in greater numbers during and after the Civil War, African Americans began to settle along the western part of Beale Street. By the 1880s and 1890s, a middle class of black professionals began to emerge, and Beale Street became the center of commerce, entertainment, and life for many of them. Together with black-owned businesses on Beale Street there were also immigrants from Eastern Europe, Ireland, China, Greece, and Germany who operated laundries, bars, restaurants, pawn shops, and more.

From the 1880s until the 1960s, Beale Street

was the epicenter of African-American life, not just for Memphians but also for the entire Mid-South region. It was here that blacks felt free from many of society's restrictions.

Beale Street's decline began in the mid-20th century and by the 1970s, it was a shadow of its former self. Investment during the 1980s and '90s led to the street's rebirth as a destination for tourists and source of pride for residents, who could now show off the street that gave birth to the blues.

Today, Beale Street has two distinct personalities. During the day it is a laid-back place for families or adults to stroll, buy souvenirs, and eat. You can also stop at one of several museums and attractions located on the street. At night, Beale Street is a strip of nightclubs and restaurants, a great place to people-watch, and the best place to catch live blues seven nights a week.

W. C. Handy Home and Museum

The story of Beale Street cannot be told without mentioning William Christopher Handy, whose Memphis home sits at the corner of Beale Street and 4th Avenue. The building was originally located at 659 Jeanette Street, but was moved to Beale Street in 1985. Now the W. C. Handy Home and Museum (352 Beale St., 901/527-3427, summer Tues.–Sat. 10 A.M.–5 P.M., winter

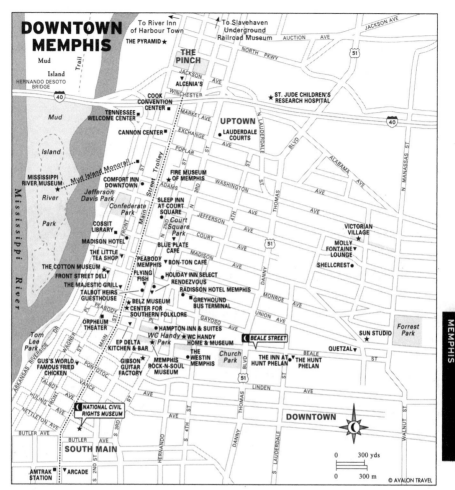

DOWNTOWN MEMPHIS

Tues.–Sat. 11 A.M.–4 P.M., adults $3, children $2) is dedicated to telling the story of Handy's life. It was Handy who famously wrote, in his "Beale Street Blues": "If Beale Street could talk, married men would have to take their beds and walk, except one or two who never drink booze, and the blind man on the corner singing 'Beale Street Blues.' I'd rather be there than anyplace I know."

The Handy museum houses photographs of Handy's family, one of his band uniforms, and memorabilia of the recording company that he founded. You can also hear samples of Handy's music.

A. Schwab

During Beale Street's dark days of the 1970s and '80s, when the clubs and restaurants closed and the pawn shops opened, one store remained: A. Schwab (163 Beale St., 901/523-9782, Mon.–Fri. 9 A.M.–5 P.M.). This landmark general store opened in

W. C. HANDY

W. C. Handy was born in a log cabin in Florence, Alabama, in 1873. The son and grandson of African Methodist Episcopal ministers, Handy was exposed to music as a child in his father's church. Handy was also drawn to the music of the black laborers of the area, and when he moved to Memphis in the early 20th century he recognized the wealth of the blues music he heard in bars, on street corners, and in back alleys around Beale Street.

Handy was a trained musician, so he was able to set down on paper the music that had, up until then, been passed from one musician to another.

In 1909 Handy composed Memphis mayor Ed Crump's campaign song "Mr. Crump," which he later published as the "Memphis Blues." But he is most famous for his composition "St. Louis Blues," published in 1914. Handy also created the "Yellow Dog Blues," "Joe Turner Blues," and "Beale Street Blues."

© SUSANNA HENIGHAN POTTER

The Memphis home of W. C. Handy was relocated to Beale Street in the 1980s and now houses the W. C. Handy Museum.

1876 and has been owned and operated by the same family ever since. Originally the source of household necessities for thousands of Delta residents, A. Schwab remains a treasure trove of goods. Here you will find practical things like underwear, hats, cookware, and tools, as well as novelties like old-fashioned candy, incense, and actual cans of Tennessee whoop-ass. Upstairs is the A. Schwab museum, a hodge-podge of old-time tools, clothes, and memorabilia of the store's 130-plus-year history.

Memphis Rock 'n' Soul Museum

Music fans should plan to spend several hours at the Memphis Rock 'n' Soul Museum (191 Beale St., 901/205-2533, www.memphis-rocknsoul.org, daily 10 A.M.–7 P.M., adults $10, children 5–17 $7), located right next to FedEx Forum off Beale Street. An affiliate of the Smithsonian Institution, this museum tells the story of Memphis music from the Delta blues to *Shaft*. Your visit starts with a short video documentary and then you can follow the exhibits with your personal audio guide, which includes recordings of dozens of Memphis-influenced artists from B. B. King to Elvis. Exhibits are dedicated to Memphis radio stations; the influence of the Victrola, Sam Phillips, and Sun Studio; and, of course, all things Elvis, among others. It takes several hours to study all the exhibits in detail and to listen to all (or even most) of the music, so plan accordingly.

There is a free shuttle that runs between the Rock 'n' Soul Museum, Graceland, and Sun Studio. Look for the black van with the Sun label's distinctive yellow sun on the side.

Gibson Guitar Factory

Across the street from the Rock 'n' Soul Museum is the Gibson Guitar Factory (145 Lt. George Lee Ave., 901/544-7998, ext. 4080, www.gibson.com), one of three in the United States. The Memphis plant specializes in the semi-hollow-bodied guitar, and a wide range of models are on sale in Gibson's retail shop. For $10, you can get an hour-long tour of the factory floor and see guitars being made, from the shaping of

the rim and panels to the painting and buffing of the finished product. Tours leave Monday–Saturday every hour on the hour 11 A.M.–4 P.M., and Sunday noon–4 P.M. Tours can sell out, so it is a good idea to buy your ticket in advance, especially during the busier summer months. Most factory workers leave by 3 P.M. and have the weekends off, so plan ahead if you want to see the factory floor in full swing.

◖ National Civil Rights Museum

If you do nothing else while you are in Memphis, visit the National Civil Rights Museum (450 Mulberry St., 901/521-9699, www.civilrightsmuseum.org, Mon. and Wed.–Sat. 9 A.M.–5 P.M., Sun. 1–5 P.M., adults $12, students and seniors $10, children 4–17 $8.50). Built on the site where Dr. Martin Luther King Jr. was assassinated on April 4, 1968, the museum makes a thorough examination of the American civil rights movement from slavery to the present day. Exhibits display original letters, audio recordings, photos, and newspaper clippings from events including the

COURTESY OF THE MEMPHIS CONVENTION AND VISITORS BUREAU

The Gibson Guitar Factory is one block away from Beale Street.

MEMPHIS

BEALE STREET WALKING TOUR

Beale Street runs from the Mississippi River to Manassas Street in midtown, but it is the three blocks between 2nd and 4th Streets that really matter, at least today. In its heyday, the Beale Street commercial and entertainment district extended farther east and west, but today, it has been condensed into the half dozen blocks from Main Street to 4th Street.

Beale Street is good for walking. Come down during the day to stroll the street and look carefully at what remains of the old architecture. Imagine the street when its cobblestones and sidewalks were jammed with African-American Memphians out doing their Saturday shopping. Then return in the evening for the modern-day experience. This walking tour begins at the intersection of Beale and Main Streets, and heads eastward.

Near the corner of Beale and Main Streets is the **Orpheum Theatre** (203 S. Main St., 901/525-7800, www.orpheum-memphis. com). This site has been used for entertainment since 1890, when the Grand Opera House opened there with a production of *Les Huguenots*. Later, the opera house began vaudeville shows and theater. Fire destroyed the opera house in 1923, but in 1928 it reopened as the Orpheum, a movie theater and performing arts venue for the likes of Duke Ellington, Cab Calloway, Bob Hope, and Mae West. The Orpheum was neglected for many years during the 1960s and '70s, but it reopened in 1984 thanks to the Memphis Development Foundation. It remains one of Memphis's premier venues for the performing arts, with Broadway productions, mainstream musical artists, movies, and much more.

A block east of the Orpheum is a statue of Memphis's most famous native son, Elvis Pres-

© SUSANNA HENIGHAN POTTER

The First Baptist Beale Street Church was built between 1868 and 1885 and was the first African-American church in the city.

ley. Depicting the King during his early career, the statue sits in **Elvis Presley Plaza.**

A. Schwab (163 Beale St., 901/523-9782, Mon.-Fri. 9 A.M.-5 P.M.) has served Memphis residents for more than 130 years, although it focuses now on odd, out-of-date, and hard-to-find items rather than general store necessities. Stop in for a souvenir, or to visit the A. Schwab "museum," a collection of old-fashioned household tools and implements.

A few doors down from A. Schwab, at the Irish pub Silky O'Sullivan's, you can see what remains of one of Beale Street's most magnificent old buildings. The facade of what was once the **Gallina Building** is held up by six steel girders. From the 1860s until 1914, this facade kept watch on the business empire of Squire Charles Gallina, who operated a saloon, restaurant, and 20-room hotel, as well as a gambling room. Gallina, who was also a magistrate, held court upstairs above the saloon, and his family lived in an apartment on the top floor. After Gallina's death in 1914, the building was used variously as a pharmacy, clothing store, dry goods shop, and dentist's office.

Beyond 3rd Street, on the northern side of Beale, is **Handy Park,** named for famous blues composer and musician W. C. Handy. Beale Street's markethouse was torn down in 1930 to build the park, which was dedicated during a ceremony attended by blues greats such as Robert Johnson and B. B. King. Since it opened, Handy Park has been a popular place for street musicians, peddlers, concerts, and community events, all of which are presided over by the life-size statue of W. C. Handy.

About midway up the southern side of the next block of Beale Street is the **Daisy Theater** (329 Beale St.). Built in 1917 as a movie house, the theater's domed front speaks of Beale's heyday. Much of the original interior remains today. The theater is closed to the public but may be rented for private events. Contact the Beale Street Development Corporation (866/406-5986) for information.

Across the street from the Daisy Theater is the **New Daisy Theater**, built in 1941 as another movie house. The New Daisy is one of Memphis's prime live music venues, and it books rock and alternative acts from around the country.

Stately and old, the **First Baptist Beale Street Church** (379 Beale St.) was built between 1868 and 1885 and is home to one of the oldest African-American congregations in Memphis. The church has its roots in praise meetings held in various locations beginning in the 1840s. In the 1860s, the congregation started to meet under brush arbors at the present location, and the first temporary structure was erected in 1865. The cornerstone was laid for the present building in 1871. The First Baptist Beale Street Church was an important force in Memphis's African-American history. It was here that black Memphians published their first newspapers, the *Memphis Watchman* and the *Memphis Free Speech and Headlight.*

Today, **Church Park** is a relatively nondescript city park with benches and some paved walks. But in 1899 when Robert Church built Church Park and Auditorium at the eastern end of the Beale Street commercial district, the park was something truly special. Church, the mixed-race son of a white steamboat captain, is said to have been the first black millionaire in the South. He made his money in real estate, and was troubled that there were no public parks expressly for Memphis's African-American residents. So in 1899 he opened Church Park and Auditorium on six acres of land along Beale Street. The park was beautifully landscaped and manicured, with bright flowers, tropical trees, and peacocks. The auditorium was a venue for black performers and speakers, and became a popular venue for conferences and meetings too. Church Park remains a venue for community events, particularly the annual Africa in April event every spring.

The Lorraine Motel, where Dr. Martin Luther King Jr. was assassinated in 1968, is now the National Civil Rights Museum.

Montgomery bus boycott, *Brown v. Board of Education,* Freedom Summer, and the march from Selma to Montgomery. Original and re-created artifacts, such as the bus where Rosa Parks made her stand in 1955 and the cell where Dr. King wrote his famous *Letter from a Birmingham Jail,* help to illustrate the story of civil rights.

When Dr. King visited Memphis in March and then again in April 1968, the Lorraine Motel was one of the handful of downtown hotels that welcomed African Americans. The room where he spent his final hours has been carefully re-created, and narration by those who were with him tell the shocking story of his death. Across Mulberry Street, in the building that was once the boardinghouse from where James Earl Ray is believed to have fired his sniper shot, exhibits probe various theories about the assassination, as well as the world-wide legacy of the civil rights movement.

Visitors to the museum can pay an extra $2 for an audio guide—a worthwhile investment. You must check your still or video camera due to restrictions on taking photographs inside the museum. This is a large museum and it is overflowing with information, so visitors who want to give the displays their due attention should plan on spending between three and four hours here. A good way to visit would be to tour the Lorraine Motel exhibits first, take a break for lunch, and then go across the street for the second half of the museum when you are refreshed.

Admission is free on Monday after 3 P.M. In June, July, and August the museum stays open until 6 P.M.

Belz Museum of Asian and Judaic Art

The Belz Museum of Asian and Judaic Art (119 S. Main St., 901/523-2787, Tues.–Fri. 10 A.M.–5:30 P.M., Sat.–Sun. noon–5 P.M., adults $5, children $4), formerly Peabody Place Museum, houses one of the largest collections of artwork from the Q'ing dynasty. Forged from the private collection of Memphis developers Jack and Marilyn Belz, owners of the Peabody Hotel and Peabody Place mall, the museum features some 1,000 objects, including an array of jade, tapestries, paintings, furniture, carvings, and other artifacts.

UPTOWN

Uptown refers to locations along Union Avenue and points north in the center city district. Here downtown workers are more common than tourists, and tall office buildings rise above the city blocks.

The Cotton Museum

The Cotton Museum at the Memphis Cotton Exchange (65 Union Ave., 901/531-7826, www.memphiscottonmuseum.org, Tues.–Sat. 10 A.M.–5 P.M., Sun. noon–5 P.M., adults $5, seniors $4.50, students $4, children 6–12 $3) is located in the broad rectangular room that once was the nerve center of the Mid-South's cotton trade. The Cotton Exchange was established in 1873, and it was here that buyers and sellers of the South's most important cash crop met, and where fortunes were

made and lost. Located just steps away from the Mississippi River, the Exchange was the trading floor of Cotton Row, the area of town that was defined by the cotton industry.

The Cotton Museum features exhibits about cotton's history, its uses, and the culture that its cultivation gave rise to in Memphis and the Mississippi Delta. There are several videos you can watch, as well as a live Internet feed of today's cotton exchange—now conducted entirely electronically. The nicest thing about the museum, however, is seeing the chalkboard where the prices of cotton around the world were written by hand. There is also a replica of the Western Union office where buyers and sellers sent telegrams using an intricate system of abbreviations known only to the cotton trade.

The Peabody Hotel Memphis

The Peabody Hotel Memphis (149 Union Ave., 901/529-4000) is the city's most famous hotel. Founded in 1869, the Peabody was one of the

© SUSANNA HENIGHAN POTTER

The lounge of the Peabody Hotel fills with people minutes before the twice-daily parade of the Peabody ducks.

MEMPHIS

first grand hotels of the South, a place as well known for its elegant balls and big-band concerts as for the colorful characters who sipped cocktails at its famous lounge. Named in memory of the philanthropist George Peabody, the original hotel was located at the corner of Main and Monroe. It closed in 1923 and a new Peabody opened two years later in its present location on Union Avenue. It remained the place to see and be seen for generations of Memphians and Delta residents. It was David Cohn who famously wrote in 1935 that "The Mississippi Delta begins in the lobby of The Peabody Hotel."

The elegant hotel lobby is gathering place for the twice-daily march of the Peabody ducks. They live on the roof of the hotel, and make the journey—by elevator—to the lobby fountain every morning at 11 A.M. At 5 P.M. they march out of the fountain, back onto the elevator, and up to their accommodations on the roof.

The hotel employs a duck master who takes care of the ducks and supervises their daily trip downstairs. Watching the ducks is free, frenzied, and undeniably fun. It is also one of the most popular activities among visitors to Memphis, so be sure to get there early and secure a good vantage point along the red carpet to watch the duck march.

Mud Island

In Memphis, it is sometimes easy to forget that you are just steps away from the great Mississippi River. A trip to Mud Island will cure this ailment once and for all. A narrow band of land in the river, Mud Island is home to the **Mississippi River Museum** (125 N. Front St., 901/576-7241, www.mudisland.com, adults $8, seniors $6, children $5), which has exhibits about early uses of the river, steam and paddle boats, floods, and much more. The museum and accompanying Mud Island Park are open daily from mid-April to the end of October. Hours in April, May, September, and October are 10 A.M.–5 P.M., and in June, July, and August 10 A.M.–6 P.M.

The museum begins with a refresher course on European exploration of this region—DeSoto, LaSalle, and Marquette and Joliet—followed by information about early settlement. The highlight is being able to explore a replica of a 1870s steamboat. In the Riverfolk Gallery there are wax depictions of Mark Twain, riverboat gambler George Devol, and steamship entertainers. The museum also remembers the numerous river disasters that have taken place along the Mississippi.

Admission to the Mississippi River Museum includes the **River Walk** at the Mud Island River Park, a five-block scale model of the entire Mississippi River—from Minnesota to the Gulf of Mexico. Walk along the model to see scale representations of cities along the river's

MUD ISLAND

Mud Island rose from the Mississippi River as a result of two seemingly small events. In 1876, the river shifted slightly about 20 miles south of Memphis, causing the currents that flowed past the city to alter course. And then, in 1910, the U.S. Navy gunboat *Amphitrite* anchored at the mouth of the Wolf River for almost two years, causing a further change in silt patterns. When the ship left in 1912, the sandbar continued to grow, and Mud Island was born.

Residents initially disliked the island, since it was ugly and proved to be a danger to river navigation.

Beginning in the 1930s, poor Memphians – black and white – squatted on Mud Island in ramshackle homes built of scrap metal and wood. Between 200 and 500 people lived on the island during this time.

In 1959, a downtown airport was built on the island, but the airport was closed in 1970 when the DeSoto Bridge was built. In 1974, plans were developed for the present-day Mud Island River Park, which includes a full-scale replica of a river boat, a monorail to the island, and the signature 2,000-foot flowing replica of the Mississippi River.

path, and read placards about the river's history. On a hot day, wear your bathing suit so you can swim in the pool at the end.

The river park is also home to an outdoor amphitheater, which in summer hosts big-name concerts. You can rent canoes and pedal boats to use in the still waters around the Mud Island harbor.

Admission to the river park is free. You cay pay $4 round-trip to ride the monorail to Mud Island, or you can walk across the monorail bridge for free. The monorail station is on Front Street at Adams Avenue.

Slavehaven Underground Railroad Museum

The legend of the Burkle Estate, a modest white clapboard house on North 2nd Street, has given rise to the Slavehaven Underground Railroad Museum (826 N. 2nd St., 901/527-3427, summer Mon.–Sat. 10 A.M.–4 P.M., winter Wed.–Sat. 10 A.M.–4 P.M., adults $6, youth $4). The museum here tells the story of slavery and the Underground Railroad, which helped thousands of slaves escape to freedom in the North (and, after the 1850 Fugitive Slave Act, to Canada). Jacob Burkle, a German immigrant and owner of the Memphis stockyard, is said to have built the Burkle Estate around 1850. Escaping slaves would have hidden in a root cellar beneath the house before making the 1,500-foot trip to the banks of the Mississippi, where they made a further journey north.

Skeptics say that there is no evidence of this story, and even point to documents that show that Burkle may not have purchased the property until 1871, well after the end of slavery. Advocates for the Underground Railroad story say that it was the nature of the railroad to be secret, so there is nothing unusual about a lack of concrete evidence.

Visitors today need not be too concerned with the details of the debate; the Slavehaven museum does a good job of highlighting the brutality of the slave trade and slavery, and the ingenuity and bravery it took for slaves to escape. Perhaps the most interesting part of the exhibit are the quilts that demonstrate the way

that slaves used quilting patterns to send messages to one another. Other displays show advertisements for Memphis slave auctions and images from the early 20th century that depict damaging racial stereotypes.

The museum is operated by Heritage Tours of Memphis and staff are available to conduct guided tours of the property.

Fire Museum of Memphis

The Fire Museum of Memphis (118 Adams Ave., 901/320-5650, www.firemuseum.com, Mon.–Sat. 9 A.M.–5 P.M., adults $6, seniors $4, children $5) is a good place to take children. There is a huge display of fire-engine toys, lots of firefighting paraphernalia, and a "fire room" that presents important lessons on fire safety. You can also see old-fashioned fire engines and youngsters will enjoy playing in the kid-friendly fire truck. The museum is located in the old Fire Station No. 1 in downtown Memphis.

St. Jude Children's Research Hospital

The sprawling complex of St. Jude Children's Research Hospital on uptown's northern fringe has been saving lives and bringing hope to children and their families since 1962. St. Jude was founded by entertainer Danny Thomas in fulfillment of his promise to God to give back to those in need. Over the years and thanks to the success of its fundraising arm—the American Lebanese Syrian Associated Charities—St. Jude has expanded many times over and now leads the world in research and treatment of catastrophic childhood diseases, especially pediatric cancers. The hospital never turns anyone away due to inability to pay, and it never makes families without insurance pay for their treatment.

Visitors can tour a small museum about Danny Thomas and St. Jude in the **Danny Thomas ALSAC Pavilion** (332 N. Lauderdale St., 901/495-4414, daily 8:30 A.M.–4:30 P.M., free), located inside a golden dome on the hospital grounds. Just outside are the graves of Danny Thomas and his wife, Rose Marie.

MEMPHIS

The Pyramid

The Memphis Pyramid is the most dominating feature of the northern city skyline. Memphis's affiliation with all things Egypt began with its name, and continued in 1897, when a large-scale replica of a pyramid was built to represent Memphis at the Tennessee Centennial Exhibition in Nashville. Pyramids were popular symbols on Memphis paraphernalia for many years.

The first serious proposal for a life-size pyramid to be built in Memphis was written in the 1970s, but the idea did not take off until the 1980s, when the city and county governments agreed to fund it. Denver developer Sidney Shlenker promoted the plan, and promised restaurants, tourist attractions, and lots of revenue for the city. The pyramid was built and opened in 1991, minus the money-making engines that Shlenker promised. Today, the $63 million Great American Pyramid sits empty, but the city is trying to attract a big-box store to turn it into a retail center.

MIDTOWN

You'll need a car to explore the attractions in midtown, which sprawls along Union, Poplar, and Madison Avenues as they head eastward from the city center.

Sun Studio

It is well worth your time to drop by Sun Studio (706 Union Ave., 901/521-0664, www.sun-studio.com, daily 10 A.M.–6 P.M., $10), where Elvis Presley recorded his first hit, "That's All Right," and where dozens of blues, rock, and country musicians were recorded during the 1950s. Founded by radio man and audio engineer Sam Phillips and his wife, Becky, the studio recorded weddings, funerals, events, and, of course, music. Phillips was interested in the blues, and his first recordings were of yet-unknown artists such as Rufus Thomas and Howlin' Wolf. In 1953, Elvis Presley came into the studio on his lunch break to record a $3 record of himself singing "My Happiness" for his mother. Phillips was not impressed with the performance, and it was not for another

year—and thanks to the prodding of Phillips's assistant, Marion Keisker—that Phillips called Presley in to record some more. When Phillips heard Elvis's version of the blues tune "That's All Right," he knew he had a hit. And he did.

But the story of Elvis's discovery is just one of many that took place in the modest homemade Sun Studio, and this attraction is not just for Elvis fans. The one-hour tour of the studio leaves every hour on the half hour, and while you are waiting you can order a real fountain drink from the snack bar or browse the shop's collection of recordings and paraphernalia. The studio is still in business; you can record here for $75 an hour at night, and dozens of top-notch performers have, including U2, Beck, and Matchbox 20.

Lauderdale Courts

The least-known Elvis attraction in Memphis is Lauderdale Courts (252 N. Lauderdale St., 901/523-8662, www.lauderdalecourts.com), the public housing complex where Presley lived

Sun Studio is where Elvis recorded his first hit in 1954, "That's All Right."

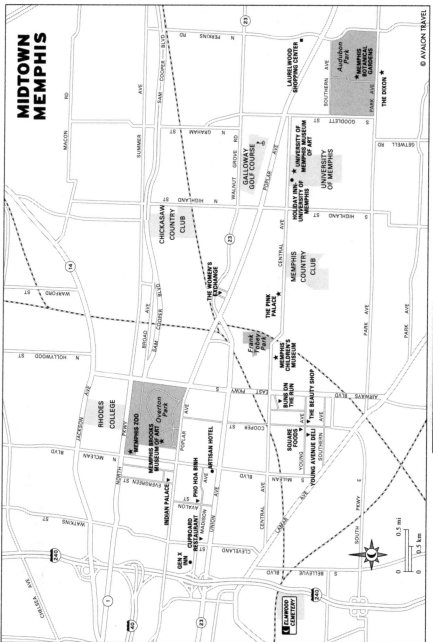

MIDTOWN MEMPHIS

© AVALON TRAVEL

MEMPHIS

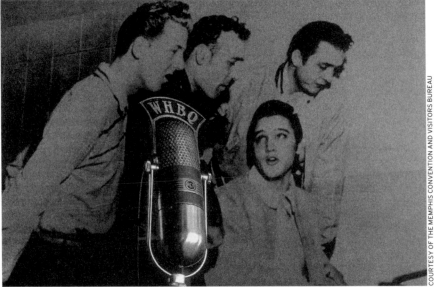

This photograph of the "Million Dollar Quartet" of Jerry Lee Lewis, Carl Perkins, Johnny Cash, and Elvis Presley was taken at Sun Studio.

with his parents from 1949 to 1953 before his rise to fame. The handsome brick building was saved from the wrecking ball in the 1990s, and the apartment where the Presleys lived has been restored to its 1950s glory. Most of the year, the Lauderdale Courts Elvis suite is rented out as a hotel room, but during Elvis's Birthday Week in January and Elvis Week in August it is open for public tours.

Victorian Village

Set on a tree-lined block of Adams Avenue near Orleans Street is Victorian Village, where a half dozen elegant Victorian-era homes escaped the "urban renewal" fate of other historic Memphis homes.

Visitors can tour the **Woodruff-Fontaine House** (680 Adams Ave., 901/526-1469, Wed.–Sun. noon–4 P.M., adult $10, seniors $8, children and students $6), one of the street's most magnificent buildings. Built starting in 1870 for the Woodruff family and sold to the Fontaines in the 1880s, the house was occupied through 1930, when it became part of the James Lee Art Academy, a precursor to the Memphis Academy of Art. When the academy moved in 1959, the building became city property and stood vacant. Beginning in 1961, city residents raised funds to restore and refurnish the house with period furniture and accessories, and it opened as a museum in 1964. This was during the period of urban renewal that saw to the demolition of many of Memphis's other old homes, and some of the house's furnishings were taken from homes that were later demolished. Visitors to the house are given a guided tour of the 1st floor, and can explore the 2nd and 3rd floors on their own. This is a good stop if you are interested in antiques.

The **Magevney House** (198 Adams Ave., 901/526-4464) and the **Mallory-Neely House** (652 Adams Ave., 901/523-1484) are two other historical homes in the district. The Magevney House is the oldest middle-class residence still standing in Memphis. It was built in 1836 by an Irish immigrant to the city, Eugene Magevney. The Mallory-Neely House is of the same vintage and is notable for the fact that it was not refurnished in more than 100 years and so remains remarkably true to the era in which it was built.

The Magevney and Mallory-Neely Houses are owned by the City of Memphis, and due to budget cuts have been closed to the public. Call to find out if they have been reopened.

Memphis Brooks Museum of Art

Memphis's foremost art museum is located in Overton Park in midtown, a short drive from downtown. Memphis Brooks Museum of Art (1934 Poplar Ave., 901/544-6200, www.brooksmuseum.org, Tues.–Fri. 10 A.M.–4 P.M., Sat. 10 A.M.–5 P.M., Sun. 11:30 A.M.–5 P.M., adults $7, seniors $6, students $3) is the largest fine art museum in Tennessee, and its permanent collection includes 8,000 works of art. This includes ancient African and Asian art, as well as European, American, and contemporary art. There are 29 galleries at the Brooks, and special exhibitions have focused on the work of Annie Leibovitz, men's fashion in Africa, and the silver work of Paul de Lamerie. There is also a museum shop and restaurant, as well as an auditorium often used to screen films. Admission to the Brooks is free on Wednesday.

The Memphis Zoo

The Memphis Zoo (2000 Prentiss Pl., 901/276-9453, www.memphiszoo.org, Mar.–Oct. daily 9 A.M.–6 P.M., Nov.–Feb. daily 9 A.M.–5 P.M., adults $13, children $8) has been expanding and is now the proud steward of two giant pandas, Le Le and Ya Ya, large cats, penguins, lions, tropical birds, and 3,500 other animal species. Its butterfly exhibit, open from May to October annually, is a popular favorite. The zoo is located on the grounds of Overton Park. Parking is an additional $3.

SOUTH MEMPHIS
◖ Stax Museum of American Soul Music

There is no place in Memphis that better tells the story of the city's legendary soul music than the Stax Museum of American Soul Music

MEMPHIS

the Memphis Brooks Museum of Art at Overton Park

SOULSVILLE

A lucky convergence of people, talents, and social forces led to one of Memphis's – and America's – most unique musical stories. Stax Records was founded in 1960 by Jim Stewart, an aspiring country fiddler, and his sister, Estelle Axton. The first two letters of the brother and sister's surnames came together to form Stax, a name now synonymous with the raw Memphis sound of performers like Rufus and Carla Thomas, Otis Redding, Sam and Dave, Isaac Hayes, Eddie Floyd, the Mar-Keys, the Staple Singers, and Booker T. & the MGs.

Jim Stewart chose a closed movie theater in a working-class South Memphis neighborhood for his recording studio. On a tight budget, he didn't fix the sloped theater floor or angled walls, and the room's reverberating acoustics came to define the Memphis sound.

The historic Stax Records studio is now the Stax Museum of American Soul Music.

Motown was known as "Hitsville" for its smooth and palatable sound, so the artists at Stax began to call their neighborhood "Soulsville" – a name that still refers to the area of South Memphis where Stax is located. The soul music that Stax recorded was raw and inventive, influenced by country, blues, gospel, and jazz.

The label's first hit was with WDIA-AM disc jockey Rufus Thomas and his daughter, Carla Thomas, who came in one day and recorded "Cause I Love You." The song became an overnight sensation.

Stax tapped into the talent of the neighborhood, and particularly the African-American Booker T. Washington High School, which graduated such greats as the members of the Soul Children and the Mad Lads. As the Stax reputation developed artists came from out of town to record, including a 21-year-old Otis Redding, who drove up from Georgia in hopes of making a record and made a career instead.

Stax also operated Satellite Records right next door to the studio, and here Estelle Axton was able to quickly test-market new recordings on the neighborhood youngsters who came in for the latest music. Wayne Jackson, a member of the studio's house band, the Memphis Horns, recalls that Estelle and Jim would invite hundreds of young people from the neighborhood into the studio to listen to their newest

recording. Based on the group's response, they would choose the single.

Stax was unique for its time as an integrated organization, where the love of music trumped racial differences. As the civil rights movement evolved, Stax artists turned to serious social themes in their music. In 1972 Stax artists organized WattStax, an outdoor black music festival in Los Angeles.

Between 1960 and 1975, when the Stax magic ran out, the studio produced 800 singles and 300 albums, including 243 Top 100 and 14 number-one R&B hits. Isaac Hayes's theme from the movie *Shaft* was the fastest-selling album in Stax history, and one of three Stax songs went to number one on the pop charts. Other big Stax hits were Otis Reddings' "(Sitting on) the Dock of the Bay"; the Staples Singers' "Respect Yourself"; and Sam and Dave's "Soul Man."

Sadly, Stax was destroyed financially by a bad distribution deal with CBS Records in 1975, and the studio was closed. Its rare master tapes were sold at auction, and the studio where soul was born was demolished.

Thankfully, the story of Stax has not been forgotten. In 2001 ground was broken for a new Stax story, one which grew into the present-day music academy and the Stax Museum of American Soul Music.

(926 E. McLemore Ave., 901/946-2535, www. staxmuseum.com, adults $10, seniors, students, and military $9, children 9–12 $7). Hours are Monday–Saturday 10 A.M.–4 P.M. and Sunday 1–4 P.M., with doors opening on weekdays at 9 A.M. from March to October.

The museum tour starts with a short toe-tapping video that sets the scene for the musical magic that took place here during the 1960s. Exhibits include the sanctuary of an old clapboard Delta church, which illustrates the connection between soul and gospel music. You can also see Booker T. Jones's original organ, Otis Redding's favorite suede leather jacket, and Isaac Hayes's 1972 peacock-blue gold-trimmed Cadillac Eldorado, Superfly.

The museum also takes you through the studio's control room and into the studio itself, slanted floors and all. If you want to try your hand, there is a karaoke machine and a dance floor in case you can't help but move to the music. The Stax museum is a must-see for music enthusiasts, but also an educational

journey for those who don't know the story behind some of America's most famous songs. It sits next door to the Stax Music Academy, a present-day music school that reaches out to neighborhood youth.

◖ Graceland

Drive south from downtown on Elvis Presley Boulevard to reach the King's most famous home, Graceland (3717 Elvis Presley Blvd., 901/332-3322 or 800/238-2000, www.elvis. com, $25–70). Graceland's summer (Mar.–Oct.) hours are Mon.–Sat. 9 A.M.–5 P.M. and Sun. 10 A.M.–4 P.M. In November it opens daily 10 A.M.–4 P.M., and from December to February it opens daily 10 A.M.–4 P.M., except Tuesday, when it is closed. Graceland is closed on Christmas and Thanksgiving Days, and sometimes on New Year's Day. There is plenty of parking.

Visitors can choose from three tour packages: The mansion-only tour takes about an hour and costs $25; the platinum tour includes

© SUSANNA HENIGHAN POTTER

The state historic marker is hardly needed at the Graceland mansion, where millions of fans have visited since it opened to tours in 1982.

the automobile museum, Elvis's two airplanes, and other special perks for $40. Enthusiasts can choose the VIP package for $70, which gives you "front of the line" access, an all-day pass, keepsakes, and access to exclusive exhibits, such as one that features Elvis's first-ever professional photographs, taken in 1955.

The Graceland complex blends into the strip malls and fast-food joints that line the boulevard in this part of Memphis. The ticket counter, shops, and restaurants are located on the west side of the boulevard, and here you board a shuttle van that drives across the highway and up the curved drive to the Graceland mansion. Graceland managers may have taken full advantage of the commercial opportunities presented by the home that Elvis left behind, but they have not overdone it. The operation is laid-back, leaving the spotlight on Elvis and, of course, his fans, who travel around the world to visit.

The mansion tour is conducted by audio guide. It includes the ground floor of the mansion (the upstairs remains closed to the public) and several outbuildings that now house exhibits about Elvis's life and career. High points include watching the press conference Elvis gave after leaving the army, witnessing firsthand his audacious taste in decor, and visiting the meditation garden where Elvis, his parents, and his grandmother are buried. There is also a plaque in memory of Elvis's lost twin, Jesse Garon. The audio tour plays many of Elvis's songs, family stories remembered by Lisa Marie Presley, and several clips of Elvis speaking. In 2008, Graceland opened two new exhibits: "Private Presley" focuses on the King's service in the army and "Elvis '68" is about the year 1968 in Presley's life and musical career.

The exhibits gloss over some of the challenges Elvis faced in his life—his addiction to prescription drugs, his womanizing and failed marriage, and his unsettling affinity for firearms among them. But they showcase Elvis's generosity, his dedication to family, and his fun-loving character. The portrait that emerges is sympathetic and remarkably human for a man who is so often larger than life.

The automobile museum features 33 vehicles, including his pink Cadillac, motorcycles, and a red MG from *Blue Hawaii*, as well as some of his favorite motorized toys, including a go-kart and dune buggy. His private planes include the *Lisa Marie*, which Elvis customized with gold-plated seat belts, suede chairs, and gold-flecked sinks. Other special Graceland exhibits include "Sincerely Elvis," which chronicles Elvis's life in 1956, and "Elvis After Dark," which describes some of Elvis's late-night passions, like roller skating.

The Graceland mansion was declared a National Historic Site in 2006. It attracts some 600,000 visitors annually.

◖ Elmwood Cemetery

Elmwood Cemetery (824 S. Dudley St., 901/774-3212, www.elmwoodcemetery.org, Mon.–Fri. 8 A.M.–4:30 P.M., Sat. 8 A.M.–noon), an 88-acre cemetery southwest of the city center, is the resting place of 70,000 Memphians—ordinary citizens and some of the city's most prominent leaders. It was founded in 1852 by 50 gentlemen who wanted the cemetery to be a park for the living as well as a resting place for the dead. They invested in tree planting and winding carriage paths so that the cemetery today is a pleasant, peaceful place to spend a few hours.

The cemetery is the resting place of Memphians like Annie Cook, a well-known madame who died during the yellow fever epidemic of 1878; Marion Scudder Griffen, a pioneering female lawyer and suffragette; and musician Sister Thea Bowman. Thousands of anonymous victims of the yellow fever epidemic were buried here, as were both Confederate and Union casualties of the Civil War. Prominent citizens including Robert Church Sr., Edward Hull Crump, and Shelby Foote are also buried at Elmwood.

Visitors to the cemetery may simply drive or walk through on their own. But it is best to rent the one-hour audio guide ($7) of the cemetery, which takes you on a driving tour and highlights 50 people buried in the cemetery. Thanks to a well-written and well-presented narration, the cemetery tour comes closer than any other single Memphis attraction to bringing Memphis's diverse history and people to life.

The cemetery offers occasional lectures and guided tours. Call ahead or check the website to find out if any are scheduled during your visit. To find Elmwood, drive east along E. H. Crump Boulevard, turning south (right) onto Dudley, which dead-ends at the single-lane bridge that marks the entrance to the cemetery.

Church of the Full Gospel Tabernacle

A native of Arkansas and longtime resident of Michigan, Al Green first made his name as one of history's greatest soul singers with hits like "Let's Stay Together," "Take Me to the River," and "Love and Happiness." Following a religious conversion in 1979, he dedicated his considerable talents to God and founded the Church of the Full Gospel Tabernacle (787 Hale Rd., 901/396-9192, www.algreenmusic. com) in Memphis, where his Sunday sermons dripped with soulful gospel.

For almost 16 years, the Reverend Al Green left secular music alone. He dedicated himself to God's music. But in 2005 Green released the first of three new secular albums on Blue Note Records. He's touring again too, in Europe and the United States.

According to his official biography, Rev. Green faced some criticism when he returned to the secular scene. "I've got people in the church saying, 'That's a secular song,' and I'm saying, 'Yeah, but you've got Monday, Tuesday, Wednesday, Thursday, Friday, and Saturday to be anything other than spiritual. You've got to live those days, too!'" Rev. Green says he has not neglected his duty to God. "The music is the message, the message is the music. So that's my little ministry that the Big Man upstairs gave to me—a little ministry called love and happiness."

Despite his rebirth as a secular soul performer, Al Green, now a bishop, still makes time for his church. He preaches regularly, but not every Sunday, and continues to sing the praises of God. The Sunday service at his Memphis church begins at 11:30 A.M. Visitors are welcome, and you can come—within reason—as you are. Please show some respect, though, by being quiet when that's called for and throwing a few bucks in the offering plate when it comes around. And don't forget that the church is a place of worship and not a tourist attraction. If you're not in town on Sunday, you can catch the weekly choir rehearsal on Thursday at 7 P.M.

National Ornamental Metal Museum

An unusual delight, the National Ornamental Metal Museum (374 Metal Museum Dr., 901/774-6380, www.metalmuseum.org, Tues.–Sat. 10 A.M.–5 P.M., adults $5, seniors $4, students and children $3) is dedicated to preserving and displaying fine metalwork. Its permanent collection numbers more than 3,000 objects, and ranges from contemporary American sculpture to works as many as 500 years old. The museum hosts special exhibits several times a year, showcasing various aspects of metalwork. There is also a working metalwork studio, and the museum grounds on the bluff overlooking the Mississippi are an attraction in themselves. This is reputed to be the site where Hernando de Soto and his men camped when they passed through the area in 1542.

Chucalissa

A group of platform and ridge mounds along the Mississippi River are the main attraction at Chucalissa (T. O. Fuller State Park, 901/785-3160, Tues.–Sat. 9 A.M.–4:30 P.M., adults $5, seniors and children $3). The mounds were once part of a Choctaw Indian community that existed between A.D. 1000 and 1550. The village was empty when Europeans arrived, and the name Chucalissa means "abandoned house."

The largest mound would have been where the chief and his family lived. The present-day museum, operated by the University of Memphis, consists of an exhibit about the Native Americans of the area and self-guided tour around the mounds and courtyard area, where games and meetings would have been held. There is also a half-mile nature trail along the bluff overlooking the river. In addition to the opening hours listed above, Chucalissa is open on Sunday afternoon during the summer months; call ahead for details.

EAST MEMPHIS

East Memphis is home to old suburbs, gracious homes, and some excellent parks and other attractions.

The Dixon

The Dixon (4339 Park Ave., 901/761-5250, www.dixon.org, Tues.–Fri. 10 A.M.–4 P.M., Sat. 10 A.M.–5 P.M., Sun. 1–5 P.M., adults $7, seniors $5, children $3), an art museum housed inside a stately Georgian-style home, has an impressive permanent collection of more than 2,000 paintings, many of them French impressionist and postimpressionist style, including works by Monet, Renoir, Degas, and Cézanne. It also mounts a half dozen special exhibits each year; previous ones have showcased the art of George Rodrigue and David Macaulay.

The Dixon is an easy place to spend several hours, immersed first in art and then in walking the paths that explore the house's 17 acres of beautifully tended gardens. There is a cutting garden, woodland garden, and formal gardens, among others.

Admission to the Dixon is free on Saturday 10 A.M.–noon.

Memphis Botanic Garden

The 100-acre Memphis Botanic Garden (750 Cherry Rd., 901/576-4100, www.memphisbotanicgarden.com, adults $5, seniors $4, children $3) is home to more than 140 different species of trees and more than two dozen specialty gardens, including a Sculpture Garden, Azalea Trail, and Iris Garden. Trails meander through the gardens, but for the greatest fun buy a handful of fish food and feed the fish and ducks that inhabit the pond at the Japanese Garden. The garden puts on a number of events, including blockbuster concerts, plant sales, and programs for children.

The Pink Palace

A good destination for families, the Pink Palace

The iris garden at the Memphis Botanic Garden blooms in springtime.

(3050 Central Ave., 901/320-6320, www.memphismuseums.org, Mon.–Sat. 9 A.M.–5 P.M., Sun. noon–5 P.M.) is a group of attractions rolled into one. The Pink Palace Museum (adults $8.25, children $5.75) is a museum about Memphis, with exhibits about the natural history of the Mid-South region and the city's development. There is a full-scale replica of the first Piggly Wiggly market, plus an exhibit about how health care became such a large part of the Memphis economy. The museum is housed within the Pink Palace Mansion, the Memphis home of Piggly Wiggly founder Clarence Saunders.

The Pink Palace is also home to the Sharpe Planetarium (adults $4.50, children $4), which is open on Saturday, and an IMAX movie theater (adults $8, children $6.25), which shows movies daily. Special package tickets are available for all the Pink Palace attractions.

Art Museum of the University of Memphis

The Art Museum of the University of Memphis (3750 Norriswood Ave., 901/678-2224, www.amum.org, free) houses excellent but small exhibits of ancient Egyptian and African art and artifacts, and a noteworthy print gallery. There are frequent special exhibitions. The museum is closed during University holidays.

Children's Museum of Memphis

You will know the Children's Museum of Memphis (2525 Central Ave., 901/458-2678, www.cmom.com, Mon.–Sat. 9 A.M.–5 P.M., Sun. noon–5 P.M., adults $8, children $7) by the large alphabet blocks outside spelling its acronym, CMOM. Bring children here for constructive and educational play: They can sit in flight simulator and real airplane cockpit, climb through the arteries of a model heart, climb a skyscraper, and more.

Lichterman Nature Center

Lichterman Nature Center (5992 Quince Rd., 901/767-7322, Tues.–Thurs. 9 A.M.–4 P.M., Fri.–Sat. 9 A.M.–5 P.M., adults $6, children $4.50) is dedicated to generating interest and enthusiasm

for the Mid-South's nature. The park encompasses some 65 acres, and visitors will enjoy seeing native trees and flowers, including dogwoods, lotus, and pine. There is a museum about the local environment, picnic facilities, and pleasant trails. Environmental education is the center's mission, and this is a popular destination for families and school groups.

TOURS
History Tours

Heritage Tours Memphis (901/527-3427, www.heritagetoursmemphis.com, $25–35) is the city's only tour company dedicated to presenting Memphis's African-American history. Operated by Memphians Elaine Turner and Joan Nelson, Heritage Tours offers black heritage, musical heritage, civil rights, and Beale Street walking tours. They can also arrange out-of-town tours to area attractions, such as the Alex Haley home in Henning, Tennessee. Most local tours cost $25 and last about three hours.

The black heritage tour starts at the W. C. Handy Home and Museum and includes a stop at the Slavehaven Underground Railroad Museum, plus narration that tells the story of black Memphians such as Ida B. Wells, Robert Church, and Tom Lee, and the events leading up to the assassination of Dr. Martin Luther King Jr. You will drive past the Mason Temple Church of God in Christ at 930 Mason Street, where Dr. King gave his famous "mountaintop" speech the night before his death.

River Tours

The **Memphis Queen Riverboat Tours** (901/527-2628, $18) leave daily at 2:30 P.M. from the Port of Memphis, located at the foot of Monroe Avenue on the riverfront. The afternoon tour lasts 90 minutes and takes you a few miles south of the city before turning around. Commentary tells some of the most famous tales of the river, but the biggest attraction of the tour is simply being on Old Man River. The views of the Memphis skyline from the water are impressive. Concessions are available onboard. The riverboats also offer dinner cruises with live music for about $35 per person.

COURTESY OF MEMPHIS CONVENTION AND VISITORS BUREAU

The *Memphis Queen* riverboat cruises the Mississippi daily.

MEMPHIS

Music Tours

Memphis just looks better from the passenger window of a 1955 Cadillac. That's as good a reason as any to call Tad Pierson for one of his **American Dream Safari** (901/527-8870, www.americandreamsafari.com) tours of Memphis. Pierson offers tours with a difference—he does not just do sightseeing, he promises experiences and memories for his guests. His tours include juke joints of Memphis, gospel churches, a Mississippi Delta day trip, a special tour for photographers, plus much more. Pierson really gets the unique appeal of Memphis, and he wants to share it with his guests.

Music fans should sign up for one of Sherman Wilmott's **Memphis Rock 'n Roll Tours** (901/359-3102, www.memphisrocktour.com), customized musical tours of Memphis. He will pick you up at any Memphis hotel and then whisk you away to some of the city's best- and least-known musical sites, such as the past and present locations of Memphis recording studios, radio stations, record stores, and even

musicians' homes. He is a fountain of music lore. If you have a special interest, speak up: Chances are that Sherman can fix you up. A former curator at the Stax museum and publisher of the *Kreature Comforts Low-Life Guide to Memphis,* Sherman recently started a partnership with Wayne Jackson of the famed Memphis Horns, who will ride along on special tours and tell firsthand stories of Memphis's musical history.

Music-themed tours are also the specialty at **Backbeat Tours** (901/272-2328, www.backbeattours.com, $25–40). You will travel on a reconditioned 1959 transit bus and be serenaded by live musicians. Tours include the Memphis Mojo Tour, which takes you to Memphis music landmarks like Sun Studio and the Stax Museum, and the Hound Dog tour, which follows in Elvis Presley's Memphis footsteps. Backbeat can also take you to Graceland and offers two walking tours of Memphis—a Memphis Ghost Tour and Haunted Pub Crawl—on Wednesday through Sunday evening for $15.

Entertainment

Memphis is a vibrant, diverse city with an entertainment scene that reflects this. Blues, rap, R&B, and gospel are just some of the types of music you can find on any given weekend. Alternative and indie rock finds a receptive audience in Memphis, as does opera, Broadway productions, and the symphony. There's always a good excuse to go out.

LIVE MUSIC AND CLUBS

Memphis may be the birthplace of the blues, but there's a lot more to the music scene than that. It's true that you can catch live blues at a Beale Street nightclub or in a city juke joint. But you can also find hard-edge rock, jazz, and acoustic music most nights of the week. The best resource for up-to-date entertainment listings is the free weekly *Memphis Flyer* (www.memphisflyer.com), which comes out on Wednesday and includes a detailed listing of club dates and concerts.

Keep in mind that big-name artists often perform at casinos in Tunica, just over the state line in Mississippi. Many of these shows are advertised in Memphis media outlets, or check out the upcoming events on the Tunica Convention and Visitors Bureau website, www.tunicamiss.com.

Blues

One of the first things you do when you get to Memphis should be to find out if the **Center for Southern Folklore** (119 S. Main St., 901/525-3655, www.southernfolklore.com, Mon.–Sat. 11 A.M.–5 P.M.) has any concerts or special activities planned during your visit. The center has been documenting and preserving traditional Memphis and Delta blues music for more than 35 years. They put on concerts and lectures, produce documentaries, offer group tours and educational programs, and organize the annual Memphis Music and Heritage Festival over Labor Day weekend. They often have live blues on Friday afternoon, and offer a variety of special shows. This is one of the best

Blues play on Beale Street seven nights a week.

places to hear authentic blues. The center has a 250-seat dining room and performance space in Peabody Place, as well as a folklore store that sells folk art, books, CDs, and hot peach cobbler, among other things. A Be Nice or Leave sign sets the tone as soon as you step into this colorful and eclectic shop, one of the best gift shops in the city. The center is a nonprofit organization, and well worth supporting.

Beale Street is ground zero for Memphis's blues music scene. While some people lament that Beale has become a sad tourist trap, it can still be a worthwhile place to spend your evening. Indeed, no other part of Memphis has as much music and entertainment packed into such a small area. On a typical night, Beale Street is full of people of all ages and races strolling from one bar to the next. Beer seems to run a close second to music as the street's prime attraction, with many bars selling

MEMPHIS JUKE JOINTS

In Memphis, there are only two reasons to go to a juke joint full of blues: because you feel good or because you feel bad. Beale Street is a reliable source seven nights a week and your visit to Memphis wouldn't be complete without checking out its scene. But if you want to sneak away from the tourist crowd and catch some homegrown talent, check out a Memphis juke joint. Live music is typical on Friday and Saturday nights and sometimes Sunday, but it gets scarce during the week. Generally music starts late (11 P.M.) and finishes early (3 A.M.).

Is it safe? Maybe not, but what is these days? Is it worth it? Most definitely yes! In fact, these clubs are far more safe and friendly than a parking lot at a shopping mall. Just be cool and come for the right reasons and you'll get home to tell the tale.

Some common-sense advice: If you're uncomfortable in a largely black crowd, don't bother. Don't be surprised if the person you've engaged in conversation sitting next to you gets called to the stage sometime during the evening and delivers a beautiful song. If you dress sexy expect results. Don't overdo the dirty dog on the dance floor. If somebody

a Memphis juke joint

© SUSANNA HENIGHAN POTTER

asks your date to dance, relax – it's bound to happen.

Remember that it's in the nature of things for these clubs to come and go. The listings below were current as of this writing, but always subject to change.

Wild Bill's (1580 Vollentine St., 901/726-5473): A legendary club in Memphis. The Patriarch himself passed away in the summer of 2007, but what he established will still carry on. The quintessential juke joint. Small, intimate, an open kitchen serving chicken wings, and ice-cold beer served in 40-ounce bottles. Home to Ms. Nikki and the Memphis Soul Survivors.

---

directly onto the street through concession windows. "Big Ass Beer" cups used by many establishments say it all.

Nearly all Beale Street bars have live music, but one of the most popular is **B. B. King's Blues Club** (139 Beale St., 901/524-5464, cover $5–7), owned by the legend himself. B. B. King performs here two or three times a year—keep your ear to the ground since the shows are not usually advertised. On other evenings, local acts and some nationally known performers take the stage. B. B. King's draws a mostly tourist crowd, but with the blues on full-throttle, you probably won't care too much.

Also on Beale Street, **Blues City Cafe** (138 Beale St., 901/526-3637, cover $3–5) books blues plus a variety of other acts, including do-wop, Zydeco, R&B, funk, and "high impact

rock-a-billy." The café-restaurant is one of the most popular on Beale Street, and the nightclub is right next door. **Rum Boogie Cafe** (182 Beale St., 901/528-0151, cover $3–5) has an award-winning house band, James Covan and the Boogie Blues Band, that performs most evenings.

Morgan Freeman is part owner of the **Ground Zero Blues Club** (158 Lt. George W. Lee St., 901/522-0130, cover varies), which opened in 2008 next door to the Westin, a few blocks off Beale Street. A satellite of the original Ground Zero in Clarksdale, Mississippi, this club offers real-deal blues seven nights a week.

Jazz

If you want a break from the blues, **King's Palace Cafe** (162 Beale St., 901/521-1851)

CC's Blues Club (1427 Thomas St., 901/526-5566): More upscale. More mirrors. But a great dance floor and don't you dare come underdressed.

One Block North (645 Marble Ave., 901/525-7505): Friday nights only for live music. Hard to find and that's why you'll be the only tourists there.

Executive Inn (3222 Airways, at the intersection with Brooks Rd., 901/332-3800): Don Valentine is the drummer and bandleader and everybody wants to sit in. This is where Preston Shannon comes to hang out. More soul than blues, but when Preacher Man closes the show you know you'll be satisfied.

Handy's Blues Hall (182 Beale St., 901/528-0150): New Orleans has Preservation Hall. Memphis has Handy's Blues Hall. Everyone bad-raps Beale Street and its jangly tourism scene. But if you catch it on a good night when Dr Feelgood warms up his harmonica and you look around the room at the memorabilia on the walls, you could be in a joint at the end of a country road in Mississippi.

The Blue Worm (1405 Airways Dr., 901/327-7947): When a legendary juke joint band gets old and disintegrates, this is where it ends up. The Fieldstones have been *the* band in Memphis since the early '60s. Now it's down to Wilroy Sanders, the Last Living Bluesman. The house band can get behind anybody and make them a superstar, for one glorious song.

Big S Bar and Grill (1179 Dunnavant Ave., 901/775-9127): They say blues is a feeling. The Big S doesn't have live music, but if you want to sink into the atmosphere of a bar that's dark with mystery and history plus the warmest vibe in town, come on home. Blues DJ on Sunday nights and the jukebox is a veritable encyclopedia of blues.

The Boss (912 Jackson Ave., 901/522-8883): Thursday nights only. Ever heard the overused term "best-kept secret in town"? Jesse Dotson on piano. Leroy Hodges on bass. Roy Cunningham on drums. An array of singers like Preacher Man, Bill Coday, O. T. Sykes. Why wait for the weekend?

Contributed by Tad Pierson, owner and operator of American Dream Safari (www.americandreamsafari.com) and purveyor of true-life expeditions into Memphis and Mississippi

specializes in jazz. Lots of wood paneling and red paint makes the bar and restaurant warm and welcoming. This is an unpretentious place to have a meal or listen to live music. There is a $1 per person entertainment charge when you sit at a table.

In South Main, **Café Soul** (492 S. Main St., 901/859-0557, cover varies) has live jazz most nights of the week, good for a relaxing evening after browsing the galleries.

Rock

Still on Beale Street, **Alfred's** (197 Beale St., 901/525-3711, cover $5 Fri. and Sat.) has rock acts five nights a week. On Sunday evening, the 17-piece Memphis Jazz Orchestra takes the stage. The dance floor at Alfred's is one of the best on Beale Street.

One of Beale Street's most historic nightclubs, **The New Daisy** (330 Beale St., 901/525-8979, cover $5 and up) books rock 'n' roll, independent, and a few R&B acts. There are shows most nights of the week; call ahead or check the entertainment listings for a schedule. The Daisy is an all-ages club, and many shows attract a young audience.

Off Beale Street, the **Hi-Tone Cafe** (1913 Poplar Ave., 901/278-8663, cover varies) is probably the best place to see live music in town. The Hi-Tone books all kinds of acts, from high-energy rockers to soulful acoustic acts. They are really committed to bringing good live music to Memphis. The cover charge for local shows is a few bucks, but tickets for bigger-name acts can run $20 and more. The bar serves respectable burgers and finger foods, excellent martinis, and lots of beer.

Also in midtown, **The Buccaneer** (1368 Monroe, 901/278-0909, cover varies) books rock acts most days a week. Cover charge rarely tops $5.

BARS
Downtown
You can head to Beale Street for a night out, even if you're not that into blues. **Coyote Ugly** (326 Beale St., 901/888-8459) attracts a youthful crowd seven days a week. The dance floor here is hot.

The best place to grab a beer downtown is the **Beale Street Tap Room** (168 Beale St., 901/527-4392). With more than 30 beers on tap, this is a great choice for beer lovers. The service is friendly and low-key, and regulars have their own mug.

Off Beale Street, the **Peabody Hotel Memphis** (149 Union Ave., 901/529-4000) may be the best place to enjoy a relaxing drink. The lobby bar offers good service, comfortable seats, and an unrivaled atmosphere.

In Peabody Place about a block from Beale Street, **The Flying Saucer Draught Emporium** (130 Peabody Pl., 901/523-7468) draws a lively happy-hour crowd. The bar offers more than 75 draft beers, plus cocktails and wine. Grab a seat along the windows and watch downtown Memphis come alive as the sun sets.

Also in Peabody Place, **Dan McGuiness** (150 Peabody Pl., 901/527-8500) offers Irish beers and sports on the telly.

In the South Main district, **Ernestine and Hazel's** (531 S. Main St., 901/523-9754) is one of Memphis's most celebrated pit stops for cold drinks and a night out. Once a brothel, Ernestine and Hazel's now has one of the best jukeboxes in town. Take a seat upstairs in one of the old brothel rooms and watch South Main Street below.

For a departure from the usual bar scene, head to the smoke-free **High Point Pinch** (333 N. Main St., 901/619-0061). Also in the Pinch neighborhood, **Precious Cargo Coffeehouse** (381 N. Main St., 901/578-8446) has a lineup of eclectic music every Friday evening starting about 9 P.M.

Midtown
The **Young Avenue Deli** (2119 Young Ave., 901/278-3123) is a friendly neighborhood bar that books occasional live acts to perform. Located in the Cooper-Young area, Young Avenue Deli has hundreds of different beers on tap or in bottles. The bar attracts a diverse crowd, from young hipsters to older neighborhood denizens.

A favorite place for music, pool, and a night out in midtown is the **Blue Monkey** (2012 Madison Ave., 901/272-2583). Grab a pizza and a beer, shoot some pool, and then rock out to the live band.

Murphy's (1589 Madison Ave., 901/726-4193) is a neighborhood bar with a nice patio, and **Zinnie's Old Place** (1688 Madison Ave., 901/726-5004) is a familiar haunt for many midtowners who are looking for a quiet spot to enjoy a cold one.

Perfect for a business date or after-work pit stop, **The Grove Grill** (4550 Poplar Ave., 901/818-9951) is popular with businesspeople and office-types.

Two of Memphis's best sports bars are found in the eastern reaches of the city. **Brookhaven Pub and Grill** (695 W. Brookhaven Cir., 901/680-8118) has big-screen plasma televisions, great beer on tap, and lots of fans. Tuesday night is quiz night. **Gill's Bar & Grill** (551 S. Highland, 901/458-2787), near the University of Memphis, specializes in cold beers and sports and has a great happy hour.

GAY AND LESBIAN NIGHTLIFE
Many gay and lesbian clubs don't get going until late in the night, after other clubs have closed.

Metro Memphis (1349 Autumn Ave., 901/274-8010, cover varies) is a gay bar and dance club that attracts both gay and straight patrons. The city's largest dance floor may be found at **Backstreet Memphis** (2018 Court Ave., 901/276-5522, cover varies), a midtown club that has light shows, drag shows, karaoke, and other high-energy entertainment.

A nightclub institution in midtown, **J Wags Bar** (1268 Madison Ave., 901/278-4313, cover varies) doesn't usually get going until the wee hours, after other mainstream clubs have closed.

Attracting mostly women patrons, **Madison Flame** (1588 Madison Ave., 901/278-9839, cover varies) has a popular karaoke night.

THE ARTS

Memphis has a growing arts scene. The **Greater Memphis Arts Council** (901/578-2787, www.memphisartscouncil.com) provides funding for more than 20 local arts groups, and is a good source of information about upcoming events.

Major arts venues include the **Cannon Center for the Performing Arts** (255 N. Main St., 901/576-1201, www.thecannoncenter.com) and the **Orpheum Theatre** (Main and Beale Sts., 901/525-3000, www.orpheummemphis.com). They regularly book major artists and Broadway performances.

Theater

For theater, check out **Playhouse on the Square** (51 S. Cooper St., 901/726-4656, www.playhouseonthesquare.com). This dynamic Memphis institution serves as home to several of the city's acting companies and puts on between 15 and 20 different performances every year. It also offers theater classes, school performances, and pay-what-you-can shows. The playhouse also screens classic movies on the first Sunday of each month.

Theatre Memphis (630 Perkins Ext., 901/682-8323, www.theatrememphis.org) is a community theater company that has been in existence since the 1920s. They stage about 12 shows annually at their theater in midtown. **TheatreWorks** (2085 Monroe Ave., 901/274-7139, www.theatreworks.org) encourages off-beat and new theater with organizations including Our Own Voice Theatre Troupe, the Memphis Black Repertory Theatre, and Playwright's Forum.

Music

The **Memphis Symphony Orchestra** (3100 Walnut Grove Rd., 901/324-3627, www.memphissymphony.org) puts on a varied calendar of performances year-round in its home at the Cannon Center for the Performing Arts at 2155 North Main Street. The symphony was founded in 1952, and today has more than 850 musicians, staff, and volunteers.

Opera

Opera Memphis (6745 Wolf River Blvd., 901/257-3100, www.operamemphis.org) performs at the historic Orpheum Theatre on Beale Street.

Dance

Ballet Memphis (901/737-7322, www.balletmemphis.org) performs classical dance at the Orpheum and other nontraditional venues throughout the city. The **New Ballet Ensemble** (901/726-9225, www.newballet.org) puts on performances around the city with "dancers in do-rags as well as tights," according to the *Commercial Appeal*.

Project Motion (901/274-7139, www.projectmotiondance.org) is a contemporary dance collective that performs at Theatre Works at 2085 Monroe Avenue.

Cinemas

There are a half dozen multiscreen movie theaters in and around Memphis, including one at Peabody Place downtown. For independent movies, try **Malco's Paradiso** (584 S. Mendenhall Rd., 901/682-1754, www.malco.com) or **Studio on the Square** (2105 Court St., 901/725-71751, www.overtonsquare.com). In the summer, check out the **Orpheum** (203 S. Main St., 901/525-7800) for classic movies, and the **Summer Quartet Drive-In** (5310 Summer Ave., 901/767-4320) for a drive-in experience.

EVENTS
Spring

Memphians celebrate their African heritage over a long April weekend in mid-April. **Africa in April** (901/947-2133, www.africainapril.org)

honors a specific country in Africa each year; activities include cooking, storytelling, music, and a parade. The festival takes place at Church Park on the east end of Beale Street.

In early May, the Memphis-based Blues Foundation hosts the annual **Handy Awards** (www.blues.org), the Grammys of the blues world.

Memphis in May (www.memphisinmay. org), the city's largest annual event, is really three major festivals rolled into one. The **Beale Street Music Festival,** which takes place at Tom Lee Park on the river during the first weekend of May, kicks things off with a celebration of Memphis music. Expect a lot of wow performers, plus many more up-and-coming talents. The festival has grown over the years, and it is now a three-day event with four stages of music going simultaneously. In addition to music, the festival offers excellent people-watching, lots of barbecue, cold beer, and festivity. You can buy daily tickets, or a three-day pass for the whole weekend.

In mid-May, attention turns to the **World Championship Barbeque Cooking Contest,** a celebration of pork, pigs, and barbecue that takes place in Tom Lee Park. In addition to the barbecue judging, there is entertainment, hog-calling contests, and other piggy antics. If you're not part of a competing team (or friends with one) you can buy barbecue from vendors who set up in the park.

Finally, at the end of the month, there is the **Memphis International Festival,** which pays tribute to a different country each year with presentations about its music, food, culture, and history.

Book your hotel rooms early for Memphis in May, since many hotels, especially those downtown, fill up.

Founded by African Americans in 1936 as an alternative to the all-white Cotton Carnival, the **Kemet Jubilee** (www.memphiskemetjubilee.com) was originally known as the Cotton Makers Jubilee. Today, the highlight of the jubilee, which takes place in May, is the parade of marching bands and costumed troupes that runs along 2nd Street in downtown Memphis.

Memphis's World Championship Barbeque Cooking Contest in May celebrates the city's favorite food: barbecue.

COURTESY OF MEMPHIS CONVENTION AND VISITORS BUREAU

Summer

Carnival Memphis (901/458-2500, www.carnivalmemphis.org), the renamed Cotton Carnival, is now racially integrated and takes place in June. The Carnival features a parade and fireworks.

The annual candlelight vigil at Graceland on August 15, the anniversary of Elvis's death, has grown into a whole week of activities throughout Memphis. More than 30,000 people visit Graceland during **Elvis Week** (www.elvisweek.com), and during the vigil his most adoring fans walk solemnly up the Graceland drive to pay their respects at his grave. Special concerts, tribute shows, and movies are shown during the week, as the city celebrates its most famous export even more than usual.

Fall

Organized by the Center for Southern Folklore, the **Memphis Music and Heritage Festival** (901/525-3655, www.memphis-musicandheritagefestival.com) held over

MEMPHIS CARNIVAL

Hoping to revive a flagging cotton industry in the early 1930s, cotton factors established the Cotton Carnival in 1931. Modeled after Mardi Gras, the weeklong celebration featured beauty pageants, parades, fireworks, and lots of cotton products on display and sale. The Cotton Carnival celebrated the Old South, its good and bad components. Black men were used to pull the floats, but blacks were otherwise not allowed to take part.

So, in 1936, African-American leaders founded the Beale Street Cotton Makers' Jubilee, which featured talent shows, beauty pageants, parades, and sporting events, many with a theme that celebrated West African civilizations, as well as cotton. In the 1960s, the NAACP protested the Jubilee for its celebration of cotton, and by implication, slavery, but the tradition continued.

In 1981, African Americans were invited for the first time to enter the annual Cotton Carnival parade. Today, both the Cotton Carnival and the Cotton Makers' Jubilee, now called the Memphis Kemet Jubilee, continue, although they are no longer racially segregated.

Labor Day weekend sticks close to the roots of Memphis music. Performers include gospel singers, bona fide bluesmen and women, rock-a-billy superstars, and much more. Performances take place in the center's shop and concert hall on Main Street, making them more intimate than other blockbuster music festivals.

End-of-summer fairs are a tradition for southern and rural communities all over the United States. The 10-day **Mid-South Fair** (www.midsouthfair.org) in September is a bonanza of attractions: livestock shows, rodeos, agricultural judging, concerts, beauty pageants, exhibitions, carnival rides, funnel cakes, and cotton candy. In 2008 it moved from the Mid-South Fairgrounds in southeast Memphis to a 150-acre site across the road from the Tunica, Mississippi, Welcome Center, about 30 miles from Memphis.

In mid-September, the Cooper-Young neighborhood throws its annual jamboree at the **Cooper-Young Festival** (www.cooperyoungfestival.com). There is an arts and crafts fair, live music, and food vendors at this street carnival.

Winter

Taking place over the weekend closest to Elvis Presley's January 8 birthday, the **Elvis Birthday Celebration** (www.elvis.com) draws Elvis fans with special performances, dance parties, and a ceremony at Graceland proclaiming Elvis Presley Day.

The two-day **Beale Street Zydeco Music Festival** (901/526-0110) takes place over the last weekend in February and features more than 20 bands paying tribute to Cajun music.

SHOPPING
Gifts and Souvenirs

Any of the half-dozen gift shops along Beale Street sell gifts and souvenirs of the city. **Memphis Music** (149 Beale St., 901/526-5047) has a good selection of CDs and DVDs for music fans. For a unique gift or something practical for yourself, **A. Schwab** (163 Beale St., 901/523-9782) is your best choice, and lots of fun to boot.

Another good place for gift shopping is the **Center for Southern Folklore** (119 S. Main St., 901/525-3655), which has books, art, and music focusing on the region. All of the city's museums have good gift shops, including the **National Civil Rights Museum, Stax Museum of American Soul Music,** and **Sun Studio,** where everything is emblazoned with the distinctive yellow Sun label.

If you have a car, head out to **Shangri-La Records** (1916 Madison Ave., 901/274-1916), the city's best record store, which specializes in Memphis music.

Bookstores

The only downtown bookstore is the aptly

named **Downtown Books** (152 Madison Ave., 901/577-6600), which trades in used books from its premises in the basement below the Memphis Coffee Exchange.

You'll need a car to reach the city's major bookstores, however. **Burke's Books** (938 S. Cooper, 901/278-7484), in the Cooper-Young district east of midtown, specializes in used and antiquarian books. **Davis-Kidd Booksellers** (387 Perkins Ext., 901/683-9801), a Tennessee-based independent bookseller, is in Laurelwood Shopping Center and is your best choice for new books. Davis-Kidd has weekly book signings and a café.

Bookstar (3402 Poplar Ave., 901/323-9332) in midtown is an outlet store for new books.

Art

For art boutiques and galleries, head south to the South Main arts district, where you will find galleries including **D'Edge Art and Unique Treasures** (550 S. Main St., 901/521-0054), which has contemporary folk art, and **Robinson Gallery/Archives** (44 Huling Ave., 901/683-1132), a photography gallery.

On the last Friday of each month the trolleys are free, the galleries stay open, and hundreds of arts-minded Memphians head to South Main to mingle into the night. For a directory of all South Main galleries, contact the South Main Association (901/578-7262, www.southmainmemphis.org).

Antiques

Head out Central Avenue, to the area between Cooper and East Parkway, for the greatest concentration of antiques stores. **Flashback** (2304 Central Ave., 901/272-2304) sells both vintage furniture and clothes, including a whole lot of Levi's jeans. **Louedau's** (2174 Young Ave., 901/722-9681) has fabric, lace, and vintage baby clothes. Another good choice is **Toad Hall Antiques** (2129 Central Ave., 901/726-0755), easy to find because of a brightly painted mural on the outside of the building.

Thrift Stores

In a city where vintage never went out of style, you can expect excellent thrift stores. The biggest and best is **AmVets** (2426 Elvis Presley Blvd., 901/775-5018). You can also try the **Junior League of Memphis Thrift Store** (3586 Summer Ave., 901/327-4777).

The most colorful shopping experience in Memphis is found at **The Memphis Flea Market—The Big One** (955 Maxwell Early Blvd., 901/276-3532), which takes place on the third weekend of each month at the Mid-South Fairgrounds. Between 800 and 1,000 vendors turn up each month with housewares, clothing, computers, jewelry, antiques, yard art, and so much more. Between 20,000 and 25,000 people come to shop. Admission is free, but you must pay to park.

Shopping Malls

Memphis proudly welcomed major retail back downtown with the opening of **Peabody Place** (901/261-7529), just a block away from Beale Street, with a Tower Records, Gap, and Victoria's Secret, as well as a movie theater and several restaurants in the food court.

The most upscale shopping mall in the Memphis area is **Wolfchase Galleria** (2760 N. Germantown Pkwy., 901/372-9409). Located in Cordova, an east-lying suburb now consumed by Memphis sprawl, the galleria celebrated its 10th anniversary in 2007. It is aging gracefully, and still boasts some of the most exclusive retailers in the city, including Brooks Brothers, Abercrombie & Fitch, and bebe. Department stores at the mall include Macy's, Dillard's, Sears, and JC Penney. You can take either exit 16 or 18 off I-40 to get to Wolfchase Galleria.

Also in Germantown, **The Shops of Saddle Creek** (West St. at Poplar Ave., 901/761-2571) has Williams Sonoma, Banana Republic, and an Apple computer store, among others.

Closer to the city center, **Oak Court Mall** (4465 Poplar Ave., 901/682-8928) was the location of the very first Starbucks in Tennessee. It is also consistently voted Memphians' favorite mall, no doubt because it offers a good selection of stores in a pleasant atmosphere, and it's relatively close to town. Department stores at Oak Court include Macy's and Dillard's; the mall also has Aveda, Jos A. Bank, Banana Republic, and dozens more stores.

And if that's not enough for you, head across the road to **Laurelwood Shopping Center** (Poplar Ave. at Perkins Ext., 901/794-6022), where you'll find specialty clothing and shoe boutiques, as well as Davis-Kidd Booksellers, Memphis's best large bookstore.

In South Memphis, **Southland Mall** (1215 Southland Mall, 901/346-1210) is Memphis's oldest mall. Built in 1966, Southland soldiers on. There is a Sears, as well as specialty shops including Radio Shack and Bath & Body Works.

Outlet Shopping

You can buy directly from name-brand retailers at rock-bottom prices at the **Lakeland Factory Outlet Mall** (3536 Canada Rd., 901/386-3180). Located at the Canada Road exit off I-40, the mall boasts a number of big-name retailers, including Bass, Van Heusen, Dress Barn, Toy Liquidators, and Old Time Pottery, which sells dinnerware and other pottery.

Sports and Recreation

With a professional basketball team, excellent downtown baseball club, and lots of city parks, Memphis is a great city in which to watch sports or get active yourself.

PARKS
Downtown

Named for the legendary blues composer, **Handy Park,** on Beale Street, between 3rd Street and Rufus Thomas Boulevard, seems a tad out of place among Beale's nightclubs and restaurants. But the park is a site of historic importance, if only because of the statue of its namesake that guards its gates. The park hosts occasional outdoor concerts and festivals, and at other times you will find places to sit and a handful of vendors.

Uptown

Tom Lee Park, a long, narrow grassy park that faces the river, is a popular venue for summertime festivals and events. It is also used year-round for walking and jogging, and by people who simply want to look out at the Mississippi River. The park is named for Tom Lee, an African-American man who saved the lives of 32 people when the steamboat they were on sank in the river in 1925. Lee, who pulled people out of the river and into his boat, "Zev," could not even swim. A dated monument erected at the park in 1954 calls Lee "a very worthy negro."

Located on the northern side of downtown Memphis, **Court Square,** three blocks from the waterfront along Court Avenue, is a pleasant city park surrounded by historic buildings. Court Square is one of four parks that was included when the city was first planned in 1819. There are benches and trees, and it is a wireless Internet hot spot.

Confederate Park, located on Front Street between Court and Jefferson Streets, commemorates Confederate soldiers who died in the Battle of Memphis, as well as other war dead. There is a statue of Jefferson Davis in the center of the park. This is where many Memphians gathered to watch the Battle of Memphis in 1862, and it remains a good place to view the river below.

Midtown

Located in midtown Memphis, **Overton Park** (1928 Poplar Ave.) is the best all-around park the city has to offer. This 342-acre park has a nine-hole golf course, nature trails through the woods, bike trails, an outdoor amphitheater (called the Overton Park Shell, which is undergoing a major restoration), and lots of green, open spaces. The park shares space with the Memphis Zoo and

MEMPHIS

NATHAN BEDFORD FORREST

Nathan Bedford Forrest is one of the most celebrated and reviled historical figures in Tennessee. An accomplished Confederate cavalry commander and the first grand wizard of the Ku Klux Klan, Forrest has come to symbolize the Old South.

Forrest was born in 1821 in Chapel Hill, a small town in Marshall County in Middle Tennessee. At the age of 16, Forrest's blacksmith father died and the young man became the head of his family. He had a mere six months of formal education in his lifetime, yet became a successful businessman, primarily as a plantation owner and slave trader.

Forrest was a staunch believer in the Southern cause, and when Tennessee seceded from the Union in 1861, he enlisted as a private in the Tennessee Mounted Rifles, together with his younger brother and 15-year-old son.

In a peculiar twist, Forrest offered freedom to his 44 slaves at the outbreak of the Civil War, if they would fight for the Confederacy. All agreed, and 43 reportedly served faithfully until the end of the war.

Forrest was daring on the battlefield, often taking great risks to avoid capture and defeat. Historian Brian S. Wills wrote: "His ferocity as a warrior was almost legendary.... Forrest understood, perhaps better than most, the basic premise of war: 'War means fighting and fighting means killing.'"

Forrest was involved in dozens of battles — small and large — during the war. In February 1862 he led his men out of Fort Donelson rather than surrender. He was wounded at Shiloh and fought at Chickamauga. In May 1863, he outmaneuvered a stronger Union force in northern Alabama by fooling Col. Abel Streight into believing that Forrest had more men than he did.

Forrest's victory at Fort Pillow in April 1864 was tarnished by the deaths of so many black Union soldiers, allegedly killed after they surrendered.

His victory at Brice's Cross Roads, in Mississippi, where Forrest defeated a much larger force of Union infantry and cavalry in June 1864, is believed by many to be his greatest success.

Forrest ended the Civil War as lieutenant general in command of cavalry in Alabama, Mississippi, and East Louisiana. His last battle at Gainsville, Alabama, in May 1865 ended in surrender.

Following the war, Forrest struggled to adapt to the changes it had brought. He supported the Ku Klux Klan in hopes of restoring the conservative white power structure that existed prior to the war and served as the Klan's first, and only, grand wizard.

His business dealings floundered. Forrest lost a fortune in the railroad industry and he spent his last years running a prison farm and living in a log cabin.

In his last years, Forrest seemed to reconsider many of his views on racial equality. In 1875 he spoke to a local group of freedmen, saying, "I came to meet you as friends, and welcome you to the white people. I want you to come nearer to us. When I can serve you I will do so. We have but one flag, one country; let us stand together. We may differ in color, but not in sentiment." Forrest kissed the cheek of an African-American women who handed him a bouquet of flowers, a gesture of intimacy unknown in that era.

Forrest died in Memphis in October 1877. He was buried at Elmwood Cemetery, but later re-interred at Forrest Park, built in his honor, in midtown Memphis.

In the years since the civil rights movement, many people have questioned Forrest's greatness. In 2005, there was an effort to move the statue over Forrest's grave and rename Forrest Park, and others have tried to get a bust of Forrest removed from the Tennessee House of Representatives chamber; both efforts failed.

the Memphis Brooks Museum of Art, making the area a popular destination for city residents and visitors.

The Madison Avenue trolley passes **Forrest Park,** along Madison Avenue, between North Manassas and North Dunlap Streets, an ample city park dedicated to the memory of the controversial Nathan Bedford Forrest. Forrest, a slave-trader, Confederate, and the first grand wizard of the Ku Klux Klan, has an uncomfortable position of prominence in Memphis and the whole of western Tennessee. Both he and his wife are buried in the park.

East Memphis

Located near the University of Memphis and Oak Court Mall, **Audubon Park** (4161 Park Ave.) has a golf course, tennis courts, walking trails, and other sports facilities. The Memphis Botanic Garden is located here.

Memphians celebrate the fact that their largest city park, **Shelby Farms,** is five times the size of New York's Central Park. But the fact is that Shelby Farms is underused, since most of its 4,500 acres are pleasantly undeveloped. There are plans to improve the park by adding more recreational facilities, but for now it is a diamond in the rough. Come here to go mountain biking, horseback riding, inline skating, walking, or running along some of the many trails. You can also fish, raft, canoe, or sail on any of the park's six lakes. There is a wheelchair-accessible trail, areas for picnicking, and a shooting range. Shelby Farms was originally set aside to be the county penal farm, and although it was not used in this way, the county jail is found on the western edge of the park. Shelby Farms is located on the eastern side of the city, just outside the I-40/I-240 loop that circles Memphis. It is easily accessible from Exits 12 and 14 off I-40, and exit 13 off I-240. Or follow Walnut Grove Road from midtown.

South Memphis

Southwest of the city center, about 15 minutes' drive from the airport, is **T. O. Fuller State Park** (1500 Mitchell Rd., 901/543-7581). The visitors

center here is open weekdays 8 A.M.–4:40 P.M. Amenities at the 1,138-acre park include sheltered picnic areas, tennis courts, a golf course, swimming pool ($3), basketball courts, softball field, six miles of hiking trails, and camping facilities. T. O. Fuller State Park was the first state park east of the Mississippi River open to African Americans, and the second in the nation.

BIKING

A few brave souls use bicycles to get around Memphis, but most cyclists in the city bike as a form of recreation. The City of Memphis has established five bike routes that circle the city and various neighborhoods. These routes are marked and have designated parking and restroom facilities at the start. They are not bike paths—you share the road with cars—and normal safety measures are necessary.

The **Memphis Hightailers Bicycle Club** (www.memphishightailers.com) organizes frequent rides for various levels, with distances ranging from 20 to 100 miles. In addition, there are rides leaving every Saturday at 8 A.M. and Sunday at 9 A.M. from the Super-Lo parking lot at Southern Avenue and Colonial Street.

For bike rentals, gear, and advice about riding in and around the city, go to **Peddler Bike Shop** (575 S. Highland, 901/327-4833, www.peddlerbikeshop.com), where owner Hal Mabray will happily help you get geared up to ride. A used-bike rental will cost about $25 per day, while a souped-up version can run $50 and up.

There are a number of parks near Memphis that are bike-friendly. **Meeman-Shelby Forest State Park** north of the city has five miles of paved bike paths, and cyclists use the main park roads for more extensive riding. Bicyclists will also find trails at **Shelby Farms.**

It is also noteworthy that the **Mississippi River Trail,** a bicycle route that will eventually run from the headwaters of the Mississippi River in Minnesota to the Gulf of Mexico, runs from Reelfoot Lake in northeastern Tennessee, through Memphis, and on to Mississippi. For maps and details, go to www.mississippirivertrail.org.

GOLF

The City of Memphis operates award-winning 18-hole golf courses at **Audubon Park** (4160 Park Ave., 901/683-6941) with gently rolling hills; **Fox Meadows** (3064 Clarke Rd., 901/362-0232), which is easy to walk but with several challenging holes; **Galloway Park** (3815 Walnut Grove, 901/685-7805); **Davy Crockett Golf Course** (4380 Rangeline Rd., 901/368-3375); and **Pine Hill Park** (1005 Alice Ave., 901/775-9434), a great course for walkers.

There are two public nine-hole courses: one at **Riverside Park** (465 S. Parkway W., 901/576-4260) and one at **Overton Park** (2080 Poplar Ave., 901/725-9905). Greens fees on the public courses are under $20.

One of the best-kept golf secrets in town is the 18-hole par-71 course at **T. O. Fuller State Park** (1500 W. Mitchell Rd., 901/543-7771) south of downtown.

TENNIS

The City operates public tennis courts at several parks, including **Bert Ferguson Park** (8505 Trinity), **Gaisman Park** (4221 Macon), **Glenview** (1813 Southern), **Martin Luther King Jr. Park** (South Pkwy. at Riverside Dr.), and **University Park** (University at Edward).

There are also four public indoor/outdoor tennis complexes: **Bellevue** (1310 S. Bellevue Blvd., 901/774-7199), **Leftwich** (4145 Southern, 901/685-7907), **Whitehaven** (Finley Rd., 901/332-0546), and **Wolbrecht** (1645 Ridgeway, 901/767-2889). Fees vary per facility; call in advance for information and court reservations.

SWIMMING

The City of Memphis operates a dozen outdoor pools that are open from June to August, and several indoor pools open year-round. Public outdoor pools are open Monday–Saturday noon–6 P.M., and admission is free. The outdoor pools include **L. E. Brown Pool** (617 S. Orleans, 901/527-3620) in southeastern Memphis; **Lester Pool** (317 Tillman Rd., 901/323-2261) in eastern Memphis; **Riverview Pool** (182 Joubert Rd., 901/948-7609) at Kansas Park in south Memphis; and **Willow Pool** (4777 Willow Rd., 901/763-2917).

Two indoor pools are open to the general public: the **Bickford Aquatic Center** (235 Henry Ave., 901/578-3732, Mon.–Fri. 8 A.M.–6 P.M.) and **Hickory Hill Aquatic Center** (3910 Ridgeway Rd., 901/566-9685, Mon.–Fri. 6 A.M.–9 P.M., Sat. 9 A.M.–2 P.M.). Admission to either pool is $5 per day or $8 for a weekly pass, although there are special free swim periods each day. The pools are closed on Sunday.

GYMS

Out-of-towners can get a day pass to the **Fogelman Downtown YMCA** (245 Madison Ave., 901/527-9622) for $10 and use the indoor pool and track and extensive gym facilities. City residents can buy one of the membership packages.

SPECTATOR SPORTS
Basketball

In 2001, Memphis realized the dream of many in the Mid-South when the Vancouver Grizzlies announced they would be moving south. The NBA team played its first two seasons in Memphis at the Pyramid before the massive $250 million FedEx Forum opened for the 2004–2005 season. The arena is one of the largest in the NBA, and hosts frequent concerts and performances by major artists.

The **Grizzlies** have yet to achieve any major titles, and attendance has been lagging. Ticket prices range from under $20 to several hundred dollars. For ticket information, contact the FedEx Forum box office (191 Beale St., 901/205-2640, Monday–Friday 10 A.M.–5:30 P.M., www.fedex.com). The NBA season runs from October to April.

The **University of Memphis Tigers** surprised many in 2008 by making it all the way to the NCAA Championship. The team's remarkable 38–2 season brought new energy and excitement to the University's basketball program.

You can watch Tigers basketball from November to April at FedEx Forum. Tickets

AutoZone Park is home to the AAA Memphis Redbirds, a Cardinals affiliate.

COURTESY OF MEMPHIS REDBIRDS

are available from the FedEx Forum box office, or contact University of Memphis Athletics (www.gotigersgo.com) for more information.

Baseball

From April to October, the **Memphis Redbirds** (901/721-6000, www.memphisredbirds.com, $6–20) play AAA ball at beautiful AutoZone Park in downtown Memphis. The stadium is bounded by Union Avenue, Madison Avenue, and 3rd Street, and is convenient to dozens of downtown hotels and restaurants. The Redbirds are an affiliate of the St. Louis Cardinals. Cheap tickets ($6) buy you a seat on the grassy berm, or you can pay a little more for seats in the stadium or boxes.

The Redbirds are owned by a nonprofit organization that also operates a number of community and youth programs in the city.

Racing

The **Memphis Motorsports Park** (550 Victory Ln., 901/358-7223, www.memphis-motorsports.com) is located a short drive from downtown Memphis in Millington, northeast of the city center. The park includes a 0.75-mile NASCAR oval, a 0.25-mile drag racing strip, and a 1.77-mile road course. It hosts some 200 race events every year, including a stop in the annual Busch Series races.

Millington is located about 30 minutes' drive north of Memphis.

Ice Hockey

The **Riverkings** (662/342-1735, $10–21) play minor-league ice hockey at the DeSoto Civic Center at 4650 Venture Drive in Southaven, Mississippi, about 20 miles south of Memphis.

MEMPHIS

Accommodations

There are thousands of cookie-cutter hotel rooms in Memphis, but travelers would be wise to look past major chains. If you can afford it, choose to stay in downtown Memphis. With the city at your doorstep, you'll have a better experience both day and night. Downtown is also where you'll find the most distinctive accommodations, including fine luxury hotels, charming inns, and an antebellum guest home.

Budget travelers have their pick of major chain hotels; the farther from the city center, the cheaper the room. Beware very good deals, however, since you may find yourself in sketchy neighborhoods. There is a campground with tent and RV sites within a 15-minute drive of downtown at T. O. Fuller State Park.

DOWNTOWN
$150-200

The ◖ **Talbot Heirs Guesthouse** (99 S. 2nd St., 901/527-9772, www.talbothouse.com, $130–250) in the heart of downtown offers a winning balance of comfort and sophistication. Each of the inn's nine rooms has its own unique decor—from cheerful red walls to black-and-white chic. All rooms are thoughtfully outfitted with a full kitchen and modern bathroom, television, radio and CD player, sitting area, desk and high-speed Internet. Little extras like the refrigerator stocked for breakfast go a long way, as does the cheerful yet efficient welcome provided by proprietors Tom and Sandy Franck. Book early since the Talbot Heirs is often full, especially during peak summer months.

Until the Westin at Beale Street opened in 2007, the **Hampton Inn & Suites** (175 Peabody Pl., 901/260-4000, www.bealestreetsuites.hamptoninn.com, $175) was the only hotel less than a block from Beale Street. The Hampton has 144 standard rooms, with high-speed Internet and standard hotel accommodations. The 30 suites ($250) have kitchens and separate living quarters.

Over $200

For several years, the Hunt-Phelan Home was a museum. Now, it is an inn and restaurant, and it provides the most unique accommodations in Memphis. ◖ **The Inn at Hunt Phelan** (533 Beale St., 901/525-8225, www.huntphelan.com, $180–300) has five rooms in the old home, plus six condo-style suites in an adjacent property. Some of the rooms have kitchens and sitting rooms; all have private baths. The Hunt-Phelan Home was built in 1828 and served as Ulysses S. Grant's headquarters while he was in Memphis during the Civil War. After the war, it was a Freedman's Bureau. Although totally modern in amenities, the rooms have been decorated in keeping with the house's history, giving the property a feeling of elegance unmatched by any other Memphis hotel. It is located about three blocks east of Beale Street in a mixed residential and commercial area.

In 2007, Memphis welcomed the **Westin Memphis** (170 Lee Ave., 901/334-5900, $220–300), located across the street from FedEx Forum and one block from Beale Street. The hotel's 203 guest rooms are plush and modern, each with a work desk, high-speed Internet, mp3-player docking station, and super-comfortable beds. The location can be noisy when Beale Street is in full swing.

Plans are afoot for a Hyatt Regency hotel at One Beale (www.onebeale.com), a $175 million mixed-use development that would sit on the riverfront at the head of Beale Street. If condo sales and other financing come through, then this would be Memphis's most luxurious hotel.

UPTOWN
$100-150

The most affordable downtown accommodations are in chain hotels. One of the best choices is the **Sleep Inn at Court Square** (40 N. Front St., 901/522-9700, $100–150), with 124 simple but clean and well-maintained rooms. Guests have access to a small fitness room, free parking, and a free continental breakfast. For those with a bigger appetite, the excellent Blue Plate Café is just across the square. It's a five-block walk to Beale Street from Court Square, but the trolley runs right past the front door of the hotel.

A little closer to the action is the 71-room **Comfort Inn Downtown** (100 N. Front St., 901/520-0583, $100–135). This hotel is within easy walking distance of all the city-center attractions. Rooms are nothing special, but the staff are often quite friendly and guests get free breakfast, Internet access, and indoor parking, and there's an outdoor pool. Ask for a room facing west and you'll have a nice view of the Mississippi River.

$150-200

Near AutoZone Park and lots of restaurants is **Radisson Hotel Memphis** (185 Union Ave., 901/528-1800, $150–200). A 272-room hotel set in the restored Tennessee Hotel, the Radisson maintains a touch of the old grandeur of the 1929 hotel from which it was crafted. Rooms are large and there's an outdoor swimming pool and fitness room. Parking is $10 or more per night.

Over $200

If you want to be in the middle of things but can't afford to stay at the Peabody, consider the **Holiday Inn Select** (160 Union Ave., 901/525-5491, www.hisdowntownmemphis. com, $200–250). Located across the street from the Peabody and near AutoZone Park, this Holiday Inn routinely gets good reviews from travelers.

(**The Peabody Memphis** (149 Union Ave., 901/529-4000 or 800/732-2639, www.peabody-memphis.com, $225–350) is the city's signature hotel. Founded in 1869, the Peabody was the grand hotel of the South, and the hotel has preserved some of its traditional Southern charm. Tuxedoed bellhops greet you at the door and all guests receive a complementary shoe-shine. Rooms are nicely appointed with plantation-style furniture, free wireless Internet, and in-room safes, as well as all the amenities typical of an upper-tier hotel. Several fine restaurants are located on the ground floor, including the lobby bar, which is the gathering place for the twice-daily march of the famous Peabody ducks.

One of Memphis's newer hotels is the **River Inn of Harbor Town** (50 Harbor Town Sq., 901/260-3333, www.riverinnmemphis.com, $245–595). A 28-room boutique hotel on Mud Island, the River Inn offers great river views and a unique location that is just minutes from downtown. Set in the mixed residential and commercial New Urban community of Harbor Town, the River Inn provides guests with super amenities like a fitness center, reading rooms, modern decor and furniture, two restaurants, a 1.5-mile walking trail, and spa. Even the most modest rooms have luxurious extras like 32-inch flat-screen televisions, chocolate truffle turn-down service, and full gourmet breakfast at Currents, one of two restaurants on the property. The River Inn offers the best of both worlds—a relaxing and quiet getaway that is uniquely convenient to the center of Memphis.

Seeking to be the finest hotel in Memphis, the **Madison Hotel** (79 Madison Ave., 901/333-1200, www.madisonhotelmemphis.com, $250–450) is appropriately snooty. The decor is modern, with a touch of art deco. Guests enjoy every perk you can imagine, from valet parking to room service from one of the city's finest restaurants, Grill 83. The daily continental breakfast and afternoon happy hour are an opportunity to enjoy the view from the top floor of the old bank building that houses the hotel. The 110 rooms have wet bars, Internet access, and luxurious bathrooms.

MIDTOWN

Midtown hotels are cheaper than those in downtown. If you have a car, they are convenient to city-center attractions as well as those in midtown itself.

Under $100

The refurbished **Artisan Hotel** (1837 Union Ave., 901/278-4100, www.artisanmemphis.com, $80–90) is a smoke-free 160-room

MEMPHIS

boutique hotel in midtown. Each room is decorated with the work of a different classical artist; common areas have lots of heavy-duty wood paneling, lots of stone, and sculpture accents. Amenities include an outdoor swimming pool, Internet access, and an on-site restaurant and lounge.

There are a few budget hotels within trolley distance of downtown. The **Red Roof Inn** (42 S. Camilla St., 901/526-1050, $70–100) is about two blocks from the Madison Avenue trolley and has a dismal, but free, breakfast. The **Motel 6** (210 S. Pauline St., 901/528-0650, $45–70) is about three blocks from the trolley. These choices are certainly not ritzy, but they're acceptable and see a large number of budget travelers.

$100-150

The **Gen X Inn** (1177 Madison Ave., 901/692-9136, www.genxinnhotel.com, $105) straddles downtown and midtown Memphis. Located about two miles from the city center along the Madison Avenue trolley line, Gen Xers can get downtown on the trolley in about 15 minutes with a little luck. The hotel, which has free parking, is also accessible to the city's expansive medical center and the attractions around Overton Park. The Gen X Inn opened in 2006 in a converted medical office building. Its rooms are standard hotel-style, enhanced with bright colors, flat-panel plasma TVs, and a general aura of youthfulness. The whole hotel is non-smoking, and guests enjoy a good continental breakfast and a special partnership with the downtown YMCA for gym use. This is a good choice for travelers who want to be near downtown but are on a budget, especially those with a car.

$150-200

If you want to cook some of your own meals and have comforts like on-site laundry facilities, **Shellcrest** (669 Jefferson Ave., 901/523-0226, www.shellcrest.com, $160) is a good choice. This handsome redbrick town house is about six blocks east of downtown. It is designed to be an extended-stay hotel—most leases are for at least one month. But if they have a vacancy and you are looking to stay for at least three nights, the owners will accommodate short-term guests at a rate of $160 per night. You get a lot for your money; the accommodations are in spacious one-bedroom apartments with a parlor, sunroom, and study, as well as a gourmet kitchen where you can cook your own meals.

The **Holiday Inn-University of Memphis** (3700 Central Ave., 901/678-8200, $150–160) is part of the university's hospitality school. All rooms are suites, with a wet bar and microwave, sitting room, and spacious bathrooms. The lobby contains an exhibit on Kemmons Wilson, the Memphis-born founder of Holiday Inn who is credited with inventing the modern hotel industry. It is located about six miles from downtown Memphis.

Over $200

You can sleep where Elvis slept at **Lauderdale Courts** (185 Winchester, www.lauderdalecourts.com, $250). The one-time housing project where Elvis and his parents lived after they moved to Memphis from Mississippi is now a neat midtown apartment complex. The rooms where the Presleys lived have been restored to their 1950s greatness, and guests can use the working 1951 Frigidaire. The rooms are decorated with Presley family photographs and other Elvis memorabilia. You can rent Lauderdale Courts No. 328 for up to six nights. It sleeps up to four adults. The rooms are not rented during Elvis Week in August or his birthday week in January when the suite is open for public viewing for $10 per person.

SOUTH MEMPHIS

There are two reasons to stay in south Memphis: the airport and Graceland. But even if you are keenly interested in either of these places, you should think twice about staying in this part of town. With strip malls, seedy neighborhoods, and lots of mediocre chain hotels, there is not much to recommend it.

Under $100

If you need a place to stay near the airport, you can't get any closer than the **Radisson Inn Memphis Airport** (2411 Winchester Rd., 901/332-2370, $90–125), which is right next door. In addition to offering a pool and fitness center, this hotel will shuttle you to the airport terminal for free. Another airport option is the **Holiday Inn Select Memphis Airport** (2240 Democrat Rd., 901/332-1130, $85–130), which caters to business travelers. There is a guest laundry, free airport shuttle, room service, business center, and good fitness room.

You can't sleep much closer to Graceland than the **Days Inn at Graceland** (3839 Elvis Presley Blvd., 901/346-5500, $70–110), one of the most well-worn properties in the venerable Days Inn chain. The hotel has amped up the Elvis kitsch; you can tune into free non-stop Elvis movies or swim in a guitar-shaped pool. There is a free continental breakfast. Book early for Elvis Week.

$100-150

For the most Elvis-y Graceland digs, why not give in and stay at the **Elvis Presley Heartbreak Hotel** (3688 Elvis Presley Blvd., 901/332-1000, www.heartbreakhotel.net, $110–125)? This 128-room hotel has special Elvis-themed suites, and the lobby and common areas have a special Elvis flair. Elvis enthusiasts should check out special package deals with the hotel and Graceland.

CAMPING

You can pitch your tent or park your RV just 15 minutes' drive from downtown Memphis at **T. O. Fuller State Park** (1500 Mitchell Rd., 901/543-7581). The park has 45 tent and RV sites, each with a picnic table, fire ring, grill, lantern hanger, and electrical and water hookups. Sites are allocated on a first-come, first-served basis; reservations are not accepted. Rates are $18.50 a night per site.

On the north side of Memphis, **Meeman-Shelby Forest State Park** (910 Riddick Rd., Millington, 901/876-5215) is a half-hour drive from downtown. Stay in one of six lakeside cabins, which you can reserve up to one year in advance. The two-bedroom cabins can sleep up to six people. Rates are between $50 and $80 per night, depending on the season and day of the week. There are also 49 tent/ RV sites, each with electrical and water hookups, picnic tables, grills, and fire rings. The bathhouse has hot showers. Campsite rates are $14.50–17.50 per night.

MEMPHIS

Food

Eating may be the best thing about visiting Memphis. The city's culinary specialties start—but don't end—with barbecue. Plate-lunch diners around the city offer delectable cornbread, fried chicken, greens, fried green tomatoes, peach cobbler, and dozens of other Southern specialties on a daily basis. And to make it even better, such down-home restaurants are easy on your wallet. For those seeking a departure from home-style fare, Memphis has dozens of fine restaurants, some old established eateries and others newcomers that are as trendy as those in any major American city.

CAFÉS AND DINERS
Downtown

You can order deli sandwiches, breakfast plates, and a limited variety of plate lunches at the **Front Street Deli** (77 S. Front St., 901/522-8943, Mon.–Fri. 7 A.M.–3 P.M., $4–9). The deli serves breakfast and lunch on weekdays only. Its claim to fame is that scenes from *The Firm* were filmed here.

For the best burgers on Beale Street, go to **Dyers** (205 Beale St., 901/527-3937, Mon.–Thurs. 11 A.M.–1 A.M., Fri.–Sat. 11 A.M.–5 A.M., Sun. 11 A.M.–1 P.M., $7–12). The legend is that Dyers' secret is that it has been using the same grease (strained daily) since it opened in 1912. True or not, the burgers here are especially juicy. Dyers also serves wings, hot dogs, milkshakes, and a full array of fried sides.

For coffee, pastries, and fruit smoothies, **Bluff City Coffee** (50 S. Main St., 901/405-4399, Mon.–Thurs. 6:30 A.M.–8 P.M., Fri.–Sat. 6:30 A.M.–10 P.M., Sun. 8 A.M.–8 P.M., $2–5) is your best bet in this part of the city. Located in the South Main district of galleries and condos, the shop is decorated with large prints of vintage Memphis photographs, and it is also a wireless Internet hot spot.

Located in the "Edge," that no-man's-land between downtown and midtown, **Quetzal** (668 Union Ave., 901/521-8388, Mon.–Thurs. 6:30 A.M.–9 P.M., Fri. 6:30 A.M.–10 P.M., Sat.

7:30 A.M.–10 P.M., Sun. 7:30 A.M.–9 P.M., $4–10) is one of the city's best coffee shops. Fair-trade coffee and cocktails make this a great pit stop, day or night. It is also an Internet café and a popular spot for meetings.

Uptown

The **Bon-Ton Cafe** (150 Monroe, 901/525-0883, Mon.–Fri. 6 A.M.–2:30 P.M., Sat. 7 A.M.–2 P.M., $4–9) serves classic diner fare with a Greek twist. For breakfast get hot cakes, waffles, or biscuits served with your choice of eggs and breakfast meat. If the plate lunch is not your first choice, try pizzas, sandwiches, pasta, or Greek specialties including moussaka or shish-kebob.

Midtown

A block off Cooper Street in a residential neighborhood, **Buns on the Run** (2150 Elzey Ave., 901/278-2867, Tues.–Fri. 7 A.M.–2 P.M., Sat. 7 A.M.–12:30 P.M., $4–8) serves breakfast and lunch. The atmosphere is homey and welcoming, and the food is made from scratch. Breakfast includes omelets, quiches, crepes, and pancakes. For lunch you can get grilled or cold sandwiches, salads with or without meat, or a plate lunch. As the name suggests, Buns on the Run specializes in baked goods, including soft and sweet cinnamon buns, lemon ice-box pie, and a rainbow of cakes.

For a wide selection of vegetarian and organic options, go to **Square Foods** (937 S. Cooper St., 901/274-4222, Mon.–Sat. 9 A.M.–8 P.M., Sun. 10 A.M.–3 P.M., $7–10). The menu here changes regularly, but includes a variety of stir-fries, sandwiches, and wraps, as well as prepared food like roasted organic free-range chickens.

No restaurant has a larger or more loyal following in midtown than **Young Avenue Deli** (2119 Young Ave., 901/278-0034, Mon.–Sat. 11 A.M.–3 A.M., Sun. noon–3 A.M., $4–8), which serves a dozen different specialty sandwiches, grill fare including burgers and chicken

PIGGLY WIGGLY

Memphian Clarence Saunders opened the first Piggly Wiggly at 79 Jefferson Street in 1916, giving birth to the modern American supermarket. Up until then, shoppers went to small storefront shops, where they would ask the counter clerk for what they needed: a pound of flour, a half-dozen pickles, a block of cheese. The clerk went to the bulk storage area at the rear of the store, and measured out what the customer needed.

Saunders's great idea was self-service. At the Piggly Wiggly, customers entered the store, carried a basket, and were able to pick out pre-packaged and priced containers of food, which they paid for at the payment station on their way out.

The Piggly Wiggly idea took off, and by 1923 there were 1,268 Piggly Wiggly franchises around the country. Saunders used some of his profits to build a massive mansion east of the city out of pink Georgia limestone, but he was never to live in the Pink Palace, which he lost as a result of a complex stock loss.

Today, Saunders's Pink Palace is home to the Pink Palace Museum, which includes, among other things, a replica of the original Piggly Wiggly supermarket.

including pancakes and omelets, all day. For lunch or later, you can order simple sandwiches or munchies like apple slices and peanut butter, potato chips, or pop tarts.

For a cold treat during the long, hot Memphis summer, head to **Wiles-Smith Drug Store** (1635 Union Ave., 901/278-6416, Mon.–Fri. 9 A.M.–5 P.M., Sat. 10 A.M.–3 P.M.) for a milkshake. The lunch counter at this old-fashioned drug store also serves sandwiches and snacks, but it is the milkshakes that draw the biggest crowd. They come in chocolate, vanilla, strawberry, and cherry and customers gets to pour the frothy treat into their own glasses.

SOUTHERN
Downtown

Tucked inside an unassuming storefront across from the valet entrance to the Peabody Hotel is **Flying Fish** (104 S. 2nd St., 901/522-8228, daily 11 A.M.–10 P.M., $5–14), your first stop for authentic fried catfish in Memphis. If catfish isn't your thing, try the grilled or boiled shrimp, fish tacos, frog legs, or oysters. The baskets of fried seafood come with fries and hush puppies and the grilled plates come with grilled veggies, rice, and beans. The tangy coleslaw is a must. The atmosphere here is laid-back; place your order at the window and come and get it when the coaster they give you starts to vibrate. The checkered tables are well stocked with hot sauce and saltines.

It would be a grave mistake to visit Memphis and not stop at **Gus's World Famous Fried Chicken** (310 Front St., 901/527-4877, $6–12) for some of their delicious fried bird. The downtown location is a franchise of the original Gus's, which is a half-hour drive northeast of town along U.S. 70, in Mason. It is no exaggeration to say that Gus's cooks up some of the best fried chicken out there: It is spicy, juicy, and hot. It's served casually wrapped in brown paper. Sides include coleslaw, baked beans, and fried pickles. They also serve grilled-cheese sandwiches. Gus's is open daily at 11 A.M., and closes at 9 P.M. on weeknights. Closing time is 10:30 P.M. on Friday and Saturday nights. The service in this

sandwiches, plus salads and sides. The Bren—smoked turkey, mushrooms, onions, and cream cheese in a steamed pita—is a deli favorite. The food is certainly good, but it's the atmosphere at this homey yet hip Cooper-Young institution that really pulls in the crowds. There is live music most weekends, and the bar serves a kaleidoscope of domestic and imported beer, including lots of hard-to-find microbrews. The deli serves lunch and dinner daily.

For a good cup of coffee in the Cooper-Young neighborhood, head to **Java Cabana** (2170 Young Ave., 901/272-7210, Mon.–Thurs. 8:30 A.M.–10 P.M., Fri. 8:30 A.M.–midnight, Sat. 9 A.M.–midnight, Sun. noon–10 P.M., $4–10). Java Cabana serves light breakfast fare,

Gus's World Famous Fried Chicken has a well-earned reputation for the best fried chicken in the city.

hole-in-the-wall establishment is slow, but friendly, so come in with a smile on.

The **Arcade** (540 S. Main St., 901/526-5757, daily 7 A.M.–3 P.M., $5–10) is said to be Memphis's oldest restaurant. Founded in 1919 and still operated by the same family (with lots of the same decor), this restaurant feels like a throwback to an earlier time. The menu is diverse, with pizzas, sandwiches, plate-lunch specials during the week, and breakfast served anytime. The chicken spaghetti is a stick-to-your-ribs favorite.

Uptown

The Little Tea Shop (69 Monroe, 901/525-6000, Mon.–Fri. 11 A.M.–2 P.M., $4.95–7.50) serves traditional plate lunches through the week. Choose from daily specials like fried catfish, chicken pot pie, and meatloaf with your choice of vegetable and side dishes. Every meal (except sandwiches) comes with fresh, hot corn bread that might well be the star of the show. This is stick-to-your-ribs Southern cooking at its best, so come hungry. If you have room, try the peach cobbler for dessert. The staff's welcoming yet efficient style makes this perfect for a quick lunch. Not to be missed.

The Blue Plate Cafe (113 Court Square S., 901/523-2050, daily 7 A.M.–2 P.M., $4–10) serves hearty breakfasts, plate lunches, and traditional home-style cooking. Its newsprint menu imparts wisdom ("Rule of Life No. 1: Wake up. Show up. Pay attention.") and declares that every day should begin with a great breakfast. It's not hard to comply at the Blue Plate. Eggs come with homemade biscuits and gravy, and your choice of grits, hash browns, or pancakes. For lunch, try a meat-and-three or vegetable plate, slow-cooked white-bean soup, or a grilled peanut butter and banana sandwich. Locals swear by the fried green tomatoes. There are three Blue Plate Cafes in Memphis: the other two are at 2921 Kirby Whitten Road in Bartlett (901/213-1066) and at 5469 Poplar Avenue (901/761-9696) in midtown.

Alcenia's (317 N. Main St., 901/523-0200, Tues.–Fri. 11 A.M.–5 P.M., Sat. 9 A.M.–1 P.M., $4–10), located in the Pinch district, is among Memphis's best Southern-style restaurants. Known for its plate lunches, fried chicken, and pastries, Alcenia's has a style unlike any other Memphis eatery, witnessed in its off-beat decor of '60s-style beads, folk art, and wedding lace. Proprietor B. J. Chester-Tamayo is all love, and she pours her devotion into some of the city's best soul food. Try the spicy cabbage and deep-fried chicken, and save room for Alcenia's famous bread pudding for dessert. Chicken and waffles is the Saturday-morning specialty.

Midtown

Just follow the crowds to the **Cupboard Restaurant** (1400 Union Ave., 901/276-8015, Mon.–Fri. 7 A.M.–8 P.M., Sat.–Sun. 7 A.M.–7 P.M., $6–18), one of Memphians' favorite stops for plate lunches. The Cupboard moved from its downtown location to an old Shoney's about a mile outside of town to accommodate the throngs who stop here for authentic home-style cooking. The Cupboard gets only the freshest vegetables for its dishes like okra and tomatoes, rutabaga turnips, steamed cabbage, and green beans. The meat specials change daily, but include things like fried chicken, chicken and dumplings, hamburger steak with onions, and beef tips with noodles. The cornbread "coins" are exceptionally buttery, and the bread is baked fresh daily. For dessert, try the lemon icebox pie.

The Women's Exchange (88 Racine St., 901/327-5681, Mon.–Fri. 11:30 A.M.–1:45 P.M., $10) feels like a throwback to an earlier era. Located one block east of the Poplar Street viaduct, the Women's Exchange has been serving lunch since 1936 and the menu has not changed much over the years. The special changes daily and always includes a choice of two entrées, or a four-vegetable plate. Classics like chicken salad, salmon loaf, beef tenderloin, and seafood gumbo are favorites, and all lunches come with a drink and dessert. The dining room looks out onto a green garden, and the atmosphere is homey—not stuffy. The Exchange also sells gifts, housewares, and other knick-knacks.

In the Cooper-Young neighborhood, **Soul**

Fish (862 S. Cooper St., 901/725-0722, Mon.–Sat. 11 A.M.–10 P.M., Sun. 11 A.M.–9 P.M., $6–15) offers traditional plate lunches, vegetable plates, and several varieties of catfish. You can get the fish breaded and fried, or blackened with a potent spice mix. Soul Fish is owned in part by Tiger Bryant, owner of the venerable Young Avenue Deli, and it has the hallmarks of a well-conceived eatery. The atmosphere is open and cheerful, with a few touches of subtle sophistication. In this case, the main attraction is good food at a good price—a combination that can be hard to find elsewhere in Cooper-Young.

South Memphis

Gayhawk Restaurant (685 Danny Thomas Blvd., 901/947-1464, Mon.–Fri. 11 A.M.–2:30 P.M., Sat.–Sun. noon–5 P.M., $6–10) serves country-style food that sticks to your ribs and warms your soul. Chef Bobo declares that his specialty is "home-cooked food" and it really is as simple as that. The best thing about Gayhawk is the luncheon buffet, which lets newcomers to Southern cooking survey the choices and try a little bit of everything. The Sunday lunch buffet practically sags with specialties like fried chicken, grilled fish, macaroni and cheese, greens, and much, much more.

◖ BARBECUE

On the northern fringe of downtown Memphis is one of the city's most famous and well-loved barbecue joints: ◖ **Cozy Corner** (745 N. Parkway, 901/527-9158, Mon.–Sat. 11 A.M.–5 P.M., $4–14). Cozy Corner is tucked into a storefront in an otherwise-abandoned strip mall; you'll smell it before you see it. Step inside to order barbecue pork, sausage, or bologna sandwiches. Or get a 2-bone, 4-bone, or 6-bone rib dinner plate, which comes with your choice of baked beans, coleslaw, or barbecue spaghetti, plus slices of Wonder bread to sop up the juices. One of Cozy Corner's specialties is its barbecued Cornish hens—a preparation that is surprising but delicious. Sweet tea goes perfectly with the tangy and spicy barbecue.

Jim Neely's **Interstate Bar-B-Que** (2265 S. 3rd St., 901/775-1045, Mon.–Thurs.

11 A.M.–11 P.M., Fri.–Sat. 11 A.M.–midnight, $5–20) was once ranked the second best barbecue in the nation, but the proprietors have not let it get to their heads; this is still a down-to-earth, no-frills eatery. Large appetites can order a whole slab of pork or beef ribs, but most people will be satisfied with a chopped pork sandwich, which comes topped with coleslaw and smothered with barbecue sauce. Families can get the fixings for six, eight, or ten sandwiches sent out family-style. For an adventure, try the barbecue spaghetti or barbecue bologna sandwich. If you're in a hurry, the Interstate has a drive-up window too, and if you are really smitten, you can order pork, sauce, and seasoning in bulk to be frozen and shipped to your home.

Although aficionados will remind you that the ribs served at the **Rendezvous** (52 S. 2nd St., 901/523-2746, Tues.–Thurs. 4:30–10:30 P.M., Fri.–Sat. 11:30 A.M.–11 P.M., $8–17) are not technically barbecue, they are one of the biggest barbecue stories in town. Covered in a dry rub of spices and broiled until the meat falls off the bones, these ribs will knock your socks off. If you prefer, you can choose Charlie Vergos's dry-rub chicken or boneless pork loin. Orders come with baked beans and coleslaw, but beer is really the essential accompaniment to any Vergos meal. The door to Rendezvous is tucked in an alley off Monroe Avenue. The smoky interior, decorated with antiques and yellowing business cards, is low-key, noisy, and lots of fun.

A Memphis chain, **Gridley's** (6842 Stage Rd., 901/377-8055, Sun.–Thurs. 11 A.M.–8 P.M., Fri.–Sat. 11 A.M.–9 P.M.,, $4–20) serves wet-style barbecue ribs, pork shoulder plates and sandwiches, plus spicy grilled shrimp. The shrimp is served with a buttery and delicious dipping sauce. Try the half-pork, half-shrimp plate for a real treat. Meals here come with baked beans, coleslaw, and hot fresh bread.

CONTEMPORARY
Downtown

The Majestic Grill (145 S. Main St., 901/522-8555, Mon.–Thurs. 11 A.M.–11 P.M., Fri.–Sat. 11 A.M.–midnight, Sun. 11 A.M.–9 P.M., $6–29)

serves a remarkably affordable yet upscale menu at lunch and dinner. Located in what was once the Majestic Theater, the white tablecloths and apron-clad waiters give the restaurant an aura of refinement. But with main courses starting at just $6, this can be a bargain. Flatbread pizzas feature asparagus, spicy shrimp, and smoked sausage. Sandwiches include burgers and clubs; specialties include pasta, barbecue ribs, grilled salmon, and steaks. Don't pass on dessert, served in individual shot glasses, such as chocolate mousse, key lime pie, and carrot cake, among others.

For a special occasion make reservations at the **Inn at Hunt Phelan** (533 Beale St., 901/525-8225, Wed.–Sat. 5:30 P.M.–1 A.M., Sun. 11 A.M.–3 P.M., $22–36), a stately and sophisticated restaurant in the historic Hunt-Phelan House. The dinner menu is always changing, but expect dishes such as butternut squash ravioli or pepper-crusted tuna with *pommes frites.* If you are feeling really special, treat yourself to the $70 seven-course tasting menu. Diners at the inn can sit inside the elegant dining room, or outside on the charming back patio.

A relative newcomer to the Beale Street dining scene, **◖ E. P. Delta Kitchen and Bar** (126 Beale St., 901/527-1444, Wed.–Sat. 5 P.M.–3 A.M., Sun.–Tues. 5 P.M.–1 A.M., $15–35) is the most upscale eatery on the famed blues drag. Located in what was once the flagship Lanksky Brothers clothing store, E. P. (that stands for Elvis Presley) Delta Kitchen has made a name for itself since opening in late 2006. The style here is spicy delta cooking with a refined twist: Imagine upscale jambalaya and bayou duck with pasta. After 11 P.M., there is a one-of-a-kind bar menu with offerings like barbecue duck quesadillas and fried green tomatoes. E. P.'s has a stylish and modern atmosphere, with live R&B on weekends. This is a popular place to start an evening out on the town, especially for the professional crowd, and don't miss some of the one-of-a-kind libations like the Memphis BBQ Bloody Mary or the Peanut Butter and Banana Cocktail.

Located on the corner of Madison and Main, **Stella** (39 S. Main St., 901/526-4950,

Mon.–Sat. 5:30–10:30 P.M., $27–48) has made a name for itself on Memphis's fine dining scene with dishes like Colorado Lamb Rack, Marinated Filet Mignon, and Oysters Stella. The dining room has expansive high ceilings, and rich wood paneling from the building's previous life as a jewelry store.

It is impossible to pigeonhole **Automatic Slim's Tonga Club** (83 S. 2nd St., 901/525-7948, $12–20), except to say that this Memphis institution consistently offers fresh, spirited, and original fare. They serve lunch Monday–Friday 10 A.M.–2 P.M. and on weekends 11 A.M.–2 P.M.; dinner is served daily 5–9:30 P.M. Named after a character from an old blues tune, Automatic Slim's uses lots of strong flavors to create its eclectic menu; Caribbean and southwestern influences are the most apparent. Take a seat and in two shakes you'll be presented with soft, fresh bread and pesto-seasoned olive oil for dipping. The Caribbean shrimp are a favorite of many diners. A meal at Automatic Slim's would not be complete without a famous Tonga Martini or one of the kitchen's delectable desserts: Pecan tart and chocolate cake are good choices. Automatic Slim's is a welcome departure from barbecue and southern food when you're ready. Its atmosphere is relaxed, and there's often a crowd at the bar, especially on weekends when there's live music on tap.

Long the standard-bearer of fine French cuisine, **Chez Philippe** (149 Union Ave., 901/529-4188, Tues.–Sat. 6–10 P.M., $65–70), located in the Peabody Hotel, now offers French-Asian fusion cuisine. The Asian influences are noticeable in the ingredients, but the preparation of most dishes at Chez Philippe remains traditional French. Entrées include grouper, bass, pork chop, and venison. Chez Philippe offers a prix fixe menu: Three courses is $65 and five courses is $70. Or opt for a seven-course tasting menu for $90; wine pairings are an addition $42 per person.

Midtown

In 2007, Memphis's foremost restaurateur, Karen Blockman Carrier, closed her fine-dining restaurant Cielo in Victorian Village, redecorated, and reopened it as the **Molly Fontaine Lounge** (679 Adams Ave., 901/524-1886, Wed.–Sat. 5 P.M.–2:30 A.M., $12–24). Carrier's vision was an old-fashioned club where guests can order upscale cocktails, relax with live music, and eat tasty Mediterranean and Middle Eastern–inspired tapas. The restaurant has an upmarket but cozy atmosphere, with equal measures of funky and fine. The live piano jazz is the perfect backdrop for the restaurant's artistic small plates.

Surprisingly good for a bookstore café, **Bronte** (387 Perkins Ext., 901/374-0881, Mon.–Sat. 9 A.M.–10 P.M., Sun. 10 A.M.–8 P.M., $8–12) offers salads, soups, and sandwiches, as well as daily meat and fish specials. The soup-and-sandwich combo is filling and good. Breakfast may well be the best meal on offer, however. The morning menu features specials designed by celebrity chefs, including omelets, baked goods, and crepes.

One of Memphis's most unique restaurant settings is an old beauty shop in the Cooper-Young area. **The Beauty Shop** (966 S. Cooper St., 901/272-7111, $8–32) takes advantage of the vintage beauty parlor decor to create a great talking point for patrons and food writers alike. The domed hairdryers remain, and the restaurant has put the shampooing sinks to work as beer coolers. At lunch, the Beauty Shop offers a casual menu of sandwiches and salads. For dinner, the imaginative cuisine of Memphis restaurateur Karen Blockman Carrier, who also owns Molly Fontaine Lounge and Automatic Slim's Tonga Club, takes over. The Beauty Shop serves lunch Monday–Saturday 11 A.M.–2 P.M. Dinner is served beginning at 5 P.M. nightly, except Sunday. It opens Sunday 10 A.M.–3 P.M.

Right next to the Beauty Shop is **Do** (966 S. Cooper St., 901/272-7111, $6–15), a trendy sushi restaurant that also offers tempura, soups, and salads. It is open for dinner only Tuesday through Saturday.

If you enjoy your beer as much or more than your meal, then head straight for **Boscos Squared** (2120 Madison Ave., 901/432-2222,

$12–22). Boscos is a brew pub with fresh seafood, steak, and pizza. Their beer menu is among the best in the city, and many of the brews are made on the premises. Boscos serves lunch daily 11 A.M.–3 P.M., dinner 3 P.M.–midnight, and the late-night munchie menu is available until 2 A.M.

East Memphis

To many minds, Memphis dining gets no better than ◖ **Erling Jensen, The Restaurant** (1044 S. Yates Rd., 901/763-3700, daily 5–10 P.M., $30–50). Danish-born Erling Jensen is the mastermind of this fine-dining restaurant that has consistently earned marks as Memphians' favorite restaurant. Understated decor and friendly service are the backdrop to Jensen's dishes, which are works of art. The menu changes with the seasons and based upon availability, but usually includes about six different seafood dishes and as many meat and game choices. Black Angus beef, elk loin, and buffalo tenderloin are some of the favorites. Meals at Jensen's restaurant should begin with an appetizer, salad, or soup—or all three. The jumbo chunk crab cakes with smoked red-pepper sauce are excellent. Reservations are a good idea at Erling Jensen, and so are jackets for men. Expect to spend upwards of $80 for a four-course meal here; $60 for two courses. Add more for wine.

Memphis's premier steakhouse is **Folk's Folly** (551 S. Mendenhall Rd., 901/762-8200, $30–70), located just east of Audubon Park. Dinner is served nightly beginning at 5:30 P.M., when diners start flocking here for prime aged steaks and seafood favorites. For small appetites, try the 8-ounce filet mignon for $28; large appetites can gorge on the 28-ounce porterhouse for $57. Seafood includes lobster, crab legs, and wild salmon. The atmosphere is classic steakhouse: The lighting is low, and there's a piano bar on the property.

ETHNIC CUISINE
Downtown

For sushi, try **Sekisui** (Union at 2nd Ave., 901/523-0001), where a roll costs between $2.50 and $8, and a filling combo plate will run you about $15. The downtown restaurant is located on the ground floor of the Holiday Inn Select. Sekisui is a Memphis chain, and there are other locations in midtown and the suburbs. The downtown location serves dinner nightly, and lunch Monday–Friday.

For Thai food, try **Sawaddii** (121 Union, 901/529-1818, daily 11:30 A.M.–9:30 P.M., $9–22), which serves a selection of thai curries, noodles, and fried rice, as well as signature dishes like grilled mahimahi. They have an extensive wine list and full bar, too. The waitstaff here is welcoming and down-to-earth, and the atmosphere stylish but not pretentious. It's a good place to come if you tire of barbecue and burgers, but don't want to break the bank.

Midtown

The **Indian Palace** (1720 Poplar Ave., 901/278-1199, daily, $7–17) is a regular winner in reader's choice polls for Indian food in Memphis. The lunch-time buffet is filling and economical, and the dinner menu features vegetarian, chicken, and seafood dishes. The dinner platters are generous and tasty. Lunch is served Monday–Friday 11 A.M.–2:30 P.M. and Saturday–Sunday 11 A.M.–3 P.M., and dinner is available nightly 5–10 P.M.

Pho Hoa Binh (1615 Madison, 901/276-0006, Mon.–Sat. 11 A.M.–9 P.M., $4–9) is one of the most popular Vietnamese restaurants in town. You can't beat the value of the lunch buffet, or you can order from the dizzying array of Chinese and Vietnamese dishes, including spring rolls, vermicelli noodle bowls, rice, and meat dishes. There are a lot of vegetarian options here.

The atmosphere at **Bhan Thai** (1324 Peabody Ave., 901/272-1538, $10–19) in midtown is almost as appealing as the excellent Thai food served there. Set in an elegant 1912 home, Bhan Thai makes the most of the house's space, and seating is spread throughout several colorful rooms and on the back patio. Choose from dishes like red snapper, masaman curry, and roasted duck curry. The Bhan Thai salad is popular, with creamy peanut dressing and crisp vegetables. Dinner here is served Tuesday–Sunday beginning at 5 P.M., and lunch Tuesday–Friday 11 A.M.–2:30 P.M.

It's the regulars who are happy at the **Happy Mexican Restaurant and Cantina** (385 S. 2nd St., 901/529-9991, Sun.–Thurs. 11 A.M.–10 P.M., Fri.–Sat. 11 A.M.–11 P.M., $7–15). Serving generous portions of home-made Mexican food for lunch and dinner, Happy Mexican is destined to become a downtown favorite. The service is efficient and friendly, and the decor is cheerful but not over the top. It's located just a few blocks south of the National Civil Rights Museum.

MARKETS

The only downtown grocery store is the **Easy-Way** (80 N. Main St., 901/523-1323, daily 7 A.M.–6 P.M.) on the corner of Main Street and Jefferson Avenue. For liquor and wine, go to **The Corkscrew** (511 S. Front St., 901/543-9463).

The closest gourmet grocery is located in Harbor Town, the residential community on Mud Island, where **Miss Cordelia's** (737 Harbor Bend, 901/526-4772, daily 7 A.M.–9 P.M.) sells fresh produce, bakery goods, and staples. A deli in the back serves soups, salads, sandwiches, and a wide variety of prepared foods.

For a full-service grocery store in midtown, look for the **Krogers** at the corner of Cleveland and Poplar.

The **Memphis Farmer's Market** (901/575-0580, www.memphisfarmersmarket.com, May–Oct. Sat. 7 A.M.–1 P.M.) takes place in the pavilion opposite Central Station in the South Main part of town.

Information and Services

INFORMATION
Visitors Centers

The city's visitors center is the **Tennessee Welcome Center** (119 Riverside Dr., 901/543-5333) located on the Tennessee side of the I-40 bridge. The center has lots of brochures and free maps and staff who can answer your questions. It is open 24 hours a day, seven days a week. The center assists more than 350,000 travelers annually.

Although it is not designed to be a visitors center, the **Memphis Convention and Visitors Bureau** (47 Union Ave., 901/543-5300, www.memphistravel.com, Mon.–Fri. 9 A.M.–5 P.M.) is a resource for visitors. You can collect maps and ask questions here. The bureau also produces videos highlighting city attractions and restaurants, which are available on many hotel televisions.

Maps

Hand-out maps that highlight key attractions are available from visitors centers in Memphis. If you are only interested in Beale Street, Graceland, and the interstates, these will be fine. The free maps provided at the concierge desk of the Peabody Hotel are especially well marked and useful.

If you want to explore further, or if you plan to drive yourself around the city, it is wise to get a proper city map. Rand McNally publishes a detailed Memphis city map, which you can buy from bookstores or convenience marts in downtown.

Media

The daily **Commercial Appeal** (www.commercialappeal.com) is Memphis's major newspaper, available all over the city. The **Memphis Flyer** (www.memphisflyer.com) is a free alternative weekly, published on Wednesday with the best entertainment listings.

Memphis magazine (www.memphismagazine.com) is published monthly and includes historical anecdotes, restaurant reviews, features on high-profile residents, and lots of advertising aimed at residents and would-be residents.

There are two independent radio stations of note: **WEVL 89.9 FM** is a community radio station that plays blues, country, and other Memphis music. **WDIA 1070 AM,** the historical Memphis station that made the blues famous, still rocks today. Another station of note is **WRBO 103.5 FM,** which plays soul and R&B.

SERVICES
Fax and Internet

Send a fax at **FedEx Kinkos** (50 N. Front St., 901/521-0261), located across from the Peabody's valet entrance.

For Internet access, try **Quetzal Internet Café** (668 Union Ave., 901/521-8388), which is open weekdays 6:30 A.M.–9 P.M. and stays open late on weekends. You can also get online at **Internet Café by Malik** (75 S. Main St., 901/575-9974).

Postal Service

There is a postal retail center, which sells stamps and offers limited postal services, at 100 Peabody Place (901/521-0159). It is open Monday–Friday 8:30 A.M.–5 P.M., and Saturday 9 A.M.–1 P.M.

The full-service downtown post office is located at 1 North Front Street (901/576-2037) and opens weekdays 8 A.M.–5 P.M.

Emergency Services

Dial 911 in an emergency for fire, ambulance, or police. The downtown police department is the South Main Station (545 S. Main St., 901/525-9800). Police patrol downtown by car, on bike, and on foot.

Several agencies operate hotlines for those needing help. They include: Alcoholics Anonymous (901/454-1414), the Better Business Bureau (901/759-1300), Emergency Mental Health Services (901/577-9400), Deaf Interpreting (901/577-3783), Rape Crisis/Sexual Assault Hotline (901/272-2020), and Poison Emergencies (901/528-6048).

Hospitals

Memphis is chock-a-block with hospitals. Midtown Memphis is also referred to as Medical Center for the number of hospitals and medical facilities there. Here you will find the **Regional Medical Center at Memphis** (877 Jefferson Ave., 901/545-7100), a 620-bed teaching hospital affiliated with the University of Tennessee; and the **Methodist University Hospital** (1265 Union Ave., 901/516-7000), the 669-bed flagship hospital for Methodist Healthcare.

In East Memphis, **Baptist Memorial Hospital** (6019 Walnut Grove Rd., 901/226-5000) is the cornerstone of the huge Baptist Memorial Health Care System, with 771 beds.

Laundry

Try any of these three laundries, which are located near downtown: **Metro Plaza Laundry** (805 S. Danny Thomas Blvd., 901/948-1673), **Crump Laundry Mat and Dry Cleaning** (756 E. Ed Crump Blvd., 901/948-7008), or **Jackson Coin Laundry** (1216 Jackson Ave., 901/274-3536).

Libraries

Memphis has 19 public libraries. The city's main library is **Hooks Public Library** (3030 Poplar Ave., 901/415-2700, Mon.–Thurs. 9 A.M.–9 P.M., Fri.–Sat. 9 A.M.–6 P.M., Sun. 1–5 P.M.), a modern, new public library with 119 public computers, an extensive collection, community programs, meeting rooms, a lecture series, and more. The central library is located on a busy thoroughfare in midtown and would be a challenge to visit without a car.

The downtown branch library, **Cossit Library** (33 S. Front St., 901/526-1712, Mon.–Fri. 10 A.M.–5 P.M.), has a good collection of new releases, and staff there are happy to help visitors looking for information about Memphis. The current building was constructed in 1959, but the Cossit Library was founded in 1888 as the Cossit-Goodwyn Institute.

Getting There and Around

GETTING THERE
By Air
Memphis International Airport (MEM; 901/922-8000, www.mscaa.com) is located 13 miles south of downtown Memphis. There are two popular routes to Memphis from the airport. Take I-240 north to arrive in midtown. To reach downtown, take I-55 north and exit on Riverside Drive. Both drives take between 20 and 30 minutes.

The airport's main international travel insurance and business services center (901/922-8090) is located in ticket lobby B and opens daily. Here you can exchange foreign currency, buy travel insurance, conduct money transfers, send faxes and make photocopies, and buy money orders and travelers checks. A smaller kiosk near the international arrivals and departures area at gate B-36 is open daily and offers foreign currency exchange and travel insurance.

There is wireless Internet service in the airport, but it is not free.

AIRPORT SHUTTLE
TennCo Express (901/345-7962, www.tenncoexpress.com) provides an hourly shuttle service from the airport to many downtown hotels. Tickets are $15 one-way and $25 round-trip. Look for the shuttle parked in the third lane near column number 14 outside the airport terminal. Shuttles depart every half hour 7:30 A.M.–9:30 P.M. For a hotel pick-up, call at least a day in advance.

By Car
Memphis is located at the intersection of two major interstate highways: I-40, which runs east–west across the United States, and I-55, which runs south from St. Louis to New Orleans.

Many people who visit Memphis drive here in their own cars. The city is 300 miles from St. Louis, 380 miles from Atlanta, 410 miles from New Orleans, 450 miles from Dallas, 480 miles from Cincinnati and Oklahoma City, and 560 miles from Chicago.

By Bus
Greyhound (800/231-2222, www.greyhound.com) runs daily buses to Memphis from around the United States. Direct service is available to Memphis from a number of surrounding cities, including Jackson and Nashville, Tennessee; Tupelo and Jackson, Mississippi; Little Rock and Jonesboro, Arkansas; and St. Louis. The Greyhound station (203 Union Ave., 901/523-9253), in downtown Memphis, is open 24 hours a day.

By Train
Amtrak (800/872-7245, www.amtrak.com) runs the City of New Orleans train daily between Chicago and New Orleans, stopping in Memphis on the way. The southbound train arrives daily at Memphis's Central Station at 6:17 A.M., leaving about half an hour later. The northbound train arrives at 10 P.M. every day. It is an 11-hour ride between Memphis and Chicago and about eight hours between Memphis and New Orleans.

The Amtrak station (901/526-0052) is located in Central Station at 545 South Main Street in the South Main district of downtown. Ticket and baggage service is available at the station daily 5:45 A.M.–11 P.M.

GETTING AROUND
Driving
Driving is the most popular and easiest way to get around Memphis. Downtown parking is plentiful if you are prepared to pay; an all-day pass in one of the many downtown parking garages costs about $10. Traffic congestion peaks, predictably, at rush hours and is worst in the eastern parts of the city and along the interstates.

Public Transportation
BUSES
The **Memphis Area Transit Authority**

MEMPHIS

© SUSANNA HENIGHAN POTTER

The Main Street trolley connects uptown and downtown.

(901/274-6282, www.matatransit.com) operates dozens of buses that travel through the greater Memphis area. For information on routes, call or stop by the North End Terminal on North Main Street for help planning your trip. The bus system is not used frequently by tourists.

TROLLEYS

Public trolleys run for about two miles along Main Street in Memphis from the Pinch district in the north to Central Station in the south, and circle up on a parallel route along Riverfront Drive. Another trolley line runs about two miles east on Madison Avenue, connecting the city's medical center with downtown. The Main Street trolleys run every 10 minutes at most times, but the Madison Avenue trolleys run less often on weekends and evenings after 6 P.M.

Fares are $1 per ride, or 50 cents between 11 A.M. and 1:30 P.M. You can buy an all-day pass for $3.50, a three-day pass for $8, or a month-long pass for $25. All passes must be purchased at the North End Terminal at the northern end of the Main Street route.

The trolley system is useful, especially if your hotel is on either the northern or southern end of downtown, or along Madison Avenue. Brochures with details on the routes and fares are available all over town, or you can download one at www.matatransit.com. The trolleys are simple to understand and use; if you have a question, just ask your driver.

SUN STUDIO FREE SHUTTLE BUS

Sun Studio runs a free shuttle between Sun Studio, the Rock 'n' Soul Museum at Beale Street, and Graceland. The first run stops at the Graceland Heartbreak Hotel at 9:55 A.M., Graceland at 10 A.M., Sun Studio at 10:15 A.M., and the Rock 'n' Soul Museum at 10:30 A.M. Runs continue throughout the day on an hourly schedule. The last run picks up at Heartbreak Hotel at 5:55 P.M., Graceland Plaza at 6 P.M., and Sun Studio at 6:15 P.M.

The shuttle is a 12-passenger black van painted with the Sun Studio logo. The ride is free, but it's nice to tip your driver. The published schedule is a loose approximation, so it's a good idea to get to the pick-up point early in case the van is running ahead. You can call 901/521-0664 for more information.

Taxis

Memphis has a number of taxi companies, and you will usually find available cabs along Beale Street and waiting at the airport. Otherwise, you will need to call for a taxi. Some of the largest companies are **Yellow Cab** (901/577-7777), **City Wide Cab** (901/722-8294), and **Arrow Transportation Company** (901/332-7769).

Expect to pay between $25 and $30 for a trip from the airport to downtown; most fares around town are under $10.

OUTSIDE MEMPHIS

From the western bank of the Tennessee River to the eastern shore of the Mississippi, Tennessee's western plains are more like the Deep South than any other part of the state. The landscape is spare; in the heart of the delta all you see for mile upon mile are cotton fields—flat with neat rows of the bushy plants. Here, you can marvel at the talents that emerged from this unforgiving place, people like Alex Haley, Tina Turner, and "Sleepy" John Estes.

In the south, not far from the Mississippi state line, is Shiloh, a monument to the scale and horror of the Civil War. In the northwest corner of the state, Reelfoot Lake attracts fishing enthusiasts, bird-watchers, and travelers curious to see the lake that an earthquake made.

PLANNING YOUR TIME

Plan a day trip or weekend getaway from Memphis and explore western Tennessee. For a quiet outdoor retreat, make it a weekend at Reelfoot Lake, stopping on the way to visit the Alex Haley House Museum in tiny Henning. If you are interested in the cultural and musical attractions of the region, don't miss Brownsville's West Tennessee Delta Heritage Center and the International Rock-a-Billy Hall of Fame in Jackson.

To explore the history of the area, start with prehistory at Pinson Mounds, mysterious Indian mounds just south of Jackson. Then head to Shiloh National Military Park, the site of the deadliest Civil War battle in Tennessee.

Driving is the best—only, really—way to

HIGHLIGHTS

◖ West Tennessee Delta Heritage Center: Gain a better understanding of cotton, the blues, and the rural way of life at this Brownsville attraction (page 187).

◖ Alex Haley House Museum: One of Tennessee's most celebrated writers grew up in the humble sawmill town of Henning. See the home where Alex Haley first imagined his ancestors (page 190).

◖ Reelfoot Lake State Park Visitor Center: Knob-kneed cypress trees, abundant wildlife, and the fresh air of the country are elixir for those who come to this quiet corner of the Delta, and the boardwalk at the state park visitors center is the best place to soak in the setting (page 193).

◖ Pinson Mounds State Archaeological Park: The sprawling and mysterious mounds at Pinson are a reminder of those who came before (page 202).

◖ Shiloh National Military Park: The scene of one of the bloodiest Civil War battles is a good place to ponder the meaning of the war and its human cost (page 205).

◖ Tennessee River Museum: The river town of Savannah is the perfect setting for this excellent museum on river life and culture (page 208).

KENTUCKY

▲ Reelfoot NWR

Reelfoot Lake State Park Visitor Center

○ Dresden

Kenton ○

○ Dyersburg

Alex Haley House Museum

◖

Henning

Brownsville

◖

West Tennessee Delta Heritage Center

○ Jackson

Pinson Mounds State Archaeological Park

◖

Tennessee River Museum ◖

Shiloh National Military Park ◖

TENNESSEE

MISSISSIPPI

Pickwick Lake

0   15 mi

0   15 km

LOOK FOR ◖ TO FIND RECOMMENDED SIGHTS, ACTIVITIES, DINING, AND LODGING.

get around West Tennessee. Even in the largest city, Jackson, attractions, restaurants, and accommodations are spread out. A good road map is all you need to find your way around, and residents are friendly and helpful if you get lost.

Unless you are in a hurry, get off I-40, which cuts a diagonal path across the plains. State routes 51, 79, 45, and 64 traverse the region and are good thoroughfares. Smaller two-lane roads are even better, since they bring you up close to the true nature of the Tennessee delta.

OUTSIDE MEMPHIS

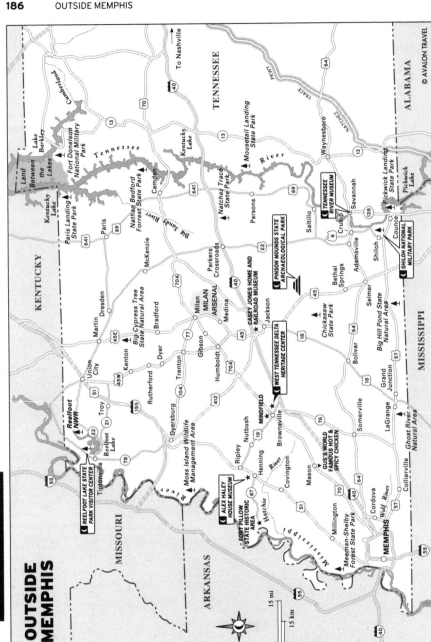

The Delta

Flat, spare, and rural, the delta region of West Tennessee was, and still is, the state's largest producer of cotton. Cotton fields spread out between small towns and farm houses.

The county seat of the largest cotton-producing county in Tennessee, Brownsville remains the unofficial "capital of the Tennessee Delta," and the commercial and cultural center for this region. The region has been fertile soil not only for farming, but for music too. Rock icon Tina Turner grew up in the rural countryside near here, and blues musicians "Sleepy" John Estes, Hammie Nixon, and Yank Rachell are from Brownsville.

BROWNSVILLE

Brownsville, the seat of Haywood County, was founded in 1824 and quickly became home to many of West Tennessee's most affluent settlers. Early leaders carefully mapped out the city lots, and they were sold to doctors, lawyers, and merchants who helped the town develop quickly during its first decades.

Brownsville's first newspaper was founded in 1837, its first bank in 1869, and in its heyday it also boasted an opera house and several hotels and restaurants. It lost hundreds of its residents to the yellow fever epidemic of 1878, and hundreds more fled to avoid becoming ill. A marker in the town's Oakwood Cemetery designates the resting place of the yellow fever victims.

◖ West Tennessee Delta Heritage Center

Half welcome center, half museum, the West Tennessee Delta Heritage Center (121 Sunny Hill Cove, 731/779-9000, Tues.–Sat. 9 A.M.–4 P.M., free) is your best stop for understanding the special music, culture, and history of the delta region. Its exhibits examine the musical heritage of the region, the ecology of

PHOTO COURTESY OF TENNESSEE DEPARTMENT OF TOURIST DEVELOPMENT

OUTSIDE MEMPHIS

The West Tennessee Delta Heritage Center pays tribute to local blues musicians.

the nearby Hatchie River, and cotton, the region's most important crop.

The cotton exhibit illustrates the process from cultivation to baling. A huge basket of picked cotton is there for you to touch, as well as the cotton both before and after being ginned. After driving past miles of cotton fields, visitors will welcome the illustration and explanations.

The heritage center also has displays about each of the counties in the region, with visitor information on each. There is also a gift shop, and you can use their Internet-enabled computer for $5, or for free with a $20 purchase.

Right next to the heritage center is the **"Sleepy" John Estes Home**, a faded clapboard home that was relocated here so tourists could see where the blues legend was living when he died in 1977. Sadly, thanks to the risk of liability lawsuits, the old building has been deemed unsafe, so you can't go inside.

The heritage center is located at exit 56 off I-40.

Historic Brownsville

It is pleasant to drive or walk around Historic Brownsville, a leafy neighborhood of antebellum homes and buildings. Each home is marked with a brown-and-white sign in the yard that is visible from the road and gives the approximate date of construction. For a more detailed guide, visit the Brownsville-Haywood Chamber of Commerce for a copy of their historical guidebook of Haywood County, which includes a walking tour of Brownsville.

Two of the city's most noteworthy old homes are the **Tripp Home** at 420 Main Street, a two-story Greek Revival home built in 1824, and the **Christ Episcopal Church** at the corner of West College and North Washington, organized in 1832. Brownsville is also home to the oldest Jewish temple in continuous service in Tennessee, the **Temple of Adas Israel** at 18 North Court Street, built in 1882.

Historic Brownsville surrounds the

"SLEEPY" JOHN ESTES

Blues musician "Sleepy" John Estes, whose home is preserved at the West Tennessee Delta Heritage Center, was born in Ripley, Tennessee, in 1904 but lived most of his life in Brownsville. A blues guitarist and vocalist, Estes had a distinctive "crying" vocal style and sounded like an old man, even on his early recordings. Estes made his recording debut in Memphis in 1929 and he recorded regularly until the outbreak of World War II in 1941. Estes spent the end of his life blind and living in poverty.

"Sleepy" John Estes, a blues legend, was living in this clapboard house in rural Haywood County when he died in 1977.

College Hill Center, where you will find the **Haywood County Museum** (127 N. Grade Ave., 731/772-4883). This museum is home to a remarkable collection of Abraham Lincoln artifacts and papers, donated by Brownsville native Morton Felsenthal. The museum is open only on Sunday 2–4 P.M., so plan accordingly or call ahead to inquire whether someone can open it for you.

The attractive redbrick College Hill Center, which houses the museum, was built in 1851 as the Brownsville Baptist Female College. After 1900 it became the Ogilvie Training School for boys and later it was the Haywood County High School from 1911 to 1970.

Mind Field

Tucked next to a payday-loan storefront and quickmart near downtown Brownsville is the *Mind Field,* a steel sculpture created by local artist Billy Tripp. At first glance it looks like an electrical transformer station, but it is truly a work of art. It stands 75 feet tall in places, and includes messages of optimism and open-mindedness from the artist. Find the *Mind Field* off U.S. 70, one block away from the town square.

Events

Brownsville hosts the **Brownsville Blues Fall Festival** in late September or early October, which celebrates blues and the culture of the delta. Come to hear some of the best Delta blues outside Memphis, and enjoy barbecue, regional crafts, and sports activities. The blues festival is followed in October by the Hatchie Fall Festival on the courthouse square in Brownsville, which offers more live music and family-oriented fun.

Accommodations

Brownsville has the greatest concentration of hotels in this part of Tennessee. Most of these are located along I-40, a five-minute drive from downtown Brownsville. The **O'Bannon Inn** (120 Sunny Hill Cove Rd., 731/772-4030, $60) at exit 56 is an independent family-run hotel located in an old Holiday Inn. The rooms are comfortable, and guests get free wireless Internet, coffee and snacks all day and night, and a full breakfast with eggs, bacon, sausage, yogurt, fruit, pastries, and biscuits. It is within walking distance of the West Tennessee Delta Heritage Center and fast-food restaurants.

Other chain hotels located here include **Econo Lodge** (2600 Anderson Ave., 731/772-4082, $50–60) and **Days Inn** (2530 Anderson Ave., 731/772-3297, $50–60).

In town, try **Lilies' Bed and Breakfast** (508 W. Main St., 731/772-9078, $100) in the historic downtown. Gail Carver has two rooms in this elegant 1855 home, each with its own private bath.

Food

If you are in town on Friday or Saturday, then don't miss the weekly fish fry at **C City Fish Market** (223 S. Washington Ave., 731/772-9952, Fri. 10 A.M.–5:30 P.M., Sat. 10 A.M.–4:30 P.M., $5–12), on a side street in the old downtown area. Watch the catfish being cleaned and cut up, then deep fried before your eyes. Dinner plates are served with hush puppies and slaw, and you can douse your fish with vinegary hot sauce. Fried catfish does not get much fresher or better than this.

For a home-cooked meal during the week, try **The Sugar Palace** (2556 N. Washington Ave., 731/772-3941, Tues.–Fri. 9:30 A.M.–6 P.M., Sat. 10 A.M.–2 P.M., $4–10) on the square, which serves lunch on weekdays and sells candy and sweets all day.

Otherwise, Brownsville has fast-food restaurants, a few barbecue joints, and at least two Mexican restaurants. **Las Palmas** (27 S. Lafayette, 731/772-8004, daily 10 A.M.–9 P.M., $5–11) is on the court square and serves combination plates, fajitas, and grilled seafood.

Information

The **West Tennessee Delta Heritage Center** (121 Sunny Hill Cove, 731/779-9000) near the interstate at Brownsville has comprehensive information about visiting not only Brownsville, but all the counties in West Tennessee. Make this your first stop for information about the area. There is also a gift shop and public Internet access.

The **Brownsville-Haywood Chamber of Commerce** (121 W. Main St., 731/772-2193, www.haywoodcountybrownsville.com) can also help with information about the city.

NUTBUSH

This rural farming community would be a mere speck on the map were it not for R&B superstar Tina Turner, who was raised in and around Nutbush from her birth in 1936 until she moved to St. Louis at age 16. Turner penned the semi-autobiographical tune, "Nutbush City Limits," in 1973, which gave rise to a popular

© SUSANNA HENIGHAN POTTER

This sign is the only evidence of Tina Turner's roots in Nutbush, a rural community west of Brownsville.

line dance called the Nutbush. Turner re-released the song in 1991.

Reality is that Nutbush is too small to even have city limits; it feels much like a ghost town today. But the lone business, the Nutbush Grocery and Deli on Highway 19 (renamed in 2001 the Tina Turner Highway), proclaims its association with the R&B superstar with a sign. The home where Tina Turner once lived in Nutbush was torn down long ago, the lumber used to build a barn elsewhere in town.

HENNING

The tiny sawmill town of Henning is a half-hour drive through the cotton fields from Brownsville. It would be unremarkable except for the fact that it nurtured one of Tennessee's greatest writers, Alex Haley.

◖ Alex Haley House Museum

The Alex Haley House Museum (200 S. Church, 731/738-2240, Tues.–Sat. 10 A.M.–5 P.M., Sun. 1–5 P.M., $5) illustrates the early childhood of the Pulitzer Prize–winning author Alex Haley. This is where Haley spent his first 10 years, and he later returned here during the summers to stay with his maternal grandparents, Will and Cynthia Palmer.

Visitors tour the kitchen where Cynthia Palmer told Haley stories of her ancestors, which he later used as inspiration for his masterwork, *Roots.* The museum has artifacts of the period, family pictures and heirlooms. You also hear a recording of Haley describing Sunday dinners served in the dining room.

The museum was established with Haley's help, and he was buried here on his death in 1991.

MASON

Along Highway 70 near Mason, one landmark restaurant attracts Memphians and residents of the delta. ◖ **Gus's World Famous Hot and Spicy Chicken** (520 Hwy. 70, 901/294-2028, Mon.–Sat. 11 A.M.–9 P.M., $8–12) has been heralded by the likes of *GQ* magazine and celebrity chef Emeril as *the* place

FORT PILLOW

The earthworks at Fort Pillow along the Mississippi River were first built by the Confederates in 1861, but the fort was soon abandoned so that the rebels could consolidate their troops farther south. Union forces occupied the fort for several years, owing mainly to its strategic position at a sharp bend in the Mississippi River. On April 12, 1864, there were some 600 Union troops stationed at Fort Pillow – 200 of them were newly freed African Americans who had volunteered to join the Union cause.

By 1864 it was clear to most that the South would lose the war, so when legendary Confederate Gen. Nathan Bedford Forrest attacked Fort Pillow on April 12, it was not a battle of strategic importance but instead a fight for supplies and pride.

Accounts are that the Confederates quickly overcame the fort by land, but that an inexperienced Union commander, Maj. William Bradford, twice declined to surrender. Whether he finally surrendered or not is a matter of debate. Regardless of whether the Union formally surrendered, there was never any question which force would prevail. Forrest had more men and the advantage of surprise. With such a clear-cut victory at hand, it is no wonder that as news of the massive Union casualties emerged, the immediate cry was of massacre.

Forrest reported that a mere 14 Union men were killed in the battle, but Union records say that some 300 men lost their lives, 200 of whom were black. Even Confederate soldiers writing home described the events as "butchery" and told of savagery so great that Forrest himself rode through the ranks and

The cannons are quiet at Fort Pillow, the site of a controversial Civil War battle in 1864.

threatened to shoot any Confederate who did not stop the killing.

The U.S. Congress immediately ordered an investigation, and after reviewing a number of accounts and interviewing witnesses, declared the battle a massacre. The Confederates dismissed this as propaganda and blamed the heavy bloodletting on poor command. The precise nature of what happened at Fort Pillow remains a matter of debate.

For Union soldiers, and especially African-American soldiers, there was no ambiguity in their minds over what took place at Fort Pillow. Recognizing that official retribution may never come, black soldiers used Fort Pillow as a rallying cry in battle. "Remember Fort Pillow," they yelled on advance.

Poet Paul Laurence Dunbar immortalized the incident in his poem "The Unsung Heroes," which reads in part: "Pillow knew their blood, That poured on a nation's altar, a sacrificial flood."

for good fried chicken. Gus's is set in an old frame house, modified over the years to accommodate the thousands of loyal patrons who can't get enough of Gus's hot and spicy fried chicken. Coated in batter and a special seasoning paste, Gus's chicken is fried so that the crust is crispy, the meat juicy, and the taste just spicy enough to be perfect with a cold beer. Just when you think it can't get

any better, someone drops a quarter in the old jukebox and the blues fill the air. Wise diners get two orders: one to eat now and one to eat on the way home.

MEEMAN-SHELBY FOREST STATE PARK

About 20 miles north of Memphis, Meeman-Shelby Forest State Park (910 Riddick Rd.,

901/876-5215) sits at the crown of the Chickasaw Bluffs along the Mississippi River. Two-thirds of the 13,500-acre park is bottomland hardwood forests of oak, cypress, and tupelo. There are two lakes, and a nature center named for Edward J. Meeman, a journalist and conservationist. The nature center includes live snakes, a fish aquarium, a touch table, and an exhibit on Native Americans. From March to April, the center is open Saturday and Sunday 1–5 P.M.; from May to October it opens Friday through Sunday 1–5 P.M.; November to February it is open Sunday only. During the busiest summer weekends, the center offers special events, including nature activities, videos, and canoe and boat rides.

Recreation

There are 20 miles of hiking trails, including one five-mile paved track used by bicycles and wheelchairs. The swimming pool is open from Memorial Day through mid-August.

There are two fishing lakes, Poplar Tree and Piersol. You can rent a johnboat from the park, or launch your own for a small fee. No gasoline motors are allowed.

Camping

Stay in one of six lakeside cabins, which you can reserve up to one year in advance. The two-bedroom cabins can sleep up to six people. Rates are between $50 and $80 per night, depending on the season and day of the week. There are also 49 tent/RV sites, each with electrical and water hook-ups, picnic tables, grills, and fire rings. The bathhouse has hot showers. Campsite rates are $14.50–17.50 per night.

FORT PILLOW STATE HISTORIC PARK

The drive along Highway 87 to Fort Pillow State Historic Park (731/738-5581) takes you through almost 20 miles of rolling cotton fields and past the West Tennessee State Penitentiary. The park, which perches atop a bluff overlooking the Mississippi River, offers group, tent, and RV camping, picnic areas, 15 miles of hiking trails, wildlife viewing, and fishing in Fort Pillow Lake. There is also a museum (daily 8 A.M.–4 P.M., free) that tells the controversial story of the 1864 Battle of Fort Pillow, which many historians say is more aptly referred to as the Fort Pillow Massacre for the brutality displayed by southern troops under the command of Nathan Bedford Forrest.

Visitors to modern-day Fort Pillow can hike to the remains of the fort itself, and see the area where the battle took place. The museum's exhibits and a short video are dated, but an interested visitor will find a great deal of information contained in them. There are reenactments of the battle in April and November. The Mississippi River Bike Trail passes through the park.

Recreation

Only fishing boats and canoes are allowed on the 15-acre Fort Pillow Lake. The lake is stocked with bass, bream, crappie, and catfish; no boat rentals are available.

There are also playgrounds, a volleyball court, horseshoes, and a softball field.

Camping

Fort Pillow's 32 campsites rent for $8 per night. There are two bathhouses and a laundry. There are no electrical or water hook-ups.

Reelfoot Lake

Tennessee's "earthquake lake" is a landscape of knob-kneed cypress trees, gently rippling water, and open spaces. It is a flooded forest, eerie-looking and peaceful. The lake is a sportsman's dream, with 54 species of fish including bream, crappie, catfish, and bass. From January to March—the best fishing season—the lake sees a steady stream of visitors who come to troll its waters.

Reelfoot Lake is home to thousands of wintering and migratory birds. Visitors cannot help but notice the daily symphony of bird calls, not to mention the sight of ducks, herons, wild turkeys, eagles, and geese around the lake. Bird-watchers have identified some 238 species of birds in Reelfoot Lake, and the April turkey hunt in the area is excellent.

Bald eagles are the most iconic of the bird species that winter at the lake, and spotting these majestic creatures is a popular pursuit from January to March. Normally, the winter eagle population on the lake numbers between 100 and 200 birds. Bald eagles had virtually disappeared from the area in the 1960s due to the effects of DDT contamination of their nesting grounds, but thanks to a nesting project started in 1988 they have returned.

Orientation

Reelfoot Lake sits in the extreme northwestern corner of Tennessee. Its northernmost finger nearly touches the Kentucky state line, and the Mississippi River is only a mile to the west. Two-lane state highways circle the lake; the entire loop is about 35 miles. The southern portion of Reelfoot is a state park, and the northern half of the lake is a U.S. National Wildlife Refuge. Several thousand residents live in lakefront communities that dot the area.

The closest town to the lake, Tiptonville is a cluster of homes and businesses at the southwestern corner of Reelfoot. The boyhood home of Carl Perkins is found here; look for a sign on Highway 78 south of town to find it.

Most accommodations, restaurants, and provisioning locales are found along the southern shore, just a few minutes' drive from Tiptonville. The state park's Airpark Inn, along with one or two private camps and inns, are set on the lake's western shore, about 10 miles from Tiptonville. The trails and visitors center maintained by the U.S. Fish and Wildlife Service are located on the more isolated northern shore.

SIGHTS
◖ Reelfoot Lake State Park Visitor Center

The State Park Visitor Center (731/253-7756, Mon.–Fri. 8 A.M.–4:30 P.M., free) provides the best introduction to the lake, with exhibits on its history, wildlife, legends, and ecology. You can see a traditional Reelfoot Lake boat and read the story of the local vigilantes who took matters into their own hands when the lake was threatened with development. This is also the place to sign up for popular lake cruises and sightseeing tours.

Outside the museum are a couple of mesh cages where you can see bald eagles, owls, and red-tailed hawks. A half-mile boardwalk trail extends out over the lake at the rear of the visitors center and is a must for anyone who wants to experience the special beauty of the lake.

Reelfoot Lake National Wildlife Refuge

On the northern side of Reelfoot, near the intersections of Highways 22 and 157, is the **National Wildlife Refuge Visitor Center** (4343 Hwy. 157, 731/538-2481, daily 8 A.M.–4 P.M., free). Here you can see exhibits about the lake, with a special focus on the flora and fauna of the area. Take note that the Reelfoot National Wildlife Refuge, which is, essentially, the northern half of the lake, is only open to the public for fishing and

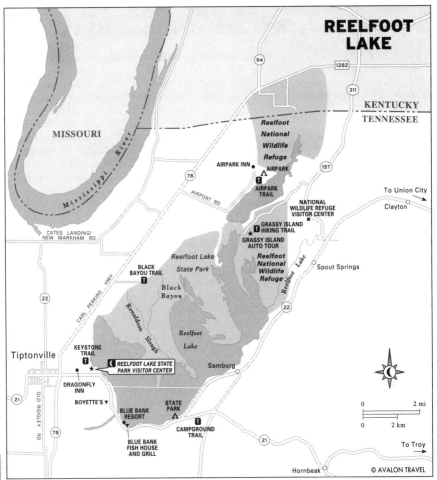

wildlife observation March 15–November 15 every year, although the visitors center remains open year-round. Contact the visitors center for specific rules about fishing, hunting, and public access to the refuge.

The wildlife refuge maintains the **Grassy Island Auto Tour,** a three-mile self-guided auto tour, year-round. The tour leads to an observation tower overlooking the Grassy Island part of the lake and is worth the detour required to reach it.

SPORTS AND RECREATION
Boating

If you can do only one thing when you visit Reelfoot Lake, get out on the water in a boat. The best cruises are provided by the state park. The cruises, which cost between $6 and $9 per person, take place from May to September and depart at 9 A.M. daily from the visitors center on the southern side of the lake. They last about three hours. Your guide will point out fish, birds, and other distinctive features of the

THE SEASONS AT REELFOOT LAKE

There are distinct variations in the type of wildlife you will see in and around Reelfoot Lake throughout the year.

In January and February, the wintering eagle and Canada goose populations peak. Cold water crappie fishing is good. In March, the eagles begin their northward migration, while osprey return from South America. Wild turkeys are often visible in March.

Spring comes to the lake in April and May, with wildflowers in abundance and the best season for bird-watching. It is also the best season to listen for frogs. By June, you may see deer fawns and the floating aquatic plants are in bloom.

July and August are the hottest months at Reelfoot Lake, and also the season of mosquitoes and deerflies. By September, it has cooled off. Fall fishing for crappie and bass begins.

During the fall, migrating and wintering birds begin to return. Short raccoon and archery deer hunting seasons take place in October; the deer gun hunt takes place in November. December is one of the best months to view ducks, geese, and eagles.

lake. It is a good idea to bring drinks (a cooler with ice is provided) and snacks.

In March and April, the park offers a deep swamp canoe float that departs on weekends at 8 A.M. and 1 P.M. The cost is $20. From January to March, special bald eagle tours are offered daily at 10 A.M. Call the state park at 731/253-7756 to make a reservation for any of the cruises.

Fishing

Fishing is the most popular recreation activity at Reelfoot Lake. With 13,000 acres of water and an average depth of just over five feet, the lake is a natural fish hatchery. An estimated 54 species of fish live in the lake. The most common fish are bream, crappie, catfish, and bass. The fishing season generally runs from March to July, although some species are plentiful into the fall.

Because Reelfoot Lake is so shallow, and because of the cypress knees that lurk below the surface, most fishermen use a specially designed Reelfoot Lake boat. If you want to fish on the lake for the first time, sign up with a local guide, who can help make arrangements for a boat rental and will share local fishing knowledge. Experienced guides include Jonathan Moore (731/538-3112), Chuck D's Professional Guide Service (731/885-5696), and Ed Hamilton (731/446-8234). For a complete and current listing of local guides, check with the visitors center or tourism council. Boat rentals usually cost $40 and up per day, and guides charge $100 and up per day.

Several hotels catering to fishermen offer special packages that include room, a boat and motor, bait, ice, and fuel for as little as $120 per night.

Hiking

For non-fishers, hiking is one of the best ways to experience Reelfoot. There are several easy and accessible trails that put hikers up close to the lake's unique environment.

Campground Trail: A half-mile trail that begins in the spillway area and ends at the state park campground on the southern tip of the lake. The trailhead is located on Highway 21/22.

Keystone Trail: This 1.5-mile path skirts the edge of the lake along part of its southern shore. Hikers should wear shoes or boots that can withstand the sometimes-muddy path. Birds are common. The trailhead is located off Highway 21/22 and is adjacent to a large picnic area.

Black Bayou Trail: This two-mile walk through the cypress swamp follows the Black Bayou Slough. The trailhead is located along Highway 78 on the western shore of the lake.

The Airpark Trail: This 1.5-mile trail winds through cypress and hardwood forest as well as open fields. The trailhead is next to the Airpark Inn off Highway 78.

Grassy Island Hiking Trail on the northern side of Reelfoot Lake explores wetlands.

Grassy Island Hiking Trail: Part of the National Wildlife Refuge at Grassy Island, this half-mile path cuts through lowland forest and over swampy wetlands. A portion follows the paved auto-tour road through Grassy Island.

Biking

The terrain around Reelfoot Lake is flat, and traffic is relatively light. Biking is a good way to get around and explore what the lake has to offer. Bring your own bike, however, since no rentals are available.

ACCOMMODATIONS

The best accommodations on Reelfoot Lake are at the state park–operated **Airpark Inn** (731/253-7756, $40), on the northwestern side of the lake. Built on a platform over the lake, the inn has 20 comfortable rooms and suites, each with a private balcony and view of the lake. Guests have reported catching fish right from their porch. Double rooms have refrigerators, microwaves, coffeemakers, and televisions; suites come with all this plus a kitchenette. All guests have access to charcoal grills and freezers as well as a fish cleaning station. Guests may also take advantage of lighted tennis courts, a swimming pool, and, for the jet-set, a 3,500-foot landing strip next to the inn. There are also meeting rooms and a boat dock, and a continental breakfast of coffee, orange juice, and pastries.

The **Blue Bank Resort** (3330 State Rte. 21E, 731/253-8976, www.bluebankresort.com) has a traditional motel as well as cabins that stand over the lake, with expansive decks and a 12-person hot tub. The cabins can sleep between 3 and 16. All rooms have a lot of exposed wood, giving the resort the feeling of a hunting lodge. The Blue Bank offers fishing packages, which cost $200–300 per person for up to four nights and include gear: boat, motor, bait, and ice for fishing. If you're just interested in a room without the add-ons, call at the last minute to find out if they have a vacancy.

For the most intimate accommodations at Reelfoot Lake, try **Dragonfly Inn** (365 Sunkist

Beach Rd., 731/442-0750, www.dragonflyinn-reelfootlake.com, $60), formerly Miss Pauline's Bed and Breakfast. Set in an old farmhouse, this friendly bed-and-breakfast is just one mile from Reelfoot Lake but feels removed from the crowds that exist during peak season. The four rooms are homey, and each has a private bath, individual heating and air-conditioning, and a queen-sized bed. Host Marianne serves a full breakfast, and accommodates fishermen with early breakfasts, freezer space, and lots of boat parking in the driveway.

Camping

The state park runs two campgrounds for RVs and tents. A small campground is located next to the Airpark Inn on the northwest coast of the lake. A larger campground is on the southern shore near the visitors center. Rates at both campgrounds are $20 for an RV site and $8 for a tent site.

FOOD

Catfish and other lake fish are the food du jour around Reelfoot Lake. **C Boyette's** (Hwy. 21, 731/253-7307, daily 11 A.M.–9 P.M., $7–15) is located across the road from the Reelfoot Lake State Park Visitor Center. The catfish platter is the specialty here, and it comes with generous portions of French fries, onion rings, hush puppies, coleslaw, and green beans. If you've worked up an appetite after a day of fishing, go for the all-you-can-eat catfish dinner, a steal at $13. You can also get frog legs, steaks, and burgers.

A little bit farther east along the lakeshore road you will find **Blue Bank Fish House and Grill** (813 Lake Dr., 731/253-8976, daily 11 A.M.–9 P.M., $6–20). The Blue Bank menu is sure to have something that will please anyone. In addition to all-you-can-eat catfish, fried quail, and country ham, you can choose from pasta, shrimp, steak, loaded potatoes, and burgers. The dinner menu is $8–20 and lunchtime entrées are $6–14. They also serve breakfast. The kitchen closes 2–4 P.M. on weekdays.

Around Reelfoot

For a break from the rustic, drive the 20 miles east to Troy, where you'll find **White House** (106 College St., 731/536-2000, $14–27), open for lunch and dinner Monday through Saturday. Set in a gracious old boardinghouse, the restaurant serves uncommonly good food in a welcoming environment. The handsome white building on the town square has a lawn and adjoining gift shop, and is a popular venue for weddings and special events. The menu includes a half-dozen different steaks, pork chops, shrimp, salmon, and chicken. At lunch, choose from sandwiches, salads, and pasta.

INFORMATION

Stop at the **State Park Visitor Center** (Hwy. 21, 731/253-7756, daily 8 A.M.–4:30 P.M.) or the **Reelfoot Lake Tourism Council** (4575 Hwy. 21E, 731/253-6516, www.reelfootlaketourism.com, Mon. 8 A.M.–5 P.M., Thurs. 9 A.M.–5 P.M., Fri.–Sat. 9 A.M.–6 P.M., Sun. 1–6 P.M.) for visitor information. The Reelfoot Lake State Park Auto Tour guide, a single-sheet handout available at any of these offices, is the most useful map of the area.

OUTSIDE MEMPHIS

Jackson

Jackson is the largest city between Nashville and Memphis, and the center of commerce and business for rural West Tennessee. Every Pringles potato chip in the world is made in Jackson, which also hosts a number of events including a Division One women's basketball tournament, the Miss Tennessee pageant, and the West Tennessee State Fair.

Jackson owes its existence to the railroads, and the city has preserved this history at a top-notch museum set right next to the railroad tracks. Jackson is also home to a museum dedicated to the life and death of famous railroad engineer Casey Jones, and another that zeroes in on that endearing art form, rock-a-billy.

SIGHTS

Jackson's city center is about five miles south of I-40, and the roadways between the interstate and downtown are cluttered with strip malls, motels, and traffic. Most of the attractions, with the exception of Casey Jones Village, are downtown on the blocks surrounding the stately courthouse square.

Casey Jones Home and Railroad Museum

In 1980, the home of the legendary railroad engineer was moved from the city of Jackson to Casey Jones Village, a plaza of shops and restaurants just off the interstate north of Jackson. The museum includes Jones's white clapboard home and a replica of the engine that he rode to his death in 1900. The home and engine form the centerpiece of the Casey Jones Home and Railroad Museum (56 Casey Jones Ln., 731/668-1222, www.caseyjones.com, Mon.–Sun. 9 A.M.–5 P.M., adults $4, children 6–12 $3, children under 6 free), which tells the story of Casey Jones's life and the legend that surrounds him to this day. Exhibits document every detail of the deadly 1900 crash that took his life, but

legendary engineer Casey Jones in the cab of an engine

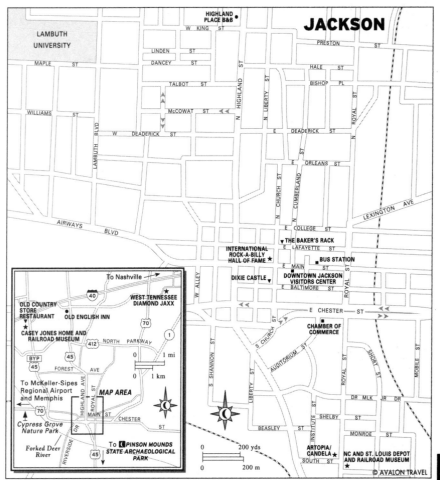

some of the most fascinating parts of the museum deal with the legend of Casey Jones that evolved after his death. There are also elaborate model train sets that you can run for a few quarters. The home and museum is open until 8 P.M. from Memorial Day to Labor Day.

N.C. & St. Louis Depot and Railroad Museum

Jackson owes it existence to the railroads that passed through the town, and the N.C.

& St. Louis Depot and Railroad Museum (582 S. Royal St., 731/425-8223, Mon.–Sat. 10 A.M.–3 P.M., free) documents much of the city's railroad history. Located inside Jackson's oldest railroad station a few blocks south of downtown, the museum walls are covered with photographs and memorabilia of the railroads. There is a large model train in the rear of the station, and outside visitors can explore a dining car and engine.

Over the railroad tracks from the Railroad

THE LEGEND OF CASEY JONES

Casey Jones was born John Luther Jones, but was better known as Casey after his hometown, Cayce, in Kentucky. He started as a telegrapher for the Mobile and Ohio Railroad in Kentucky, and worked his way up to be brakeman, fireman, and eventually engineer. Casey had a reputation for running the trains on time, whatever it took.

In the early-morning hours of April 30, 1900, Jones was running a passenger train from Memphis to Canton, Mississippi, when he crashed into the tail end of a freight train that was blocking a portion of the track near Vaughn, Mississippi. Jones died when his engine No. 382 collided with the freight train and veered off the tracks. Jones was the only person killed in the accident.

The story of Casey Jones did not end with his death, however. An African-American engine wiper, Wallace Saunders, started to sing a song that he composed about the dead engineer, and soon "The Ballad of Casey Jones" was a well-known folk song. The professional songwriting team Sibert and Newton copy-

Casey Jones Home and Railroad Museum

righted the song in 1909 and it became one of the most famous songs in America. Neither the Jones family or Wallace Saunders ever received a penny from its success.

The story of Casey Jones's life and death was immortalized on television, film, and stage. His widow, Janie Jones, and accident survivor, Simeon Webb, remained minor celebrities for the rest of their lives.

The story of Casey Jones is told at the Casey Jones Home and Railroad Museum in Jackson.

Museum is a covered fountain whose waters once drew thousands of people to Jackson. The **Electro Chalybeate Well** (604 S. Royal St.) was discovered in the late 1800s and its waters were reputed to cure a host of ailments. In recent years the city of Jackson built the fountain, gazebo, and benches around the well. You can drink the water from a circle of water fountains if you like.

International Rock-a-Billy Hall of Fame

As the city that lays claim to Carl Perkins, Jackson is home to the International Rock-a-Billy Hall of Fame (105 N. Church St., 731/423-5440, www.rockabilly.org, Mon.–Fri. 10 A.M.–4 P.M., adults $10). This storefront museum features exhibits about a number of the genre's famous performers. There is also a room of Elvis memorabilia, and a performance space for concerts and dancing. A tour with

enthusiastic guide Linda McGee costs $10 and is best-suited for hard-core rock-a-billy fans. There are line-dancing lessons Monday beginning at 6 P.M., and live music on Friday night starting at 6:30 P.M.

ENTERTAINMENT
Shopping

Across Royal Sreet from the N.C. & St. Louis Depot and Railroad Museum is **Artopia** (575 S. Royal St., 731/554-2929), a gallery housed in an old hotel. Each old guest room is filled with the work of different artists, and items include paintings, sculpture, fabric, and much more. There is also a salon, coffee shop, and restaurant. Artopia is open every day, and stays open until 9 P.M. on Thursday, Friday, and Saturday.

Events

Jackson puts on three major annual events. The **Shannon Street Blues and Heritage**

Festival (731/427-7573, www.jackson-downtown.com) takes place in June at the West Tennessee Farmer's Market and is the work of the Downtown Development Corporation. The Rock-a-Billy Hall of Fame organizes an **International Rock-a-Billy Festival** (731/427-6262, www.rockabilly-hall.org) every August, and the Casey Jones Village puts on an **Old Time Music Fest** (731/668-1223, www.caseyjonesvillage.com) in September.

Every September sees the **West Tennessee State Fair** (731/424-0151), a week of competitions, amusements, performances, and rides at the Jackson Fairgrounds Park.

SPORTS AND RECREATION

Parks

A few miles southwest of downtown Jackson is **Cypress Grove Nature Park** (Hwy. 70 West, 731/425-8316), a pleasant park with boardwalks, picnic facilities, walking paths, and an observation tower.

Spectator Sports

The **West Tennessee Diamond Jaxx** (4 Fun Pl., 731/988-5299, www.diamondjaxx.com) play in Pringles Field just off I-40 in Jackson. A farm team of the Chicago Cubs, the Jaxx put on a good show for fans during their season from April to October. Admission is $4.50–9.50.

ACCOMMODATIONS

For the most luxurious accommodations in Jackson, choose ❰ **Highland Place Bed & Breakfast** (519 N. Highland Ave., 731/427-1472, www.highlandplace.com, $145–175). Set in a stately redbrick historic home along central Highland Avenue, a five-minute drive from downtown, the inn has four rooms ranging from a three-room suite to single rooms. Each room has a private bath, cable television, and wireless Internet access. The rooms are decorated with antique and modern handmade furniture. All guests have the run of the numerous public rooms, including a living room, library, and breakfast room. It sure beats a standard hotel room.

The Old English Inn (2267 N. Highland Ave., 731/668-1571, www.oldenglishinn.com, $60–75) is set a mile or so south of the interstate. Its 103 rooms include suites and handicapped-accessible rooms. The lobby and common areas enjoy distinctive flair, included stained glass and a fireplace, and all the rooms are nicely furnished with dark wood. The Old English Inn calls itself a Christian hotel, although guests of all religious affiliations are welcome.

FOOD

❰ **Dixie Castle** (215 E. Baltimore, 731/423-3359, Mon.–Fri. 10:30 A.M.–2 P.M., Mon.–Sat. 5–9 P.M., $5–12) attracts a large local crowd for lunch and dinner. This diner-style restaurant serves plate-lunch specials, burgers, and sandwiches. The food is home-style, with large portions. You'll be hard-pressed to find a table at the peak of the lunch rush. At dinner, they offer steaks, pork chops, and chicken dinners. They do a brisk take-out trade as well, and the servers are some of the friendliest in town.

Also downtown, **The Baker's Rack** (203 E. Lafayette, 731/424-6163, Mon.–Thurs. 7 A.M.–5 P.M., Fri. 7 A.M.–3 P.M., $2.50–9) serves a diverse menu of hot or cold sandwiches, baked potatoes, plate lunches, and salads. They also make decadent desserts: Try the red velvet cake or "better than sex" cake. For breakfast, choose from biscuits, eggs on toast, oatmeal, French toast, or a generous breakfast platter with all the fixings.

In Casey Jones Village off I-40, the **Old Country Store Restaurant** (56 Casey Jones Lane, 731/668-1223, www.caseyjones.com, daily 6:30 A.M.–9 P.M., $5–9) serves specials like country ham, smothered chicken, and fried catfish, plus burgers and barbecue. The breakfast bar is a popular choice for those with a big appetite. They also have a fruit bar and the usual breakfast choices of eggs, biscuits, pancakes, and omelets.

One of the best new restaurants in town is **Candela** (575 S. Royal St., 731/554-3663, Tues.–Sat. 11 A.M.–2 P.M., Thurs.–Sat. 5–9 P.M.). Located in Artopia, Candela takes a creative approach to dining, and the results are usually excellent. Lunch ($7–12) features tortellini pasta, seared salmon, shrimp salad, and a variety of sandwiches. For dinner ($7–17) try the stuffed mushrooms, lobster ravioli, or fish of the day.

The **West Tennessee Farmer's Market** (91 New Market St., 731/425-8310) takes place under shelters in downtown Jackson daily 7 A.M.–4 P.M. in the summer.

INFORMATION AND SERVICES

Maps and general information on Jackson can be found at the **Jackson Downtown Development Corporation** (314 E. Main St., 731/427-7573) or the **Jackson Area Chamber of Commerce** (197 Auditorium St., 731/423-2200).

The **Jackson-Madison County Library** (433 E. Lafayette St., 731/425-8600) is one of the nicest public libraries in West Tennessee.

GETTING THERE AND AROUND

Jackson is located about midway between Nashville and Memphis along I-40, and most people drive here. The regional McKellar-Sipes Airport (MKL, www.mklairport.com) has on-and-off commercial air service, subject to the ups and downs of the airline industry. Check with airport officials to find out if commercial service is available.

Photographers have been known to make a detour to photograph the iconic Jackson Main Street Greyhound bus terminal, with its retro art deco style. The station is convenient to several attractions and restaurants, but not close to any hotels. There is daily service to Memphis and Nashville; Paduch, Kentucky; and Jackson, Mississippi.

While trains still travel on Jackson's famous tracks, there is no passenger service to or from the city.

◖ PINSON MOUNDS STATE ARCHAEOLOGICAL PARK

One of the largest complexes of mounds ever built by Woodland Indians is found 10 miles south of Jackson. Pinson Mounds (460

© SUSANNA HENIGHAN POTTER

The tallest of the mounds at Pinson Mounds, shown here, is 33 feet.

Ozier Rd., 731/988-5614, free), now a state park, is a group of at least 17 mounds believed to have been built beginning around 50 B.C. The mounds were discovered in 1820 by Joel Pinson, part of a surveying team that was mapping new territory bought from the Chickasaw Indians in 1818. Early archaeological digs were carried out in the late 1800s, but it was not until 1961 that the first major investigation of the site was completed by scientists from the University of Tennessee.

Despite continuing archaeology on the site, many mysteries remain: Among them is the significance of the design and arrangement of the mounds and why the mound-builders abandoned the site around A.D. 500. Some scientists have argued that the mounds were arranged as markers for the solar equinox and winter solstice.

Visitors to Pinson Mounds begin within a mound replica, which houses a museum and bookstore. The museum is dedicated to telling the story of what is known about the mysterious mounds and the people who built them. The mounds themselves are spread out along six miles of hiking trails that meander through the archaeological park. Many of the trails are across open fields, and walking can be hot during the summer months. A bike is an ideal way to get around, but you need to bring your own since there is no rental facility.

The park museum is open Monday–Saturday 8 A.M.–4:30 P.M. and Sunday 1–5 P.M. The rest of the park, including its hiking trails and picnic area, are open until dusk.

Events

Archaeofest is a festival celebrating Native American culture. It takes place every September and includes artistic demonstrations, food and craft vendors, storytelling, flintknapping, and more. Contact the park office for more information.

Camping

Pinson Mounds has a group camp facility that can accommodate up to 32 people. There is also a day-use picnic area.

BETHEL SPRINGS

About 30 miles south of Jackson on Highway 45, near the community of Bethel Springs, is **Ada's Unusual Country Store** (9653 Hwy. 45, 731/934-9310, Mon.–Sat. 8 A.M.–5 P.M.), which is unusual indeed. The shelves are packed with organic and natural food items, including grains, flour, pastas, and snacks. You can buy fresh local eggs, honey, and milk; Amish cheese and cookbooks; and homemade breads and sweets. For a meal on the go, you can get cold drinks, fresh-made sandwiches, and ice cream.

Shiloh and Vicinity

The Civil War battle fought in the woods and fields around the Shiloh Methodist Meeting House on Sunday, April 6, and Monday, April 7, 1862, has been etched in the nation's memory ever since. The first major battle of the western theater and one of the bloodiest of the entire Civil War, Shiloh demonstrated to both North and South that the war would be a longer and harder fight than either side imagined.

Visitors to this famous battleground, now a national park, can study the details of the engagement, consider its significance in the Civil War, and ponder the meaning of so many deaths.

In addition to Shiloh, this part of West Tennessee offers wonderful opportunities for recreation on the Tennessee and Wolf Rivers, and the lovely old towns of La Grange and Savannah.

Information

The **Tourism Association of Southwest Tennessee** (866/261-7534, www.tast.tn.org) produces brochures and stocks information stands at interstate rest stops and other crossroads. Their guide to the region has helpful listings and a map.

LA GRANGE

La Grange, a mere speck of civilization 50 miles east of Memphis, feels like the town that time forgot. Old homes—some elegant, some ramshackle—line narrow drives. The post office, town office, and an old-fashioned country store constitute the business district. Unfortunately, since the closure in 2007 of Cogbill's Store and Museum, there is not much to do here except look. If you are here on Saturday morning, stop at the La Grange General Store for a cup of coffee and conversation. The town office is open weekday mornings.

Despite the dearth of outright attractions, La Grange, also called "La Belle Village," delivers an experience unlike any other town in this part of Tennessee. Its lovingly preserved antebellum homes, rural landscape, and charming people are truly unique.

History

La Grange, named in honor of the Marquis de

LaFayette's ancestral home in France, seemed destined for great things when it was chartered in 1829. Its population quickly swelled to more than 3,000. The first Episcopal church in West Tennessee was founded here, and in 1835 stockholders chartered the La Grange & Memphis Railway. The plans for a railroad faltered, however, and La Grange suffered from Union occupation during most of the Civil War. A tornado destroyed part of the town in 1900, and La Grange lost its telegraph station and express mail delivery to nearby Grand Junction. Hopes for La Grange to grow into a city dwindled.

Despite its size, La Grange was and is known for a special refinement and pursuit of the arts and education. In 1855, the La Grange Female College and the La Grange Synodical College for Men were chartered. The town's local newspapers, *The Monitor* and, later, the *Spirit of the Age,* were respected in the region. During the Civil War, La Grange native Lucy Pickens was depicted on the face of the Confederate $1 note, and three different $100 notes. Pickens, whose childhood home at 290 Pine Street is still standing, was known as the "Queen of the Confederacy."

In 1998, La Grange dedicated a 2.5-ton bronze and limestone monument to the nearby Wolf River. The **Wolf River Monument,** located near the post office and fire department, was rendered in the shape of a wolf's head and was created by Memphis sculptor Roy Tamboli.

Information

La Grange City Hall (20 Main St., 901/878-1246, Mon.–Fri. 8 A.M.–noon) is the best source of information about the town. They can provide you with a large fold-out map of the town's historic homes.

Ghost River State Natural Area

The Ghost River is a 14-mile section of the Wolf River that meanders through bottomland forest, cypress-tupelo swamps, and open marshes. The river got its name from the loss of river current as the water flows through marshes and swamps.

© SUSANNA HENIGHAN POTTER

the Ghost River

GENERAL JOHNSTON

Gen. Albert Sidney Johnston, the Confederate commander of the western department of the army, was concentrating all available forces at Corinth, Mississippi, in early April 1862. His objective was to launch an offensive against the Union army under the command of Gen. Ulysses S. Grant at Pittsburg Landing, Tennessee, before Union reinforcements arrived.

On April 3, Johnston ordered his troops to march north, towards the engagement. Heavy rains and bad roads slowed their forward progress, and the Southern troops lost a day on their journey, a delay that would prove significant in the coming days.

The Confederates arrived at their camp south of Pittsburg Landing on the late afternoon of April 5, and Johnston decided to delay the attack until morning. During the evening, he and his second-in-command, P. G. T. Beauregard, disagreed about the coming fight; Beauregard argued against attack, saying that the Union army would not be surprised. But Johnston would not be deterred. He wanted to attack the Union forces before reinforcements from Nashville arrived.

As it turned out, the Union army was surprised by the Confederate attack in the early-morning hours of April 6. Soldiers described the disorder and chaos of the Union camps as word was quickly spread about the advancing fighters. Gen. Grant, who was breakfasting at the Cherry Mansion in Savannah, a few miles north of Shiloh, was surprised by the sound of gunfire and rushed to the scene.

Gen. Johnston would not live to see the outcome of the battle that he orchestrated. In the middle of the afternoon on the first day of fighting, just before the Confederates reached the high-water mark of their efforts, Johnston was struck by a mini-ball in the leg. His companions did not realize at first the seriousness of his injury, and neither did Johnston. But at 2:45 P.M. on April 6, the Confederate general died, passing command to Beauregard.

Johnston was the highest-ranking officer on either side of the Civil War to be killed in active duty.

About a three-mile drive south of La Grange you can hike or canoe in the Ghost River State Natural Area. To find the 600-foot boardwalk and hiking trail, drive south from La Grange on Yager Road, and then turn west on Beasley Road. The parking area is about 1.5 miles down the road. There is another parking area and a place to put in a canoe along Yager Road, and a marked canoe path so you don't get lost in the swamp. There is another parking area at the canoe take-out on Bateman Road. You can get a map from the La Grange town office, or from the State of Tennessee website (www.state.tn.us).

◀ SHILOH NATIONAL MILITARY PARK

The Shiloh National Military Park (1055 Pittsburg Landing Rd., 731/689-5696, www.nps.gov/shil, daily 8 A.M.–5 P.M., $3) is set along the western shore of the Tennessee River about eight miles south of Crump. Shiloh today is a landscape of alternating open fields and wooded forest, populated by hundreds of monuments to soldiers who fought and died at Shiloh on April 6–7, 1862. The peacefulness of the present brings into even greater focus the violence of the battle that took place here almost 150 years ago and claimed nearly 24,000 casualties.

You can drive around the battlefield, but some of the most important sites are a short walk from the road. At the visitors center there is a small museum and you can watch a 25-minute video about the battle. The film, made in 1956, was one of the first park service films to use live actors. A new movie is in the works.

Sights within the park include the peach orchard, now being regrown, where soldiers described the peach blossoms falling like snow

© SUSANNA HENIGHAN POTTER

Some two-thirds of the 3,695 people buried at the Shiloh National Cemetery are unidentified.

on the dead and injured; the "bloody pond," where injured men crawled for water, and in some cases, to die; and the Hornet's Nest, the site of some of the most furious fighting.

The 10-acre **Shiloh National Cemetery** is located next to the visitors center. Two-thirds of the 3,695 bodies interred here are unidentified. Most are Union soldiers killed at Shiloh, but there are others from nearby battles, the Spanish-American War, both World Wars, and the Revolutionary War. The Confederate dead were buried in five

trenches around the battlefield, and remain there today.

Nearly 800 years before the Civil War, the riverbank near present-day Shiloh was home to a mound-building Mississippian Indian community. The **Shiloh Indian Mounds** that they left behind sit along the west bluff of the riverbank, and are one of the largest mound groups in the country. A remarkable effigy pipe was discovered here in the 1890s and is on display at the Tennessee River Museum in Savannah. The mounds are accessible on foot from two points in the park.

DEATHS AT SHILOH

	Present for Duty	Killed	Wounded	Missing
Union	65,085	1,754	8,408	2,885
Confederate	44,699	1,728	8,012	959
Total	109,784	3,482	16,420	3,844

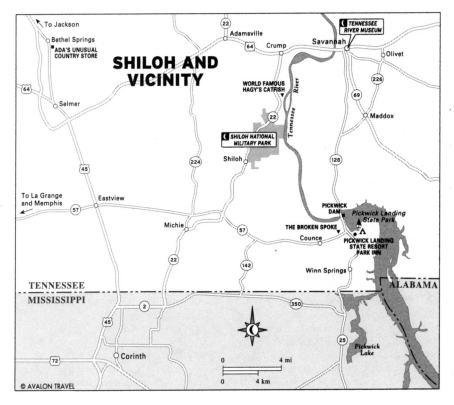

Practicalities

A printed guide and map to the battlefield is available at the visitors center, and it takes about an hour to follow it. For a more detailed examination, you can buy an audio tour from the park bookstore for $12. This tour takes about two hours to complete and includes narratives by soldiers, historians, and civilians.

Shiloh National Military Park is closed on Christmas Day. The bookstore is one of the best in the area, and has an extensive collection of books on the Civil War, Tennessee, Native Americans, and African-American history.

There are snack and drink vending machines at the visitors center, and a picnic area in the park. The closest restaurants are in Shiloh, Savannah, and Counce. For accommodations, look in Savannah.

With its miles of flat roads and restrained traffic, Shiloh is a good place to bicycle. There are no rental facilities nearby, however, so plan on bringing your own wheels.

SHILOH

There is not much to the modern town of Shiloh, except a few souvenir shops and one excellent catfish restaurant. **World Famous Hagy's Catfish Restaurant** (off Hwy. 22, 731/689-3327, Tues.–Sat. 11 A.M.–10 P.M., Sun. noon–9 P.M., $9–15) is set off by itself in a beautiful clearing overlooking the Tennessee River. You can stretch your legs with a walk down to the water's edge. Hagy's menu has fried and grilled catfish, plus other favorites like chicken and steak. But choose the catfish, which is nicely seasoned and expertly fried. It comes with hush puppies and coleslaw. This will be a meal to remember.

Find Hagy's by looking for the large sign for the turn-off along Highway 22 on the northern side of Shiloh National Military Park.

SAVANNAH

A picturesque town on the eastern bank of the Tennessee River, Savannah has historic homes, a good museum, and the greatest selection of restaurants and accommodations in this part of the state.

In its early life, the town was Rudd's Ferry, named for James Rudd, who operated a ferry across the river. The ferry was taken over by David Robinson, whose wife is said to have renamed the town Savannah after her hometown in Georgia. In 1830, Savannah became the seat of Hardin County and soon developed a reputation as a wealthy, cultured town.

C Tennessee River Museum

Savannah is a river town, and the river is one of its main attractions. The Tennessee River Museum (507 Main St., 731/925-2364, Mon.–Sat. 9 A.M.–5 P.M., Sun. 1–5 P.M., $2) documents the history of the region and the river. Exhibits detail the prehistoric peoples of the region, and include an original red stone effigy pipe found inside one of the Shiloh Indian Mounds a few miles south. There are also exhibits on Shiloh and the river during the Civil War, riverboats, and the economic uses of the river, including pearl farming and mussels. Some of the most interesting items on display are receipts issued by Savannah merchants to the U.S. Army party that was escorting 2,500 Cherokee Indians down the river on the Trail of Tears in 1838.

The museum is a good first stop for visitors to the area, and staff can provide information about other nearby attractions. Through a partnership with Shiloh National Military Park, guests who show their Shiloh parking pass receive free entry to the museum.

Historic Homes

David Robinson built the **Cherry Mansion** (265 W. Main St.) on the riverbank, on top of what historians believe was an Indian mound. Robinson gave the mansion to his daughter when she married William H. Cherry. The house, which is closed to the public, is where U.S. Gen. Ulysses S. Grant stayed during the days leading up to the battle of Shiloh. William Cherry was a noted Union sympathizer, and the mansion remained a Union headquarters and field hospital during the war. Although the house is privately owned, visitors are welcome to stop and look. There is a river overlook next door.

Savannah was settled between 1830 and 1850, but many of the old houses were damaged or destroyed during the Civil War. However, beautiful homes were rebuilt and many of these remain in the leafy residential area just north of Savannah's Main Street. The homes are elegant examples of fine houses of the late 19th century.

Pick up a guide to the **Savannah Walking Tour** at the Tennessee River Museum (507 Main St., 731/925-2364).

Haley Memorial

Savannah is where the paternal grandparents of Pulitzer Prize–winning author Alex Haley are buried. Alex Haley Sr. operated Rudd's Ferry, and his wife, Queen Haley, worked in the Cherry Mansion for the Cherry family. Haley's novel *Queen* was inspired by his grandmother's life. The couple's shared tombstone is located in the Savannah Cemetery. To find the Haley Memorial, take Cherry Street from downtown Savannah and over a small bridge and enter the cemetery. Take the first gravel road to your right, and then walk over the hill, taking a right at the Y. The Haleys, as well as Alex Haley Sr.'s first wife, Tennie, share a gravestone.

Accommodations

You can get a comfortable bed at the **Savannah Lodge** (585 Pickwick St., 731/925-8586, $35–55), a motel that boasts the basics for its guests. Several national chains also have locations in Savannah.

TENNESSEE PEARLS

The fast-running rivers of Tennessee are home to freshwater mussels, and these mussels sometimes create beautiful pearls.

Native Americans were the first to discover Tennessee's pearls; Indians harvested mussels for food and used the pearls in jewelry. Tennessee history knows many stories of simple folks who stumbled upon a pearl, getting an unexpected payday in the process. In one such story, Charles Bradford and James Johnson were looking for bait to go fishing in the Caney Fork River in the early 1880s. They had pulled up several mussels and inside one found a large white pearl. The boys sent the pearl to Tiffany's in New York and received a check for $83.

Stories such as this one fueled the Tennessee pearl industry for many years. The industry peaked between 1882 and 1914, when special musseling boats would ply the Tennessee and other rivers, dragging a "brail" (resembling an underwater rake) that captured river mussels. In more modern times, diving is the most popular way to harvest wild mussels from the watery depths.

Tennessee pearls were a variety of colors and shapes, and the mother-of-pearl from the mussel shells was used in button manufacturing during the early part of the 20th century, before plastic buttons became common.

Tennessee pearls declined following the establishment of the Tennessee Valley Authority and the damming of many rivers in the state. Dams caused rivers to flow more slowly, elimi-

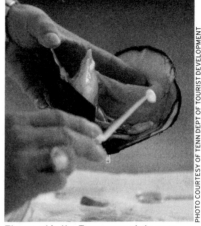

PHOTO COURTESY OF TENN DEPT OF TOURIST DEVELOPMENT

The pearl is the Tennessee state gem.

nating the fast-moving water habitat required by freshwater mussels. Pollution also hurt wild mussels, as did overfishing and the rise of pearl cultivation in Asia.

The Tennessee River Pearl Farm near Camden, Tennessee, still harvests pearls from the river, although they are cultivated. Some of the pearls harvested here are fashioned into jewelry, but most are exported to Asia where they are used in the cultivation of high-grade pearls.

The pearl was named the Tennessee state gem in 1979.

Food

Worleybird Cafe (990 Pickwick St., 731/926-4882, Mon.–Sat. 5 A.M.–9 P.M., Sun. 5 A.M.–2 P.M., $5–12) is a popular choice for Savannah's locals. Named for beloved son of the soil, country musician Daron Worley, the café serves sandwiches, Cajun catfish, steaks, chicken cordon bleu, and salads, plus eggs, biscuits, and pancakes in the morning.

Another good choice for home-style cooking in Savannah is **Toll House Restaurant** (610 Wayne Rd., 731/925-5128, Mon.–Sat. 5 A.M.–9 P.M., Sun. 6 A.M.–2 P.M., $4–9), whose home fries and eggs draw a crowd in the morning. At lunch and dinner, there is an ample buffet with traditional favorites like macaroni and cheese, fried catfish, and beef tips.

For a more refined dining experience, go to the **Uptown** (390 Main St., 731/926-1911, Mon.–Sat. 11 A.M.–8 P.M., $12–19), a wine bar and bistro with seafood, pasta, and steak, as well as superb desserts.

Information

Stop at the **Tennessee River Museum** (507 Main St., 731/925-2364, Mon.–Sat. 9 A.M.–5 P.M., Sun. 1–5 P.M.) to pick up maps and other information about Savannah.

You can also contact the **Hardin County Convention and Visitors Bureau** (731/925-8181, www.tourhardincounty.org) for information.

PICKWICK LANDING STATE PARK

Pickwick Landing was a riverboat stop from the 1840s until the 1930s when Pickwick Dam was built and the lake formed. Pickwick Lake was created in December 1937 when the Tennessee Valley Authority dammed the Tennessee and flooded farmland in the valley. The lake was dedicated in 1940, and a crowd of 30,000 people attended the services on the southern earth dam. Today it attracts vacationers from around the region who enjoy the laid-back atmosphere and top-flight bass fishing.

The lake lies in Tennessee, Alabama, and Mississippi and is one of the premier spots for recreation in the area. Boating, fishing, and swimming are especially popular. There are several nearby golf courses, and opportunities to camp, hunt, and hike.

Pickwick Landing State Park (Rte. 57, 731/689-3129) is one of Tennessee's resort parks, with a new hotel, conference center, golf course, and marina.

Hiking

There is an easy three-mile hiking trail that meanders along the lakeshore.

Golf

The Pickwick Landing State Park golf course is a par 72, champion's 18-hole course. The pro shop rents clubs and carts and sells golf accessories. Call 731/689-3149 to reserve a tee time. Greens fees range $13–22, depending on the season and day of the week.

Boating

Pleasure riding, sailing, waterskiing, and

Pickwick Dam

OUTSIDE MEMPHIS

fishing are all popular activities on Pickwick Lake. There are three public boat launch ramps at Pickwick Landing State Park, and marine fuel and other boating items are available from the park marina.

You can rent a pontoon boat from **Pickwick Boat Rentals** (731/689-5359) for $175 and up per day.

Fishing

Fishing on Pickwick Lake is best in the spring and fall. Conditions here include shallow stump flats, well-defined channels, active feeder creeks, steeply falling bluffs, rocky ledges, and long grass beds.

Pickwick Outdoors, Inc. (877/214-4924) organizes fishing vacations for groups. For a fishing guide, contact **Big Orange Guide Service** (731/689-3074) or **Rick Matlock's Guide Service** (731/689-5382).

Swimming

Pickwick Landing State Park has three swimming beaches. Circle Beach and Sandy Beach are in the day-use area; Bruton Beach is in the primitive area, which is located across the lake from the main park.

Accommodations

(Pickwick Landing State Resort Park (Hwy. 57, 731/689-3135, $70–80) is the home of one of Tennessee's newest state park inns and conference centers. The modern hotel has 75 rooms, each with a balcony looking out over the lake and the dam. Cabins are available for between $100 and $125 per night, and campsites are available for under $20. There is a pool and a 135-seat restaurant at the inn, which serves three meals a day.

COUNCE

This humble town is the western gateway to Pickwick Lake. It is also a hub in the region's hardwood timber industry, and you will smell the fumes of the local paper plant at certain times of the day.

Accommodations

If you're planning to stay more than a few days at Pickwick Lake, consider renting a cabin. **(Pickwick Lake Cabin Rentals** (11268 Hwy. 57, 731/689-0400, www.pickwicklake-cabins.com) represents the owners of two dozen one-, two-, and three-bedroom cabins on and around the lake. Lakefront cabins will cost from $300 to $400 per night; water-view cabins will cost $200 to $300, and cabins off the water cost between $100 and $200. Many lakefront cabins come with a private dock and can accommodate large groups.

Food

Don't be mistaken by the rustic appearance of the **(Broken Spoke** (7405 Hwy. 57, 731/689-3800, Wed.–Sat. 11 A.M.–10 P.M., $12–27). This is the most upscale and creative dining around Pickwick Lake. The decor is comfortably eclectic, but not trashy, and there is tasteful live music several nights a week. The menu is remarkably diverse: You can choose from catfish, po-boys, and burgers, or steaks, pork chops, and chicken cooked expertly on the grill. There are also salads, pasta, and daily specials. Come with an appetite—there are no small portions. The adjacent bar is a popular hangout spot any night of the week, and **Mombie's Pizza** (731/689-8646, Tues.–Sat. 11 A.M.–10 P.M., $9–15), right next door, serves the best pizza, burgers, and wings in Pickwick. You will find the Broken Spoke and Mombie's one mile west of the dam on Highway 57.

BACKGROUND

The Land

Tennessee is a long, narrow state. Shaped roughly like a parallelogram, it is 500 miles from east to west, and 110 miles from north to south. Partly due to its unusual shape, Tennessee, along with Missouri, borders more states than any other in the United States. Its neighbors are North Carolina, Virginia, Kentucky, Missouri, Arkansas, Mississippi, Alabama, and Georgia. Tennessee is the 36th-largest state in the United States, with a land mass of 44,169 square miles.

GEOGRAPHY

If you ask a Tennessean where they are from, the answer is never as simple as "Tennessee."

Tennessee is divided by the Tennessee River into three "Grand Divisions": East Tennessee, Middle Tennessee, and West Tennessee. These three regions are set apart by more than geography; they have unique histories, politics, and identities.

East Tennessee

East Tennessee is defined by the Appalachian Mountains and their foothills. The culture in this region was historically that of small farms, isolated mountain communities, and Scotch-Irish heritage. East Tennessee is the least racially diverse part of the state. It opposed secession during the Civil War and votes overwhelmingly Republican.

© SUSANNA HENIGHAN POTTER

Within East Tennessee are two geographic regions. The Unaka Mountains are part of the Appalachian Mountain Chain, which peak along the state's border with North Carolina. This zone includes the Great Smoky Mountains National Park. It is also where you will find Clingman's Dome, which at 6,642 feet above sea level is the highest point in Tennessee.

West of the Unaka Mountains is the Great Valley of East Tennessee, home to Knoxville and Chattanooga. This region is characterized by picturesque low ridges and a wide, fertile valley.

Middle Tennessee

Middle Tennessee is home to Tennessee's capital city, Nashville, and some of its most fertile farmland. Before the Civil War, great plantation mansions dotted the countryside south of Nashville. Today, Tennessee Walking Horse farms, new industries, and the economic success of Nashville continue to make Middle Tennessee prosperous.

Geographically, Middle Tennessee begins with the Cumberland Plateau, which rises to about 2,000 feet above sea level and lies west of East Tennessee's Great Valley. Despite its name, the plateau is not flat; there are a number of steep valleys in the plateau, the largest being the Sequatchie Valley.

The Highland Rim is a region of hills, valleys, and fertile farmland, which lies west of the plateau. The largest physical region of Tennessee, the Highland Rim contains some 10,650 square miles of land, or almost 25 percent of the state. Almost entirely surrounded by the Highland Rim is the Central Basin, a low, flat, and fertile region in north-central Tennessee. Nashville is located in the Central Basin.

West Tennessee

West Tennessee is more like the Deep South than any other part of the state. Mostly flat and rural, this was the epicenter of the state's cotton industry both before and after the Civil War. The Gulf Coastal Plain, an area of 9,000 square miles, is drained by the Mississippi River and its tributaries. Memphis lies in the southwestern corner of this area.

Memphis sits on a low bluff over the Mississippi River, keeping it safe from flooding. Economically and socially, Memphis has more in common with the delta regions of Arkansas and Mississippi than with parts of Tennessee, especially the eastern regions. The city's location near the center of the continental United States and within a day's drive of most of the U.S. population has given rise to a large distribution and transportation industry.

RIVERS AND LAKES

The largest river in Tennessee is the Mississippi River, which forms the western border of the state. The Hatchie River is among the smaller tributaries that drain West Tennessee and flow into the Mississippi.

The state's two most important rivers are the Cumberland and Tennessee. The Cumberland River flows through Nashville and along the north-central portion of the state. The Tennessee River flows in a U shape, first flowing south through East Tennessee, through Knoxville and Chattanooga, and then northward, defining the boundary between Middle and West Tennessee. Both the Cumberland and the Tennessee Rivers empty into the Ohio River, which flows to the Mississippi.

The Cumberland River supplies Nashville's drinking water. Memphis's water comes from the Memphis Sand Aquifer, a huge underground reservoir of water that is pumped to the surface with wells. Memphis is the largest city in the world to rely exclusively on artesian wells for its water supply.

All but one of Tennessee's major lakes are man-made, having been created by the Tennessee Valley Authority during the last century. TVA impounded rivers to control flooding, generate electricity, and to create recreational opportunities around the new lakes. The only large, natural lake in Tennessee is Reelfoot Lake in the northeastern corner of the state. Reelfoot was formed from the 1812 New Madrid earthquake when the mouth of what had been Reelfoot Creek was closed off and

THE NEW MADRID QUAKE

The most powerful earthquake to strike the continental United States in historic times was the New Madrid quake of February 7, 1812. In fact, the earthquake that on that date created Reelfoot Lake was the final in a series of quakes that began in December 1811. While the present-day scale for measuring the magnitude of earthquakes did not exist, scientists believe that between December 1811 and February 1812 at least three magnitude 8.0 earthquakes shook the central United States.

The first major quake struck on December 16, 1811, and caused the ground to split open around New Madrid, Missouri. A sulfurous gas filled the air, and witnesses saw thousands of birds flying away from the area. On this day the *New Orleans*, one of the nation's first steamboats, was voyaging down the Mississippi River. The crew were no doubt alarmed to find that as they entered the earthquake-stricken area, riverbanks were shaking and waves were rocking the boat. The steamboat weathered the effects of temblors on December 19, and on December 21 the crew woke to find that the mooring that they had cast the night before was no longer secure because the very island

The New Madrid earthquake in 1812 created Reelfoot Lake.

PHOTO COURTESY OF TENN DEPT OF TOURIST DEVELOPMENT

they had anchored to had disappeared under the water.

The final quake in the series gave birth to Reelfoot Lake. The most violent of all the quakes, it caused dishes to shake in Montreal, Canada, and rang bells in Boston. The Mississippi riverbed rose and sank; boats capsized or were sucked into fissures that appeared suddenly in the earth. The quake was so powerful that it caused the Mississippi River to flow northward for a period and diverted a large amount of water onto once-dry land, creating Reelfoot Lake.

the creek's water spread out to cover the surrounding land.

CLIMATE

Tennessee has a mild climate. The average temperature statewide is 58 degrees; in winter temperatures generally hover between 30 and 40 degrees and in summer between 80 and 90 degrees. Summer days can feel very hot, however, especially in Middle and West Tennessee. Of the state's three major cities, Memphis is the hottest; its average temperature is 60 degrees. Knoxville is the coolest city.

The state receives an average of 50 inches of rain per year, and only a few places in the Appalachian Mountains receive more than 10 inches of snow per year. Nashville and Memphis receive little snow or ice precipitation annually.

Tornadoes are the most common form of severe weather in Tennessee. In 2008, tornadoes on Super Tuesday destroyed homes, leveled businesses, and killed 33 people in Tennessee. Five years earlier, a freak storm, dubbed by some "Hurricane Elvis," hit Memphis, destroying homes, uprooting trees, and leaving much of the city without power. Heavy rains associated with tropical weather systems can sometimes affect the state, and winter weather can close roads in the higher elevations along the Cumberland Plateau and the Smoky Mountains.

History

NASHVILLE

The land surrounding present-day Nashville was rich hunting territory for successive waves of Native Americans. Paleoindians lived here as early as 11,000 years ago, hunting large game animals and gathering nuts and berries. Successive waves of native groups lived in the area of modern Nashville. The last group of Indians to live around Nashville was the Mississippians, who, like the earlier Woodland Indians, built earthen mounds, some of which survive to this day. John Overton's home, Travellers Rest, in South Nashville was built upon an Indian mound.

Early Settlement

The earliest Europeans to use the area were French fur-traders, who came in the 1700s and called the area "The Bluffs." In 1710 Charles Charleville opened a trading post near a salt lick just north of town. Fifty years later, a French-Canadian hunter named Timothy Demonbreun moved into the area. The region became known as the French Lick.

Owing to the topography of the Appalachian Mountains and Cumberland Plateau, it was difficult for people to get to French Lick over land from the east. Early hunters and traders arrived from the north, passing through the Cumberland Gap that sits along the present-day border between Tennessee and Kentucky.

Settlers in North Carolina and Virginia had heard of the fertile territory and favorable location of the French Lick. In 1778 James Robertson led a scouting party to the area. Based on his report, Robertson and Col. John Donelson embarked to establish a permanent settlement on the banks of the Cumberland River in Middle Tennessee.

Robertson and the first group of settlers,

© SUSANNA HENIGHAN POTTER

Fort Nashborough, the first settlement in Nashville, was founded on Christmas Day, 1779. A re-creation of the original fort remains on the riverfront in Nashville.

mostly men, traveled overland and arrived at French Lick on Christmas Day, 1779. The second group of settlers, led by Donelson, followed a water route down the Holston and Tennessee Rivers and up the Ohio and Cumberland Rivers. It was a torturous journey. Approximately 30 families, including dozens of women and children, started the trip from Fort Patrick, North Carolina, on December 22, 1779, aboard the *Adventure*. Joined by another group of settlers at the Clinch River, the flotilla amounted to 30 vessels, including canoes, flatboats, and dugouts. The group also included 30 African-American slaves. During a four-month journey, the party suffered Indian attacks, a smallpox outbreak, hunger, extreme cold, and dangerous river conditions. Some 33 people died on the journey, and the party that arrived on April 24, 1780, was exhausted and in low spirits.

Within a week of Donelson's arrival, 256 men signed the Cumberland Compact to create the first civil government of the area. They first named the settlement Fort Nashborough after Gen. Francis Nash of North Carolina, a Revolutionary War hero. It was later felt that Nashborough sounded "too British," and so, in 1784, the name was changed to Nashville.

The Nashville settlement sat on what had been Cherokee Indian territory. While the settlers had purchased it from the Cherokee a few years before, they were not immune from Indian attacks. Cherokee and Chickamauga Indians led by Dragging Canoe continued to resist white settlers' encroachment on their land.

In April, 1781, the "Battle of the Bluffs" took place when an estimated 700 Cherokee attempted a surprise attack on the Nashville settlement. The settlers' response was disorganized and ill-conceived, and had it not been for the decision of Mrs. Charlotte Reeves Robertson, the wife of commander James Robertson, to loose the fort's dogs on the attackers, the fort's defeat would have been certain.

Statehood

Tennessee became the 16th state in 1796, and settlers moved quickly to claim territory there.

During this period, Nashville and the countryside around it remained the western frontier of the state; the capital was in East Tennessee where a greater number of settlements existed.

In May 1797, a 24-year-old Louis Phillippe d'Orleans visited Nashville. The visitor would eventually rise to be the last king of France, ascending to the throne in 1830 and reigning until 1848. The prince's visit was unremarkable—he and his two traveling companions arrived on horseback and slept in a single bed at the home of a Captain Maxwell. Later, in 1845, King Louis Phillippe commissioned a portrait of Gen. Andrew Jackson by the painter P. A. Healy. Healy traveled to the Hermitage and completed the painting during the final days of Jackson's life. It was regarded by Jackson and many of his peers as the best likeness of him ever made.

By 1818 all Native American claims on Tennessee were gone, and settlers felt secure putting down roots in the rich Tennessee frontier. During the early 19th century, life slowly became easier for Nashville's residents. The first steamboat arrived in 1819, opening up trade with cities like New Orleans and Pittsburgh. The city became a trading hub for the whole region. Banking, printing, and publishing industries grew. The Hermitage, Belle Meade Plantation, and Travellers Rest were all built during this period, evidence of the city's growing prosperity and sophistication.

This sophistication was evident by the fact that, in May 1825, the city hosted a visit from the Marquis de LaFayette. The Frenchman was treated to the best that the city could offer; $3,000 was budgeted for his entertainment. There was a parade, a military review, ball, tea at the Hermitage, and a dinner, where LaFayette reportedly toasted: "Tennessee beauty—equal to Tennessee valor."

The visit was judged a success, but the Marquis' exit from the city less so. LaFayette and his party, including Tennessee governor William Carroll, sailed out of town on a steamship. Overnight on May 8, 1825, it struck a snag and the Frenchman and his companions and the governor and his party were rescued by lifeboat and placed on the riverbank. The steamer sank in 18 feet of water; some of the crew and some of the passengers drowned. The Marquis lost his hat, many of his papers, some of his baggage, and a little dog.

In 1828, Nashville resident Andrew Jackson was elected the seventh president of the United States. Jackson's success testified to the growing prominence of Tennessee and of the nation's westward expansion.

During the state's early years, the capital was in East Tennessee, home to the greatest number of settlers. But as the population expanded westward, Nashville became the natural choice for state capital. In 1843, the city became the permanent capital of Tennessee and 14 years later William Strickland was hired to design the capitol.

The 1850s were a period of growth for the young city. The first locomotive arrived in Nashville in 1850, the Medical School of the University of Nashville opened in 1851, and the publishing arm of the Methodist Episcopal Church South opened in 1854.

The city's first public school, named for educator Alfred Hume, opened in 1855. A number of prominent historic buildings were constructed during this period, including the Downtown Presbyterian Church, Holy Trinity Episcopal Church, and Belmont Mansion.

By 1860, on the eve of the Civil War, Nashville was a thriving city home to 14,000 residents. The advent of streetcars led to the establishment of the first city suburbs: Edgefield in East Nashville and the Cameron-Trimble area in South Nashville were founded around this time.

The Civil War

When Civil War broke out in 1861, Nashville was quickly identified as an important strategic center for the distribution of supplies. Union forces occupied the city in February 1862 and held it for the remainder of the war. President Abraham Lincoln appointed Andrew Johnson, himself a future president of the United States, to be military governor of Tennessee during the war. Johnson established his offices in the state

capitol in Nashville. Despite sporadic guerrilla attacks from Confederate sympathizers in the city, the Union occupation of Nashville was mostly peaceful.

Union Gen. Grenville M. Dodge spent Christmas of 1863 in Nashville along with other Federal commanders, who were summoned by Gen. Ulysses Grant to meet with him there. Gen. Dodge's account of the few days spent in Nashville describes paying a courtesy call on the military governor Andrew Johnson, going to see a production of *Hamlet* in the "Old Theater," and eating dinner at a saloon in town. They had Christmas dinner at the home of Gen. R. S. Granger.

During the Battle of Nashville, fought in the city's southern suburbs on December 15 and 16, 1864, Confederates under the command of Gen. John Bell Hood failed to re-take Nashville from the Federals. The battle was the final chapter of the Confederacy's disastrous 1864 Middle Tennessee campaign, and was the end of fighting in the whole western theater of the Civil War.

Reconstruction

Nashville fared better than many of the other major Southern cities during the Civil War. Its infrastructure was largely intact. The city rebounded economically; its printing industry remained strong and new distribution and wholesale businesses developed. Four different universities were founded during the 1860s and 1870s: Fisk University and Meharry Medical College became prominent centers for the education of African Americans. Vanderbilt University was founded in 1873 and Peabody College, a teacher's college, was established two years later.

During the period from 1860 to 1900, the city's population grew from 17,000 to almost 81,000 people.

In 1880, Nashville celebrated its 100th anniversary with the unveiling of the statue of Andrew Jackson that remains in front of the state Capitol. Seventeen years later, the city hosted the Tennessee Centennial Exposition on grounds west of the city center. The event drew hundreds of thousands of people to the city and left two major legacies: Centennial Park and the only full-scale replica of the Parthenon in the world.

The Early 20th Century

During the first two decades of the 20th century, Nashville dealt with two national issues: Prohibition and the movement for women's suffrage. The two issues were linked since the movement for temperance and Prohibition brought many women into the political sphere for the first time.

Tennessee had a long history with the temperance movement, having effectively banned liquor sales in many rural areas with the passage, in 1887, of the Four Mile Law. The law stopped the sale of liquor anywhere within four miles of a rural school, and required towns to give up and then reapply for their charter in order to enact the Prohibition. As the years passed, the Four Mile Law was amended so it would apply to more and more towns. In 1907, it was amended to extend to cities of 150,000, which included Nashville and the other major cities in the state. However, only Knoxville acted to turn in and reapply for its charter; Nashville and Memphis were not interested in stopping the sale of alcohol, despite emotional and fervent pressure from temperance advocates. The failure of the law thus far to effectively stop alcohol sales was fuel for the Prohibitionists' fire.

The state went "bone-dry" in 1917 with a law that forbade the receipt, possession, or transportation of liquor. When the 18th Amendment to the U.S. Constitution, which banned alcohol at the national level, passed in 1919, Tennessee had been dry for two years. As in the rest of the country, bootleggers in Tennessee found ways around Prohibition, especially in the large urban centers like Nashville.

Prohibition was reversed nationally and locally in 1933, although its legacy remains; many rural counties continue to have conservative laws regarding alcohol sales.

In 1914, Nashville was the site of a national convention on women's suffrage. Six years later, in 1920, it was at the heart of a national firestorm on the issue when Tennessee stood to be the 36th and final state required to ratify the 19th Amendment.

This historic vote took place on August 18, 1920, and the victory was slim: The House approved the measure by a vote of 50 to 49. It had been a hard-fought and, in many respects, unexpected victory, which made Tennessee suffragists proud.

Also during this period, Nashville experienced the Great Train Wreck of 1918, when an inbound local train collided with an outbound express, killing 101 people.

Music City USA

Nashville's path to Music City USA begins with National Life and Accident Insurance Company. In 1924 Nashville-based National Life invested money in an AM radio station. The call letters WSM stood for National Life's slogan—We Shield Millions—and the station was considered a novel tool to reach millions of customers and potential customers in the southeastern United States.

On November 25, 1925, WSM disc jockey George Hay invited a 78-year-old fiddler, Uncle Jimmy Thompson, to perform live on Saturday night over the radio waves. The response was electric, and WSM continued to broadcast live old-time music every Saturday night. In May 1927, the program was named the Grand Ole Opry.

The program hit a nerve with people all across the country. They were hungering for a form of music that was uniquely theirs, and country was it. During the rough times of the Great Depression in the 1930s, people looked forward to sitting around the radio on Saturday night, listening to the Opry. After World War II, record company executives began to take notice of country music. They opened offices and recording studios in Nashville and the city's music business was born.

The Great Depression and World War II

The Great Depression of the 1930s exacerbated

already bad economic times in Tennessee and the rest of the South.

New Deal programs like the Public Works Administration and the Works Progress Administration left an indelible mark on Nashville. The PWA built new public housing complexes and schools, including West End and Pearl High Schools. PWA grants were used to finance dozens of buildings in the city, including the Tennessee Supreme Court Building, the State Office Building, and the Davidson County Public Building and Court House.

Under the Works Progress Administration, unskilled and semi-skilled laborers, who would otherwise have been unemployed, were put to work on public projects. Crews built roads, sewer systems, bridges, waterways, dams, viaducts and overpasses. In Nashville, WPA crews built the airport, restored Fort Negley, improved Percy and Edwin Warner Parks, worked at the Hermitage, and built or restored 25 miles of streets.

It was the economic impact of World War II that finally did away with the Depression. Industrial complexes were converted to military factories and land was set aside for military bases. Nashville's "war baby industry" included Consolidated Vultee Aircraft Corporation, which employed 3,000 people and opened in 1945. Two existing manufacturers—the Nashville Bridge Company and the DuPont plant in Old Hickory—altered production to war-related products. Despite these economic impacts, Nashville experienced less war-related industrialization than other Tennessee cities.

Close to Nashville, 20 Middle Tennessee counties were used for the so-called Tennessee Maneuvers. More than 800,000 men and women took part in these full-scale training exercises, which were headquartered in Lebanon and involved "red" and "blue" armies facing off against each other in the countryside. The army officially referred to them as taking place "somewhere in Tennessee."

Camps Forrest, near Tullahoma; Tyson, near Paris; and Campbell, near Clarkesville, were the largest and most important army bases in Tennessee during World War II. The camps were used for training, and, as the war progressed, to house German, Italian, and Austrian prisoners of war. POWs were also held in Nashville.

Post-War Years

World War II spurred myriad social and political changes in Nashville and the rest of the nation. Women developed a taste for work. African Americans moved from the countryside to the city—between 1940 and 1950 Nashville's non-white population grew by 7,000 to 59,000. The economic depression of the 1930s was totally gone by the end of the war, with bank deposits and incomes up to the highest levels they had ever been.

With the growth of early suburbs and the effects of the Great Depression, downtown Nashville experienced economic decline. In 1949 the city launched the first-ever postwar urban renewal program, called the Capitol Hill Redevelopment Project.

Civil Rights

The heightened expectations created by World War II gave rise to the civil rights movement that took place in the 1950s and '60s.

In 1960, Nashville became the first Southern city to desegregate its public services. The change came as a result of a historic campaign of sit-ins and economic boycott led by young African-American students from colleges and universities in the city. The campaign, which was both peaceful and successful, inspired other non-violent protests throughout the Deep South.

When the U.S. Supreme Court struck down the practice of segregated schools in 1954, Nashville, like dozens of other major cities, had a school system that was deeply unfair. Schools established for blacks were rundown, unsanitary, and inadequate. There were not enough teachers, books, or sanitary facilities for the students.

As a result of the court order for schools to be desegregated "with all deliberate speed," an East Nashville barber named Alfred Z. Kelley filed a lawsuit seeking permission for his son to

THE PERFECT 36

On August 18, 1920, the Tennessee general assembly voted to ratify the 19th Amendment to the U.S. Constitution: "The right of citizens of the United States to vote shall not be denied or abridged by the United States or any State on account of sex." With those words, women now had the right to vote.

Tennessee was the 36th state to ratify the 19th Amendment, and the final approval needed for the amendment to become law. Suffragists dubbed Tennessee "the perfect 36" because of this.

The struggle for women's rights in Tennessee had begun with Elizabeth Avery Meriwether, of Memphis, who briefly published a journal on women's rights in the early 1870s and attempted to cast a ballot in the 1876 presidential election. Later, Meriwether's sister-in-law, Lide Meriwether, rose to prominence as the president of the Women's Christian Temperance Union and became an outspoken proponent of women's suffrage. While they advocated for temperance, some women began to feel that they had a rightful place in politics.

Lide Meriwether founded the first women's suffrage organization in Memphis in 1889. The second was in Maryville, near Knoxville, in 1893, and the third in Nashville in 1894. Suffragists met in the Women's Tent during the Centennial Exhibition in Nashville in 1897, where they formed the first statewide women's suffrage organization.

Despite these early steps, the movement for women's voting rights stalled after Lide Meriwether resigned and the Women's Christian Temperance Union withdrew its support for women's rights. During the first decade of the 20th century, there was no organized statewide effort to promote women's rights, although local organizations were formed and began to grow.

In 1914, the National American Woman Suffrage Association held its national convention in Nashville. The event received positive coverage in the press, and helped to generate support for the suffrage movement. When the United States entered World War I in 1917, suffragists threw their support behind the troops. They sold war bonds, raised funds for luxuries for soldiers, organized Red Cross chapters, and supported European orphans. Their actions demonstrated that women had a role to play in matters of national defense.

Despite the advances, the suffrage movement in Tennessee faced challenges. Suffrage groups were plagued by internal conflicts. Opponents of suffrage were plentiful and powerful. In 1916, the National Association Opposed to Woman Suffrage opened a Tennessee branch. The anti-suffragists, or "antis," as they were called, were supported by the deep pockets of distilleries, textile manufacturers, and railroad companies, all of whom opposed giving women the right to vote.

Tennessee's suffragists won their first battle in 1918, when the general assembly approved an amendment to the Tennessee constitution that would give women the right to vote in municipal and presidential elections. But it was Tennessee's vote on the U.S. Constitutional amendment that would cement its place in history.

It was the spring of 1920, and 35 states had already approved the amendment; one more ratification was required. When Delaware unexpectedly voted "no" in June, all eyes turned to Tennessee. The state was an unlikely source of hope, since opposition to suffrage was strong in the South, and Tennessee was far from a sure bet.

The first step was for the governor, Albert H. Roberts, to announce a special session of the general assembly. Roberts, who feared giving women the vote because he thought they would vote against him, was lobbied hard by

COURTESY OF LIBRARY OF CONGRESS

"I DID NOT RAISE MY GIRL TO BE A VOTER"
Soprano Solo With Vociferous Supporting Chorus of Male Voices

This 1915 cartoon, published in *Puck* magazine, depicts anti-suffragist women being manipulated by big business.

local, regional, and national figures, including U.S. president Woodrow Wilson. Eventually he bowed to pressure from the suffragists and announced that a special session would begin on August 9.

The announcement set off a political firestorm, the scale of which had never been seen in Tennessee before, and has scarcely been seen since. Suffragists and antis converged on Nashville. Every member of the House and the Senate was lobbied. Suffragists and antis kept close tabs on each member's position, counting votes for and against. Newspaper editors, businessmen, and politicians were lobbied. National figures on both sides came to town to lend support, and suffragists accused the antis of underhanded tactics, including bribes.

As expected, the measure easily passed in the Senate. The House was just too close to call, however.

The House vote took place on August 18, and the atmosphere in the chamber could not have been more tense. Members voted by roll call, and when the seventh name was called, Harry Burn, a Republican from McMinn County, voted to ratify. It was one of three unexpected affirmative votes that gave the suffragists their win. As it turned out, Burns, who had previously opposed women's suffrage, carried with him a letter from his widowed mother urging him to vote for the amendment. That letter very well may have secured the suffragists' victory.

When the votes were cast, the 19th Amendment passed by the slimmest of margins: 50-49. On August 26, 1920, U.S. secretary of state Bainbridge Colby issued a proclamation declaring the 19th Amendment ratified and part of the Constitution.

It was a victory made all the sweeter by the remarkable odds that had been overcome. Abby Crawford Milton, a Tennessee suffragist and one of the leaders of the campaign, later wrote: "I shall never be as thrilled by the turn of any event as I was at that moment when the roll call that settled the citizenship of American women was heard. Personally, I had rather have had a share in the battle for woman suffrage than any other world event."

In August 2006, the Suffrage Coalition unveiled a memorial to Tennessee's suffragists in downtown Knoxville. The life-sized bronze sculpture depicts three leading suffragists, Lizzie Crozier French of Knoxville, Anne Dallas Dudley of Nashville, and Elizabeth Avery Meriwether of Memphis.

attend East High School, which was in walking distance of their home, rather than Pearl High School, the African-American school on the other side of town.

Kelley's case was argued in federal district court by Nashville lawyer Alexander Looby and his partner Avon Williams Jr. The court ordered that the Nashville School Board prepare a plan for desegregation and submit it to the court by January of 1957.

Between January and September 1957, the court, the school board, and members of the community debated exactly how the Nashville schools would be desegregated. It was a period of heightened tensions. Eventually, on September 9, 1957, desegregation began with 19 black boys and girls enrolling at white schools. Police escorted the students past jeering crowds, and the first day of school passed without incident.

Overnight, however, things became violent. A few minutes past midnight a bomb destroyed part of East Nashville's Hattie Cotton School. The next day, police arrested an out-of-town agitator, John Kaspar, who had come to protest desegregation. There were no further incidents of violence. Over the next decade, hundreds of black students enrolled in white schools, ending the era of segregated schooling in Nashville.

Modern Nashville

In 1968, Hospital Corporation of America (HCA) was founded in Nashville as one of the first for-profit hospital companies in the country. By 1979, HCA owned or managed 140 hospitals; by the mid-1980s the company owned more than 200 hospitals and held contracts to manage 200 more. HCA remains one of Nashville's most important corporations, and it gave rise to the city's modern health-care industry. A scandal erupted in 1997 that caused HCA and its related companies to pay a total of $840 million to the U.S. Justice Department. The company's Nashville hospitals are now operated under the name TriStar Health System.

What is now Tennessee State University was founded in 1912 as the Tennessee A&I State Normal School for Negroes. The schools educated thousands of African Americans with funds raised from within the African-American community and meager state appropriations. In 1951 the school became the Tennessee A&I State University, then in 1968 it became Tennessee State University. That was the same year that a lawsuit was filed arguing that the recent establishment of the University of Tennessee at Nashville, located downtown, furthered segregation in higher education and competed with TSU. A decade later, in July 1979, UT Nashville merged with Tennessee State University. Today, TSU remains the city's only public university.

One of TSU's most famous graduates was Oprah Winfrey, who spent her teenage years in Nashville. Winfrey, who lived with her father, Vernon, and his wife, Velma, graduated from East High School and enrolled at TSU. She was active in speech and drama clubs, and worked for WVOL Radio and as a reporter for Channel 5 television. Winfrey left TSU in 1975 one class shy of her graduation requirement. Ten years later she completed the course, a senior project, and is still one of TSU's most celebrated alumni.

During the 1970s and '80s, Nashville's publishing and music industries grew. Religious publishing was a stronghold of Nashville's economy since before the Civil War, when the Southern Methodist Episcopal Church was established. Today, the United Methodist Publishing House publishes hundreds of new books, church school curriculums, and tapes annually. The world's largest publisher of religious materials, the School Board of the Southern Baptist Convention, is located in Nashville, along with the National Baptist Publishing Board, an African-American publishing house. The world's largest publisher of Bibles, Thomas Nelson Publishers, opened in Nashville in 1972. In 1982, Rutledge Hill Press, a non-religious regional publishing house, opened its doors.

In 1996, Tennessee marked 200 years of statehood with the establishment of the Bicentennial

Mall State Park. The 19-acre park is part monument, part museum. During this period, Nashville attracted the then Houston Oilers, who became the first National Football League franchise to be located in Tennessee. The decision to invite the team was controversial because of the upfront cost to taxpayers. Nashville was required to build a 65,000-seat stadium, which the Oilers would rent for at least 30 years. The agreement required the approval of Nashville voters, who voted in favor by a margin of 59 percent to 42 percent in July 1996. To the consternation of Nashville residents, the Oilers played their first season not in Nashville, but in Memphis, at the Liberty Bowl. In 1999, the team changed its name to the Tennessee Titans.

The first decade of the 21st century has been defined by major new downtown developments, including the Schermerhorn Symphony Center and the Country Music Hall of Fame; the Frist Center for the Visual Arts; the Sommet Center, home to the Nashville Predators ice hockey team; and the new Nashville Public Library, to name a few. By mid-decade, new residential projects were underway, too; for the first time in a long time, people wanted to live Nashville. Urban condos and residential projects like Rolling Hill Mill, SoBro, and the Gulch created a new vibrancy to the city as people started to move here. It is yet to be seen, however, whether the downtown building boom will weather the economic slowdown that began in late 2007.

MEMPHIS
Prehistory and Exploration

The area around Memphis was first settled by Native Americans 10,000 years ago. During the Mississippian period beginning around A.D. 1000, the Native American town of Chucalissa was settled just south of present-day Memphis.

It is believed that the first Europeans to visit the area of Memphis were members of Hernando de Soto's party, who arrived on the Chickasaw Bluffs in 1542. The party camped on the bluff for a few weeks while they built rafts to cross the Mississippi River.

HERNANDO DE SOTO.

Hernando de Soto camped at the present-day site of Memphis in 1542.

Forty years later a Frenchman, Robert Cavalier de La Salle, stopped on the bluff on his way down the Mississippi to New Orleans. A member of La Salle's party, Pierre Prudhomme, disappeared, and La Salle built a small fort for the company while they searched for the missing man. Prudhomme returned two days later and La Salle and his men continued south. Their small Fort Prudhomme is considered the first European building in Memphis.

The Chickasaw Indians claimed the Fourth Bluff (the bluff over the Mississippi River on which Memphis now sits) and its surrounding areas, but used the lands mostly for hunting; their settlements were farther south. Though the Revolutionary War was far from this part of the American frontier, the war gave rise to a period when the Spanish, Americans, and British competed for the Indians' loyalty, while the Chickasaws struggled to keep their land.

As they had in other parts of the Americas, white settlers, who were moving westward towards Memphis in great numbers, introduced a "factor" system of trade designed to put the Indians in debt so they would be forced to abandon their lands in repayment of their debts. In 1818 the Chickasaw Indians ceded their land in western Tennessee, including the bluff where Memphis sits today.

Early Settlement

Businessmen and political leaders moved quickly to survey, sell, and settle lots on the Fourth Bluff, which they had already realized would be the location of a city of strategic importance in the expanding western frontier. James Winchester, Andrew Jackson, and James Overton met at Jackson's home, the Hermitage, near Nashville, in 1819 to make plans for the new city. Winchester suggested the name Memphis because he considered the Mississippi to be the "American Nile." The city of Memphis was incorporated in 1826, and Winchester was elected Memphis's first mayor a year later.

Memphis quickly grew into the important city its founders had predicted. By the 1850s, Memphis was the biggest inland cotton market in the world, and on the eve of the Civil War some 400,000 bales left the city's wharves each year. Cotton arrived by barge on the river and was graded and sold at the city's famed Cotton Exchange on Front Street. Cotton factors provided seed and other capital to farmers all over the Mid-South, creating great wealth in the city. Memphis's first private bank, Farmers and Merchants Bank, opened in 1833.

Meanwhile, transportation links to the surrounding area were developed. In 1831 the first stagecoach service opened between Nashville and Memphis. Railroads followed, and by the 1850s, Memphis was connected by rail to Nashville, Bowling Green, Charleston, and Grenada, Mississippi.

Memphis's population was diverse. The city attracted migrants from Virginia, the Carolinas, and Georgia, as well as a number of Irish and German immigrants. In 1860, nearly one-quarter of the city's population was Irish.

Memphis owed its prosperity to slavery, which fueled the plantation economy of the Delta as well as many of the small plantation farms in western Tennessee. Memphis was the largest slave-trading center in the Mid-South, although the market relied less on public auctions than on private sales. Nathan Bedford Forrest and Byrd Hill ran one of the city's largest slave-trading companies in the years before the Civil War.

The Civil War and Reconstruction

Memphis fell to the Union Army on June 6, 1862. The Battle for Memphis began before dawn and was finished in time for many Memphians' breakfast. Thousands watched the lopsided sea battle from the bluff, as a Union force of 16 mortar boats, six rams, and eight iron-clads defeated a Confederate navy of just seven gunboats. At the end of the fighting, which consisted mainly of boats ramming each other, all but one of the Confederate ships were sunk or destroyed.

Memphis was occupied by the Union Army from 1862 until the end of the war in 1865.

Just one year after the end of the Civil War, Memphis experienced its most bitter race riot. Sparked by a fight between four Memphis police officers and four members of the U.S. Colored Heavy Artillery in April 1866, the three-day riot was an assault on the city's black population and its property. A reported 46 blacks were killed—although the actual number is probably much larger. Seventy-five people were wounded, five black women were raped, and more than 100 homes, churches, businesses, and schools were destroyed. It was a violent and uneasy start to the city's post–Civil War period.

While Memphis suffered racial unease after the Civil War, its physical infrastructure was relatively unscathed by the war compared to other Southern cities. Commercial activity recovered quickly, although Memphis was not insulated from economic hardships experienced in other parts of the South.

The period between 1880 and World War I was marked by accomplishment and growth for the city. In 1892, the 8,000-foot "Frisco Bridge" opened between Memphis and Arkansas, the first bridge across the Mississippi south of St. Louis. Electricity and telephone service came to the city. Street lamps were installed and roads

YELLOW FEVER STRIKES

It was not economic hardship, but disease-carrying mosquitoes that would most seriously stunt Memphis's recovery from the Civil War. In the late summer of 1878, Memphis was struck by a yellow fever epidemic that killed thousands and caused tens of thousands to flee. Memphis had experienced smaller yellow fever outbreaks in 1855 and 1873, so when reports of an outbreak in New Orleans reached the city in the summer of 1878, Memphians were on guard.

This was 20 years before the link between yellow fever and mosquitoes was known, and many people believed the disease was related to filthy and unsanitary conditions in the city. When the first cases of yellow fever were detected in Memphis in July 1878, hundreds of Memphians left the city, and within a few days, 25,000 more followed. In many cases, the exodus caused the further spread of the disease into smaller towns in western Tennessee and northern Mississippi.

In Memphis, 20,000 people remained during the epidemic. Some 5,000 of these people died, and a further 12,000 were stricken but survived. Of those who survived, 10,000 were African-Americans, causing many people to believe that blacks had greater natural immunity to yellow fever than whites.

A number of heroes emerged from the 1878 epidemic. The Howard Association, made up of black volunteers, collected and dispensed assistance, hired nurses and doctors, and organized burials. The nuns from St. Mary's Episcopal Cathedral turned their nunnery into a makeshift hospital, and two local madams turned their brothels into hospitals for the sick.

When the epidemic ended with the first frost in October, Memphis had been gutted. The population was decimated by disease and flight. The city's tax base was gone, and in January 1879, Memphis lost its charter. The rebuilding period was slow but eventually fruitful. By 1893, when Memphis regained its charter, the city was in the midst of an economic and cultural rebirth.

---

around the city were paved. By 1892, Memphis had 63 miles of sewers and 10,000 connections. The discovery of a huge reservoir of water underneath the city gave rise to waterworks, breweries, and ice-making factories.

During this period, Memphis opened its first public library. The Peabody Hotel, Grand Opera House, and Lyceum also opened. The city's cotton industry grew in the 1890s, thanks to better facilities to market, finance, sell, and transport cotton. Three-quarters of U.S. cotton was produced within 200 miles of Memphis, and the city became the financial epicenter of this booming industry. This was the period when many of the large, airy cotton-related buildings were constructed along "Cotton Row" on Front Street.

Race Relations

Despite the city's economic and social gains, Memphis's African-American residents still experienced racial violence, political intimidation, and economic injustice. Some 44 percent of the city was black in 1890. Most black men worked as laborers in the cotton industry, and black women worked as domestic servants, midwives, nurses, and laundresses. Memphis had developed distinct black neighborhoods, and schools, churches, and small businesses were largely segregated.

Black men were the victims of racial violence, especially lynchings. When Mississippi native Ida B. Wells was editor of the Memphis *Free Speech,* she wrote vehemently against lynching and was eventually run out of town for her strongly worded views. She settled in New York where she continued to campaign against racial violence.

The end of Reconstruction marked the beginning of an increasingly repressive legal and social regime against Memphis's blacks. Blacks were forbidden from the city's newly built Overton Park, Memphis Zoo, and Tri-State Fair. In 1901, the city hosted the 11th national reunion of Confederate veterans, and dedicated a statute and park in memory of Confederate Gen. Nathan Bedford Forrest, a slave-trader and founder of the Ku Klux Klan.

While Memphis's blacks were unwelcome in many of the city's public spaces and white neighborhoods, they developed their own communities and economies. There were major black business districts all around the city, but none outshone Beale Street, "the Main Street of the American Negro." Beale Street was a 15-block area, home to barber shops, groceries, drug stores, saloons, pool halls, juke joints, restaurants, churches, and dry-goods stores. Above the storefronts there were offices belonging to black dentists, doctors, businessmen, bankers, lawyers, tailors, insurance brokers, and teachers. The neighborhood was not strictly black; many of Memphis's recent Irish, Greek, German, and Chinese immigrants lived in black neighborhoods and ran businesses catering to black customers.

The turn of the 20th century was, in many respects, the birth of the blues. The musical form inexorably linked to the city of its birth, the blues combined African-American spirituals, ragtime rhythms, work songs, and ballads. W. C. Handy composed the political campaign song "Mr. Crump" in 1909 for a political newcomer, Ed Crump, who was running for mayor. Handy later published the song in 1912 as the "Memphis Blues," and it was the first published blues composition.

The political career of Ed "Boss" Crump, the mayor who Handy helped elected in 1909, would be, in many respects, the story of Memphis for the next five decades. Crump, who arrived in Memphis a pauper from Mississippi, built one of the most powerful political machines in the nation. His machine was so powerful that it controlled not only city and county elections, but statewide contests as well.

The Great Depression and World War II

Following the good economic times of World War I and the subsequent Roaring Twenties, Memphis experienced economic decline.

Thousands of black and white sharecroppers fled rural poverty for the urban variety. The cotton market bottomed out and closed in 1933, with a three-year supply of unsold cotton.

Memphis benefited from several New Deal programs. More than $8 million in Public Works Administration funds were used to build John Gaston Hospital, a new grain elevator, juvenile court, and several public schools. In 1935, Riverside Drive was built. Two major public housing centers were built in the 1930s: Lauderdale Courts for whites and Dixie Homes for blacks. More public housing was funded at the end of the decade. The Civilian Conservation Corps established parks, and Works Progress Administration workers built roads, sidewalks, a new airport terminal, and flood protection for the city of Memphis.

World War II completed Memphis's economic recovery. The city's industries converted to wartime production. With many men overseas, women went to work—in the case of many white women, for the first time. Wartime also saw the first signs of easing of social segregation between black and white. In 1948, Memphis radio station WDIA adopted black programming, which was a major commercial success. WDIA was soon the second-largest radio station in the Mid-South, and it was listened to by both blacks and whites. At the same time, whites were beginning to discover Beale Street. Thursdays there were known as "Midnight Rambles," the night when whites were welcome at black bars and shows.

Post-War Years

In the 1950s, record producer Sam Phillips and his wife, Becky, laid down some of the first recordings of "race music," or music by African Americans. Phillips was looking for hits that would appeal to white audiences, and he found what he was looking for in a poor white man who sang with the soul of the blues. Elvis Presley recorded "That's All Right" in Phillips's Sun Studio in 1954.

Memphis's musical history is much more than Elvis Presley, however. Memphis-based Stax Records recorded hit after hit during the early 1960s. An interracial organization, Stax catapulted artists like Otis Redding, Isaac Hayes, the Staple Sisters, and Booker T. and the MGs to fame.

Post-war Memphis was the era of the automobile, drive-in, and suburbanization. It was also the beginning of so-called urban renewal, in whose name the Memphis Housing Authority took over 560 acres and destroyed more than 3,000 buildings, many of them historic structures sorely missed today.

Modern Memphis

Beginning in the 1970s, Memphis slowly emerged from the ashes of economic depression, racial polarization, and the stain of the 1968 Dr. Martin Luther King assassination. Community organizations began to push for the preservation of historic downtown buildings. Investment slowly trickled in to rebuild the Memphis downtown. In 1975 developer Jack Belz bought the derelict Peabody Hotel for $75,000 and began a $24 million renovation. The Peabody is now the cornerstone of Peabody Place, a large downtown mall. The Cook Convention Center opened in 1974 on the north end of town, and in the same year Main Street was made into a pedestrian corridor. In 1982, Mud Island River Park opened, finally giving a purpose to the river island that frustrated city residents for so many years. But more importantly for the city's tourist industry, Elvis Presley's Graceland mansion opened for tours in 1982. The same year, efforts began to convert what remained of historic Beale Street into a tourist attraction.

AutoZone Park, home of the Memphis Redbirds, opened in 2000 in the heart of downtown Memphis. A year later, Memphis finally attracted a professional basketball team. The Memphis Grizzlies now play in FedEx Forum just off Beale Street. As it turned out, 2003 was an important year for the city; that was when the Cannon Center for the Performing Arts and the Stax Museum of American Soul Music opened. It was also the year that straight-line winds of more than 100 miles per hour devastated parts of the city and knocked out power to thousands of subscribers. The freak storm, dubbed "Hurricane Elvis," was the most destructive natural disaster in the city's history.

In 2005, five local politicians, including state senators John Ford and Kathryn Bowers, and former state senator Roscoe Dixon, were netted in a federal corruption probe nicknamed "Operation Tennessee Waltz." Ford, a member of the politically powerful Ford family, was convicted following a 2007 trial. He was sentenced to 66 months in prison.

In 2008, the 40th anniversary of the assassination of Martin Luther King brought national and international attention to Memphis, as celebrities, presidential candidates, and journalists parachuted in. It was an opportunity for the city to show off its jewels—like the National Civil Rights Museum—but also an opportunity to reflect on how much remains to be done: One local commentator pointed out that in Memphis today 9 out of 10 African-American students attend all-black schools, the same number that did in 1968.

Government and Economy

GOVERNMENT

Tennessee is governed by its constitution, unchanged since 1870 when it was revised in light of emancipation, the Civil War, and Reconstruction. Nashville is the state capital, and local and statewide politics are intertwined here.

Tennessee has a governor who is elected to four-year terms, a legislature, and a court system. The lieutenant governor is not elected statewide; he or she is chosen by the Senate and also serves as its Speaker.

The legislature, or general assembly, is made up of the 99-member House of Representatives and the 33-member Senate. The Tennessee State Supreme Court is composed of five members, no two of whom can be from the same Grand Division. The Supreme Court chooses the state's attorney general.

Nashville Government

In 1962 Nashville and Davidson County residents voted to approve a consolidated city-county government. Nashville was the first large U.S. city to adopt this structure.

Karl Dean, a Democrat, was elected the sixth mayor of the Metropolitan Government of Nashville and Davidson County in 2007. He defeated Frank Clement, also a Democrat, the son of former Tennessee governor Frank G. Clement.

The legislative arm of city-county government is the Metropolitan Council. There are 40 council members—35 are elected in district races and 5 are elected at-large. They serve a four-year term.

Metro Council meetings take place on the first and third Tuesday of each month. They are open to the public and are held in the Metro Courthouse. Many meetings are broadcast live on the local-access television channel.

Memphis Government

In 2008, five-term Memphis mayor William W. Herenton announced that he would step down, but only if he could get his old job as schools superintendent back. The political furor that erupted following his surprise announcement was deafening, and the future of Memphis's first African-American mayor—as well as his legacy—remains uncertain.

Memphis's legislative responsibilities rest with the City Council. There are 13 council members; nine districts elect a single council member and two "super districts" elect three members each. The City Council meets on the first and third Tuesday of each month at City Hall.

Shelby County has its own mayor and County Commission. A. C. Wharton was elected to a second four-year term as mayor of Shelby County in 2006. The 13 members of the Shelby County Board of Commissioners are part-time legislators, elected to four-year terms. The Shelby County Administration Building is located on Main Street in downtown Memphis.

POLITICS

Like other Southern states, Tennessee has seen a gradual shift to the political right since the 1960s. The shift began in 1966 with Howard Baker's election to the U.S. Senate, and continued with Tennessee's support for Republican presidential candidate Richard Nixon in 1968 and 1972. Despite a few exceptions, the shift has continued into the 21st century, although Nashville, Memphis, and certain parts of Middle and West Tennessee have traditionally been Democratic territory.

East Tennessee holds the distinction as one of a handful of Southern territories that has consistently supported the Republican Party since the Civil War.

The supremacy of the Republican Party in Tennessee has not been complete, however. Voters elected a Democrat, Phil Bredesen, governor in 2002 and again in 2006, and the senate candidacy of Harold Ford Jr., a Democrat and an African American, in 2006

NASHVILLE CORPORATIONS

A good number of U.S. companies are headquartered in Nashville. They include:

- American General Life & Accident Insurance/AIG
- Asurion
- Bridgestone/Firestone Americas
- Caremark
- Caterpillar Financial
- Cracker Barrel Old Country Stores and Logan's Roadhouse
- Dollar General Corporation
- Gaylord Entertainment Company
- Genesco Inc.

- Gibson Guitar Corp./Baldwin Pianos
- HCA
- Ingram Industries Inc.
- Lifeway Christian Resources
- Louisiana Pacific
- O'Charley's Inc.
- Primus Automotive Financial Services
- Shoney's Inc.
- Thomas Nelson Inc.
- United Methodist Publishing House

was closely followed around the country. Ford was unsuccessful, but the close contest exposed widespread disaffection with the Republican Party.

Tennesseans on the National Stage

Andrew Jackson may still be the most prominent Tennessean in American political history, but Tennessee politicians continue to play a role on the national stage. Albert Gore Jr., elected to the U.S. House of Representatives in 1976, served as vice president under president Bill Clinton from 1992 until 2000, and lost the highly contested 2000 presidential contest to George W. Bush. Gore famously lost his home state to Bush, but went on to champion global climate change and win the Nobel Peace Prize.

Lamar Alexander, a former governor of Tennessee, was appointed secretary of education by the first President Bush in 1990. Alexander—famous for his flannel shirts—ran unsuccessfully for president and was later elected senator from Tennessee. Bill Frist, a doctor, was also elected senator and rose to

be the Republican majority leader during the presidency of George W. Bush, before quitting politics for medical philanthropy.

The most recent Tennessean to seek the Oval Office was former senator and *Law and Order* star Fred Thompson, from Lewisburg in Middle Tennessee.

ECONOMY
Nashville

Nashville's biggest industry is not music or tourism—it is health care. Nashville is the headquarters of Hospital Corporation of America, the largest private operator of hospitals in the world, plus more than 250 other health-care corporations. Health care contributes an estimated $18.3 billion to the Nashville economy and employs more than 95,000 people.

Music recording is the second-largest industry in Nashville, and Music City is home to the nation's second-largest music recording hub (the largest is in New York City). Music recording contributes $6.4 billion to the Nashville economy annually and employs more than 19,000 Nashvillians.

With 17,881 workers, the largest employer in

Nashville is Vanderbilt University and Medical Center. The State of Tennessee is a close second with some 17,000 employees in Nashville.

Nashville is the North American headquarters of Nissan; has large insurance, finance, and religious publishing industries; and is home to the headquarters of several Christian denominations, including the Southern Baptist Convention and the National Baptist Convention.

According to the U.S. Census Bureau's American Community Survey on Nashville, the city's median household income is $47,204. An estimated 11 percent of people in Nashville live below the federal poverty line. This includes 14 percent of children under 18 years and 11 percent of senior citizens.

Memphis

Memphis International Airport is the world's busiest cargo airport, in terms of tonnage, thanks to FedEx, which was founded here and makes Memphis its headquarters and transit hub. Other major companies that are headquartered in Memphis are AutoZone Incorporated and International Paper. Memphis also manufactures textiles, heating equipment, pianos, and automobile and truck parts.

According to the U.S. Census Bureau, the most common occupations for Memphians are management and professional (30 percent); sales and office (25 percent); service (21 percent); production, transportation, and material moving (16 percent); and construction (8 percent). Seventeen percent of the city's residents are employed by the federal, state, or local governments.

The median household income in the city is $32,285. An estimated 24 percent of people in the city live in poverty. Thirty-four percent of children under 18 were below the poverty level, and 20 percent of senior citizens were poor.

People and Culture

The people of Nashville and Memphis are at once diverse and of a kind. Both cities are noticeably friendly, and definitively Southern. But they are also urban, with growing immigrant populations and also an increasing number of city residents who are not Tennessee natives, or even Southerners.

If you were to pigeonhole the two cities, Memphis would emerge as the city of the Deep South with a much greater African-American influence. Questions of race are omnipresent in Memphis. Equally, visitors will notice an exciting energy that comes from the convergence of different cultures: the rural and urban Souths, African-American and white culture, and the added impact of new transplants. It was a milieu that gave rise to rock 'n' roll in the 1950s, and it is still magical today.

Nashville, on the other hand, is the capital city of Middle Tennessee, a region that has been associated with affluence, power, and traditional country living through successive generations. The city has a perpetual identity crisis: Is it a bastion of high culture and wealth—the Athens of the South—or is it the hillbilly big city, the City of Oz for country folks? Nashville is, of course, both, and this tension is alive in the city and its people.

POPULATION

Tennessee was home to 6.2 million people in 2007, 82 percent white and 17 percent black. It is the 17th fastest-growing state in the country.

Nashville

Nashville's metropolitan area—which includes 13 counties—counted just over 1.4 million people in 2007. Some 80 percent of these are white; 15 percent are African-American, and 5 percent are Latino or Hispanic. Nashville's foreign-born population tripled during the decade between 1990 and 2000. According to a 2006 Census

Bureau survey, almost 11 percent of city residents, some 60,000 people, were born abroad. These immigrants come from countries including Mexico, Vietnam, Laos, and Somalia. Nashville is also home to more than 11,000 Iraqi Kurds. Sixty-two percent of Nashville residents were born in Tennessee.

Memphis

Greater Memphis, including parts of Mississippi and Arkansas, counted 1.26 million people in 2007. More than 62 percent of Memphians are African-American, a greater proportion than is found in any other American city. An estimated 5 percent of people living in Memphis were foreign-born; 69 percent of residents were born in Tennessee. Memphis has the youngest population of the four major cities of Tennessee.

RELIGION

Tennessee is unquestionably part of the U.S. Bible Belt; the conservative Christian faith is both prevalent and prominent all over the state. Eighty-three percent of Tennesseans call themselves Christians and more than half of these identify as Baptist. The second-largest Christian denomination is Methodist. Nashville is the headquarters of the Southern Baptist Convention, the National Baptist Convention, and the United Methodist Church. Memphis is the headquarters of the mostly African-American Church of God in Christ.

While Tennessee's urban centers are the home of church headquarters, religious fervor is strongest in the rural communities. Pentecostal churches have been known for rites such as speaking in tongues and snake handling, although these activities are not as widespread as they once were.

Non-Christians will feel most comfortable in urban areas, where religious minorities have grown in recent years and where the influence of churches is not as great.

One practical effect of Tennessee's Christian bent is that many counties and even some cities are totally dry, while most bar the sale of alcohol on Sunday.

ARTS
Music

Tennessee may be more famous for its music than for anything else. Blues was born on Beale Street; the Grand Ole Opry popularized old-time mountain music; and the Fisk Jubilee Singers of Nashville introduced African-American spirituals to the world. Rock 'n' roll traces its roots to Elvis Presley, Carl Perkins, Jerry Lee Lewis, and the city of Memphis.

The blues became popular in cities from New Orleans to St. Louis at the turn of the 20th century. But thanks in large part to composer and performer W. C. Handy, the musical form was forever associated with Memphis and Beale Street. Early blues greats like Walter "Furry" Lewis, Booker T. Washington, "Bukka" White, "Little Laura" Dukes, and Ma Rainey started in Memphis.

Sun Records in the 1950s recorded some of the first commercial blues records, but the label is most famous for discovering Elvis Presley. Stax Records created a new sound—soul—in the late 1950s and early 1960s.

Country music was born in Bristol, Tennessee, where the earliest recordings of Jimmie Rodgers and the Carter Family were made in the 1920s. In the decades that followed, Nashville became the capital of country music, thanks in part to radio station WSM and dozens of rural musicians who trekked to town to play on the radio. America was hungry for a type of music to call its own, and country music was it. First called "hillbilly music," country was popularized by barn-dance radio shows, including the Grand Ole Opry.

Over the years, country music mellowed out, adopting the Nashville Sound that softened its edges and made it palatable to a wider audience. Today, the city is second only to New York as a center for recorded music; and many country music stars still live in and around the city.

While Memphis's prominence on the musical map is mostly historical, the city continues to have a vibrant and happening music scene. Indie rock, rap, and blues are played in nightclubs around the city, and the recent success of movies like *Hustle & Flow* generated an aura of urban-Memphis glam.

Visual Art

Early Tennessee artists were itinerant craftsmen whose main specialty was portraiture. The rural nature of Tennessee and the agricultural nature of its economy made it impossible for early artists to support themselves year-round in one location.

Ralph E. W. Earl was probably the state's first resident painter. Earl, a portraitist, lived with Andrew Jackson at the Hermitage and, later, the White House. In 1830, Washington Bogard Cooper, also a portraitist, established a studio in Nashville and became its preeminent painter. Washington Cooper's brother, William Cooper, later established a studio in Memphis. A decade later, John Wood Dodge, a miniaturist, established a Nashville studio, although he continued to travel in the region.

The names Cooper and Dodge appear on virtually all the paintings and miniatures to emerge from Tennessee during this era. In 1858 the Tennessee Historical Society raised funds to purchase Washington Cooper's series of portraits of Tennessee governors.

During the 1850s and after the Civil War, different types of painting were popularized. Canvases now depicted historical events, still lifes, "negro studies," and landscapes. *Tennessee*, a sweeping landscape, was painted by New Yorker Alexander Wyant and is now in the Metropolitan Museum of Art's collection. John Stokes's *Smoky Mountain Wedding* (1872), now at the Tennessee State Museum, depicted stereotypical images of both white and black southerners. Gilbert Gaul, who moved to Tennessee in 1881, won a bronze medal at the 1889 Paris Exposition for *Charting the Battery*, a Civil War painting.

In 1878, the Nashville Art Association was founded and the state's first coeducational arts school opened in 1885 in Nashville.

Tennessee lagged behind art trends. Impressionism did not take off in Tennessee until it was well-established in Europe and America. Knoxville artist Catherine Wiley, the state's first impressionist, did not become fashionable until the turn of the century. Postimpressionism fared little better; abstract painting did not appear in full force on Tennessee canvases until the 1960s.

The New Deal provided an outlet for new realist painting. Murals were commissioned in some 30 Tennessee post offices. The finished works included *Farm and Factory* by Horace Day at Clinton, *Manpower and the Resources of Nature* by William Zorach in Greeneville, and *Farmer Family* by Wendell Jones at Johnson City. The Davidson County Courthouse and John Sevier Office Building in Nashville also received murals. Carroll Cloar, one of Tennessee's best-known painters of the 20th century, painted in a realistic, semi-pointillist style. His work *Historic Encounter Between E. H. Crump and W. C. Handy on Beale Street* is owned by the First Tennessee Bank in Memphis.

Aaron Douglas was Tennessee's first major African-American artist. Douglas was a painter in the Harlem Renaissance of the 1930s, and he joined the faculty at Fisk University in Nashville in 1936. Douglas painted several murals that are still displayed at Fisk, and the University's African art gallery is named in his honor.

Perhaps the most famous Tennessee artist of the 20th century is Charles Roger "Red" Grooms, who was born in Nashville in 1937. Grooms attended school in Tennessee before moving to Chicago and, later, New York. His playful images of urban life seem far removed from his Tennessee childhood.

The 20th century was good for the establishment of institutions of art. Brooks Museum in Memphis opened in 1913 and remains the state's largest fine-arts museum. The Nashville Museum was founded 1924 and moved to the Fine Arts Center at Cheekwood in 1957. The Tennessee State Museum, founded in 1937, came under the umbrella of the Tennessee Arts Commission in 1971 and has sponsored retrospective exhibits on certain Tennessee artists.

Despite the strides, Tennessee arts remain poorly funded, relying largely on private donations and sponsorships.

ESSENTIALS

Getting There and Around

Driving is the easiest way to get to, and around, Memphis and Nashville. A good road map, or in-car navigation system, is all you really need to find your way around.

If you are flying into either city, you should consider renting a car at the airport to get around. Getting a car is a good idea if you want to see a lot of sights, feel like having an adventure, or are in town for more than a few days. If, on the other hand, you plan to hit only one or two sights over a short weekend, then you should consider taxis and walking to get around. In both cities there are downtown hotels that are within walking distance of major attractions, restaurants, and nightlife.

BY AIR
Nashville

The **Nashville International Airport** (BNA; 615/275-1675, www.nashintl.com) has 16 airlines serving 86 markets. It sees an average of 404 daily departures and arrivals. Legacy carriers that serve the city include American, Continental, Delta, Northwest, United, and U.S. Airways.

Low-cost carriers serving Nashville include Frontier, which flies direct from Denver to Nashville and from Nashville to Cancun, Mexico. Southwest Airlines flies to Nashville from more than two dozen American cities.

Nonstop international service is provided on Air Canada to Ontario and Toronto.

PHOTO COURTESY OF TENNESSEE DEPARTMENT OF TOURIST DEVELOPMENT

Memphis
Memphis International Airport (MEM; 901/922-8000, www.mscaa.com) is a hub for Northwest Airlines, and local officials hope it will remain so even if a proposed merger between Delta and Northwest goes through.

KLM Royal Dutch Airlines provides international direct flights from Memphis to Amsterdam.

Low-cost carrier AirTran flies from Memphis to Atlanta and Orlando. Legacy carriers serving Memphis include American Airlines, United, Continental, and Delta.

BY CAR
Nashville and Memphis are 220 miles apart by car.

Nashville
No less than three major interstate highways converge in Nashville. I-40 runs east–west, connecting Nashville with Knoxville and Memphis. I-65 runs north–south, and connects the city with Louisville, Kentucky, and Birmingham, Alabama. I-24 travels at a southeastern angle down to the city, connecting it with the cities of Clarkesville and St. Louis in the north, and Chattanooga and Atlanta in the south.

The city is 250 miles from Atlanta, 330 miles from St. Louis, 400 miles from Charlotte, 550 miles from New Orleans, and 670 miles from Washington, D.C.

Memphis
Memphis is located at the intersection of two major interstate highways. I-40, which runs east–west across the United States, and I-55, which runs south from St. Louis to New Orleans.

The city is 300 miles from St. Louis, 380 miles from Atlanta, 410 miles from New Orleans, 450 miles from Dallas, 480 miles from Cincinnati and Oklahoma City, and 560 miles from Chicago.

BY BUS
Nashville
Greyhound (800/231-2222, www.greyhound. com) serves Nashville with bus service to the city from Memphis, Jackson, Chattanooga, and Knoxville, Tennessee, as well as Paducah and Bowling Green, Kentucky.

Expect to pay about $40 for a one-way ticket from Memphis to Nashville.

Memphis
Greyhound (800/231-2222, www.greyhound.com) runs daily buses to Memphis from around the United States. Direct service is available to Memphis from a number of surrounding cities, including Jackson and Nashville, Tennessee; Little Rock, Tupelo, and Jackson, Mississippi; Jonesboro, Arkansas; and St. Louis.

BY TRAIN
Amtrak (800/872-7245, www.amtrak.com) runs the City of New Orleans train daily between Chicago and New Orleans, stopping in Memphis on the way. It is an 11-hour ride between Memphis and Chicago and about eight hours between Memphis and New Orleans.

There is no Amtrak service to Nashville; the closest passenger train station is in Memphis.

ORGANIZED TOURS
Package tours are a popular way to visit Nashville. The **Gaylord Opryland Hotel** (615/889-1000) offers a wide variety of packages, which often include transports, hotels, and entertainment. These tours are good for travelers who don't want to waste any time making their own plans or who aren't keen on driving around an unfamiliar city. They are not good for people who are looking to really get to know Nashville.

Sweet Magnolia Tours (901/369-9838, www.sweetmagnoliatours.com) offers group and individual tour packages to Memphis and Nashville. Popular packages include hotel accommodations and admission to attractions such as Graceland and the Grand Ole Opry. They offer special all-Elvis packages and special event packages that coincide with Elvis Week in Memphis and the CMA Festival in Nashville.

Tips for Travelers

CONDUCT AND CUSTOMS
Etiquette

The standard rules of etiquette that have faded in other parts of the country have retained a foothold in Memphis and Nashville. If you wish to make a good impression on your hosts, strive to be considerate of others at all times. Show deference to people who are older than you: Open doors for them, address them with courtesy, and yield to their wishes when you can.

Men should remove their hats while the national anthem is being played (such as at a sports game), and you should show respect by being fully dressed and putting a stop to foul language if you enter a church, even if there's no service going on; remember that this is a place that some people consider to be sacred.

Communication

You will be addressed as "sir" or "ma'am" routinely in Memphis and Nashville. It is nice to employ these courtesies yourself, especially if you are addressing someone who is older than you are. In many situations, it is customary to refer to people as Mr. or Mrs. So-and-so unless the person has asked you to call them otherwise.

While you will, no doubt, encounter a harried store clerk or less-than-friendly waiter, Tennesseans are, by and large, friendly people. They appreciate a smile, a statement of welcome or greeting, or a joke as much as the next person. The people you meet will be eager to help you, so always speak up if there is something special that you need or want. Asking questions about the city is a good way to develop a positive rapport, but avoid delving too deeply into a stranger's personal life unless he or she encourages it.

TRAVELING WITH CHILDREN

Both Nashville and Memphis have attractions designed for children, plus others that will be appreciated by them. There are zoos, children's museums, and interactive science, fire, and history museums in both cities. During the summer months, swimming and other outdoor activities are good for families.

Parents will enjoy Dining with Monkeys, a blog by Memphis writer Stacey Greenburg, in which she describes eating out with her two sons, "the monkeys," ages five and three. Greenburg's columns (http://diningwithmonkeys.blogspot.com) offer good real-life information for parents, such as restaurants where kids' drinks are brought with a lid and where crayons and paper placemats are provided. The columns are also so entertaining that even those without monkeys will find them riveting.

WOMEN TRAVELERS

Women are unlikely to experience discrimination or harassment out of line with what exists in other major American cities.

Women should avoid walking alone at night, especially in neighborhoods that are not well lit or that feel off the beaten track. In high-traffic areas, such as Beale Street in Memphis or the District in Nashville, keep alert to what is happening around you. Take a friend if you're heading out to a juke joint or any other nightclub that is off the beaten track.

GAY AND LESBIAN TRAVELERS

Both Nashville and Memphis have happening queer scenes, with gay and lesbian bars, dance clubs, and civic organizations. Despite the conservative nature of both these Southern cities, gays and lesbians will feel relatively comfortable.

Discretion is advisable, however. Public displays of affection may draw stares or even harassment in places like a Memphis juke joint or a country music dance hall. Be aware that while most people are willing to live and let live, there is a minority who object to homosexuality.

Nashville

Three different publications cover the gay, lesbian, bisexual, and transgender community. The **Church Street Freedom Press** (www. churchstreetfreedompress.com) and **InsideOut Nashville** (www.insideoutnashville.com) are free weeklies; **Out and About** (www.outandaboutnewspaper.com) is a free monthly newsmagazine.

To meet other gay people and find out about events, stop by the **Outloud Café and Bookstore** (1703 Church St., 615/340-0034, www.outloudonline.com).

In Nashville, the **Doubletree Downtown** welcomes lesbian and gay guests. They also offer commitment ceremonies. **International Travel Inc.** (4004 Hillsboro Rd., 615/385-1222) is a Nashville-based gay-friendly travel agency.

Memphis

The **Memphis Gay and Lesbian Community Center** (892 S. Cooper St., 901/278-4297, www.mglcc.org) is a clearinghouse of information for the gay and lesbian community. They have a directory of gay-friendly businesses, host social events, and promote tolerance and equality.

Mid-South Pride (www.midsouthpride. org) organizes Memphis Pride in June. The **Memphis Triangle Journal** is a free weekly paper available at local bookstores, libraries, and other locations.

SENIOR TRAVELERS

Elderhostel (800/454-5768, www.elderhostel.org), which organizes educational tours for people over 55, offers tours in Memphis and Nashville.

For discounts and help with trip planning, try the **AARP** (800/687-2777, www.aarp.org), which offers a full-service travel agency, trip insurance, a motor club, and AARP Passport program, which provides you with senior discounts for hotels, car rentals, and other things.

Persons over 55 should always check for a senior citizen discount. Most attractions and some hotels and restaurants have special pricing for seniors.

TRAVELERS WITH DISABILITIES

More people with disabilities are traveling than ever before. The Americans with Disabilities Act requires most public buildings to make provisions for disabled people, although in practice accessibility may be spotty.

When you make your hotel reservations, always check that the hotel is prepared to accommodate you. Airlines will also make special arrangements for you if you request help in advance. To reduce stress, try to travel during off-peak times.

Several national organizations have information and advice about traveling with disabilities. The **Society for Accessible Travel and Hospitality** (www.sath.org) publishes links to major airlines' accessibility policies and publishes travel tips for people with all types of disabilities, including blindness, deafness, mobility disorders, diabetes, kidney disease, and arthritis. The Society publishes *Open World*, a magazine about accessible travel.

Wheelchair Getaways (800/642-2042, www.wheelchairgetaways.com) is a national chain specializing in renting vans that are wheelchair accessible, or otherwise designed for drivers and travelers with disabilities. Wheelchair Getaways has a location in Memphis (901/795-6533), and they will deliver to Nashville and other locations in the state.

Avis offers **Avis Access,** a program for travelers with disabilities. Call the dedicated 24-hour toll-free 800/879-4273 for help renting a car with features such as transfer boards, hand controls, spinner knobs, and swivel seats.

Though formed primarily to serve residents, the government-funded **Disability Information Office** (615/743-7300 or 800/342-1117) in Nashville can help visitors too. They are a clearinghouse of information about services for people with disabilities.

Nashville's public transit authority operates AccessRide, a paratransit van service for people with disabilities. You must qualify for the service, but special arrangements are in place for visitors who need the service for a short-term stay in the city. Call 615/880-3970 for more information.

In Memphis, the Main Street trolleys are equipped with wheelchair lifts and each station has a wheelchair ramp. For a ride with MATA Plus, a bus service for persons with disabilities, you have to submit an application and make prior reservations. Call 901/722-7105 for more information.

FOREIGN TRAVELERS

Memphis and Nashville attract a fair number of foreign visitors. Elvis and the international popularity of blues and country music bring people from all over the globe to these two cities.

Communication

Foreign travelers will find a warm welcome. Those in the tourist trade are used to dealing with all sorts of people, and will be pleased that you have come from so far away to visit their city. If you are not a native English speaker, it may be difficult to understand the local accent at first. Just smile and ask the person to say it again, a bit slower. Good humor and a positive attitude will help at all times.

Visas and Officialdom

Most citizens of a foreign country require a visa to enter the United States. There are many types of visas, issued according to the purpose of your visit. Business and pleasure travelers apply for B-1 and B-2 visas respectively. When you apply for your visa, you will be required to prove that the purpose of your trip is business, pleasure, or for medical treatment; that you plan to remain in the United States for a limited period; and that you have a place of residence outside the United States. Apply for your visa at the nearest U.S. embassy. For more information, contact the **U.S. Citizenship and Immigration Service** (www.uscis.gov).

Nationals of 27 countries may be able to use the Visa Waiver Program, operated by Customs and Border Protection. Presently, these 27 countries are: Andorra, Australia, Austria, Belgium, Brunei, Denmark, Finland, France, Germany, Iceland, Ireland, Italy, Japan, Liechtenstein, Luxemburg, Monaco, the Netherlands, New Zealand, Norway, Portugal, San Marino, Singapore, Slovenia, Spain, Sweden, Switzerland, and the United Kingdom.

Take note that in recent years the United States has begun to require visa waiver participants to have upgraded passports, with digital photographs and machine-readable information. Check to make sure that your passport is acceptable. For more information about the Visa Waiver Program, contact the **Customs and Border Protection Agency** (www.travel.state.gov).

All foreign travelers are now required to participate in U.S. Visit, a program operated by the Department of Homeland Security. Under the program, your fingerprints and photograph are taken—digitally and without ink—as you are being screened by the immigration officer.

Nashville

At the Nashville International Airport, you can exchange currency at SunTrust Bank near A/B concourse, or at the Business Service Center (Wright Travel) (615/275-2660) near C/D concourse.

Outside the airport, you can exchange currency at most banks.

Memphis

The Memphis airport is well equipped for foreign travelers. The lone international airline, Northwest/KLM Royal Dutch Airlines, provides interpreters for the Customs Clearance Facility and the boarding areas for international flights. They can accommodate Dutch, German, Arabic, Spanish, and French-speaking passengers.

International travel services are provided at the Business Service Center (Ticket Lobby B, 901/922-8090, Mon.–Fri. 7 A.M.–7:30 P.M., Sat. 7:30 A.M.–7:30 P.M., Sun. 11 A.M.–7:30 P.M.). Here you can exchange currency, buy travel insurance, make telephone calls and send faxes, wire money, and buy travelers checks. An additional kiosk is located in Concourse B near the international gates (gate B-36). Here you can buy travel insurance and exchange currency. The hours are daily 4:30–7:30 P.M.

Memphis International Airport is a "Transit Without Visa" Port of Entry. This means that foreign travelers whose flight will connect through Memphis on the way to another foreign destination beyond the United States no longer need a U.S. transit visa just to connect to their outbound flight.

CRIME AND HARASSMENT
Nashville

Nashville's problems with crime are on par with a city of its size, although increased gang activity is a cause for concern. Aggressive policing and other factors led to a decrease in major crime in 2007; police said it was at the lowest level in 17 years.

In 2007, Nashville tallied 73 homicides, a slight decline over previous years. South Nashville precincts experienced the greatest concentration of killings, a fact that police attributed to changing demographics, social ills, and the proportion of rental properties in the area.

Downtown Nashville is well patrolled by police day and night. If you keep your head and pay attention to your surroundings, you should have little to worry about. Avoid exploring unknown parts of town after dark, and always trust your instincts.

Memphis

Memphis has fought a long battle with crime; the controversial city crime ratings published by Congressional Quarterly, Inc., and based on FBI statistics, pegged the city as the 8th "most dangerous" in the United States in 2007. Local police dismiss these types of one-dimensional assessments, however, and say that new aggressive policing methods are helping to reduce crime.

The good news for visitors is that the city is serious about keeping order in the areas of the city frequented by tourists. Beale Street and all parts of downtown are heavily patrolled at all times, and champions of downtown development are quick to point out that downtown Memphis is the safest part of the city. While you can expect a certain level of security downtown, always be aware of your surroundings and trust your instincts.

Visitors should avoid north and south Memphis, especially at night. If you do decide to venture out, do so with a local guide or friend.

Information and Services

MONEY
Banks

Dozens of local and regional banks are found throughout Memphis and Nashville. Most banks will cash travelers checks, exchange currency, and send wire transfers. Banks are generally open weekdays 9 A.M.–4 P.M., although some are open later and on Saturdays. Automatic Teller Machines are ubiquitous; many are compatible with bank cards bearing the Plus or Cirrus icons. There is usually a fee of $2–4 for withdrawing cash from an ATM that does not belong to your bank.

Sales Tax

Sales tax on food and groceries is 8.25 percent and 9.25 percent on all other goods.

The sales tax you pay is split between the state and local governments. Tennessee's sales tax is 6 percent on food and groceries, and 7 percent on all other goods. Cities and towns add an additional "local use tax," usually between 1.5 percent and 2.75 percent. The local use tax in both Memphis and Nashville is 2.25 percent.

Cost

Nashville and Memphis are routinely ranked favorably on cost-of-living indexes; they fall between 89 and 94 percent of the national cost-of-living average. Visitors can comfortably eat their fill in casual restaurants and coffee shops for $25 a day, although it is possible to spend much more if you prefer to eat in upscale restaurants.

The most expensive hotels are found downtown in both cities. Here you can expect to pay upwards of $150 per night. The most affordable hotels are found along interstates 10–15 minutes from the city centers. In Nashville, Music Valley has a lot of cheap hotel rooms in a safe and relatively family-friendly environment. Even the budget hotels will usually wind up costing between $50 and $60 per night.

If you are not coming in your own car, one of your most substantial expenses will be a rental car. Most rentals bottom out at $30 a day, and rates can be much higher if you don't reserve in advance or if you are renting only for a day or two.

Discounts

Most historic sites, museums, and attractions offer special discounts for senior citizens and children under 12. Some attractions also have discounts for students and servicemen and women. Even if you don't see any discount posted, it is worth asking if one exists.

Many chain hotels offer discounts for AAA members.

Bargaining

Consumer Reports magazine reported that you can often get a better hotel rate simply by asking for one. If the rate you are quoted sounds a little high, simply say that that is more than you were planning to spend and ask if they can offer a better rate. Many times, especially if it is out of season, the answer will be yes. Your negotiations will be more successful if you are willing to walk away if the answer is no.

Tipping

You should tip waiters and waitresses between 15 and 20 percent in a "sit-down" restaurant. You can tip 5 to 10 percent in a cafeteria or restaurant where you collect your own food from the counter.

Tip a bell hop or bag handler $1 per bag, or more if they went out of their way to help you.

TOURIST INFORMATION

In addition to local sources, the **Tennessee Department of Tourist Development** (615/741-2158, www.tnvacation.com) is a source of visitor information about Nashville and Memphis.

The **Nashville Convention and Visitors Bureau** (615/259-4126 or 800/657-6810, www.musiccityusa.com) publishes an annual guide to the city, maintains a list of upcoming concerts and events, and operates two visitors centers in the city. Contact them before you arrive to request their guide, which includes a map and discount coupons.

The **Memphis Convention and Visitors Bureau** (800/462-8366, www.memphistravel. com) produces its own visitors guide and operates several visitors centers. They will send you a visitors guide by mail if you request it.

AAA

The American Automobile Association provides free maps, travel information, and roadside assistance to its members.

Contact Nashville's AAA (2501 21st Ave. S., 615/297-7700) or Memphis's AAA (5138 Park Ave., 901/761-5371) for maps, guidebooks, and emergency roadside assistance.

COMMUNICATION
Area Codes

The Memphis metropolitan area code is 901; the rest of West Tennessee—stretching to the Tennessee River—is 731.

Nashville and the 13 counties that form the Nashville Metropolitan Area have the same area code: 615. The rest of central Tennessee has 931 as an area code.

Cell Phones

Cell phone service in the urban areas of Nashville and Memphis is good, and so is service along I-40 connecting the two cities. Service in the countryside is hit or miss, especially in rural areas. If you plan to explore the countryside, buy a phone card or arrange a back-up way to get in touch with family and friends.

TIME ZONE

Nashville and Memphis are in the Central Standard Time zone, one hour earlier than Eastern Standard Time and six hours earlier than Greenwich Mean Time. They observe daylight saving time during the summer months. Take note that the Eastern Standard Time zone begins just east of Crossville, Tennessee, between Nashville and Knoxville.

RESOURCES

Suggested Reading

PHOTOGRAPHY AND ART

Escott, Colin. *The Grand Ole Opry: The Making of an American Icon.* New York: Center Street, 2006. An authorized (and somewhat sanitized) look at the Grand Ole Opry. Lots of pictures, reminiscences, and short sidebars make it an attractive coffee table book.

McGuire, Jim. *Nashville Portraits: Legends of Country Music.* Guilford, CT: The Lyons Press, 2007. Sixty stunning photographs of country music legends including Johnny Cash, Waylon Jennings, Doc Watson, and Dolly Parton. The companion book to an eponymous exhibit that debuted in 2007 at the Frist Center.

Sherraden, Jim, Paul Kingsbury, and Elek Horvath. *Hatch Show Print: The History of a Great American Poster Shop.* San Francisco: Chronicle Books, 2001. A fully illustrated, beautiful book about Hatch Show Print, the Nashville advertising company and letterpress founded in 1897.

GUIDES

Brandt, Robert. *Touring the Middle Tennessee Backroads.* Winston-Salem, NC: John F. Blair, Publisher, 1995. Robert Brandt is a Nashville judge and self-professed "zealot" for Middle Tennessee. His guidebook details 15 driving tours through back roads in the Heartland of Tennessee. Brandt's knowledge of local history and architecture cannot be surpassed, and his enthusiasm for his subject shines through the prose. While some of the entries are now dated, the guide remains an invaluable source of information about small towns in the region.

The WPA Guide to Tennessee. Knoxville: University of Tennessee Press, 1986. The Works Progress Administration guide to Tennessee, written in 1939 and originally published by Viking Press, is a fascinating portrait of Depression-era Tennessee. Published as part of a New Deal project to employ writers and document the culture and character of the nation, the guide contains visitor information, historical sketches, and profiles of the state's literature, culture, agriculture, industry, and more. The guide, republished as part of Tennessee's "Homecoming '86," is a delightful traveling companion.

TENNESSEE HISTORY

Bergeron, Paul H. *Paths of the Past: Tennessee, 1770–1970.* Knoxville: University of Tennessee Press, 1979. This is a concise, straight-up history of Tennessee, with a few illustrations and maps.

Corlew, Robert E. *Tennessee: A Short History.* Knoxville: University of Tennessee Press, 1990. The definitive survey of Tennessee history, this text was first written in 1969 and has been updated several times by writers including Stanley J. Folmsbee and Enoch Mitchell. This is a useful reference guide for a serious reader.

Dykeman, Wilma. *Tennessee.* New York: W. W. Norton & Co., and the American Association for State and Local History, 1984. Novelist and essayist Wilma Dykeman says more about the people of Tennessee and the events that shaped the modern state in this slim and highly readable volume than you would find in the most detailed and plodding historical account. It becomes a companion, and a means through which to understand the Tennessee spirit and character.

HISTORY

Arnow, Harriet Simpson. *Seedtime on the Cumberland.* Lincoln, NE: Bison Books, 1995. Originally published in 1961, this is the classic narrative of the settlement of southern Kentucky and Middle Tennessee. A classic of Tennessee history, Southern culture, and the act of settlement, this is truly a must-read for those seeking to understand rural life.

Beifuss, Joan Turner. *At the River I Stand.* Brooklyn: Carlson Pub., 1985. This account of the Memphis sanitation strike of 1968 is told from the ground up. It places the assassination of Dr. Martin Luther King in its immediate, if not historical, context.

Bond, Beverley G. and Janann Sherman. *Memphis in Black and White.* Charleston, SC: Arcadia Publishing, 2003. This lively history of Memphis pays special attention to the dynamics of race and class. The slim and easy-to-read volume contains interesting anecdotes, and lots of illustrations. It is an excellent introduction to the city.

Branch, Taylor. *Parting the Waters: America in the King Years 1954–63.* New York: Simon and Schuster, 1989. The most authoritative account of the civil rights movement, told through the life of Dr. Martin Luther King. The first in a three-volume account of the movement, *Parting the Waters* includes descriptions of the Nashville Sit-Ins of 1960. The final volume, *At Canaan's Edge,* includes his assassination in Memphis.

Crosby, Molly Caldwell. *The American Plague.* New York: Berkley Books, 2006. A portrait of "the epidemic that shaped our history": the yellow fever epidemic of 1878 that wiped out New Orleans and Memphis.

Egerton, John. *Speak Now Against the Day: The Generation Before the Civil Rights Movement in the South.* Chapel Hill: University of North Carolina Press, 1995. Nashville native John Egerton tells the relatively unacknowledged story of Southerners, white and black, who stood up against segregation and racial hatred during the years before the civil rights movement.

Egerton, John. *Visions of Utopia.* Knoxville: University of Tennessee Press, 1977. An accessible and fascinating portrait of three intentional Tennessee communities: Ruskin in Middle Tennessee, Nashoba in West Tennessee, and Rugby in East Tennessee. Egerton's usual sterling prose and sensitive observations make this volume well worth reading.

Honey, Michael. *Going Down Jericho Road: The Memphis Strike, Martin Luther King's Last Campaign.* New York: W. W. Norton & Co., Inc., 2007. Labor historian Michael Honey depicts with academic detail and novelistic drama the Memphis sanitation strike of 1968. He documents Memphis of the late 1960s, and the quest for economic justice that brought Dr. King to the city. King's assassination and its aftermath are depicted in devastating detail.

Potter, Jerry O. *Sultana Tragedy: America's Greatest Maritime Disaster.* Gretna, LA: Pelican Publishing Co., Inc., 1992. The end of the Civil War and the assassination of Abraham Lincoln grabbed the headlines in April 1864, so much so that the sinking of the *Sultana* and the death of more than 1,800 men in the Mississippi River near Memphis went almost unnoticed. This book tells a tale more poignant and moving than the loss of the *Titanic.*

Sword, Wiley. *The Confederacy's Last Hurrah: Spring Hill, Franklin and Nashville.* Lawrence, KS: University Press of Kansas, 2004. This is a well-written and devastating account of John Bell Hood's disastrous campaign through Middle Tennessee during the waning months of the Confederacy. It was a campaign that cost the South more than 23,000 men. With unflinching honesty, Sword describes the opportunities lost and poor decisions made by Gen. Hood.

MUSIC

Carlin, Richard. *Country Music.* New York: Black Dog and Leventhal Publishers, 2006. This is a highly illustrated, well-written, and useful reference for fans of country music. It profiles the people, places, and events that contributed to country's evolution. With lots of graphic elements and photographs, it is a good book to dip into.

Gordon, Robert. *It Came From Memphis.* Boston: Faber and Faber, 1994. Memphis resident Robert Gordon takes the back roads to tell the remarkable musical story that emerged from Memphis during the 1950s and '60s. He paints a textured picture of the milieu from which rock 'n' roll eventually rose.

Guralnick, Peter. *Last Train to Memphis: The Rise of Elvis Presley.* Boston: Little, Brown, and Co., 1994. Quite possibly the definitive biography of the King. In volume one, Guralick re-creates Presley's first 24 years, including his childhood in Mississippi and Tennessee, his remarkable rise to fame, and the pivotal events of 1958, when he was drafted in the army and buried his beloved mother.

Guralnick, Peter. *Careless Love: The Unmaking of Elvis Presley.* Boston: Little, Brown, and Co., 1999. Volume two of Peter Guralnick's biography of Elvis Presley. Guralnick writes in the introduction that he "knows of no sadder story" than Presley's life from 1958 until his death in 1977. The book examines un-

flinchingly the gradual unraveling of America's greatest pop star.

Handy, W. C. *Father of the Blues.* New York: The Macmillan Co., 1941. This memoir by Memphis's most famous blues man depicts Memphis during the first quarter of the 20th century. It is an entertaining and endearing read.

Kingsbury, Paul, ed. *Will the Circle Be Unbroken: Country Music in America.* New York: DK Adult, 2006. A collection of articles by 43 writers, including several performing artists, this book is a useful reference on the genre's development from 1920 until the present. Illustrated.

Kossner, Michael. *How Nashville Became Music City: 50 Years of Music Row.* Milwaukee, WI: Hal Leonard, 2006. Forget about the stars and the singers, this profile of country music focuses on the people you've never heard of: the executives, songwriters, and behind-the-scenes technicians who really make the music happen. An interesting read for fans who don't mind seeing how the sausage is made, and a good introduction for people aspiring to be a part of it.

Raichelson, Richard M. *Beale Street Talks: A Walking Tour Down the Home of the Blues.* Memphis: Arcadia Records, 1999. A slim, well-written tome that describes Beale Street as it was, and Beale Street as it is. This is a handy companion for exploring the street.

Sharp, Tim. *Memphis Music: Before the Blues.* Charleston, SC: Arcadia Publishing, 2007. Part of the Images of America series, this work includes rare and evocative photographs of Memphis people. The result is a painting of the backdrop on which the Memphis blues were born in the early 20th century.

FICTION

Grisham, John. *The Firm.* Boston: G. K. Hall, 1992. Probably the most celebrated Memphis-set novel in recent years, especially following the success of the eponymous film. Mitchell McDeere takes on corrupt and criminal mob lawyers. It includes references to many city landmarks.

Jones, Madison. *Nashville: 1864*. Nashville and Chicago: J. S. Sanders & Co., 2005. This engrossing tale of Nashville during the Civil War is told through the eyes of a 12-year-old boy whose father is off fighting in the war. It deals well with difficult issues of slavery, race, and loss. Appropriate for young people and adults.

Roberts, Nora. *Blue Dahlia*. New York: Jove, 2004. Mass-market novelist Nora Roberts uses Memphis as backdrop for this off-beat romance, whose characters include the Harper Bride ghost.

Taylor, Peter. *Summons to Memphis*. New York: Knopf Publishing Group, 1986. Celebrated and award-winning Tennessee writer Peter Taylor won the Pulitzer Prize for fiction for this novel in 1986. Phillip Carver returns home to Tennessee at the request of his three older sisters to talk his father out of remarrying. In so doing, he is forced to confront a troubling family history. This is a classic of American literature, set in a South that is fading away.

Wright, Richard. *Black Boy*. New York: Chelsea House, 2006. The 1945 memoir of African-American writer Richard Wright recounts several years of residency in Memphis. His portrayal of segregation and racism in Memphis and Mississippi are still powerful today.

FOOD

Lewis, Edna and Scott Peacock. *The Gift of Southern Cooking: Recipes and Revelations from Two Great American Cooks*. New York: Knopf Publishing Group, 2003. Grande dame of Southern food Edna Lewis and son-of-the-soil chef Scott Peacock joined forces on this seminal text of Southern cuisine. It demystifies, documents, and inspires. Ideal for those who really care about Southern foodways.

Lundy, Ronnie, ed. *Cornbread Nation 3*. Chapel Hill, NC: University of North Carolina Press, 2006. The third in a series on Southern food and cooking. Published in collaboration with the Southern Foodways Alliance, which is dedicated to preserving and celebrating Southern food traditions, the Cornbread Nation collection is an ode to food traditions large and small. Topics include paw-paws, corn, and pork. *Cornbread Nation 2* focused on barbecue. *Cornbread Nation 1* was edited by restaurateur and Southern food celebrant John Egerton.

Stern, Jane and Michael. *Southern Country Cooking from the Loveless Café: Biscuits, Hams, and Jams from Nashville's Favorite Café*. Nashville: Rutledge Hill Press, 2005. Road-food aficionados wrote the cookbook on Nashville's most famous pit stop, the Loveless Café. Located at the northern terminus of the Natchez Trace Parkway, the Loveless is quintessential Southern cooking. Now you can take some of that down-home flavor home with you.

Internet Resources

Tennessee State Parks
www.state.tn.us/environment/parks
An online directory of all Tennessee state parks, this site provides useful details, including campground descriptions, cabin rental information, and the lowdown on activities.

Tennessee Department of Tourist Development
www.tnvacation.com
On Tennessee's official tourism website you can request a visitors guide, search for upcoming events, or look up details about hundreds of attractions, hotels, and restaurants.

Tennessee Encyclopedia of History and Culture
http://tennesseeencyclopedia.net
The online edition of an excellent reference book, this website should be your first stop for information on all topics Tennessee. Articles about people, places, and events are written by hundreds of different experts. Online entries are updated regularly.

Nashville Convention and Visitors Bureau
www.visitmusiccity.com
The official tourism website for Nashville, this site offers concert listings, hotel booking services, and useful visitor information. You can also order a visitors guide and money-saving coupons.

The Tennessean
www.tennessean.com
Nashville's major newspaper posts news, entertainment, sports, and business stories online. Sign up for a daily newsletter of headlines from Music City, or search the archives.

The Nashville Scene
www.nashvillescene.com
Nashville's alternative weekly has a great website. The dining guide is fabulous, the stories interesting and archived, and the entertainment calendar is the best in town. Go to "Our Critics' Picks" for a rundown on the best shows in town. The annual manual, reader's choice awards, and other special editions are useful for newcomers and old-timers alike.

Memphis Convention and Visitors Bureau
www.memphistravel.com
The official travel website for Memphis offers listings of hotels, attractions, and events. You can download coupons, request a visitors guide, or book hotels.

The Memphis Flyer
www.memphisflyer.com
Memphis's alternative weekly newspaper publishes entertainment listings and article archives on its website.

Memphis Magazine
www.memphismagazine.com
Good restaurant reviews and useful event listings. Subscriptions available online ($15 annual).

Index

Map Index

Acknowledgments

It has been a joy getting to know the cities of Nashville and Memphis so closely over the past few years. Tennessee may have been flowing through my veins, but I had a lot to learn. Many people helped me along the way.

Thanks to Tad Pierson of American Dream Safari and Sherman Willmott of Shangri-La Projects for showing me the Memphis they love, and to Jackie Reed of the Memphis Convention and Visitors Bureau for pointing me in the right directions. I appreciated the hospitality of the Peabody Memphis and the Talbot Heirs Guesthouse.

In Nashville, I am grateful for the warm welcome and hospitality of Phil and Dikkie Schoggen, old friends who became new ones. Thanks also to Ed Hamlett for sharing his thoughts on what makes his city special. Finally, thanks to all those wonderful and friendly people in Memphis, Nashville, and beyond who cheerfully answered my questions and shared a little something of themselves.

I would like to thank the staff of Avalon Travel Publishing for believing that I was the right person for this job, and for making this a better book.

Friends and family in Tennessee, the Virgin Islands, and beyond encouraged me during this project. In particular, my parents, Lucy and Rich Henighan, listened patiently to my progress reports and believed I could get it done. They were the best traveling companions I could have asked for.

I could not have written this book without the support of my husband, Amarro, who forgave my absences and tolerated my preoccupation with all things Tennessee, including country music.

Finally, this book is dedicated to my grandparents. It is dedicated to Louise Barker, whose tenacity and perseverance continues to set an example for all her grandchildren. It is dedicated to the memories of Roger Barker, and to Richard and Susan Henighan. You were travelers, long before me.

www.moon.com

HMNTW 917
.6804
05
M818

**MOON HANDBOOKS
NASHVILLE & MEMPHIS**
MONTROSE
03/09

For helpful advice on planning a trip, visit www.moon.com for the **TRAVEL PLANNER** and get access to useful travel strategies and valuable information about great places to visit. When you travel with Moon, expect an experience that is uncommon and truly unique.

MAP SYMBOLS

▦	Expressway	◖	Highlight	✗	Airfield	⚲	Golf Course
▤	Primary Road	○	City/Town	✈	Airport	🅿	Parking Area
▬	Secondary Road	◉	State Capital	▲	Mountain	▲	Archaeological Site
┄┄┄	Unpaved Road	⊛	National Capital	✚	Unique Natural Feature	▮	Church
------	Trail	★	Point of Interest			⛽	Gas Station
⋯⋯⋯	Ferry	•	Accommodation	🌿	Waterfall		Glacier
▬▬	Railroad	▼	Restaurant/Bar	▲	Park		Mangrove
▦	Pedestrian Walkway	■	Other Location	ⓘ	Trailhead		Reef
▥	Stairs	Λ	Campground	⛷	Skiing Area		Swamp

CONVERSION TABLES

$°C = (°F - 32) / 1.8$

$°F = (°C \times 1.8) + 32$

1 inch = 2.54 centimeters (cm)

1 foot = 0.304 meters (m)

1 yard = 0.914 meters

1 mile = 1.6093 kilometers (km)

1 km = 0.6214 miles

1 fathom = 1.8288 m

1 chain = 20.1168 m

1 furlong = 201.168 m

1 acre = 0.4047 hectares

1 sq km = 100 hectares

1 sq mile = 2.59 square km

1 ounce = 28.35 grams

1 pound = 0.4536 kilograms

1 short ton = 0.90718 metric ton

1 short ton = 2,000 pounds

1 long ton = 1.016 metric tons

1 long ton = 2,240 pounds

1 metric ton = 1,000 kilograms

1 quart = 0.94635 liters

1 US gallon = 3.7854 liters

1 Imperial gallon = 4.5459 liters

1 nautical mile = 1.852 km

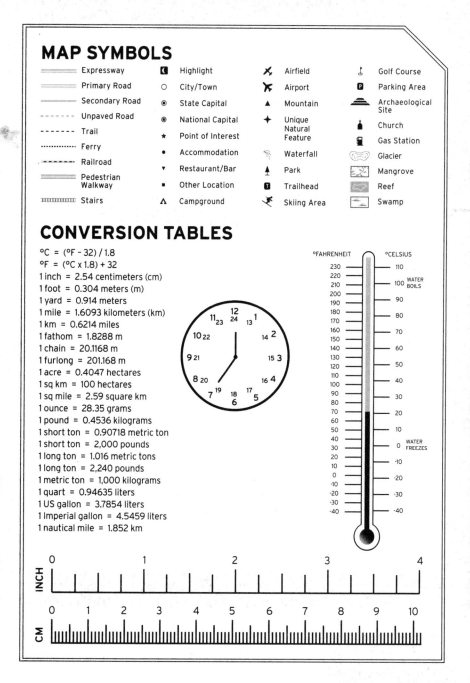

MOON NASHVILLE & MEMPHIS
Avalon Travel
A member of the Perseus Books Group
1700 Fourth Street
Berkeley, CA 94710, USA
www.moon.com

Editor and Series Manager: Kathryn Ettinger
Copy Editor: Amy Scott
Graphics Coordinator: Sean Bellows
Production Coordinator: Sean Bellows
Cover Designer: Sean Bellows
Map Editor: Albert Angulo
Cartographers: Chris Markiewicz, Kat Bennett, and Brice Ticen
Indexer: Greg Jewett

ISBN-10: 1-59880-102-3
ISBN-13: 978-1-59880-102-6
ISSN: 1942-9584

Printing History
1st Edition – October 2008
5 4 3 2 1

Front cover photo: Banjo Player at Ryman Auditorium, Grand Ole Opry © Danita Delimont/ Digital Railroad

Title page photo: Elvis tribute, Courtesy of Tennessee Department of Tourist Development

Color interior photos: pg. 4 (top), 5 (top left, bottom), 6, 7 (top, bottom right), 8 (top), 9, 11, 16, 18, 19, Courtesy of Tennessee Department of Tourist Development; pg. 4 (bottom middle and right), 5 (top middle), 8 (bottom), 10, 12, 14, 17, 20 © Susanna Henighan Potter; pg. 4 (bottom left), 5 (top right), 6-7 (bottom middle), 13, 15, Courtesy Memphis Convention and Visitors Bureau.

Printed in USA by RR Donnelley

KEEPING CURRENT

If you have a favorite gem you'd like to see included in the next edition, or see anything that needs updating, clarification, or correction, please drop us a line. Send your comments via email to feedback@moon.com, or use the address above.